Key Concepts in
Transactional Analysis
Contemporary Views

EGO STATES

Edited by **Charlotte Sills**
and **Helena Hargaden**

Worth Publishing
www.worthpublishing.com

First published 2003 by Worth Publishing Ltd
6 Lauderdale Parade, London W9 1LU
www.worthpublishing.com

Printed and bound in Great Britain by Bath Press, Bath, UK

British Library Cataloguing in Publication Data
A catalogue record for this book is available from the British Library

ISBN 1-903269-05-9 (pbk)

Illustration of the developing brain in Chapter 1, Fig 3, by Tom Sills
Text and cover design by Caroline Harper

CONTENTS

ACKNOWLEDGEMENTS

Thanks and appreciations go to all the contributors to this book, who have generously given their energies and their ideas to produce this exciting contemporary volume; and to the clients who gave us permission to learn from them (their identities, naturally, have been disguised). We especially wish to acknowledge Keith Tudor for his helpful and supportive suggestions in shaping this book.

Our thanks go also to all the many other transactional analysis practitioners and writers – some of whom are listed in the introduction and mentioned throughout the book – who have contributed over the years to the development of ego states as a rich and multi-faceted concept.

Last but by no means least, we are enormously grateful to Andrea Perry – publisher extraordinaire – who gives the term 'multi-tasking' a whole new meaning! From managing the whole project through to noticing the detail at the copy editing stage, she has steered us through with warmth, encouragement and humour. In particular, her knowledge and experience of psychotherapy made her feedback and perceptive suggestions invaluable.

Key Concepts in
Transactional Analysis
Contemporary Views

This is the first book in the series, *Key Concepts in Transactional Analysis, Contemporary Views*. Each volume will address a key concept or issue that challenges today's practitioners. Leading thinkers, as well as new writers in the field of transactional analysis psychotherapy and counselling will be invited to contribute their ideas. It is hoped that the series will both honour the roots and foundation of this approach, and also celebrate and foster the ways in which it is being developed and used throughout the world.

Series Editors

Charlotte Sills MSc (Psychotherapy), Teaching and Supervising Transactional Analyst, is Head of the Transactional Analysis Department at Metanoia Institute, London and a psychotherapist and supervisor in private practice. She is the author or co-author of a number of books and articles in the field of counselling and psychotherapy including *Transactional Analysis Counselling* (Lapworth, Sills & Fish, Winslow Press 1993) and *Transactional Analysis – A Relational Perspective* (Hargaden & Sills, Routledge 2002)

Helena Hargaden MSc (Psychotherapy), Teaching and Supervising Transactional Analyst, lives and works in south-east London where she has a private practice in psychotherapy and supervision. She teaches on the MSc in Transactional Analysis Psychotherapy programme at Metanoia Institute, is the author of a number of articles and the co-author *of Transactional Analysis – A Relational Perspective* (Hargaden & Sills, Routledge 2002). She is particularly interested in forms of the unconscious.

NOTES ON CONTRIBUTORS

William F. Cornell MA, Teaching and Supervising Transactional Analyst, maintains a private practice in psychotherapy, supervision and consultation near Pittsburgh, USA and runs an ongoing training group in Geneva, Switzerland. He is the author of numerous articles and a frequent speaker at conferences relating to transactional analysis, bodywork and psychoanalysis.

Fanita English Teaching and Supervising Transactional Analyst, is a Fellow of the American Group Psychotherapy Association. She had a private clinical practice in Chicago (where she also taught at the University of Chicago) and then in Philadelphia, where she founded her own Institute in 1970. After 1981 she worked primarily in Europe – (Germany, France, Italy, Austria and Switzerland) training professionals in the application of her methods in clinical settings and business organisations. She is the author of several books in German, French and Italian, and has published numerous articles and chapters in professional books. She is the recipient of two Eric Berne Scientific Awards for her theoretical work (1978 and 1998) and has been an invited Keynote speaker at each of the three World Council of Psychotherapy meetings held every three years in Vienna, Austria.

Richard G. Erskine PhD, Teaching and Supervising Transactional Analyst, is the Training Director of the Institute for Integrative Psychotherapy in New York City and a visiting professor at the University of Derby, UK. He is the co-recipient with Marilyn Zalcman of the 1982 Eric Berne Memorial Award for their development of intra-psychic (racket) analysis, and with Rebecca Trautmann in 1998 for eight articles published in the *Transactional Analysis Journal* and for *Theories and Methods of an Integrative Transactional Analysis: a volume of selected articles* (TA Press, 1997).

Maria C. Gilbert is a chartered clinical psychologist and UKCP registered Integrative psychotherapist. She is currently Head of the Integrative Department (Psychotherapy and Counselling Psychology) at Metanoia Institute in West London. She has a private practice as a psychotherapist, supervisor, consultant and trainer. Maria is the co-author with Kenneth Evans of *Psychotherapy Supervison: an Integrative Relational Approach,* (Open University Press, 2000).

Katarina Gildebrand MSc (Psychotherapy), Dip COT, is a Provisional Teaching and Supervising Transactional Analyst. She works as a counsellor, psychotherapist and supervisor, and is a trainer in Transactional Analysis Counselling and Psychotherapy at Metanoia Institute in London. She is registered with the UKCP, and accredited by the BACP. Born in Sweden, she came to the UK to train as an Occupational Therapist in 1977. Following 10 years working in the Mental Health Services, she set up in private practice in 1990. Her particular interests include understanding the process of change in relation to the structure and processes of the brain.

Helena Hargaden - see *Series Editor biography*

Mita Hiremath MSc (Psychotherapy), Certified Transactional Analyst, is a BACP Accredited and UKCP registered psychotherapist. She works part-time at an Asian Women's Counselling Service and has a private practice. She also works as a freelance trainer and consultant.

Adrienne Lee BA, PGCE, Teaching and Supervising Transactional Analyst is a psychotherapist and also a Master Practitioner in Neuro-Linguistic Programming. Adrienne has been a University teacher and psychotherapist for more than 25 years and was one of the first people in the UK to practise transactional analysis. She is a Founder Member and past Chair of the UK's Institute of Transactional Analysis (ITA). She has been running training programmes in TA since 1975; together with Ian Stewart, she has founded and is co-director of The Berne Institute in Nottingham, UK. The Berne Institute represents their dedication to standards of excellence in Transactional Analysis psychotherapy and training, combined with creativity, ease of learning and a community of mutual respect.

Michele Novellino Teaching and Supervising Transactional Analyst is a psychiatrist and psychologist. He lives and works in Rome and is the Director and President of Eric Berne Institute (IEB). With Carlo Moiso, he is the principle proponent and developer of the Psychodynamic School of Transactional Analysis, and founded the Transactional Psychoanalytic approach. He has written widely on aspects of Transactional Analysis psychotherapy theory and practice. His last two important books are *La Sindrome di Pinocchio* (1996) and *L'Approccio Clinico all'Analisis Transazionale* (1998) (Franco Angeli Editore).

Steff Oates BA, PGCE, is a Provisional Teaching and Supervising Transactional Analyst. She runs a private psychotherapy and supervision practice in South Manchester, and is co-director of the Cheshire Institute for Psychotherapy and Counselling Training. She continues to be fascinated by the range of possibilities that lie in the therapeutic relationship when the dignity and integrity of both therapist and client are honoured.

Suhith Shivanath MSc (Psychotherapy), is a Provisional Teaching and Supervising Transactional Analyst, UKCP and BACP accredited psychotherapist. She works for the National Health Service in inner City London where the majority of her clients are from Black, white working class and other minority communities. She has worked in the field of equal opportunities for over 20 years. She has a private practice as a psychotherapist, and freelance trainer.

Diana Shmukler PhD, Teaching and Supervising Transactional Analyst, is a former Associate Professor of applied psychology at the University of Witwatersrand, Johannesburg, SA. She currently teaches and practices in London, England. In addition to a clinical and supervision practice, she teaches in integrative psychotherapy training programmes and consults in the United Kingdom, South Africa and Australia.

Charlotte Sills - see *Series Editor biography*

Rebecca L. Trautmann RN, MSW, practices psychotherapy in New York City and is co-founder, with Richard Erskine, of the Institute for Integrative Psychotherapy. In 1998, the International Transactional Analysis Association awarded Rebecca and Richard the Eric Berne Scientific Award for a collection of articles they wrote. Rebecca is a former editor of the *Transactional Analysis Journal*.

Keith Tudor MA, MSc (Psychotherapy) Provisional Teaching and Supervising Transactional Analyst is a qualified social worker and psychotherapist with over 25 years in the helping professions. He has a small private practice in Sheffield, England offering psychotherapy, supervision and consultancy, and where he is also a co-Founder of and Partner in Temonos, which offers graduate and post-graduate training courses in Person-Centred Psychotherapy and Counselling. He is interested both in the integrity of different theoretical approaches to therapy as well as dialogue between them.

AN INTRODUCTION, SOME REFLECTIONS AND A CHALLENGE!

Charlotte Sills and Helena Hargaden, Editors

This book, the first in the *Key Concepts in Transactional Analysis: Contemporary Views* series, focuses on ego states, and originally started as an exploration into transactional analysis approaches in Britain. During the nineties, as we (the editors) were developing our own model based on our shared thinking, reading and clinical experience, periodically another view of ego states would emerge in the literature, and the psychotherapy it facilitated was exciting and persuasive. By the time we published the first account of our model (Hargaden & Sills 1999), we had begun to be intrigued by how differently people could view ego states and how effective their work could be. In our view, these differences reflect the versatility of transactional analysis, with its capacity to assist the therapist in working either intrapsychically or interpsychically, of addressing early development or the 'here-and-now', and of helping individuals, couples, groups and families – let alone teachers and students, managers and organisational consultants. We were inspired by the extent to which transactional analysis had developed in so many directions, both in Britain and abroad. Our first idea for this book, therefore, was to make it a 'state of the ego' in Britain, a book that would bring together all these different models into one volume. In 1999 we put out a call for contributions to the British TA association – the ITA – and were pleased by the interest that it stimulated. For this reason, the reader will find a preponderance of British contributions in these pages, and we extend our appreciation to our colleagues who have been willing to take part in the enterprise.

However, we quickly realised that the emphasis upon British writers meant that we unintentionally neglected exciting developments in other parts of the world and we decided to cast a wider net and include models and their applications on an international level. How were ego states being used in other countries, other cultures?

Inevitably, this involved some difficult decisions. To include the different approaches of all TA's authors would require not one but several volumes. Reluctantly, for reasons of space, we did not approach authors who have recently published their ideas about ego states in the *Transactional Analysis Journal,* as these articles are accessible to the transactional analysis world already; for example, Drego (1993), Hine (1997), Avery & Milhollon (1997), Thunissen (1998), Cox (1999), Woods (1999), Allen (2000,2001) Allen & Allen (2000), Jacobs (2000) Summers & Tudor (2000) and others. Nor, in the main, do we have contributions by those whose models, while not very recent, have been firmly established as part of TA's canon – for example, Haykin (1980), Blackstone (1993). The one exception to this parameter, as our model of the self has been recently published (Hargaden & Sills 2001), is our own chapter in this volume. Shamelessly, we decided that we still had more to say and granted ourselves a special dispensation!

What we have done is approach some of the authors whose recent work invites inference of a particular way of using ego states. In other words, practitioners whose description of their therapeutic style implies a distinctive understanding or use of this basic concept.

Consequently, the reader will find in these pages chapters from a variety of therapists, some of whom have already influenced the shape of transactional analysis psychotherapy in recent years, some of whom are bringing new ideas and visions.

Ego states - a multi-faceted concept

The concept and use of ego states is the heart of transactional analysis. According to Berne (1970) ego states are 'its foundation stones and its mark. Whatever deals with ego states is transactional analysis, and whatever overlooks them is not' (1970, p. 243). Ego states are also perhaps the richest area of difference and diversity in the approach. In 1983, only twenty years after Berne's first detailed articulation in 1961, Trautmann & Erskine wrote an overview of the different ego state models described by Berne and others. Identifying four types of model within the Bernean literature (conceptual, structural, functional and second-order) they reference no fewer than sixteen different authors who, by that time, had already described slightly or largely different models. Another twenty years have passed and the theory has continued to develop as more and more clinicians find new perspectives on the original premises. In 1987, a 'great debate' took place at the ITAA Chicago conference on the nature of ego states, subsequently written up by the contributors Richard Erskine, Petruska Clarkson, Bob Goulding, Martin Groder and Carlo Moiso (Erskine et al 1988). This debate was continued in the 1988 *Transactional Analysis Journal* special issue on Ego States (edited by Marjory Friedlander); and at the ITAA Stamford conference in 1991 (described in Novey et al 1993) in a panel discussion about ego states and the concept of self. This dialogue continued throughout the next decade in *The Script* and elsewhere.

We do not intend here to give a depth overview of ego states and their origins. The literature – including many of the chapters in this book – contains a wealth of such studies and suggestions for ways of classifying or organising the different models. To mention a few: Schegel (1998) organises transactional analysis theory in terms of methodology, describing it as a creative combination of cognitive, behavioural and psychodynamic therapy. Oller-Vallejo (1977) offers an integration of the three major models in contemporary transactional analysis. Erskine (1998) looks at motivation and personality theories in order to integrate the theory. Allen (2003), and Allen & Allen (2000) link ego states to structures of the brain and to the creation of narrative.

Pearl Drego (1981, 1993, 2000) goes 'behind' Berne's models to identify the paradigms from which they are developed. She describes what she calls Berne's primary 'Cowpoke Paradigm' (Berne 1957/1977) from which emerge four views of ego states which correspond to Berne's four methods of ego state diagnosis. These viewpoints are the *experiential paradigm* which gives rise to phenomenological models, the *biographical paradigm* which leads to historical models, *the metaphorical paradigm* which leads to behavioural models, and the *relational paradigm* which, in Drego's view, is manifest in social models. Drego stresses, as Trautmann & Erskine (1983) did, that all the models can be useful depending on the context, the client, the problem, and the contract.

We want to take this idea further and take another step 'behind' the models. We suggest that there is a further level of reflection to be made, before identifying ways of viewing ego states, their models and their application. This step involves the psychotherapist asking herself about her view of human beings and how they develop. It involves asking: What do human beings search for in their lives? What motivates them? How does personality develop? What causes distress? How can change happen? And finally, what can a therapist do to facilitate this change? We believe that the answers to these questions will lead to a choice of ego state model and a method of using it. And we believe that there is no such thing as one right answer to the questions. Human beings have many complexities and at different stages in their lives, the answer to what makes them the way they are, can vary.

It is not uncommon to hear transactional analysts declare that no debate or discussion can take place until an agreement has been found about the definitive definition of ego states. We, on the contrary, agree with Jung, for whom uniformity of meaning is the same as spiritual weakness (Jung 1968). The lack of a uniformity of meaning is, in our view one of the major strengths of transactional analysis, and not its weakness. We want to celebrate the fact that transactional analysis is an approach to psychotherapy and counselling (as well as education and organizational work) that has many ways of looking at the human being and its functioning. As an approach, it is ready to be flexibly responsive to the individual and his/her unique circumstances.

In this endeavour, we are inspired by the work of Pine (1990) in *Drive, Ego, Object and Self*. Pine describes the four major psychoanalytic views of understanding intrapsychic processes and how they inevitably lead to different theories of personality and different methodologies in the practice of psychoanalysis. Pine sees them as four types of motivation. He offers the idea that these four visions, sometimes seen as incompatible, sometimes as inseparable, are in fact aspects of human functioning which might at different times – rather in the way of the Gestalt idea of figure and ground – become figural in a person's development or in their life. These four are drive theory, ego psychology, object relations theory and self psychology. They are four approaches that have originated from development in the psychoanalytic world, and also guided the thinking of those developing the other major forces of psychology.

Why are these relevant to transactional analysis? Because most of TA is predicated upon the same assumptions as psychoanalytic theories. That is: a) whatever transpires is personally motivated and b) the adult personality is significantly shaped by early bodily-based and object-connected experiences. In other words, how a person behaves is dictated from within himself and is likely to be largely influenced by his experiences in early life. The four psychologies outlined here each describe a significant way in which the mind functions. In fact, they encompass the foundation of understanding human personality of almost all the approaches to psychotherapy. What is more, they seem to offer a rationale for the existence of several different models of ego states. In this introduction, we will briefly describe the four theories as elucidated by Pine, then link them to models of ego states.

A very brief history of psychoanalysis
Psychoanalysis started as a *drive theory*. Freud (1905, 1915) believed that the human being is driven by the libido (understood to be predominantly a sexual drive) and mortido (the urge to destroy and ultimately to die). Most of his theories centred around the idea that man (and woman) seeks constantly to achieve gratification of his urges, thereby increasing pleasure and avoiding pain. While the basic drives he described were sexuality and aggression, they can be understood as giving rise to a variety of urges and instincts which, while biologically based, achieve psychological representation and form throughout life. Freud also believed that a separate part of the mind (later named the super-ego in the tripartite system) feels instinctive shame and guilt about these urges and attempts to repress or at best sublimate them. The urges are therefore subject to a wide variety of attempts to delay, transform, displace or sublimate them. The repressed material, held insecurely in the unconscious, continuously attempts to re-emerge and the individual tries again and again to repress or deny. These are the beginnings of the notion of the repetition compulsion. The individual is seen as struggling with the vicissitudes of his instincts.

Already this description of drive theory implies a need to understand how the individual is required to manage his urges and function successfully in the world. This was the beginning of the development of *ego psychology*, which mapped the growth and functions of the ego – the part of the mind that would integrate reality, drive and conscience (Freud 1926, A. Freud 1937, Hartmann 1939). The functions of the ego involve building defences against drives, but they also include managing adaptation to the environment, containing impulses and learning to delay gratification, undertaking reality testing and developing autonomy. These capacities, which are not found in the infant but exist in the adult, are seen as expanding over time as a result of learning. Problems in this developmental process lead to problems in ego function, such as overly rigid adaptation or, conversely, an inability to be self-contained or to test reality. No transactional analyst can discuss ego psychology without, of course, mentioning Federn (1952) and his pupil Weiss (1950), who described ego states and introduced the notion that they were not simply a concept, but phenomenological and historical realities.

While psychoanalysts continued to hold drive theory as central, their study of how the ego functions were established and what facilitated the human being in their development, revealed the importance of the early relationship in the individual's psyche. Klein (1948) began to describe the libidinal and destructive drives in terms of the taking in or getting rid of the 'good' or 'bad' object. Freud had recognised the importance of the significant 'other', but only as a vital source of gratification. Fairbairn (1941), who coined the term *object relations theory*, proposed that in fact the infant's primary drive was object-seeking rather than pleasure-seeking. In other words, the relationship with the mother (or chief caretaker) was of fundamental importance. These views were supported and enhanced by the work of Winnicott (1958, 1965) and later Bowlby (1969, 1973, 1980), whose studies of infants and children in relationship to their mothers shed light on the centrality of the infant-object dyad. Object relations theorists see human experiences and behaviour as being a result of internalised representations of early relationships as they were experienced, which are repeated again and again in later life. Where these early relationships have been inadequate, abusive or neglectful, the individual will be drawn to people who will recreate that dynamic. This urge to repeat was included in drive theory as the breakthrough of repressed material, with the urge to complete, to find gratification and relief from pain. It was also part of ego psychology as a way of achieving mastery in the world and justifying modes of reaction that have become instinctual. In the repetition of object relations, it was now viewed as central to human functioning both in its attempt to keep the original relationship alive (even if painful), and in its attempts to wrestle with intrapsychic and interpersonal relationships.

The fourth development of psychoanalysis was the focus on the subjective experience of the *self* in relation to such phenomena as the attainment of boundaries of self-definition, self-esteem, agency and history. The notion of the cohesive and coherent sense of self, while developing essentially in relationship with the environment, was considered to be the essential developmental task of the growing infant and child. While the concept is included by the psychoanalytic authors already mentioned, especially the object relations theorists, it became central in the works of Kohut (1971, 1977) and his followers, and again, later, in the research-based work of Stern (1985). The role of the mother (or significant other) was stressed as vital in the establishment of confidence in the individual's worth and in his capacity to relate, to develop goals and values. The infant's pro-activity in establishing and regulating relationships was seen as proof of the existence of at least an 'emergent self' from birth. The mother's responsiveness and her ability to soothe, to contain, manage, and attune to feelings, laid down patterns of relating which the infant then appeared to repeat. Again, the urge to repeat patterns of relating to self and other is recognised, but in a psychology of self-experience, this is understood as the need to maintain the homeostasis of the syntonic sense of 'I'. Recent neuroscientific findings, in describing the establishment in relationship and subsequent fixing of neural pathways, do much to explain this inevitability of repetition.

Pine (1990) sees these four psychologies as being different aspects of human functioning, which are, in many ways, intertwined and overlapping. Any piece of behaviour can be viewed from any standpoint. For example, the crying infant may be expressing his hunger drive, or testing how to manipulate his environment; or he could be calling for contact with his mother or he could be expressing the anxiety provoked by loss of stable self-experience. A child who avoids his mother's contact may be managing an aggressive urge, trying to achieve mastery over a situation, playing out a dynamic of rejection or attempting to preserve his self boundary. Indeed the behaviour may well be understood in a multilayered way rather than as having discrete meaning – all could be equally true.

Similarly, in the consulting room a human being, a symptom or a problem could be understood from any of the viewpoints. A client's demand for the therapist's approval may be understood as exhibiting a need for gratification or poor impulse control. Again, he may be understood to be enacting an old relational dynamic in which finally he is rejected as 'too much' or he may be manifesting an unmet developmental yearning for appreciative mirroring from the idealised other.

Pine (1990) sees the four psychologies existing from the earliest moments of infancy as four types of motivation which develop throughout life, each linked to different developmental stages and tasks, and each becoming figural at different times, depending on the particular experiences of the person. He therefore believes that each individual develops *his/her own personal hierarchy of motivations*, which will emerge in the consulting room. For one person, drives will seem to be figural, for another some defect of ego functioning, for a third the repetition of destructive relationships, and for a fourth, a struggle with distance and closeness in relation to self definition. Pine (1990) urges the analyst to pay careful attention to his patient in order to notice which motive is central in any particular session. He warns against 'applying' the theories but says 'I listen with evenly hovering attention until I feel I understand something' (p. 51). This notion of 'evenly hovering attention' (Freud, 1912) evokes the phenomenological enquiry of existential or Gestalt therapy (see Spinelli, 1989; Sills, Fish & Lapworth 1995) in which the assumptions and presuppositions are bracketed in favour of listening with 'horizontal' attention. A method of inquiry and a sense of openness in the therapist's mind have now become core concepts of transactional analysis (Erskine, 1993). They are also implied in Berne's descriptions (1961, 1966) of attending to the client.

Drawing upon Pine we propose, therefore, that no one understanding would be complete. Although traditionally the transactional analyst does not normally aim to make her unconscious available for the patient's unconscious in the way Freud intended, there is inevitably an unconscious process occurring between patient and therapist. It seems to us that the extent to which the therapist pays attention to this process depends upon the influences upon her, her own imaginative and creative propensity, personality type and historical influences that have formed her as a person. For example, if the therapist is alive to her own unconscious, then the therapy is more likely to take that route (Hargaden & Sills, 2002). If the therapist is not so alive to her own unconscious processes, then the therapy will more likely take a cognitive route. The role of theory – such as the concept of ego states – will also be a different for different people. When therapists work strongly with imagination and intuition, then theoretical constructs and explanations provide a valuable tool by which to test and think about their hunches and feelings. For those who are naturally more given to sorting, solving and focussed thinking, theory provides a tool which supports their existing cognitive structures and can point the way to opening up other avenues of communication through feeling or intuition.

Thus, how one therapist might interpret, for example, the crying baby or the patient with symptoms, will be influenced, most importantly, by the unique presentation of that patient, but also, inevitably, by who the psychotherapist is as a person. Implicit in Pine's paradigm is an understanding that there are multiple lines of psychic interest. Which one the therapist chooses to pursue will probably be the one which most elicits her attention. It is this flexibility of transactional analysis, with its lack of rigidity, which has allowed for the development of a wide variety of different attitudes and theoretical leanings to develop. And as we will see, transactional analysis has grown from a number of different approaches.

We now turn to transactional analysis, and ego states in particular, in order to locate these approaches to psychology.

Drive in transactional analysis

'Drive psychology emphasises the taming, gratification and socialisation of drives' (Pine 1990, p.50). Berne (1961) did not include the 'id' in his model of ego states. He rebelled against the inflexible dogmatism, as he saw it, of the psychoanalytic world, and was attempting to create an accessible and useable body of theory and practice that would be immediately useful to his patients, whom he wanted very much to empower. He was a doctor and a pragmatist, and he prided himself on taking a scientific approach. He was no doubt influenced also by the growth of cognitive behavioural methods in the U.S. at the time, methods that stressed the factual and the observable.

Therefore, we may hypothesise that the notion of turbulent, overpowering drives, insecurely repressed in the unconscious, did not seem particularly helpful. However, Berne did describe the Child – the seat of the hungers, authentic feelings, needs and wishes, which would need to be mediated by the rest of the personality. He described the Parent, not the super-ego, but the authentic Parent ego state – the internalisation of the socialising force. This notion moved away from the theory of drive. Yet Berne said 'The function of the Parent was to conserve energy and diminish anxiety by making certain decisions 'automatic' and relatively unshakeable'. (Berne 1961, p. 76). This description pulls us straight back to the idea of the defence against anxiety that is the heart of drive theory. In this volume, drives are discovered in the connection between ego states and the brain described by Gildebrand (pp. 1-27) whose chapter brings together the neuroscientific evidence which, under different nomenclature, is increasingly supporting the validity of psychotherapeutic ways of viewing mankind. This is followed by Cornell (pp. 28-54) who moves naturally from the mind to the body as the oft-neglected element of the Child ego state. The notion of drives – not in the original Freudian sense, but in the sense of wishes, needs and hungers – is also found in the work of English (pp. 55-72) who links sub-systems of the Child ego state with dynamic motivating forces.

Ego psychology in transactional analysis

'Ego psychology emphasises the development of defence with respect to the internal world, adaptation with respect to the external world, and reality testing with respect to both' (Pine 1990, p. 50). It is clear that transactional analysis is an ego psychology. Not only do the words 'ego state' imply as much, but so many of the central ideas of the approach are compatible with the theories of ego psychology. Adaptation, reality testing, autonomy, self-responsibility are all key features of transactional analysis. The 'simple structural' model, and particularly its occasional reduction to 'values, facts and feelings', is a tool that rapidly increases 'the patient's ability to tolerate and control his anxieties and circumscribe his acting out.' (Berne 1961, p. 77). As this was developed into the functional model, which divided the Parent into Nurturing and Controlling and the Child into Free or Natural and Adapted (including compliant and rebellious), a simple yet sophisticated tool was provided for the client who needed, for example, to free his Natural Child feelings and urges (see English's Expressive Drive pp. 65-66), develop his Parental control or his Adult planning.

To an extent, ego psychology is represented throughout this book, and certainly in the work of Lee (pp. 73-82), who describes a dynamic technique based on a constructivist approach to transactional analysis; also Erskine (pp. 83-108), who offers a rich conceptualisation of the Parent ego state and goes on to describe the theory and practice of psychotherapy; and Erskine & Trautmann (pp. 109-134), whose chapter provides a 'live' example of Parent ego state work. All of these chapters also include object relations and, in Erskine & Trautmann's theory of relational needs, elements of self psychology.

Philosophically, Berne and other humanists, proposed that human beings were born 'OK'. There was, then, a fundamental philosophical difference between Berne and Freud, which is reflected in the theory. In transactional analysis, for instance, drivers, injunctions, script, games and so on are seen as creative responses to difficulties which arise in a person's life. Mental health, and the innate striving towards health as denoted by Berne's understanding of *physis*, are juxtaposed alongside pathology, so that a person in difficulties can be understood in a more balanced, even and human way than had sometimes been the case in psychoanalysis.

In terms of methodology, the central psychoanalytic techniques of free association, dream analysis and interpretation were not the tools of TA. Berne believed in the importance of the unconscious but considered that it is most usefully recognised as operationalised in script. Therefore he worked with the 'specified' material (Berne 1966). However, his focus on intuition and ego image demonstrate a continuing respect for the power, not only of the patient's unconscious, but also that of the therapist. The fact that Berne studied psychoanalysis – and it is clear that he also expected his students to do so – accounts for some of the multiplicity of theoretical routes open to the transactional analyst. It also explains the, at times, bewildering number of contradictions contained within TA. In addition, elements of the theories and ideas from both drive theory and ego psychology can be clearly recognised in transactional analysis's understanding of human beings and human motivation.

Object relations in transactional analysis

Similarly, object relations theory and the concept of the developing self are also evident.

> Object relations theory focuses on the task of simultaneously – carrying within us (through identification and internalised object relations) the record of the history of our object relationships – which is essential to our humanness and is a basis for social living – and on the other hand of freeing ourselves from the absolute constraints of those relationships so that new experiences can be greeted as new, within limits, and responded to on their own, contemporary terms. (Pine 1990, p. 50)

Pine also describes the development of early object relations as 'an internal drama, derived from early childhood, that is carried around within, as memory (conscious or unconscious) and in which the individual enacts one or more of all the roles' (Pine 1990, p. 35). This could be a pure definition of ego states and script. Certainly, as soon as second order structure was introduced (Berne 1961) and built on the notion of the real internalised parent (Federn 1952; Berne 1961), transactional analysts were provided with a working model of object relations. The focus in the early days was on how those early relationships were replayed through transactions and games. Later, the intrapsychic processes behind these dynamics became more the focus of the therapist's attention, for example in the works of Haykin, (1980), Moiso (1985), Novellino (1984, 1985) Blackstone (1993) and others.

In this book, object relations and unconscious processes are the focus of Shmukler (pp. 135-148), who reflects on the usefulness of ego states in a variety of contexts, and raises important issues in relation to unconscious communication in the psychotherapeutic relationship. Novellino (pp. 149-168) proposes an unconscious level of communication in the Adult to Adult therapeutic relationship. Shivanath & Hiremath (pp. 169-184) describe their ego state model in relation to race and culture. Erskine (pp. 83-108) describes the Parent ego state as a real, accessible internalised object; this is illustrated in the transcript and commentary of Parent ego state psychotherapy in Erskine & Trautmann (pp. 109-134). Hargaden & Sills (pp. 185-200) propose three domains of transference relating to early object relations as a way to chart forms of the unconscious.

The self in transactional analysis

Psychologies of the self focus on the diverse tasks of forming a differentiated and whole sense of self (both in contra-distinction to and in relation to the other), of establishing the self as a centre of initiative and as the owner of one's inner life, and of developing an ongoing sense of subjective worth.   (Pine 1990, p. 50)

As for the self, the literature is full of implications that the transactional analysis psychotherapist focuses on the developing self and self-experiences. Ideas drawn from self psychology (Kohut 1971, 1977 and his followers) have emerged perhaps only in the last decade (for example, Erskine, 1993, 1997, Blackstone, 1993, Erskine & Trautmann, 1996, Hargaden & Sills 2001). However, the concept of self-experience, of a growing child becoming himself in a changing environment, developing his identity and sense of himself in relation to others is implicit in the work for example of any therapist who works with the idea of early decisions.

In this book, chapters that have a focus on the development and needs of the self are the contributions by Erskine (pp. 83-108) who describes the relational needs, Erskine & Trautmann (pp. 109-134)) who illustrate working with those needs and Hargaden & Sills (pp. 185-200), who offer a model of the self as Child ego state.

Other chapters of the book build on all of the categories discussed here while adding new dimensions. Tudor (pp. 201-230) proposes a reformulation of the Adult ego state based on co-creativity and 'present centred' relating. Gilbert (pp. 232-246) stresses the importance of distinguishing phenomenological narrative from autobiographical memory and cautions against the concretisation of ego states. Oates (pp. 247-249) describes a personal journey in her understanding and use of ego state models – a journey that is encapsulated in her sense of an Adult self, which resonates with both the past and the potential future.

The implication for transactional analysis practice

Transactional analysis is born out of psychoanalytic thought, yet it was also developed at a time when the world of psychology was dominated by respect for the scientific, the observable and the measurable (the fore-runner of evidence-based practice of today). Berne and his colleagues were exposed to all the theories described above. He must also have been influenced by more pragmatic methods; his medical training and the high priority given in mid-twentieth century America to the 'do-able', the observable and the provable, tended to lead him away from approaches that allowed for the 'unexplainable'. This then coincided with the new post- Second World War optimism and confidence, the cult of the individual and the primacy of doing one's own thing. People were encouraged to 'lose ... your mind and come to your senses' (Perls 1969, p. 50) and to move away from 'oughtisms and shouldisms'.

Berne, in developing his own model, clearly intended his method to be a way of understanding the operationalisation of the unconscious and the development of ego function. However, we believe that he was also trying to discover an approach that would contain *all* the ideas about human beings and their functioning; the philosophy of OKness and self-responsibility, the pragmatic methodology of cognitive analysis, as well as the complexities of analytic theory.

The result of this versatility is that TA is well placed to support a flexible attitude in the therapist to the client's needs. For example, a woman complains of her inability to maintain intimate relationships. On investigation, it appears that she begins to feel anxious and irritable when her partner becomes close to her. It would be possible to make sense of the phenomenon as the manifestation of a wish for freedom and self-expression or even for control, which is defended with an anxious, tense response. The client might need help in recognising her Child feelings and responses. Equally, it could be said that the partner's presence made demands on her for adaptation, which she resented. In this case, the functional model of ego state modes may be used to explore the full range of the client's responding, in order for her to express her feelings in a way that maintains respectful relating as well as integrating the learned 'social behaviours'. She might be encouraged to question the force and strength of the Parent ego states, using Adult to choose an appropriate response, and exercising emotional literacy.

Another way of understanding the problem would be to see the relationship with the partner as recalling, for the client, the relationship she had with her father - a relationship in which she had felt used and abused. The therapist in this case may use the transactional diagram of games to facilitate understanding of the dynamics; or she may identify a type two impasse, and invite the client to 'find an early scene' (Goulding & Goulding 1979) in which the relationship was originally experienced, in order to re-experience the feelings and make a redecision about future relationships. If the early object relationship is deemed to be pre- or non-verbal, then the therapist might carefully analyse its manifestation in the therapeutic relationship in order to help the client bring awareness and understanding to her repeating patterns.

Finally, in terms of Pine's taxonomy, the client's discomfort may be understood as a fear of invasion of her self boundaries, a clue perhaps that as a young person, she had been somewhat engulfed and 'possessed' by her mother. In this case again, the therapist might explore manifestations of this discomfort as it occurred in the relationship between them, or she may think in terms of type three impasses. Or she may decide that a deficit had occurred in the early relationship that could be addressed through a careful empathic relationship.

Any or all of these interpretations may be sound. Each of them takes a different lens in understanding the issue, each uses a different model of ego states and each calls for a somewhat different treatment plan. At different times in the client's life, a focus on one or another of these aspects would be appropriate. It is the psychotherapist's duty to explore the material with the client, using ego state diagnosis to help discover the meaning of the symptom to the client at this time in her life. Ego state diagnosis will take into account how the problem is manifesting in the 'here-and-now' (behavioural diagnosis), the phenomenological truth of the client (phenomenological diagnosis), and the developmental stage and past experience of the ego states that are emerging (historical diagnosis). Use of the counter-transferential response of the therapist (social diagnosis) is also a vital aspect, for this brings feelings into the therapeutic partnership, which can give clues as to the nature of the problem. For instance, the therapist might notice that she found her client irritating, or that she started to feel a deep-seated sense of anxiety in the session. She may even notice feelings that do not seem related to anything that has been said. It may take time to understand, with all of the above, what exactly is the 'matter'.

Part of any accurate diagnosis has to integrate a cultural perspective. In common with many psychologists, psychiatrists, psychotherapists, and counsellors we have noticed that the profile of our clients has changed. Just as Freud's era differed from Berne's, we are now in a different time again. Berne lived in a time of Depression, then war, poverty and deprivation, followed, in the triumphant aftermath, by the surge of confidence and the desire to celebrate the individual and to free him from his constrictions. The typical client of this era was invited to free his Free Child and moderate his Controlling Parent. Things have since changed – we could say that Pandora's box has been opened, and of course, as we know, what was released from the box can never be put back in again. From an era of repression and authoritarian control we have moved into times where it seems nothing is contained, controlled or repressed. Sociologists may chart the breakdown of the family as the cause, others blame feminism, drugs, the hippy, the punk or just the rolling stone! Whatever the reason, the average client has a different profile from the one he had twenty or thirty years ago. The therapist needs to be aware and responsive to his needs. Clients are presenting with a more fractured sense of self. Common features expressed are a loss of security, a lack of identity, unstable experiences of self and lack of containment. The contract – that essential element of the working alliance – must reflect a careful exploration by therapist and client into the particular issues and problems of that individual. The therapist does not try to apply a 'one therapy fits all' approach, but listens with the client to her story, identifying which area of human motivation or functioning is involved. The therapist will use his intuition to see the ego image, to think Martian; he will use the evidence of his senses, and his feelings as well as his thinking to make sense of what he hears. He will be ready to develop a treatment plan based on all of this including, above all, the client's sense of what the problem is and what the remedy.

The Challenge!

'*C'est magnifique mais ce n'est pas la guerre*', commented an awed but appalled witness to the Charge of the Light Brigade. It is magnificent, but it is not war. It is not uncommon these days, to hear transactional analysts complaining that this or that approach to the work is – "Not transactional analysis!" We believe that the many diverse models of ego states available to us are in fact a strength, not a weakness, for they enable us to respond to the client where and who she is. It is exciting to see the concept of ego states responding to new understandings of human beings, new research evidence and new discoveries.

We are put in mind of the Christian teachings of *process theology,* in which God is seen as someone or something whose nature changes over time. He (or She) is described not as an immutable entity, because how could S/He be truly loving if S/He remained unchanging? Love exists in a relationship where both parties affect and are affected by the other. Instead, process theology sees God as a being that evolves in response to Her/His people. Richardson & Bowden (1983) describe God in terms reminiscent of descriptions of a projection of the needed object. Thus, as humanity has changed and developed over the centuries, its experience of God has changed. At first there was the very involved 'Controlling Parent' God of the early books of the Old Testament; a God who talks and appears directly to the people, telling them clearly what to do, punishing them for disobedience. Later He becomes a distant, more benign God who invites His people to write their own laws and take responsibility for themselves; recently S/He has been viewed as many things – a feminist, a political activist – in short, a God who is responsive to the needs of the people. We believe that psychotherapy theory, and in this instance, transactional analysis theory, evolves in a similar way, according to the developing ideas of its practitioners and the needs of their clients. This means that the challenge for transactional analysts is to let ego states be as responsive as God!

References

Allen, J.R. (2000) Biology and transactional analysis: integration of a neglected area. *Transactional Analysis Journal* 29(4)250-259

Allen, J.R. (2001) Biology and transactional analysis II: a status report on neurodevelopment *Transactional Analysis Journal* 30(4) 260-69

Allen, J.R. & Allen, B.A. (2000) Every revolution should have dancing: biology, community organisation, constructionism and joy, *Transactional Analysis Journal* 30(3)188-191

Allen, J.R. (2003) Introduction to the section on neurology in Allen, J.R. & Allen, B.A. *Therapeutic Journey: Practice and Life.* Oakland, CA: TA Press

Avery, B. & Milhollon, B. (1997) The altered state: a missing link in ego state theory? *Transactional Analysis Journal* 27(4) 295-97

Berne, E. (1961) *Transactional Analysis in Psychotherapy,* New York: Ballantine Books

Berne, E. (1966/1994) *Principles of Group Treatment,* Menlo Park, CA. Shea Books

Berne, E. (1970) *Sex in Human Loving,* New York: Simon and Schuster

Berne, E. (1977) 'Ego states in psychotherapy' in P. McCormick (ed) *Intuition and Ego States: the origins of transactional analysis.* (pp.121-144) San Francisco: TA Press. (article first published 1957)

Blackstone, P. (1993) 'The dynamic Child: integration of second order structure, object relations and self psychology', *Transactional Analysis Journal* 23(4):216-234

Bowlby, J. (1969) *Attachment and Loss Vol 1. Attachment,* New York: Basic Books

Bowlby, J. (1973) *Attachment and Loss Vol 2. Anger and Anxiety,* New York: Basic Books

Bowlby, J. (1980) *Attachment and Loss Vol 3. Loss and Depression,* New York: Basic Books

Cox, M. (1999) The relationship between ego state structure and function and diagrammatic formulation' *Transactional Analysis Journal,* 29(1) 49-58

Drego, P. (1993) Towards an ethic of ego states *Transactional Analysis Journal,* 30(3)192-206

Drego, P. (1981) Ego state models in *Tasi Dahan* 1(4)119-145

Drego, P. (1993) Ego state paradigms and models, *Transactional Analysis Journal* 23(1)5-29

Drego, P. (2000) Toward an ethic of ego states *Transactional Analysis Journal* 30(3)192-206

Erskine, R.G. (1988) Ego structure, intrapsychic function and defense mechanisms: a commentary on Berne's original theoretical concepts *in Transactional Analysis Journal* 18(1)15-19

Erskine, R. G. (1993) Inquiry, attunement and involvement in the psychotherapy of dissociation, *Transactional Analysis Journal* 23(4)184-190

Erskine, R.G. (1997) *Theories and Methods of an Integrative Transactional Analysis - a Volume of Selected Articles,* San Francisco: TA Press

Erskine, R.G. (1998) The therapeutic relationship: integrating motivation and personality theories in *Transactional Analysis Journal* 28(2)132-42

Erskine R.G., Clarkson, P, Goulding, R.L., Groder, M.G. and Moiso, C. (1988) Ego state theory: definitions, descriptions and points of view in *Transactional Analysis Journal* 18(1)6-14

Erskine, R.G. & Trautmann, R. L. (1996). Methods of an integrative psychotherapy, *Transactional Analysis Journal* 26 (4) 316-328

Fairbairn, W. R. D. (1941) A revised psychopathology of the psychoses and psychoneuroses *International Journal of Psychoanalysis* 22, 250-79

Federn, P. (1952) *Ego Psychology and the Psychoses.* New York. Basic Books

Freud, S. (1905) Three essays on the theory of sexuality. *The Complete Psychological Works: Standard Edition* 7:135-243. New York: Norton

Freud, S. (1912) Recomendations to physicians practising psychoanalysis. *The Complete Psychological Works: Standard Edition* 12:111-120. New York: Norton

Freud, S. (1915) Instincts and their vicissitudes. *The Complete Psychological Works: Standard Edition* 14:117-140. New York: Norton

Freud, S. (1926) Inhibitions, symptoms and anxiety, *The Complete Psychological Works: Standard Edition* 20: 87-172. New York: Norton

Freud, S. (1926) Analysis terminable and interminable, *The Complete Psychological Works: Standard Edition* 23: 216-52. New York: Norton

Frielander, M. (ed) (1988) Theme Issue: Ego States. *Transactional Analysis Journal* 18(1)

Goulding M. M. & Goulding R. L. (1979) *Changing Lives Through Redecision Therapy,* New York: Grove Press

Hargaden, H. & Sills, C. (1999) The Child ego state: an integrative view. *ITA News, Spring Edition*

Hargaden, H. & Sills, C. (2001) Deconfusion of the Child ego state *Transactional Analysis Journal* 31(1)55-70

Hargaden, H. & Sills, C. (2002) *Transactional Analysis – A Relational Perspective.* London: Routledge

Hartmann, H. (1939) *Ego Psychology and the Problem of Adaptation* New York: International Universities Press

Haykin, M. (1980) Typescasting: the influence of early childhood experience on the structure of the Child ego state, *Transactional Analysis Journal* 10(4) 354-64

Hine, J. (1997) Mind structure and ego states *Transactional Analysis Journal*, 27(4)278-89

Jacobs, A. (2000) Psychic organs, ego states and visual metaphors *Transactional Analysis Journal 30(1)10-22*

Jung, C.G. (1968) *The Collected Works*, Vol.12 edited by H. Read, M. Fordham, and G. Adler, translated by R.F.C. Hull, London: Routledge & Kegan Paul

Klein, M. (1975/88) *Envy and Gratitude and Other Works 1946 -1963* London: Virago Books

Kohut, H. (1971) *The Analysis of the Self*. New York: International Universities Press

Kohut, H. (1977) *The Restoration of the Self*. New York: International Universities Press

Luborsky; L., Singer, B., & Luborsky, L. (1975). Comparative studies of psychotherapies: Is it true that "Everyone has won and all must have prizes"? *Archives of General Psychiatry; 32,* 995-1008

Moiso, C.M. (1985). Ego states and transference. *Transactional Analysis Journal* 15(3)194-201

Novellino, M. (1984). Self-analysis of countertransference. *Transactional Analysis Journal* 14(1)63-67

Novellino, M. (1985). Redecision analysis of transference: a TA approach to transference neurosis. *Transactional Analysis Journal* 15(3)202-206.

Novey, T.B., Porter-Steele, N., Gobes L. and Massey, R.F. (1993) Ego States and the Self Concept in *Transactional Analysis Journal* 23(3)123-38

Oller-Vallejo, J. (1997) Integrative analysis of ego state models *Transactional Analysis Journal* 27(4) 290-94

Oller-Vallejo, J. (2001) The ego states and the three basic functions *Transactional Analysis Journal* 31(3)167-71

Perls, F.S. (1969) *Gestalt Therapy Verbatim*. Moab, UT: Real People Press.

Pine, F. (1990) *Drive, Ego, Object and Self: A Synthesis for Clinical Work*. New York: Basic Books

Richardson, A. & Bowden, J. (1985) *The Westminster Dictionary of Christian Theology*. London: Westminster John Knox Press

Schegel, L. (1998) What is Transactional Analysis? *Transactional Analysis Journal* 28(4) 269-287

Sills, C., Fish, S. & Lapworth, P. (1995) *Gestalt Counselling*. Oxon: Winslow Press

Spinelli, E. (1989) *The Interpreted World: an Introduction to Phenomenological Psychology*. Sage London

Stern, D. N. (1985) *The Interpersonal World of the Infant*. USA: Basic Books

Stewart, I. (2001) Ego states and the theory of theory: the strange case of the Little Professor *Transactional Analysis Journal*, 31(2)133-47

Summers, G. and Tudor, K. (2000) Co-creative transactional analysis *Transactional Analysis Journal* 30(1)23-40

Thunnissen, M. (1998) The Structural development of the Child ego state *Transactional Analysis Journal* 28(2)143 - 51

Trautmann, R. & Erskin, R. G. (1981) Ego state analysis: a comparative view. *Transactional Analysis Journal* 11(2)178-185

Weiss, E. (1950) *Principles of Psychodynamics,* New York: Grune & Stratton

Winnicott, D. (1956) Primary maternal preoccupation. In *Collected Papers* (pp300-305). New York: Basic Books

Winnicott, D. (1958) *Collected Papers*. New York: Basic Books

Winnicott, D. (1965) *The Maturational Processes and the Facilitating Environment*. New York: Basic Books

Woods, K. (1999) A retrospective on states of the ego *Transactional Analysis Journal*, 29(4) 266-72

Chapter I

AN INTRODUCTION TO THE BRAIN AND THE EARLY DEVELOPMENT OF THE CHILD EGO STATE

Katarina Gildebrand

There have been significant developments in recent years in our understanding of ego states, developments that inform our work and our expectations of psychotherapy. In particular, new research methods have allowed for important strides into the understanding of the structure and function of the brain.

As practitioners, we are involved with processes of change, both in terms of possibilities and limitations. A conceptual framework for thinking about ego states in relation to the processes of the brain may be useful to underpin our work as clinicians. Questions about what works, and what doesn't, with whom, and why, are central to our work, and yet to date our understanding is often based on speculative assumptions, reached through the use of clinical enquiry as the main tool for research. Some of those assumptions, such as the importance of the quality of the therapeutic relationship, are gaining validation through contemporary research, whilst others need updating.

Freud, himself a neuroscientist, suggested that the field of neurology, then in its infancy, was too crude and not at that time a very useful tool for developing an understanding of the mind from a psychological point of view. Instead he proposed and embarked on an in-depth study of mental phenomena. The resulting observations, by him and many others, with their associated theories, have formed the basis for our understanding of psychopathology, and the therapeutic process.

However, in the last decade in particular, our understanding of the brain from the neurological point of view has progressed enormously. New research methods, such as functional brain imaging and molecular biology have allowed our understanding of the brain and how it functions to take a giant leap forwards. Of course, these exciting developments are in their infancy, and, no doubt, new findings will update some of the hypotheses and understanding that are described in this chapter.

The fields of psychology and neurology now begin to inform each other, as Freud himself had envisaged would one day take place. As clinicians, we are beginning to realise that we can make use of what we learn from the field of neurology to validate, update and change the assumptions on which we build clinical practice. As TA practitioners, we have inherited the concept of ego states as developed by Eric Berne, which was based in part on neurological findings limited to the research methods available at that time.

In this chapter, I will present a model based on two inter-related, but separate memory-systems. One system is concerned with 'higher' levels of functioning[1], and is potentially, in part at least, available to awareness. The other is concerned with more 'primitive' levels of functioning, is more instinctual and not in itself available to awareness. I link these memory systems to a conceptualisation of the Child ego state, related to Daniel Stern's model of child development. I also comment on the Parent and Adult ego state as relevant to this chapter, drawing on Jenny Hine's (1997) theory of ego states.

Throughout this chapter, I use clinical examples to illustrate the material presented. Through these discussions, I hope to help the reader develop a conceptual framework for thinking about ego states, and the possibilities and limitations of psychotherapy and change in general. I do not propose to suggest a complete model of ego states, but to provide an overview of relevant material about the brain, so that the reader may embark on further exploration of the concept of ego states. The chapter by Helena Hargaden and Charlotte Sills in this volume, *Who am I for you?*, can usefully be linked to this chapter to provide a comprehensive model of the Child ego state in relation to the brain.

Background
The way we were

We owe much of our inherited understanding of ego states to the now famous experiments by the neurosurgeon Wilder Penfield in the early 1950s. These findings informed and inspired Eric Berne in his development of ego state theory. Penfield hypothesised that ego states were the functional manifestations of underlying neurological structures which he referred to as psychic organs. By today's standards, Penfield used rather crude methods for studying brain function. Patients about to undergo surgery to relieve symptoms of epilepsy had the surface of their temporal lobe exposed. With their consent, Penfield was able to stimulate different sites of the bared surface of the brain of his subjects using an electrode. When stimulated in the area of the temporal lobe, the subjects reported vivid past memories.

Berne (1965), reflecting on Penfield's findings, wrote that:

> electrical stimulation of certain areas of the human temporal cortex leads to the re-experiencing of past events in a totality whose sense corresponds exactly to what is here called an ego state.
>
> (p. 281)

He goes on to say that Penfield speculated that:

> in this respect the brain functions like a tape recorder to preserve complete experiences in serial sequence, in a form recognised as ego states – indicating that ego states comprise the natural way of experiencing and of recording experiences in their totality. (*ibid*)

Berne was clearly attracted by this seemingly straightforward idea of ego states in action: 'press here, and activate ego state X'.

However, Berne does not describe in depth his thinking about the relationship between Penfield's findings and ego states. There were indeed aspects of Penfield's findings that indicated a more complex situation. For example, Susan Greenfield (1997) argues that 'the memories themselves were *not* like highly specific recordings on a video and were a far cry from the memories on a computer'. She also cites the fact that when the same area was stimulated on different occasions, different memories were elicited, and that occasionally the same memory emerged when a different area was stimulated. These findings seem to indicate a more dynamic, less static situation than indicated by Berne[2].

The way we are

It used to be assumed that, at birth, our brain was more or less fully developed, with a vast number of brain-cells waiting for their turn to mature. Reflecting this way of thinking, Berne (1964), in *Games People Play*, discussed the possibility of freeing ourselves from our early (negative) influences:

> Indeed, such liberation is only possible at all because the individual starts off in an autonomous state, that is, capable of awareness, spontaneity and intimacy...   (p. 161)

Berne here appears to assume, as was commonly thought at the time, that the functional structures supporting the capacity for autonomy were there from birth, and will therefore remain in adult life, ready to be activated under the right conditions.

However, in recent years there has been a shift in our understanding of the brain. Whilst it is known today that the brain has numerous 'potential' neural networks in early life[3], most of these networks are never activated, and therefore wither away and die, rather than lying dormant. The networks present in early infancy are not yet connections as such. The brain starts off with an almost infinite number of possibilities, in the form of *potentials* for functional structures. However, these neural networks are unable to function until they are 'primed', through repeated stimulation. Like an electric appliance, which is not yet plugged into a socket, these networks are by themselves as good as useless. Where these networks are not sufficiently stimulated, these early possibilities for neural connections disappear.

Some of the children who were kept in orphanages in Romania, where the level of stimulation they had been given was grossly inadequate, appear to have sustained what may well be permanent damage to their brains. A person who is born blind cannot learn to use their sight if it is restored in adult life, because the neural connections for learning to use vision were not established at the critical time in the infant's development. Glaser (2001) has demonstrated that severe neglect impacts the actual neural architecture of the brain.

Berne's assertion then that we are born *"capable* of awareness, spontaneity and intimacy" does not bear up to closer scrutiny in the light of today's knowledge. We are not truly *capable* until the neural wiring has been established through repeated stimulation. While our brain is formed with infinite possibilities for developing connections, some develop through sufficient stimulation, but others are never realised. For some, autonomy in terms of the capacity for spontaneity, awareness and intimacy may well be an unattainable goal, if the neural networks which would support such a capacity were not sufficiently stimulated at the critical point of development. As psychotherapists, we may need to re-adjust our expectations of what can be achieved with certain types of clients, and re-evaluate how best to work with them.

How the brain develops
The brain develops according to pre-programmed developmental tasks, such as learning to walk and talk. The motivation to develop certain skills and capacities, and the direction that the learning takes is innate, and unfolds according to pre-set patterns. Whilst some children start to speak or walk earlier than others, the overall pattern of development is universal.

However, the brain cannot develop without encouragement from outside. It is now recognised that the brain matures in response to environmental influences, in particular the mother-infant[4] relationship (Schore 1994). This relationship directly influences the structuring of the brain and how the various parts interconnect.

Specific aspects of the brain are pre-programmed to develop connections during spurts of growth in childhood (Glaser 2001), the infant actively seeking the type of stimulation it needs. Interestingly, stimulation is not, by itself, sufficient for sculpting to take place in the brain. Changes in neural structures require that we pay attention (Robertson 1999). By being fully engaged, we are more likely to imprint the experience in terms of learning, or the development of neural pathways.

The process by which the brain responds to demands by growing and adapting is known as 'Hebbian plasticity'[5] or just plasticity (LeDoux 1998). As described above, the infant is born with an infinite number of possibilities for neural connections to develop. It is through a process of enforcing and pruning connections between neurones that the brain develops. The old saying "use it or lose it"[6] holds very true of our minds; 'neurones which fire together survive together and wire together' (Post and Weiss 1997). The traditional division between 'nurture' and 'nature' no longer seems helpful in thinking about the brain. Nature and nurture are instead in constant interaction, both affecting and being affected by the other. It is like a dance without a leading partner, both setting the pace and following the other[7].

It has become clear that parts of the brain are more capable of re-moulding themselves in adult life, than previously thought (as long as sufficient development of the basic structures has taken place). However, the level of plasticity varies in each region of the brain. It appears that the higher centres, and in particular the pre-frontal lobes, retain a far higher level of plasticity, than do the more primitive structures associated with the limbic system. It would follow that it is, generally speaking, less difficult to make changes to pathology which has arisen from a later developmental period.

The three-tier brain
One easy way of conceptualising the structure of the brain is as a three-tier system of inter-related structures. In brief, the human brain (Fig. 1) consists of:
• the brain stem and cerebellum - controls vegetative processes
• the limbic system - the emotional brain
• the cerebral cortex - responsible for rational thought.

Ego states, here conceptualised as neural networks, are likely to be the result of activation of certain combinations of the neural wiring of the brain, which form part of these systems. I will focus on the latter two, the limbic system and the cerebral cortex, as these have most direct relevance to ego states. However, at some other time, it would be interesting to explore the role of our vegetative processes in their development.

Below I present a brief outline of these structures, and their inter-relationships:

The brain stem and cerebellum
These structures control vegetative processes (such as breathing, heart rate and blood-pressure) and automatic movement. It may be that clients with early developmental issues display disturbances in these processes, e.g. high blood pressure, or conditions related to some failure of the immune system.

The limbic system
Situated deep inside the skull, beneath the cortex, is a network of neurological structures known collectively as the limbic system[8]. This part of the brain is unconscious, and not in itself available to awareness. However, it affects our experience profoundly, linked through dense connections to the cortex above.

In brief, the limbic system consists of the *thalamus* (a kind of relay station, which co-ordinates sensory input, such as sight, smell, hearing etc.), the *hypothalamus* (which keeps the body adjusted to the environment), the *amygdala*, the seat of our primary emotions, and the *hippocampus*, responsible for laying down of long-term memories.

In an exploration of the applications of the limbic system to our understanding of ego states, it is worth taking a closer look at the latter two structures, the amygdala and the hippocampus. Together with the cortex they are intimately involved in the functioning of the three collections of neural networks creating the different states of the mind that we refer to as ego states.

The amygdala
The *amygdala* is crucial for our survival. It generates our primary emotions,

happiness, sadness, fear, anger, surprise and disgust[9] (Damasio,1999). Without our primary emotions, and fear in particular, we would soon succumb to the dangers our environments present, and probably die out as a species. Without the capacity to feel fear, we would not learn how to protect ourselves.

The amygdala is thought to be close to maturity at birth. Memories held here are crude and over-generalising, and cannot distinguish between past and present.[10] These memories are not by themselves accessible to conscious recall. For example, I might feel vaguely anxious whenever I am in the presence of a man dressed in a dark suit, but not know why. The influence of an early infant memory of being roughly handled by a man in dark clothing has been activated, although I have no conscious memory of such an event. This sort of memory is generally known as 'implicit memory', which we will explore further later in this chapter. Early emotional memories appear to be laid down here, supported by the developing cortical structures, in the form of a blueprint for emotional life.

The hippocampus

The hippocampus stores recent conscious memories, and is essential for learning and for the laying down of long term memories in the cortex.

If sufficiently repeated or significant enough, memories, with the help of the hippocampus, are laid down in the cortical structures as long term memories. Emotionally laden memories are easier to learn, which explains why most of us can recall what we were doing when we learned of the September 11th (2001) terrorist attacks on New York and Washington. Other memories may be lost, such as facts we learn for an exam, but then do not revisit.

The hippocampus plays a central role in co-ordinating memories, so that memories held in different cortical structures are remembered as one event (e.g. sound and vision). It allows us to understand the significance of what we see, so that we know not to be scared of fire burning in the fireplace, but get scared when seeing our house on fire.

During severe stress, the hippocampus appears to 'close down' so that the person is unable to recall the traumatic event. A period of prolonged stress also has detrimental affects on the hippocampus and its capacity for contributing to the laying down of memories.

For example, Vietnam veterans, who suffered from PTSD (post traumatic stress disorder) were found to have 8% less hippocampal tissue than comparable veterans. Adult survivors of sexual abuse were found to have 12% less hippocampal tissue (Bremner et al 1997). It is reasonable to conclude that children who live in an atmosphere of constant threat of physical or emotional abuse, will have poor functioning of the hippocampus in terms of the holding onto and laying down of conscious memories. In other words, they are not fully available for learning, and may suffer consequences such as poor impulse control, inability to plan or learn from their experiences and hold fragmented memories of their lives.

The hippocampus becomes sufficiently mature at about the age of three when it can begin to hold memories that are available to consciousness[10]. The inability of adults to recall memories from before this age, is referred to as 'childhood amnesia'. Our earliest memories appear to be held solely in our unconscious amygdala-based memory system.

Gabriella sought help from psychotherapy because of non-specific symptoms such as low self-esteem, relationship difficulties and a sense of internal emptiness. Nothing in her early history appeared to fully explain her symptoms. However, some years into treatment, she was in bed at a friend's house one night, just about to fall asleep. Perhaps it was the unfamiliarity of the surroundings, or some similarity of the room to a room where she had stayed with friends of the family at the age of two-and-a-half, which led her to re-experience the bodily and emotional experience of having been sexually abused. She felt scared, with a sensation of being held down and manipulated around her pelvic area and of choking, as if her mouth had been stuffed too full. From re-experiencing these early sensations, and putting together what she knew from her history, Gabriella became convinced that she had been sexually abused. For her, it was the missing piece to the puzzle, which helped her make sense of her difficulties, and allowed her to move on in her development. Whether or not the events, as we put them together, are historically accurate, will never be known. However, the reliving of her early memory, her early history and her presenting symptoms, allowed her to make new meaning of her symptoms.

Sometimes, people claim to remember early memories from before the age when the hippocampus becomes functional. However, the experience is often narrated "from the outside looking in", as if observing oneself from an outsider's viewpoint (perhaps because someone else has suggested the events) .

My client Elsa got in touch with an early childhood experience during a recent session. She burst into tears, saying: "I can see myself, only one-and-a-half years old, standing there in the doorway, bewildered. I felt completely alone, abandoned and confused, wondering why no-one was noticing me". In remembering this event, Elsa was drawing on her implicit memory of her abandonment and confusion, but adding to it a later construction; that of herself as a toddler in the doorway, visualising herself from the external view point of the adult self.

The cerebral cortex

The cortex, and in particular the frontal lobes, supports a greater complexity of processing and the capacity to learn from and adapt to the environment. From about 1.5 million years ago (Carter 1998) we gradually developed a very large skull with a brain, which allows us to think, plan, organise and communicate. We are truly the most big-headed members of the animal kingdom, as any woman who has given birth will know.

Conscious experience[11] (Damasio 1999) now becomes a possibility. In

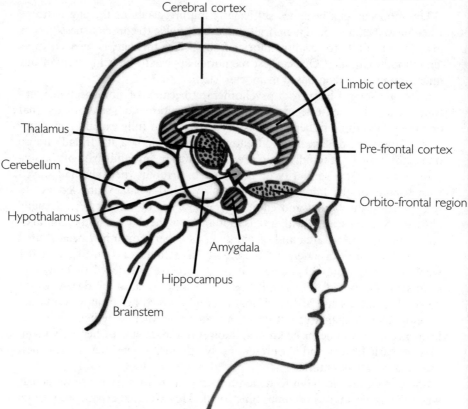

Fig. I: Anatomical regions of the brain

particular, the pre-frontal lobes (Fig. 1), situated at the front of the cerebral cortex, endow us with our specifically 'human' qualities. The pre-frontal lobes allow us to learn sophisticated lessons from experience. They are reality oriented, and act as the seat for our here-and-now consciousness, as well as our awareness of what is in the past and expectations of the future. Hine (1997) relates this uniquely human trait to the Adult ego state:

> ...the capacity of the Adult[12] to evaluate danger and choose upcoming action plans based on past experience gives humans an enormous advantage over other creatures, many of which are bigger, faster and stronger. (p. 286)

With the aid of the pre-frontal lobes, man has developed an impressive capacity to manipulate the environment. However, damage to this part of the brain can affect our capacity for logic. It has been shown that patients with an injury to parts of the pre-frontal lobes are capable of accommodating striking contradictions without concern. A patient treated by Dr. Mark Solms (2000 - 2001) following a brain injury, was delighted to have met up with an old friend, also a patient on the ward, who had died 20 years previously in another country. The patient, who could see that there was a problem with this situation, stated "It must cause some difficult legal problems to be dead in one country and alive in another". This patient demonstrated an unusual tolerance for contradictions, typical of injury to this part of the brain. Such contradictions are normally not tolerated by the well-functioning mind. It appears that the pre-frontal lobes are crucial for Adult ego state functioning, and damage to this part of our brain can make it difficult for us to learn from our experiences.

Of particular interest to us as psychotherapists, is the orbito-frontal region (Fig. 1). Situated on the underside of the pre-frontal lobes, it is thought of by some as part of the limbic system, to which it is closely situated and densely connected. It plays an important role in affect regulation, and is referred to by Schore (2001a) as the "Senior Executive" of social interactions, involved in managing behaviour, in particular in relation to emotion.

How we can remember what we can't remember

In the early part of the 20th century, a woman who had suffered a head injury, affecting her hippocampus in particular, was a patient in a French hospital. This injury had left her unable to lay down new conscious memories. Every day her doctor, Edouard Claparede (1911/1951), would go to see her, introducing himself by shaking hands. Each time, she had no conscious recollection of having met him before, even after only a few minutes of separation. Each day, as he introduced himself again, she responded to him as if they had never met before. One day, and no doubt in the name of science, he hid a pin in the palm of his hand. On shaking hands that day, she got a nasty pinprick. A short while later, she had no recollection of this at all. However, the next day when the doctor came to see her, she declined to shake his hand. When asked why, she was completely at a loss to explain why she felt apprehensive.

What was going on here? The woman clearly *did* remember at some level what had happened, or she would have shaken his hand as normal.

The explanation lies within the different structures, which hold our memories. The memory of the pinprick had been laid down in her amygdala, the seat of fear reactions, but not in her injured hippocampus; hence the lack of conscious memory of the recent past event. She had formed a clear, but unconscious memory of being hurt, whilst having no conscious memory of the event at all. For this woman, the link between the unconscious memory and the conscious mind, formed by the holding onto and laying down of long-term and potentially conscious memories, had been severed.

It is thus quite possible to perceive stimuli of which our conscious self has no awareness, but to which we still respond. Much of our early learning will be activated in this way, without an accompanying conscious memory. Outside awareness, these unconscious memories are constantly active, and will, to a greater or lesser extent, affect our total experience in the here-and-now.

Explicit and Implicit Memory Systems

The various parts of the brain interact with each other, creating *two* main memory systems that are of interest in this context: namely unconscious or *implicit memory,* and conscious or *explicit memory* (Fig. 2).[13]

The conscious or *explicit* memory system is mediated by the *hippocampus* and related cortical areas as described above. When we refer to remembering something, we are usually referring to our explicit memory system. It contains facts, concepts and ideas, and relies on the use of language. It allows us to assess the emotional significance of a stimulus, and decide on our response according to the meaning we attach to it, as mentioned in the example of the fire in the fireplace and the burning house.

The emotional or *implicit* memory system[14] involves internal states, automatic procedures and skills. It is related in particular to the learning of the fear response, but also includes all the six primitive or universal emotions [9].
It involves the *amygdala* and related structures. It was referred to by LeDoux (1998) as "the quick and dirty route", referring to the quarter of a second by which it is able to respond ahead of the hippocampal-based system, but without the sophistication of which the latter is capable.

For example, the soldier, returning from the war, is exposed to a car backfiring. His implicit amygdala-based memory system responds to the sound, which he has learnt to associate with danger. Before he has had time to assess the reality of the situation with his explicit memory system, he reacts automatically to protect himself from the perceived threat, throwing himself onto the ground.

A client came to me for help with PTSD following a serious physical assault. He was extremely distressed when telling me how, some weeks following the attack, he had punched a woman who innocently approached him to ask for directions. Having been pre-occupied with tying his shoe-laces at the time, he had not seen her approach until she was standing over him. Clearly, the assault had 'taught' him to be frightened of unexpected closeness, triggering the 'fight or flight' response.[15] He responded with a punch before he could assess the situation with the help of his explicit memory system. Luckily she was not seriously hurt, if understandably upset. However, my client was terrified he might attack someone again "despite himself", and was very disturbed by what he had done. He was very distressed because he had no deep-seated violent tendencies which may have inured him to committing violent acts. Clearly, in some ways he was innocent. His learned response for self-protection was too quick for his conscious self to have time to assess the situation and decide on more appropriate action. The ego state, which was in charge[16], was based on his defensive emotional implicit memory system.

However, our implicit memory response does not usually get us into trouble in such a dramatic way. Although the quicker route, it does not cause us to act so hastily, unless we have learned to do so through some fear-inducing experience.

As mentioned earlier, the functioning of the amygdala is imperative for our

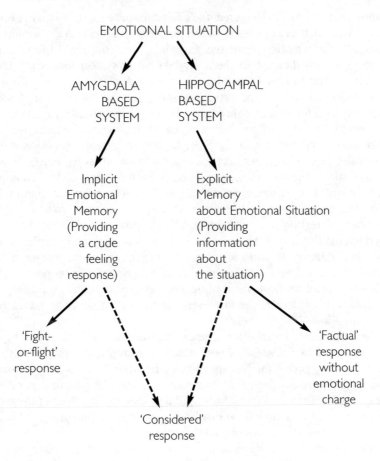

Fig. 2: Implicit and explicit memory systems, (based on LeDoux 1998, p. 202)

The figure above demonstrates how the emotional situation triggers a response in the amygdala-based memory system, and in the hippocampal-based memory system. The former causes a body based response, such as accelerating heart-rate and a tensing up of muscles, as part of the activation of primary emotion[5]. The latter stimulates a potentially conscious memory, of similar situations from the past and what that meant to you. Likewise, you will lay down a new memory of this particular situation in both memory systems. Should the amygdala-based system assess the level of danger involved in the situation as potentially life-threatening, it will activate the fight-or-flight response before the hippocampal-based system has had time to activate. On the other hand, should the hippocampal-based system become activated without the involvement of the amygdala-based system, the person will report themselves as not experiencing the expected feeling response. Most commonly, however, the two responses occur more or less simultaneously, and work in tandem to produce a response.

emotional life. When triggered, the amygdala-based system will fire our body-responses, such as changes in blood pressure, heart-rate etc. Should we lose access to information from the amygdala, our emotional life will atrophy. Someone with damage to the amygdala-based system may say: "It's a sad situation, and I know I should feel sad, but I don't".

Usually, the implicit and explicit memory systems, although separate, act in tandem to inform each other (see Fig. 2). For example, my client, Laura, always looks awkward and embarrassed when entering the therapy room, her movements indicating that she is attempting to 'disappear' and 'not be seen'. She can't explain why, but says she needs a few minutes to 'warm up' with me, before she can relax. Having suffered from abuse as a child, she appears to have learnt that people represent danger. When entering the room, it is likely that the 'mental blueprint', held in her implicit memory system, is activated for her protection and ultimately for her survival. Her implicit memory system, mediated by her amygdala, has learnt to associate people, in this case me, with danger. In these moments of entering the room, she cannot distinguish between friend and enemy, all people appearing to her as a threat. However, after we relate for a while, and her explicit memory system has time to assess the situation, she 'discovers' that I am not about to attack her, and she can allow herself to relax.

On other occasions the converse can be true, i.e. the feelings you experience are triggered by the *meaning* you attach to a situation, rather than the situation itself triggering the feeling. When a friend fails to keep an appointment, the feelings you experience whilst waiting for your friend will depend on what you make of the situation. The amygdala, while not involved in triggering the response, will nonetheless be involved in generating the affect. This is likely to be the mechanism producing racket feelings[17].

These examples of the influence of one system over the other seem to add new dimensions to our understanding and treatment of what Berne (1961) called Structural Pathology - in other words contaminations, exclusions and lesions.

The development of the Child ego state
From what we have touched on already, the laying down and activation of ego states involves two interconnected, but qualitatively different, memory systems; one potentially available to conscious recall, the other not.

The child develops and learns in interaction with the environment, building up its earliest memory system. At birth, the cortex is far from mature. During the first three years of life, the right side of the brain develops at a fast rate[18]. The memory structure that is closest to maturity at birth is the amygdala-based system. The amygdala and related structures will hold the blueprint of mental life, wired into its neural network, reflecting our experiences in the first few years of life.

The baby relates to its environment through his primitive emotions. The baby who is frightened or hungry, cries and attracts the attention of the mother. The mother's role in this symbiosis is to tune in to the infant's communication, to respond to, hold and soothe the distressed child, both physically and emotionally, as well as to provide stimulation. In other words, she acts as a container and caretaker for the child's affective expressions. Stern (1985) describes this role of the mother, as "the self-regulating other".

Allan Schore (2000) has shown that the attachment relationship directly shapes the infant's right brain stress-coping mechanisms. The orbito-frontal region, or the "Senior Executive" of the social-emotional brain, is especially expanded in the right cortex, and is heavily involved in affect attunement. If damaged in the first year of life, it influences social and moral behaviour[19].

It is the right side of the brain which we use when we 'tune in' to the underlying affectual state of the other, in the form of ulterior transactions. Eye contact and the interpretation of facial expressions and subtle shifts are of great importance for attunement to another's mental state.

By letting herself be impacted by her child in this way, the mother will respond to emotional signals given. Her response influences the infant, who responds in turn, again impacting on the mother's affectual state. It is in this dance, right-brain-to-right-brain, in interaction with another that neural pathways are laid down. Schore (2000) has demonstrated that the development of the right hemisphere is affect-dependent. He claims that the self-organisation of the developing brain occurs in the context of a relationship with another self, another brain.

It is during the first three years of life that the right side of the brain develops the most. This right-brain-to-right-brain receptive state of mind is familiar to many therapists, and described originally by Freud (1912) as "evenly suspended attention". We are listening for the communications from the (nonverbal) Child ego state.

The earliest scripting takes place outside the reach of conscious awareness. It is more than likely that these early unconscious memories, in the form of generalised representations[20], are activated frequently in our more significant relationships. These unconscious memories manifest as a developmentally early form of transference[21]. Held in this primitive part of the brain, these memories, which lack the sophistication of the cortex, tend to be crude and over-generalising.

The implicit memory-system, in interaction with a perceived authority figure, such as the therapist, may give rise to early memories of neglect, abuse and humiliation (as may become manifest in the transference relationship). These memories are outside conscious awareness, and if left un-tempered by later corrective experiences will be activated and experienced as 'real' in that moment. In other words, to that client, the therapist *is* an abuser at that moment. The memory itself holds little awareness of the experience being an intrusion from the past, as the awareness of time is a product of our explicit memory system. Understanding alone will not remove the impact of this early memory. One of my clients, who was angry with me after she had experienced a very difficult journey to her session, said: "I *know* it isn't your fault (explicit memory system), but it *feels* as if it is" (implicit memory system).

The bad news for the implicit memory system is that what is learnt tends to remain. This is particularly true in cases of abuse or neglect. This phenomenon is likely to be related to the survival function of the amygdala as the seat of our 'fight, flight or freeze' reactions. The good news is that is seems possible to re-mould the affect regulatory structures in the pre-frontal lobe. The exception may be where the brain has been too badly damaged through the early experience. A relationship with a therapist over time, focussing on attunement and containment of early emotion, may forge new neural pathways, offering an alternative response to a situation. Here the therapist would take on the temporary role as "the self regulating other" (Stern 1985). Future research will hopefully throw more light on the neural responses to such a relationship. In normal development, the right side of the brain becomes responsible for generating *awareness* of emotion, expressing itself through affect representational systems, such as symbols and metaphors (Allen & Allen 1999), as utilised by artists of all kinds, including musicians.

The left hemisphere focuses more on the *reasons* behind the emotion, and uses language as its representational system. At 18 months, the left hemisphere develops fast as the child begins to learn to speak, as the centres responsible for the development of language are situated here. As the child grows and develops towards adulthood, these developing neurological structures gradually take over responsibility for satisfying the needs of the organism. This can be understood as the gradual dissolving of the (healthy) symbiotic relationship.

Ego states as neural network hierarchies

The infant is pre-programmed to learn to master its environment specifically in terms of pre-programmed developmental tasks. As mentioned earlier, this is manifest by critical periods in brain development, during which the infant is engaged in specific tasks, such as learning to walk or talk. Berne recognised this as a drive, which is with us from birth, manifested as a need for *stimulation* (stimulation-hunger). The infant also needs to keep safe. Our safety relies on forming bonds with other humans, in particular the mother, and later the father and other close family members. We are hard-wired to seek out *relationships* (Johnson 1994). Berne recognised this drive as manifest in recognition-hunger (Berne 1982). Hine (1997) conceptualises the Adult ego state as arising from the experience of mastery and understanding of the environment (related to stimulation and structure hunger), and the Child ego state as arising from the experience of engaging in relationship (related to recognition hunger).

The Parent ego state, thought of by Hine (1997) as "internalised parent figures" allows us to fall back on skills and relationships which we 'borrow' from authority figures around us. Being born with limited genetically inherited skills and knowledge, it may be to our advantage to be able to 'draw on' others' experience and knowledge.

Throughout life, we oscillate between exploring the new, in order to learn more, and rushing back to base to find our sense of safety. Problems may arise where the very safety we need in our early relationships to support our learning is compromised.

Hine (1997), proposes that ego states:

> ... form progressively out of generalised representations that develop as the individual interacts with the environment and with his or her perceptions of self and others through the period of infancy and childhood. (p. 278)

Based on recent findings in the field of neural development, Hine goes on to describe her understanding of ego states to be:

> discrete systems of mental activity that build up progressively from lived perceptual experience and that have continuity, coherence, and a certain stability over a lifetime. *(ibid)*

She suggests that ego states can be usefully conceptualised as the manifestation of three underlying neurological network hierarchies; the Child, the Adult and the Parent ego states respectively. She describes healthy functioning as occurring when the three ego state networks interact harmoniously. In other words, like a team of three, with very different qualities, but each contributing with their unique characteristics. This proposition is moving away from the more common view of the Adult ego state as responsible for integrating, or holding the integration of the Parent and the Child.

The term 'ego' was used by Freud to describe our conscious selves, the part of our experience which is available to awareness, and which was the focus of Berne's method of clinical work more than his theories. However, Berne also used the term in ways that implied the inclusion of unconscious processes. The term ego state as used in TA often appears to include what some theories refer to as the 'self'. It seems that the word 'ego state' in TA has been and is used in different ways [22]. It may be useful for TA as a body of theory to update and, as far as possible, reach some agreement of what is meant by the term.

Some thoughts on brain development and developmental phases of the infant, as described by Daniel Stern

Stern (1995) describes the evolution of early aspects of what transactional analysts might call the Child ego state based mainly in the implicit memory system. He developed a theory of infant development of the self [23], based on numerous in-depth observations of infants and infant-and-mother interactions. He identified four developmental phases, each characterised by a specific developmental task. Each phase represents the start of a life-long period of development and also a critical period during infancy when a specific aspect of self-experience develops with particular intensity. Each sense of self will be laid down in the form of neural networks. These networks will continue to change and develop throughout life; new networks get established, neural connections which are frequently used will remain and strengthen, whilst those not activated will diminish. He named the four aspects of self: the emergent self, the core self, the inter-subjective self and the verbal self respectively. The resulting early ego states will form an important part of the Child ego state, and be mostly pre-verbal and unconscious.

The Emergent Self (0 months - 2/3 months)
This can be understood as the early establishment, through repeated activation, of neural pathways. This developmental phase is likely to prepare the ground, by serving as a reference point, for the development of a sense of Core Self which follows. The Emergent Self has its roots in the baby's somatic, or body self.

Stern describes the Emergent Self as a period when the infant is specifically concerned with making connections, leading to the "*emergence of organisation*" or the most rudimentary experience of a sense of self being in the process of "*coming into being*" (Stern 1995 p. 28). The baby can be observed to occupy a state referred to as *alert inactivity* (Wolff 1966, Stern 1985). The baby, satisfied and awake, appears alert, as if 'taking in' what goes on around them.

At this stage of development, the baby is mostly concerned with internal stimuli, regulated by the limbic system. However, the propensity for bonding behaviour by actively seeking stimuli generated by the mother (such as turning towards the outline of a face, or the smell of the mother's milk) is present from the first hours after birth.

The emergent sense of Self, like the other senses of self, continues to develop throughout life, although not at the same level of intensity. For example, the moment of understanding which follows the period of blankness when pondering a problem, is an example of an emergence of a connection.

Fig. 3: Brain development in the young infant

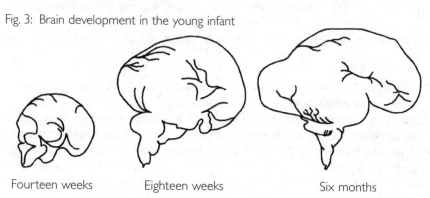

Fourteen weeks   Eighteen weeks   Six months

During the first few months of life, the brain is busy forging connections with such intensity that the baby sometimes appears to 'blank out'. It is speculated that, for short intervals, the brain appears to go into overload, as demonstrated by a temporary flat-line readout on an EEG (Channel Four UK TV, 2000). Perhaps our need for periods of withdrawal, which form an important aspect of our capacity for affect regulation, has its roots in the need of the organism to 'digest' our experiences in order to create optimal neural connections. Indeed, one of the potent sources of stress in modern life has been identified as the lack of access to periods of inactivity, which appear to be necessary for the brain to effectively process past events.

The Core Self (2 months - 7/9 months)

Stern (1995) describes our Core Self as the baby learning to experience themselves as whole and complete physical beings[24]. The child's physical needs, limitations and capabilities are the focus for development during this stage. The brain continues to grow at an incredible rate (see Fig. 3). Sills (1995) and Hargaden and Sills (in this volume) describe how the child, who experiences sufficiently attuned interplay with the primary care-giver, develops a cohesive and fundamentally OK sense of core self, which will form part of the infant's developing 'blueprint of emotional life'.

Where the level of non-attunement has been experienced by the helpless baby as threatening to its survival, the memory of the relationship becomes engraved as a traumatic experience. The infant's developing sense of himself as physically whole and complete is likely to be fragmented, and his sense of trust in being safe in the world will have been impaired. The baby experiences himself as not OK. This trauma will be stored in the implicit memory system, only to be unconsciously evoked in relationships in later life.

As we have seen above, the memory activated is ingrained in the amygdala based memory systems, but these early experiences will also influence the development of the child's cortex. The cortex is not yet sufficiently mature to hold the conscious memories we come to expect from the older child, and he will not be able to recall these events in adulthood. However, the child's neural pathways are continually moulded in response to experience, affecting his later capacity to function.

The infant is an active partner interacting with his mother. An OK experience of this relationship will result in an OK sense of core self. It is likely that such 'good enough' experiences form the solid base on which the Adult ego state develops, drawing on the early experience of mastery from the interaction with the mother.

Client Jonathan, whose mother had suffered from post-natal depression, was left for long periods in discomfort. Even when the mother did respond, it is likely that her level of responsiveness would have been dulled by her internal state. He eventually learnt not to cry; he became a 'good baby'. His father, on the other hand, was more prone to interact with the boy. However, he was very loud and abrupt, often frightening to Jonathan. He appeared not to have noticed his son's distress, and Jonathan soon learnt to hide his fear rather than losing the attention his father did give him. He grew up harbouring a deep sense of emptiness. As an adult, he started to compensate for his lack of internal structure by seeking high levels of stimulation, riding fast motor-bikes and living 'close to the edge' generally. This gave him the sense of exist-ing that he lacked internally. "I am excited/frightened[25], therefore I exist." He commented that underneath the excitement, he was not at all sure who he was, and he carried a fear of going mad; probable signs that his sense of core self was fragmented and lacking the experience of wholeness striven for by the organism at this phase of development.

Inter-subjective Self (9 months - 15/18 months)
At about 7-9 months, the baby reaches a developmental milestone. With a developed sense of itself as a physical, complete being, the child can perceive 'the other' as a separate entity. The frontal lobes have developed sufficiently to deliver the first glimmers of cognition, and the infant has begun to develop a generalised representation of the mother as existing over time. The infant's core self, is now sufficiently developed to allow the emergence of 'other' as external or separate to itself (Hargaden & Sills 2001). At this stage of devel-opment the pre-frontal cortex, of great importance in our human experience, is deeply involved. Edme (1988) argues that the greatest promoter of growth lies in this early experience of intimacy, shaping and developing the pre-frontal cortex.

The pre-frontal cortex contains the orbito-frontal region, which is activated when we experience empathy and soothing. During this critical period for its development, the orbito-frontal area is busy forging connections with the limbic system that will help the infant manage distress. It is speculated that with sufficient repeated episodes of being comforted, the infant will inter-nalise the experience and learn how to self-soothe.

Infants now become shy of strangers, especially if the mother is not there to reassure them. They now 'know' in a rudimentary way (as contained in the developing neural structures of the pre-frontal lobe), that they have a mind, and that others have one too, and that this state of mind can be shared. For example, it is now possible to point at an object and the infant will follow the implied direction given by the finger and look at the object pointed at (Stern 1985). A few months earlier, the child may have been fascinated by the dis-play of the finger, but not much else. It is now possible to share the focus of attention with another, to hold a shared abstract idea.

At this time in the infant's development, a now famous experiment was carried out (Stern 1985). A crawling baby was enticed to crawl across a glass top towards a desired object. To get to it, they had to crawl across a 'visual cliff'. Typically, when the infant encountered the 'cliff' below, they hesitated, and looked towards the mother for feedback. They recognised potential dan-ger, but looked for maternal instruction on how to react. Where the mothers had been instructed to smile encouragingly, it resulted in the infant crawling across the chasm. We can speculate that the experience gave rise to a sense of mastery as contained in the relational interaction. When the mother showed fear, the infant retreated, and became upset, experienced perhaps by the infant as a failed attempt at mastery. In both these incidents, the child took instruction from the mother to guide him on how to react.

This sharing of affective states is typical of this stage of a child's development, and appears, as mentioned earlier, to engage the right hemisphere of both mother and infant, and to contribute towards the neural development in the infant in particular. In healthy development, the mother and infant typically resonate with each other, co-creating a psycho-physiological inner state similar to each other's (Allen 2000).

The possibilities for failure of attunement, or empathic failure [26] however, are immense. In the example of Jonathan, his need for containment had been neglected by his unresponsive mother, as well as by his intrusive and insensitive father. Both parents, each in their own way, failed to 'read' and respond to his affectual state. Working with Jonathan, I experienced a non-specific sense of anxiety or fear in our relationship, presumably a result of his watchfulness for the signs of abandonment or intrusion to which he had had to adjust as a small boy.

The pre-frontal lobe is now developed sufficiently to allow the child some capacity for simple reasoning. If the mother in the example above is responsive to the infant's distress, she will be able to re-attune and help the infant to repair the rupture. The infant is likely to begin to use early reasoning to establish a belief about himself as OK. When the rupture is not managed, however, the potential for an early belief about himself as not OK is much greater.

The experience of attunement in the relationship with the mother influences the development of the orbito-frontal region of the brain (Fig. 1). Referred to by Schore (2001) as the "Senior Executive" of social interactions, he claims that the early environment, and the relationship with the mother in particular, has a direct influence on the final wiring of circuits in the cortex of the brain. Bowlby (Holmes 1993/95) also argues that the orbito-frontal region of the brain executes the highest level of control of behaviour, in particular in relation to emotion. It appears that our capacity to manage our feelings is laid down in the brain during this developmental phase. In all likelihood, a relationship in adult life, such as may be provided in the therapeutic relationship or in a loving partnership, can provide an opportunity for learning to contain and manage emotion by drawing on the attunement provided through this 'right-brain-to-right-brain' interaction.

It is interesting to speculate that the 'therapeutic tension', often thought to support optimal change, does not come about through the client experiencing the therapist as perfectly attuned, but, in addition to a 'good enough' attunement, requires manageable chunks of ruptures and repairs in the relationship. In this way, each experience of successful mastery of a rupture is likely to contribute to the development of new neural pathways. Such experiences may contribute to an early sense of mastery (Hine 1997) of the environment, of 'being in charge', an experience attributed by her to the Adult ego state.

Luke came to me for psychotherapy following a suicide attempt. A very successful businessman, he was married with two children. His work involved extensive travel around the globe. He was highly regarded for his energy and competence, having received awards for his contribution to the company. His home and family were very important to him, but more a symbol of security than as real people. He carried treasured photographs in his wallet, but managed to spend minimum time actually being with them. As a personality, he was enthusiastic and engaging, with an exaggerated sense of self-worth. He got his needs for closeness and sex met through a succession of mistresses, each time falling madly in love until he met the next one.

It was a bubble waiting to burst, and when it did, Luke's whole existence lost its meaning - his wife filed for divorce. Following a suicide attempt, he went into a deep depression, questioning everything he had ever done and deeming his whole life to date a failure. He came face-to-face with his belief about himself as un-lovable, and the pain of early abandonment, which he had successfully defended against until now.

The crisis motivated him to seek help through therapy. Together, we explored his early belief systems, as manifest in his story and in the quality and expectations of his relationships (including in our relationship). Slowly and painfully, and through a lot of grief, he began to learn about being in a relationship where abuse and neglect was not the norm. For the first time in his adult life, he chose not to be in a sexual relationship, as he began to build up his tolerance for closeness and intimacy.

It transpired that Luke carried a deep-seated belief about himself as not OK. He had defended against his sense of not OK-ness by being successful, and being able to tell himself that he had a successful marriage. However, he was terrified of intimacy. His mother, though superficially supportive of him as a child, was subtly but consistently denigrating of much of his experiences. She was more invested in having a little boy who could bring her pride, whom she could "show off" to others as an affirmation of her own worthwhile-ness. She failed to attune to the "real" Luke, as she selectively attuned only to aspects of his experience of which she could feel proud. As a result, he developed a "false self" through which he related to the world.

After more than 10 years of therapy, Luke in now beginning to develop a close relationship with a woman he has known for some time through his work.

The Verbal Self (15/18 months onwards)

From about 15 months, the child starts to speak. This developmental leap coincides with a spurt of growth in the left hemisphere, responsible for language development. Before this age, a child, on seeing itself in a mirror, does not fully know that it is looking at itself. It typically points to the mirror to draw attention to something it sees.

After 18 months or so, the child, on seeing its reflection in the mirror, will point to itself (Stern 1985). It is now able to be truly self-conscious, to see itself as an outsider might. This capacity for abstract thinking is vital for the development of the symbolic media of language, and the cortex will be relied on to provide the necessary neural connections. The child learns to communicate like never before. It can share its experience with others, and construct a narrative of its own experiences. Hine (1997) suggests that the Adult ego state, A_2, develops as the child learns about 'cause and effect' in its striving for mastery and understanding of the external world and of its own organism. The use of language is imperative in this process.

Language as an emotional regulator

Language can now begin to serve as an emotional regulator. Parents instinctively begin to give verbal explanations to their child, to help the child to understand what is happening and why. Through this process the child begins to build up its capacity to use verbal reasoning and understanding to help contain its feelings.

I recently visited some friends who had a four-year-old daughter. At the end of a long day of excitement, the mother left the room to make a private phone call. The little girl burst out crying, trying to follow her mother. Her father, sensitive to the girl's distress, picked her up and explained why her mother had left the room, and when she would be back. The girl listened attentively, then cried a little more. But soon she got on with playing again, and was heard saying to herself "Mum will be back soon, she's talking on the phone". She had learnt to use the information given to soothe her upset.

This process is further illustrated by an experiment measuring activity in the implicit memory system, using brain-imaging techniques (Robertson 1999). Subjects were asked to match the facial expression of fear displayed on photographs shown to them. Activity in their amygdala increased accordingly. However, when asked to name and successfully label the expression seen as fear, the activity in the amygdala decreased. It appears that the act of symbolising the experience through words is one way in which we learn to manage our primitive responses; in this way language can be used as an emotional regulator.

Interestingly, the right cortex is more densely connected to the limbic system than is the left[27], and appears to play an important role for our awareness of emotion. The left hemisphere can then name and identify the reason for the emotion, thereby playing its part alongside the containing functions of the right hemisphere in managing the feelings experienced. In this way, both hemispheres are involved and contributing to the regulation of emotions and primitive urges arising from the 'unruly' amygdala.

Summary and conclusions

Berne (1972) spoke of three major drives or hungers; structure hunger, stimulation hunger and recognition hunger. These relate to two tasks, which are paramount to us as human beings. The first, related to structure and stimulation hunger, is the striving to master our environment. The second, related to recognition hunger, is our need to be in relationship.

Using Hines' conceptualisation (1997), the Parent ego state arises by internalisation of parental figures, with the advantage of allowing us to get on with things without having to learn them first.

The drive towards mastery of the environment involves mainly the Adult ego state, an important part of the related neural networks located in the frontal lobes. Explicit memory forms an important aspect of this process.

The Child ego state, on which this chapter primarily focuses, relies mainly on the more primitive processes involved in implicit memory, and is probably, therefore, to a greater extent, unconscious. These processes arise out of, and are involved in negotiating our relationships (including our experience of ourselves). For the Child ego state the implicit memory system is paramount, holding our 'blueprint for emotional life'.

My understanding of ego states is informed by recent findings from the study of the brain. Ego states are here conceptualised as the activation of neural networks, which have become established over time. These neural networks draw on two interrelated, but separate memory systems.

The implicit memory system, crude and over-generalising in its recall, is by definition unconscious. The explicit memory system is at least theoretically accessible to conscious awareness. Normally the two systems operate together, informing each other, so that they appear to be part of a unified system. There appears to be an intrinsic 'desire' to integrate experience through the hippocampus and the explicit memory system, to make meaning of experience.

In health, it appears that the different memory systems work together, informing each other, but with the pre-frontal lobes managing the primitive impulses arising from the amygdala (an exception would be in situations when the faster 'fight or flight' response is called for in response to real here-and-now danger). Often, this has been referred to as 'integrated Adult' or 'integrating Adult' functioning. However, with an understanding of ego states as integrating neural networks, the idea of healthy functioning as an Adult ego state process may need rethinking [28].

At birth, the implicit memory system is believed to function well. The explicit memory system develops gradually and in response to experience, in particular through the relationship with the mother, but also through other stimulation and exploration. The cortex, in particular in the right hemisphere, grows very fast in the first few years, developing the capacity to lay down conscious memories from around three years old, when the hippocampus becomes sufficiently mature.

Early in life, and in relationship with the mother, we establish our life position and beliefs about ourselves, others and the world (held in a non-verbal form, in the implicit memory system). Our basic sense of OK-ness is developed through our experience of the interaction of our needs and body functions and the mother's response.

As the cortex begins to function at around 6 months old, we develop our early belief about ourselves dependent on our early perception of the nurturing relationship and of the outcome of ruptures in the relationship with the care-giver. A sufficiently attuned (through right-brain-to-right-brain interaction), and 'good enough' mother allows, through her emotional holding, the child to gradually develop a coherent sense of self with a growing capacity for self-regulation of affect.

As language begins to develop in the left hemisphere, at around the eighteenth month, the infant can symbolise his or her experience sufficiently to be truly self-conscious. Language can now act as a regulator of emotion working alongside the affect regulation provided by the developing right orbito-frontal region of the pre-frontal cortex.

The cortex gradually develops the capacity to 'care take', or to regulate and deal with emotion and social interactions. In healthy development there will be a gradual dissolving of the symbiosis with the mother. For the less fortu-nate, the need for symbiosis will, to a lesser or greater extent, remain un-resolved.

Early learning, in particular if resulting from trauma, is held in the implicit memory system and seems to be difficult, if not impossible to 'undo'. However, the explicit system retains a greater level of plasticity. Here we may establish new neural pathways, which, through repeated use, can begin to over-ride the early ingrained primitive responses.

Evidence for the possibility of creating new neurological structures in our right hemisphere (which is responsible for the regulation of affect) is begin-ning to emerge. It appears that by engaging in a relationship, which provides the experience of empathy and intimacy, we provide the conditions, which are believed to be particularly growth promoting[29]. This is not a new idea, but is now beginning to find support in neuroscience. Schore (2000) argues that for therapy to be effective, it needs to involve the client's "unconscious affect-reg-ulating structures", activated as part of the Child ego state, and developing in the pre-frontal structures of the right hemisphere in particular.

In addition, language plays an important role to help us make meaning of experience, and to challenge outdated unhealthy belief systems. Cognitive re-structuring involves the speech-centres situated in the left hemisphere. In the early days of classical transactional analysis, these processes were the main approach to treatment. However, cognitive restructuring alone may not be sufficient. For clients where early ruptures of the relationship with the moth-er means that they have developed a fragmented and/or hostile blueprint, negative aspects of developmentally early transference[21] will need to be worked through in the therapeutic relationship. In addition to cognitive restructuring, a healing relationship appears to allow the client to establish alternative neural pathways, which can, in part at least, over-ride and contain some of the old primitive 'blueprint' responses. The door is open for trans-actional analysts to expand and refine their treatment choices so that they can respond to the subtle complexity of their individual clients.

Notes

1 The use of the word 'higher' (memory system) is here used in relation to its later emergence in evolution. It is not intended as a value judgement in terms of bringing superior levels of functioning, as was commonly thought in the past. In fact, recent research points to the paramount importance of our more 'primitive' memory system to our overall functioning as effective human beings, particularly in relation to our capacity for engaging in relationships and in generating emotions.

2 Allen (2000) suggests that psychic organs "are best regarded as possibilities or probabilities of specific neural network activations rather than as static structures" (p. 261); this encompasses a wider understanding of the fluid complex connections of neural pathways.

3 At eight months, the infant has the maximum numbers of neural networks (Nilsson, 2000). By the age of about three, the 'pruning' process begins to remove un-activated neural networks.

4 The word 'mother' will be used throughout the document to mean the primary carer.

5 Hebbian Plasticity is named after Donald Hebb, who, in 1949, proposed that learning involves changes in neural function brought about when two cells are active at the same time, through a mechanism called long-term potentiation, LTP.

6 An example of this process was found through study of the brains of typists, machine-operators, and appliance repairmen. The research showed that the brain cells in the areas of the brain which corresponds to their hands (responsible for co-ordinating hand movements) were more richly branched when compared with brain cells responsible for other parts of the body. (Robertson 1999, p. 47).

7 Perhaps Eric Berne may have had an intuitive sense of how the brain is sculpted in relationship with the outside world, when he wrote: 'Parents, deliberately or unaware, teach their children from birth how to behave, think, feel and perceive. Liberation from these influences is no easy matter, since they are *deeply ingrained...*' (Berne 1964/82, p. 161).

8 There is some disagreement in the world of neurology about what structures should be included in the limbic system, or even if such a term is useful. The brain is in reality too complex to be neatly divided into separate sub-systems. There are implications here for ego states. Perhaps the focus needs to be on function, rather than structures (or psychic organs).

9 Antonio Damasio (1999) describes six *primary* or universal emotions: happiness, sadness, fear, anger, surprise and disgust. Those are emotions, which are inherently human, and common to all cultures. He distinguishes these from what he terms *secondary*, or social emotions, such as embarrassment, jealousy, guilt or pride, and *background* emotions, such as calm or tension. There is immediate relevance here for the concept of the Natural and Adapted Child.

10 Memories based in the amygdala memory system are experienced as happening *now*. When experiencing the activation of the memory, there is no awareness of time. The car backfiring is interpreted by the ex-soldier as a gunshot happening right now (thus the potential for re-traumatisation for patients suffering from PTSD).

11 Mark Solms (2000) describes a unit of consciousness as a bringing together of a moment of awareness of 'me' with an internal or external object, or event. Antonio Damasio expands on the subject of consciousness in *The Feeling of What Happens* (1999).

12 Hine (1997) argues for a new understanding of the three ego states, the Adult ego state being the neural networks concerned with a striving for mastery and understanding of the external world.

13 Freud referred to these forms of memory in terms of primary and secondary process respectively.

14 There are a number of implicit memory systems, but for the purpose of this discussion, we shall concentrate on the *emotional* implicit memory system, referred to in the text as the implicit memory system.

15 It appears that the appropriate amygdala inhibiting responses have not developed sufficiently in some people who have suffered severe emotional abuse or neglect, probably due to faulty development of parts of the pre-frontal lobe, which would normally inhibit such responses.

16 The ego state in charge here would traditionally be thought of as a fixated Child ego state, arising from a past traumatic experience, i.e. the assaults he had experienced.

17 Racket feelings are defined as "inauthentic feelings involving the substitution of one feeling for another" (English 1971).

18 The brain continues to grow into maturity well into our twenties

19 In cases of severe abuse or neglect early in life, the pre-frontal cortex does not fully develop. The right orbito-frontal region has been found to be severely damaged in murderers, linked to abuse and neglect in childhood. In addition, functional imaging studies have shown that murderers exhibit less activity in the frontal lobes, which is likely to affect their capacity to control their impulses (Raine et al 1997). However, these studies are yet in their infancy and inconclusive. It is becoming clear that empathic attunement is necessary for the development of the brain-structures which we employ in our socio-emotional life, as we attempt to master the demands of the outside world and manage internal impulses and drives.

20 Hine (1997) describes a generalised representation of an event as "the knowledge, and reactions to that knowledge, that are synthesised from perceptions of several different occurrences of similar events until it becomes the expected stereotype for future occurrences of the same experience" (p. 297). Daniel Stern also referred to such representations in terms or RIGS, or "Representations of Interactions which have become Generalised" (1984). (Maria Gilbert explores this concept in more depth in her chapter in this volume.)

21 Allen & Allen (1991) explore four different types of transference, suggesting three types of transference as arising from the implicit memory system, and one arising from the explicit memory system.

22 William Cornell explores the concept of ego states in greater depth in his chapter in this volume.

23 Stern speaks of a crucial period of development for each particular sense of self. He postulates that each sense of self continues to develop throughout life. The brain is pre-disposed to the neurological wiring supporting the particular phase, of development of self-experience, engaged in at that particular time.

24 .... in terms of self-agency (ownership of actions), self-coherence (being a non-fragmented, physical whole), self-affectivity (experiencing one's own affect as belonging to oneself) , and self-history (knowing I exist over time).

25 The physiological response arising from fear and excitement is similar, whilst the *meaning* a person attaches to the experience places it into one category or the other.

26 Stern speaks of non-attunement, selective attunement, mis-attunement, un-authentic attunement and over-attunement as examples of the various forms of empathic failure.

27 There are denser neural connections going up from the limbic system to the cortex, than there are connections from the cortex to the limbic system. As the limbic system is largely a product of bodily reactions, the old saying that 'the heart rules the head' has merit in the wiring of our brains.

28 Hine (1997) suggests the introduction of the term "integrating ego state networks" when referring to mature functioning of the individual.

29 Rogers (1951/1994) was, in my view, before his time in claiming that the quality of relationship was a major tool (or *the* tool, according to his model) for facilitating therapeutic change. He described the desired quality of relationship in terms of the three "core conditions" of empathy, congruence and unconditional positive regard.

References

Allen, J. R. (2000)Biology and transactional analysis II: a status report on neurodevelopment. *Transactional Analysis Journal*, 30(4)260-269

Allen, J & Allen, B (1991) Concepts of transference: a critique, a typology, an alternative hypothesis, and some proposals. *Transactional Analysis Journal*, 21(2)

Berne, E. (1961) *Transactional Analysis in Psychotherapy.* New York: Grove Press

Berne, E. (1964) *Games People Play.* Harmonsdworth: Penguin

Berne, E. (1965) *Principles of Group Treatment.* New York: Grove Press

Berne, E. (1982) *What Do You Say After You Say Hello?* London: Corgi Books (First published 1972)

Bremner, J.D., Randall, P., Vermetten, E. and Staib, L. (1997) *Biological Psychiatry* 41(1), 23-32

Carter, R. (1998) *Mapping the Mind.* London: Weidenfeld & Nicolson

Claparede E. (1951) Recognition and "me-ness". In D. Rapaport (Ed.), *Organization and Pathology of Thought* (pp. 58-75) New York: Columbia University Press. (First published in 1911)

Coleman, D. (1995) *Emotional Intelligence.* London: Bloomsbury

Damasio, A (1999) *The Feeling of What Happens.* Reading, Berks: Cox & Wyman

Edme, R. N. (1988) Development terminable and interminable. Innate and motivational factors from infancy. *International Journal of Psycho-analysis*, 69, 23-42

English, F. (1971) The substitution factor, rackets and real feelings. *Transactional Analysis Journal* (4), 225-230

Freud, S. (1912) Recommendations to physicians practicing psychoanalysis. *The Complete Psychological Works.* Standard edition (12)111-120

Glaser (2001) in Balick, A. (2001), "The 7th UKCP Professional Conference"(Warwick University, UK) The Psychotherapist, Issue No. 17

Greenfield, S. (1997) *The Human Brain – a Guided Tour.* Guernsey: Guernsey Press.

Hargarden, H. and Sills, C. (2001) Deconfusion of the Child ego state. *Transactional Analysis Journal*, 31(1), 55-70

Hickman, D. and Klein, L. (1994) *Baby, It's You.* Channel Four TV UK 25 May, part one.

Hine, J. (1997) Mind structure and ego states. *Transactional Analysis Journal* 27(4)

Holmes, J. (1995) *John Bowlby & Attachment Theory.* Routledge: London. (First published 1993)

Johnson, S (1994) *Character Styles.* New York: Norton

Karplan-Solms, K. & Solms, M. (2000) *Clinical Studies in Neuro-Psychoanalysis - an Introduction to Depth Neuropsychology.* London: Karnac Books

LeDoux, J. (1998) *The Emotional Brain.* London: Weidenfeld & Nicolson

Nilsson, A. (2000) Digital Högertrafic i Tankens Nätverk. *Psycholog Tidningen* 12-13/00

Pinker, S. (1997) *How the Mind Works.* Harmondsworth: Penguin Press

Post, R. and Weiss, S. (1997) Emergent properties of neural systems: how focal molecular neuro-biological alterations can effect behaviour. *Development and Psychology*, 9, 907-930.

Raine, A., Buchsbaum, M. S., Stanley, J. and Lottenberg, S. (1997) Selective reductions in prefrontal glucose metabolism in murderers. *Biological Psychiatry*, 36(6): 365-373

Robertson, I. (1999) *Mind Sculpture – Unleashing your Brain's Potential.* London: Bantam Books

Rogers, C. (1994) *Client Centered Therapy.* London: Constable and Company Ltd. (First published in 1951)

Schore, A. (1994) *Affect regulation and the Origin of the Self.* Lawrence Erlbaum: New Jersey

Schore, A. (2000) *Attachment, the Developing Brain and Psychotherapy.* The Bowlby Conference, London

Schore, A. (2001a) The effects of a secure attachment relationship on right brain development, affect regulation, and infant mental health. *Infant Mental Health Journal*, 2001, 22, 7-66.

Schore, A. (2001b) The effects of early relational trauma on right brain development, affect regulation, and infant mental health. *Infant Mental Health Journal*, 2001, 22, 201-269.

Sills, C. (1995) From ego states and transference to the concept of setting in transactional analysis: reviewing the healing relationship, *Panel Presentation Chair: Carlo Moiso. San Francisco. ITAA conference.*

Solms, M. (2000-2001) Lectures: *A Beginners Guide to the Brain.* The Anna Freud Centre, London.

Stern, D. (1985) *The Interpersonal World of the Infant; a View from Psychoanalysis and Developmental Psychology.* New York: Basic Books.

Wolff, P. H. (1966) The causes, controls, and organization of behaviour in the neonate, in *Psychological Issues 5, 17*

Chapter 2

BABIES, BRAINS, AND BODIES:
somatic foundations of the Child ego state
William F. Cornell

Babies were never like pathological adults....If pathology is not infantile, then patients cannot be thought of as babies. Pathology develops in an individual who has been experiencing the world longer than the infant has....Thinking that pathology is a linear outcome of an infantile/child experience is, as Kagan (1998) put it, a seductive idea but one that is incorrect. Adults are not infants, and pathology is not infantile - it is "adultile."

(Tronick 2001, p.189)

Babies and brains have been getting a good deal of attention in the laboratory over the past couple of decades. Contemporary neurophysiological research and studies of infant/parent interaction are leading to radical revisions of theories of psychic development, with equally radical implications regarding the nature of the psychotherapeutic process with adults.

In this chapter, I hope to convey some of the clinical and theoretical implications of such research for Eric Berne's model of the Child ego states, which is at the heart of the clinical practice of transactional analysis. Although Berne developed his theory of ego states as an extension of the work of Federn (1952) and of the brain research carried out by Penfield (1952), the clinical corollaries Berne based on Penfield's speculations no longer hold up. Taking this into account, and drawing on my understanding of current research and my experience, in addition to transactional analysis, as a body-centered psychotherapist, I will suggest a significant revisioning of what TA therapists have come to think of as the Child ego state.

Most clinical writing in the transactional analysis literature emphasizes the historical, fixated and regressive nature of Child ego state functions. Parallel to this emphasis on the nature of the Child ego state are the models (or metaphors) of the therapeutic relationship, common among transactional analysts, as some sort of parenting, corrective or compensatory relationship, intended to be responsive to the traumas and environmental failures of childhood. In this chapter, I hope to demonstrate the limits and errors in conceiving of the Child ego state as a fixated repository of childhood experiences, and as the infrastructure for characterological games and defensive scripts. I will also challenge the corrective/compensatory models of therapeutic relationships that seem to be an outgrowth of an out-of-date conceptualization of the Child ego state.

I do not deny regressive aspects of some Child ego state patterns, but in my view there are also powerful *progressive* and *exploratory* functions to those aspects of the human psyche that we transactional analysts have come to label as the Child ego state. I have come to think that it is a fundamental error to conceptualize the Child ego state as a repository of historical experience. I have come to understand that the level of mental organization transactional analysts call the Child ego state forms *subconsciously* and *unconsciously* within a matrix of emotionally and somatically based motivational forces, which are organized and reorganized throughout the course of one's life. I suggest that what we have come to call the Child ego state involves subsymbolic (Bucci 1997a, 1997b, 2001) neural, emotional, and sensorimotor processes that are crucial forms of psychic development and organization. These processes are perhaps not best conceptualized as states of the ego or even as functions of the ego but are better understood within some of the more recently emergent language in the transactional analysis literature, such as activation states (Hine 1997, 2001) or states of mind (Allen 2000).

I want to emphasize at the start of this chapter that baby and brain research is unfolding at an extraordinarily rapid rate (Tronick 1998, 2001; Fonagy 1999, 2001; Lyons-Ruth 1998, 1999; Panskepp 1993, 2001; Emde 1999; Lachmann 2001). While I am not an expert in either field, I have been reading in both for many years as a fascinated clinician, drawing upon a now rather distant academic background. The clinical implications are exciting, but since clinicians are in the earliest stages of digesting this work, its generalizability to psychotherapy with adults is not at all clear. Green (2000), among others, offers an especially compelling critique of the too-literal applications of mother/infant research. Similarly, Panksepp (2001), a psychobiological researcher with decades of experience, cautions, 'Despite remarkable advances in neuroscience and psychology during the past few decades, our attempts to relate core psychological processes to neural processes remains rudimentary' (p. 139). Therefore, this chapter is speculative in intent, falling far short of a definitive statement. With these caveats in mind, I offer the following musings about babies, brains and bodies, in order to raise important questions and thus contribute to the evolution of ego state theory in transactional analysis.

The roots of transactional analysis in ego psychology

Berne's own training in the late 1940's and early 1950's was in psychoanalysis, which was then dominated in the United States by models of ego psychology, a departure from the drive theories of classical Freudian analysis. In fact, Paul Federn and Erik Erikson, Berne's two training analysts, were among the leading theoreticians of the ego psychology movement at that time.

In the glossary of terms in Berne's (1947) first book, *The Mind in Action*, which he wrote when he still identified with psychoanalysis, Berne defined ego this way:

[It is] that part of the mind which is in contact with the outside world on the one hand and with the Id and the Superego on the other. It attempts to keep thoughts, judgments, interpretations, and behavior practical and efficient in accordance with the Reality Principle. Here we have used the word somewhat inexactly as almost synonymous with the conscious part of the mind. (p. 303)

In the body of the text itself, writing in his typically more informal fashion, Berne characterizes the ego as '...a system which in some mysterious way can look at itself' (p. 66). When *The Mind in Action* was revised in 1968, with Berne now famous for creating transactional analysis, sections on TA were included and Berne added a definition of ego states to the glossary. However, his definitions and descriptions of the ego in both glossary and text remained unchanged. Freud's own understanding of the ego and its functions was complex and changed over the course of his writings (Laplanche & Pontalis 1973, pp.130-143). The understanding of the ego as 'an agency of adaptation which differentiates itself from the id on contact with external reality' (Laplanche & Pontalis 1973) was brought to the United States before and after the World War II by emigrant analysts. The ego psychology school of psychoanalysis became dominant in the U.S. through the middle of the 20th century. Berne's understanding of the ego seemed to change little over the course of his writings.

In leaving psychoanalysis to create transactional analysis, Berne sought to create a metapsychology and a therapeutic process that were more interpersonal and phenomenological than the dominant analytic models of his day. Nevertheless, his new model was based squarely within the tenets of ego psychology. Reviewing Berne's theory of the ego and ego states, Rath (1993) concluded that: '...ego psychology represents the basis of the theory of personality structure and dynamics in transactional analysis' (p. 209). Today this grounding in ego psychology seems taken for granted by transactional analysts, even as they graft on subsequent (and often contradictory) psychoanalytic models, such as self psychology, object relations and attachment theories.

The problematic Child ego state

The tenets of ego psychology served much of Berne's efforts quite well, but he ran into trouble with the limits of this model as he attempted to delineate what he first called the archeopsyche, and subsequently described as the Child ego state. The Child ego state, as conceptualized by Berne, has been the problem child of TA theory from the beginning. Berne himself never resolved his understanding of the Child ego state, and his writings about the Child are full of contradictions.

Berne's varying descriptions of the archeopsyche and the Child ego state created a theoretical hash that has profoundly affected clinical assumptions and techniques ever since Berne's original writings. The concept of a psychic organ suggests a *capacity* of the mind with a sense of the potential for action, whereas the concept of an ego state suggests a *structure within* the mind with a sense of fixation. Although Berne tended to use the terms of archeopsyche and Child almost interchangeably, I think that the archeopsyche conceived as a "psychic organ" is a more inclusive concept that can incorporate some of the aspects of mental development that I will discuss in this chapter. In fact, with his idea of the Child, Berne hypothesized a supposed state of the ego that was founded in realms of experience that I suggest are far more accurately described as both pre-ego and sub-ego; that is, preceding the developmental capacities for ego organization and underlying the functions of the ego throughout the course of life.

Berne's conceptualization of ego states evolved during the writing of a series of early papers in the late 1950s, which were collected together after his death and published as *Intuition and Ego States* (1977). However, even then, before he had articulated the TA model, his efforts to distinguish between the archeopsyche as a mental capacity, and the Child ego state as a more clearly bounded mental/emotional structure, were already in trouble. The Child ego state was presented as a sort of homunculus of the past, seated in the brain: 'The Child in the individual is potentially capable of contributing to his personality exactly what a happy actual child is capable of contributing to family life' (1977, p. 149). Later, in *Transactional Analysis in Psychotherapy*, Berne put it this way:

> When a previously buried archaic ego state is revived in its full vividness in the waking state, it is then permanently at the disposal of the patient and the therapist for detailed examination. Not only do 'abreaction' and 'working through' take place, but the ego state can be treated like an actual child. It can be nurtured carefully, even tenderly, until it unfolds like a flower, revealing all the complexities of its internal structure. (1961, p. 226)

This version of the Child ego state seems to suggest a sort of resident child in the adult client's psyche and a visiting child in the psychotherapist's office. The clinical consequences of Berne's creation of direct parallels between the Child ego state and child*hood* and his reification of the Child ego state as a virtual little being in the brain have been theoretically rather troublesome, to put it mildly.

Confusion about the nature of the Child ego state is intensified in Berne's more colloquial style of writing within the texts themselves. For example, Berne writes:

> Each person carries within a little boy or little girl, who feels, thinks, acts, talks, and responds just the way he or she did when he or she was a child of a certain age. This ego state is called the Child. The Child is not regarded as "childish" or "immature," which are Parental words, but as childlike, meaning like a child at

a certain age, and the important factor here is the age, which may be anywhere between two and five years in ordinary circumstances. It is important for the individual to understand his Child, not only because it is going to be with him all his life, but also because it is the most valuable part of his personality.   (1972, p. 12)

Here we have conceptual confusion and a reification of the Child ego state as an actual child-like presence and as childhood remnants within the adult psyche, remnants that can be both fixated (on a bad day?) and precious (on a good day?). Also, we have in this formulation the crucial, formative years of the Child ego state identified as two to five, when the developing youngster is becoming motorically and linguistically autonomous and does, indeed, have the beginnings of true ego functions. Significantly, however, much of Berne's writings seemed to ignore the significance of the years from birth to two, which are emerging in current brain and infant research as crucial to psychological development, as well as to the psychotherapeutic process.

In contrast to some of his more informal, colloquial writings, the formal definitions of the Child ego state Berne presented in his books were more consistent. 'Child ego state is a set of feelings, attitudes and behavior patterns which are relics of the individual's own childhood,' stood as the original definition provided *in Transactional Analysis in Psychotherapy* (1961, p. 77). In *Principles of Group Treatment* (1966), he defined the Child ego state as 'An ego state which is an archaic relic from an early significant period of life' (p. 362). And in *What Do You Say After You Say Hello?* (1972), he wrote that the Child is '.....an archaic ego state. The Adapted Child follows Parental directives. The Natural Child is autonomous' (p. 442). (One wonders how an ego state can be simultaneously archaic and autonomous?)

Many transactional analysis clinicians have emphasized the archaic, fixated, defensive functions of the Child. Rath (1993) extended this perspective as follows:

> The archeopsyche or Child ego state (colloquially known as the Child) is defined by a set of inadequate (pathological) states of the ego displayed in thoughts, feelings, and behaviors, which manifest themselves in the here-and-now during the development of the elements stored in the archeopsyche and which are, from the phenomenological point of view, regressive elements and psychic reactions to earlier stages (of development).   (p. 210)

Erskine (1998), in a similar fashion, has argued:

> The archaic state of the ego is the result of developmental arrest which occurred when critical early childhood needs for contact were not met. The child's defenses against the discomfort of unmet needs became egotized-fixated; the experience cannot be fully inte-

grated into the Adult ego state until these defense mechanisms are dissolved. (p. 17)

According to this view, the archeopsyche/Child is viewed as a kind of storage container for archaic psychopathology, seemingly more of a container for weeds than the tenderly unfolding flowers sometimes suggested by Berne.

Clarkson and her colleagues at the Metanoia Institute (Clarkson & Gilbert, 1988; Clarkson & Fish, 1988) struggled perhaps the most mightily among TA practitioners with the theoretical dilemmas created by Berne's writings about the Child. Clarkson (1992) wrote:

> Ego states were initially conceived of as vividly available temporal recordings of past events with the concomitant meaning and feelings which are maintained in potential existence within the personality (Berne, 1980/1961: 19). However, he distinguishes from this multitude of Child ego states: (1) Child as archaic ego states and (2) Child as fixated ego states....Child ego states might be better referred to as *'historical ego states'* since a person's vivid experiences of today will be stored in natural psychological epochs, archaic by tomorrow. (pp. 44-45)

Although in this conceptualization the Child is still understood as a phenomenological repository of the experiences of history consistent with Berne's basic definitions and his emphasis on childhood, we also see some effort to resolve the question of how the Child can be viewed both as fixated, adapted, *and* as autonomous in function and expression.

Transactional analysis theoreticians and clinicians have been aware of this quandary for a long time now, but it has yet to be resolved satisfactorily. Some have challenged the conceptualization of the Child as an archaic, fixated ego state. Schiff and her colleagues (Schiff et al., 1975), for example, viewed the Child this way:

> The Child ego state is the source of all energy and is in control of cathexis. ...Psychopathology can be thought of as the development of adaptations which control the Child as opposed to the Child controlling the adaptations. (p. 26)

The Gouldings (1979) argued:

> Some TA therapists believe that the Child ego state stops developing at an early age. We see the Child as ever growing and ever developing, as the sum total of the experiences he has had and is having in the present ....The Child develops. We have stressed that the *Child* does the work. The Child both experiences and copies, and then incorporates. (p.20, italics in original)

Blackstone (1993) extended the argument for the activity and changeability of the Child ego state, and presented a model of the intrapsychic dynamics of the Child ego state, drawing upon object relations theories.

I am not arguing that it is mistaken to include historical and fixated elements within the definition of the Child ego state. Rather, I am suggesting that an emphasis on these elements does not sufficiently account for the nature of the Child ego state, and that continued reliance on Berne's definitions maintains a serious limitation in theory and significant bias in clinical work.

Implicit and explicit knowing

Our earliest means of learning and mental organization occur at the level of sub-symbolic, sensorimotor and affective experience which cannot be accurately described as states or functions of the ego. These realms of organization developmentally precede the capacities of the ego and underlie/accompany/inform/shape/color the nature of the Child, Adult and Parent ego states throughout the course of life. Seen from the perspective of current neurophysiological and memory research, the psychological states of organization that transactional analysis calls the Child ego state does not develop until the middle of the second year of life. An immense amount of enduring learning is occurring in those first eighteen months of life and throughout the life span through avenues other than the functions of the ego.

Brain and memory researchers (McClelland 1998; Milner, Squire, & Kandel 1998), while often using different terminologies, are converging on a quite consistent differentiation of implicit (procedural) and explicit (declarative) memory processes. Implicit memory precedes the evolution of explicit memory, which requires cortical functions that develop later. Implicit memory is not replaced by explicit memory but continues to operate in parallel with explicit memory, providing the unthought realms of knowing. Siegel (2001) summarizes contemporary research this way:

> The process of memory and those of development are closely aligned. For the first year of life, the infant has available an "implicit" form of memory that includes emotional, behavioral, perceptual, and perhaps bodily (somatosensory) forms of memory.... When implicit memories are activated, they do not have an internal sensation that something is being recalled. They merely influence our emotions, behaviors, or perceptions directly, in the here and now, without our awareness of their connection to some experience from the past.
>
> By the middle of the second year, children begin to develop a second form of memory, "explicit" memory (Bauer, 1996). Explicit memory includes two major forms: factual (semantic) and autobiographical ("episodic") (Tulving, Kapur, Craik, Moscovitch, & Houle 1994). For both types of explicit memory, recollection is

associated with an internal sensation of "I am recalling something
now."   (p. 74)

The felt sense of implicit memory is captured in Bollas' (1987) now famous
phrase of the "unthought known." Implicit knowledge is formed and sustained through somatic activity and emotional experience. As summarized by
Pally (2000), implicit memory is understood as memory for aspects of experience, historical *and current*, that are not processed consciously, that is, patterns of learning and experience that influence functioning but are not experienced as conscious remembering. Kihlstrom (1990) and Izard (1993) define
a broader range of forms of implicit *cognitions*, which includes perception,
memory and learning. These realms of implicit experience and learning are
also taken up and extended within models of both research and clinical practice by Bucci (1997a, b) as sub-symbolic processes, Ogden (1989) as the autis-
tic-contiguous mode, Mitrani (1996) as unmentalized experience, Tronick
(1998) and Lyons-Ruth (1998, 1999) as implicit relational knowing, Shahar-
Levy (2001) as emotive motor memory clusters, and La Barre (2000) as non-
verbal behaviour.

Berne's writings about the Child ego state and script theory were primarily
rooted in explicit memory, though what he defined as the script protocol is
more reflective of implicit memory. Current transactional analysis perspectives based in attachment and empathic attunement models reach back into
realms of implicit memory, although these have little to say about the infant's
sensory, affective, and motor organization (i.e., the baby in relation to its own
body, outside of relational experiences). In articles on the implications of
neurodevelopmental research for transactional analysis, Allen (1999, 2000)
also discussed the relevance of implicit and explicit memory for transactional
analysis theory and observed:

> Implicit memory develops earlier than explicit memory. It is non-
> verbal and nonsymbolic, but it is not less rich or more primitive. It
> is not replaced by explicit knowledge. It involves how we feel and
> is a major element in relationships. Complicated music is under-
> stood implicitly.   (2000, p. 262)

It is important to note that implicit, nonverbal, subsymbolic experiences are
not limited to the first year of life. They are constant elements in the psychic
organization of experience, co-existing side by side with explicit and declarative realms of experience in the here-and-now. Life that can be languaged is
not necessarily healthier, richer, or more mature; it simply has a different kind
of psychic organization. Healthy functioning requires both implicit and
explicit knowing, subsymbolic/nonverbal and symbolic levels of organization. A complete psychotherapy must work within both levels of mental
organization. While it is certainly a primary therapeutic task to foster the
development of the capacity for symbolic and verbal representation, it is not

necessarily true that sensate and subsymbolic experience is in some way regressed and pathological or will be improved by the achievement of symbolic or languaged knowing. Just consider how societies build museums and concert halls for the work of those who are able to carry us through sensation, sight, and sound into unthought and unlanguaged realms of experience.

In actual life and in psychotherapy, the realms of implicit knowing and subsymbolic experience can simultaneously contain elements of past, present, and future. I offer a case example to illustrate.

Ben, an accomplished physicist, began individual therapy as an adjunct to marital therapy. Both he and his wife had engaged in extra-marital relationships at the time of their youngest child entering college. While the marital crisis had precipitated therapy, Ben's attention quickly turned to the pervasive deadness in all aspects of his life. The brief but intense sexual liaison with a new partner had startled him with an experience of his own vitality and passion. "Most of the time," Ben said, "I'm so dead to the world, lost in my head, that I could fall off the edge of the world and not notice."

Therapy proved extremely difficult. Sessions were filled with bitter and deadening complaints about himself, his marriage, his work, his colleagues, me, the therapy. "Just what was it that I am paying you for?" was the disdainful question that ended most of sessions. My efforts at observation, confrontation or empathic elaboration were typically met with some version of, "I think we already know that one. Perhaps you could come up with something new the next time we meet." His impatience and disdain colored everything. He saw no purpose in talking about his parents or his history, as he "knew all of that already." I found it increasingly difficult to speak. I didn't know what to speak about, our talking seemed useless. I wondered to myself how it was that I found myself so often speechless in the presence of a man I both liked and admired, whom I was also quite certain felt considerable regard and affection toward me.

Then one evening I ran into Ben and his wife at a baroque concert. He opened the next session with, "I feel a bit silly saying this, but I was watching you during the concert. You never sat still. It was like you were dancing in your seat. What was going on in you?" Rather hesitantly I replied, "I can't listen to that music and sit still. I don't think that music was written to settle people down. I think it was written to inspire people, to move them. It moves me, and I move when I'm moved." Then Ben asked, "What goes on inside of you when you listen to music?". "I think I'm supposed to ask you that sort of question," I parried. "I asked you first," Ben persisted. I told him, describing body sensations, dancing in my seat, humming aloud, feeling a range of emotions, imagining what the original rooms and audiences looked like, wishing at moments I had a sort of belief in a god that seemed to inspire that sort of music, anger at my parents for never letting me learn to play an instrument, wondering if the performers travelled with their lovers or if some of them slept with each other. "What," I then asked Ben, "goes on inside of you?" "I analyze the structure of the music and try to see the notes on the page. Quite a contrast, huh? It's what I do with every aspect of my life. I analyze it and kill it."

"Kill it:" suddenly the session was filled with memories, sensations, and images of Ben's childhood: the deadness of his parents; his inability to somehow move his parents; his desperate and ultimate bitter wish to somehow touch and inspire his parents (and then his wife); the atmosphere created by his mother's depression and bitterness, which was ever present and always unspoken, his father's constant withdrawal and solitude, including images of father sitting alone at the breakfast table to start his day and finishing alone in the garden reading the newspaper. Ben felt how he himself was killing off so much of his life, his own vitality, that the deadness of which he so often complained was of his own making. Like his parents, Ben was a "killer." He now knew why he was in therapy.

This example illustrates both the regressive and progressive aspects of the Child ego state. Rarely in psychotherapy do we create new patterns of emotional and relational processes for the future without first circuiting back, if even briefly, into memories of the past (perhaps a powerful factor in why it has been so easy to equate the Child ego state with actual childhood and psychopathology). As we wrestle in psychotherapy with wishes for a future different from the past, the possibilities of the future seem inextricably bound up and blinded by the strictures of the past. Dropping into the realm of sensory experience that our discussion of the baroque concert opened up for him threw Ben back in time, into a wealth of visceral/sensate/visual memories, and threw him forward into a realm of unthought desires that had long seemed unthinkable, foolish and impossible. Would I suggest that this conversation and the subsequent therapy brought him out of a Child ego state into an Adult ego state (an integrated or integrating Adult, as is often suggested in current transactional analysis theory)? I would not. Rather, I think these experiences strengthened his Adult ego state, deepening his self-reflective capacities. I would also suggest that these experiences strengthened his Child ego state functions in the here-and-now, providing an intensification and enrichment of his sensate and emotional capacities. I see these somatic experiences as inherent to the nature of the Child ego state, not simply as remnants of childhood but as current and constant accompaniments of other aspects of psychic and interpersonal functioning.

Emotion and the brain

I have come to understand the Child ego state in procedural rather than structural and historical terms, which is to say, as a coherent and enduring system of organization and motivation. This system has deep, often compelling, historical roots, but it is a system that lives and changes in the present. The complexities and apparent contradictions of the simultaneously old and current elements in our emotional reactions are examined by Levenson. Levenson asked, "Is the human emotion system a masterpiece of design or the ultimate kludge?" (1999, p. 482). He answered in this way:

> This conundrum results from the fact that of all of the building
> blocks that make up human beings, some of the evolutionarily

oldest as well as some of the newest, are found in the emotion system. This confluence of old and new makes an extremely complex
system, one that often serves us extremely well as we navigate the
stresses, challenges and opportunities of life, but at other times
bedevils and plagues us, even undermining our health.   (p. 482)

The implications of this two-system design of the brain, as discussed in such
pivotal books as Lichtenberg (1989), Schore (1994,), LeDoux (1996), Bucci
(1997), Demasio (1999), and Pally (2000), as well as in countless articles in
professional journals, have profoundly deepened and altered my understanding of the nature of the psychotherapeutic project in general and, as I attempt
to address in this chapter, of the Child ego state in particular.

Berne developed a theory and therapy of primarily the conscious mind,
with ego states as manifestations of different levels and kinds of consciousness. Like most ego psychologists of his era, he viewed emotions and affect
with ambivalence, suspicious of their disruptive, regressive, irrational qualities. But things have changed since then! Levenson (1999), for example,
offered a contrasting perspective that is rich in its clinical implications:

> Emotion appears to function as a master choreographer, the
> ultimate organizer of disparate response systems. Emotion orches-
> trates the action of multiple response systems so that they act in a
> unified way in the service of solving problems. This view of emo-
> tion as an *organizer* stands in stark contrast to the oft-expressed
> view of emotion as a *disorganizer* or *disrupter*. In this latter view,
> emotion is the enemy of purposeful behavior and rational thought
> (p. 495, italics in the original).

Likewise, Emde (1999) challenged the long-held biases of classical psychoanalysts and ego psychologists about affect and emotion to emphasize,
'Affective processes enhance developmental change in an everyday sense, not
just at times of transition, and they are linked to cognitive processes' (p. 323).

Panksepp (2001) pushed this perspective on the organizing and motivating
functions of emotions even further, concluding in language that is uncannily
familiar to transactional analysts:

> Because emotionality is remarkably ancient in brain evolution,
> there is every reason to believe that the underlying brain systems
> served as a foundation for the emergence of basic social and cog-
> nitive abilities. The basic emotion systems of the brain imbue
> environmental events with values (i.e., "valence tagging"), and defi-
> ciencies in emotions may lead to psychiatric problems character-
> ized by distinct cognitive and social idiosyncrasies. In developing
> infants such processes may be psychologically decisive. Infants
> may fundamentally project their emotions into the world, and

initially assimilate cognitive structures only in highly affective ways....The rich interpretation of emotions and cognitions establish the major psychic scripts for each child's life. (p. 141)

How do we reconcile these views of the role of emotion and affect in the organization of the brain and in the motivation of behavior with the ego state model of transactional analysis? This is not an easy task as the ego state model now stands. Clearly the researchers just cited see emotion as *rooted* in the very earliest stages of life, but this is quite different from seeing it as *fixated* or *archaic*. They suggest that emotions and affective states shape and inform cognition throughout the life span. Does Berne's (1961) definition of the Adult ego state as 'characterized by an autonomous set of feelings, attitudes and behavior patterns which are adapted to current reality' (p. 76), or the subsequent theoretical elaborations of an integrat*ed* or integrat*ing* Adult ego state, adequately embrace the models of emotion and cognition that these researchers describe? I think not. I see the Child ego states as *a matrix of emotionally, somatically based organizing and motivating systems*. Grounded in sensorimotor and implicit, procedural forms of knowledge, the Child provides systems of organization and motivation quite distinct from Adult and Parent states of the ego.

Movement and sensorimotor organization

One thing that babies and brains have in common is that they are firmly and permanently attached to a body, although the actions and organization of this body receive remarkably little attention in clinical theorizing. As one of the consistent voices on behalf of considering the body in theory, (not to mention the consulting room), Boadella (1997) reminded psychotherapists:

Every patient brings to the session not only his problems but also his body: he can never leave it behind, even if he forgets it's his (as in depersonalization); or treats it as a mechanical object (as in the schizoid process); or as a source of threat (as in hypochondria).
(p. 33)

Significantly, the psychological and relational significance of sensorimotor organization and activity is now receiving attention in the body-centered literature (Marcher 1996; Boadella 1997; Downing 1996; Rothschild 2000; Frank 2001). Within the transactional analysis literature there have been a few writers touching upon the senorimotor realms (Steere 1981, 1985; Ligabue 1991; Waldekranz-Piselli 1999). Downing speaks to the rather obvious but often overlooked fact: that for the infant, the body is the means, the vehicle, to all that is outside. Seen from a developmental perspective, the inattention in clinical theory to sensorimotor processes is a curious oversight, one reflecting a long history of bias and blindness against the body within psychology and psychoanalysis, many philosophical traditions, and countless religions of associating the brain and the mind while setting the body and mind in opposition.

Researchers Thelen and Fogel (1989) threw down a conceptual gauntlet:

> Developmentalists, like other psychologists, have been concerned primarily with the formation of the complex symbolic and affective processes of the "life of the mind" and have paid less attention to the translation of ideas into movement - a "life of the limbs." Infants, however, are born with much movement and few ideas and, for the first year or so, lack symbolic and verbal mediating mechanisms between their mental state and the expressions of their bodies and limbs. At this stage of the life cycle, then, the link between the developing mind and the developing limbs may be especially direct. We see this formulation in no way competing with theories that focus more directly on mental structures but rather as a complement and supplement to understanding the development of cognition. (p. 23)

A substantial body of research has been developed within the general rubric of "dynamic motor theory" which suggests that many psychological phenomena presumed to arise from brain processes may actually develop more fundamentally from the activities of the muscles and limbs (Fischer & Hogan 1989), that the movements of the body organize and reorganize the brain.

Fischer and Hogan (1989) described the unfolding of levels of cognitive development linked the sequencing of sensorimotor competencies. In the first weeks of life the infant has a limited repertoire of reflex movements, such as turning the head to orient toward the mother's face, which come quickly under voluntary control. By 10 to 11 weeks, babies have the capacity to carry out a limited but flexible sensorimotor sequence of action, such as following a ball with gaze while opening a hand and extending an arm in the direction of the moving ball, in contrast to a singular movement of one part of the body. Sensorimotor activities quickly reach more complex layers of activities, or "mappings," and by the end of the first year have become flexible systems of sensorimotor competencies, such as 'complex systems of sensorimotor actions: infant moves a rattle in different ways to see different parts of it' (p. 280). Not until some time between 18 to 24 months are young children able to translate complex sensorimotor systems into representational systems (i.e., a child can pretend a doll is walking, walk the doll, and say, "Doll walk.") As Boadella (1997) observed, 'The movement vocabulary of the child, during the first year and a half, is the foundation of his communicative rapport with the world: he interacts by means of motoric and vocal signs long before there is the capacity for semantic use of language' (p. 33). Call (1984) referred to this process as the 'grammar of experience,' by which he suggested that the development of language is grounded in the sensorimotor organization of the infant and toddler in relation to caregivers and the physical world.

Downing (1996), drawing on the work of Winnicott, Stern, Mahler, and others in particularly creative ways, writes with clarity and specificity about the importance of sensorimotor organization in the patterns of infant/parent interactions and its significance for adult psychotherapy. He stresses the importance of the infant's development of 'affectmotor schemas' and 'affect-motor beliefs' that are an elaboration and integration of the infant's sensori-motor development within the relational and affective patterns with the care-givers. These patterns are not encoded in language but in literal affective and motoric experiences, that is, the somatic infrastructure. Downing conceptual-izes these affectmotor schemas as forming prelinguistic, sensorimotor belief systems for connectedness, differentiation and bodily effectiveness. He hypothesizes 'that certain physical parent-infant bodily interactions...leave a trace....that this trace can be understood as a shaping, an influencing, of the infant's motor representational world....that the vestige of these early motor beliefs will later affect adult behavior and awareness.' (p. 150). He stresses the importance of the parent-infant relationship fostering for the infant a sense of embodied agency, that 'the infant's ability to impinge upon the other must equally be unfolded' and that the infant 'must build up a motoric representa-tion of the other as engagable, and of himself as able to engage' (1997, p. 169).

Attention to the sensorimotor regions of the brain and realms of mental organization remind us in a very important way that the infant is developing a relationship not only to an other(s) but also, equally importantly, to one's own body and developing sense of selfhood. Infants spend many waking hours alone with themselves, discovering the pleasures of their bodies (Lichtenberg 1989, p. 234) in relation to the body itself and the inanimate world as well as the interpersonal world. This becomes even more pro-nounced when the child begins walking, and the world opens up dramatically. As Call (1984) describes it, 'for the first time the child experiences what must be something like a kinesthetic art gallery. The world changes as the child moves in the world' (p. 19). Thus, as the research of Thelan and her col-leagues also demonstrates, while the brain and its neural activities can direct the movements of the body, the movements of the body and the acquisition of new sensorimotor patterns change the brain and its neural paths as well.

All of this is to underscore the tremendous amount of learning and organ-ization occurring during infancy *and throughout childhood and adult life* that is outside of the purview of the traditional definitions of the ego and most def-initions of the Child ego state. The body brings the world to life not only for the developing baby and the growing child, but also for adults and their psy-chotherapists. Shapiro (1996), as an example, has attempted to bring aware-ness of the body - both of the client and the therapist - into the consulting room and the therapeutic process. She has criticized other psychoanalytic theorists who have attempted to include a sense of somatic experience within the therapeutic process as having tended 'to view these experiences as more primitive and pathological than verbally symbolized experience' (p. 299). She described the range of bodily experiences that are present in the therapist's office (whether they are attended to or not) as 'a complex experience which includes the whole range of somatosensory phenomena: our breath, pulse, posture, muscle strength, fatigue, clarity and speed of thought, sense of boundedness, our skin, mucous membranes, bodily tension, facial expression, taste, smell, pulse, vitality' (p. 298) that have the potential to enliven the therapeutic process and its participants, to have an 'interanimating and interpenetrating' experience of somatic and verbal interplay. In this regard, Waldekranz-Piselli (1999) has made a major contribution to TA clinical technique, elaborating - within transactional analysis theory - an accounting of sensate and affectmotor explorations and the client's being 'active in the process of discovering his or her being and living his or her own body as well as how this affects relating to others' (p. 46).

Sensorimotor processes clearly provide a means of knowing and relating to 'reality' from the there-and-then *as well as* in the here-and-now. These are not patterns that are simply 'remnants' from childhood, though they begin in childhood. These are means of exploring, knowing and shaping the world throughout one's life. As Thelan wryly observes, 'the motor system is capable of generating novel form, as even an ageing psychologist can learn to tap dance or to ski or to play a musical instrument' (Thelan & Fogel 1989, p.28). I recall the first time I stood at the age of 45 at the top of a black diamond ski slope, which a friend of mine (an expert skier) had decided I was ready to manoeuver. I was terrified, and as I tried to follow his instructions, I fell repeatedly. Finally my friend told me to simply follow him and "Do whatever I do." No words, no thinking, just doing, physically imitating his movements, developing a *sense* of how to use my body, my sensorimotor systems, in Thelan's language, generating novel forms and new possibilities. I made it to the bottom of the slope without falling, acquiring in the process substantial new skills in the life of my limbs. Skiing, like so many aspects of life involving the body, improves by doing it, rather than talking about it.

Subsymbolic experience

We are just beginning to develop terms and concepts that adequately convey the nature of prelinguistic, subcognitive experience. As transactional analysts have extended and deepened the reach of their clinical work, they have come to increasingly work within these realms of subsymbolic experience. Many transactional analysis theorists have desperately stretched the conceptualization of the Child ego state to address these arenas of developmental and clinical experience, as we see in the common notations of P_0, A_0, C_0. Taken from Berne's effort to establish a standard nomenclature for the TA literature, these zero-based ego states were meant by Berne to signify 'at birth' (1969, p. 111). The notations was taken up by Schiff and her colleagues (1975), to try to reflect the very earliest stages of motivation and organization within the ego state model. This notation was extended and formalized within Mellor's account of third degree impasses, which 'relate to primal protocols (Berne

1972); that is, they originate during very young experiences, perhaps even pre-natal' (1980, p. 214). As TA theorists have attempted to describe these earli-est, precognitive realms of experience, the concept of the third degree impasse has taken an important place in the literature (Levin-Landheer 1982; Giuli 1985; Clarkson 1992; Cox 1999; Waldenkranz-Piselli 1999). Waldenkranz-Piselli accounts for the P_0, A_0, C_0 levels of organization purely in terms of sensate levels of experience, reflective of the development of affectmotor schema in a way that is more consistent with direct body experience than with ego function. I find this extension of an ego state model more obfuscating than clarifying and think we find far more accurate and clinically viable models outside of conceptualizations of the ego. Here I have found the work of Bucci most useful.

Bucci (1997a, 1997b, 2001), through her explication of subsymbolic processes, has made an especially important contribution from cognitive psy-chology to clinical theorizing and research within the realms of sensorimotor learning, implicit knowledge and psychotherapy with adults. Subsymbolic processes refer to those means of mental organization and learning that are not dependent on language. This perspective has much to offer transactional analysis. According to Bucci (2001):

> Subsymbolic processing accounts for highly developed skills in athletics and the arts and sciences and is central to knowledge of one's body and to emotional experience....Balanchine communi-cated to his dancers primarily through these modalities. His com-munication was intentional, conscious, systematic and complex - within the motoric mode....he did not resort to motoric or sensory modalities because verbal representations were repressed, but because the information existed only in a form that could not be captured in words....We should emphasize that the prefix "sub" here denotes the subsymbolic as *underlying* symbolic representa-tion, not as an inferior or primitive processing mode.
>
> (pp. 48-49, italics in the original)

Bucci (1997a) effectively evokes a sense of the body that is deeply familiar within the experience of doing body-centered psychotherapy:

> These sensory experiences occur in consonance with somatic and visceral experience of pleasure and pain, as well as organized motoric actions involving the mouth, hands, and the whole body - kicking, crying, sucking, rooting and shaping one's body to another's....these direct and integrate emotional life long before language is acquired   (p. 161)

We kick, cry, suck, experience pain and pleasure, shape one's body to another's (with any luck at all!) throughout the course of life. These are not simply manifestations of infancy or archaic remnants of childhood, but also of intimacy, play, eroticism, fighting, sexuality, and nurturing throughout the full span of one's life. In these subsymbolic realms, the therapeutic process becomes a kind of exploratory, psychosomatic partnership (quite different and distinct from a corrective, pseudo-parent/child relationship) that can be often wordless, rich in meaning nonetheless. A clinical example further illustrates the organizing and reorganizing potential of sensorimotor and subsymbolic activity.

Abby was one of four siblings, two sons and two daughters, born to ambitious, upper middle-class parents. The family prided itself on its social and political accomplishments, the children pressured to be outgoing, independent, socially competent, and academically accomplished. Abby, both as a child and as an adult, felt she often fell short of the mark. Her therapy tended to focus on professional concerns and self-doubts and the stresses of being a professional woman while raising very active children. In discussing struggles with colleagues or family members, Abby was intensely self-critical, rarely feeling or expressing anger or disappointment toward those around her. She was able to express anger and disappointment toward me, though with considerable apprehension and difficulty. The issues she raised with me were substantial and brought up in a way that enhanced the work rather than disrupted it or distanced from it. Sessions were productive, and yet no underlying theme seemed to emerge. Abby remained uncertain as to why she was "really" in therapy, whether she could justify the time and expense.

During one session, she mentioned in passing that she had become preoccupied with a photograph she'd seen in a magazine, one that both fascinated and disturbed her. She thought several times of bringing it up with me but hesitated, feeling embarrassed and uncertain of what to say about it. She finally decided to draw it, hoping she could then discover its meaning. After drawing, redrawing, and reworking the image several times, she asked to bring the drawing to a session.

The image was of three football players walking off the field, hunched over, soaked in rain and covered with mud. The figures were somewhat obscured in the rain and mist, their faces hidden by their helmets. The figures communicated both a menace and a fatigue. The men were physically close, touching each other, clearly part of a team. The drawing was very finely rendered and quite moving as a drawing in and of itself.

As Abby began to associate to the picture, she thought of her father, his pride in his body and his athleticism, his preference for his sons over his daughters, his bullying and narcisstic authority and self-righteousness. All of this was familiar material from her previous therapy, Abby reported, and she expressed bewilderment at not being able to get through to whatever it was that made the image so compelling for her. I suggested that rather than drawing the image or talking about it, she become it physically, literally taking it on with her body.

A series of sessions ensued in which she worked standing up, mimicking each of the figures, gradually entering the posture of each, walking and moving in the way she imagined they would move. Each session would begin with her discussing whatever events of the week she wanted me to know about or that she needed to think through, and then she would stand up, put the picture on the floor, and begin to do some part of the picture. We spoke very little. I stood near her, offering no interpretations, simply asking her to relate what she experienced if she was so inclined. She did a lot and said very little, occasionally commenting on sensations in her body, on what she was feeling, on what she sensed the men in the picture might be feeling. No new memories or insights emerged, but she did begin having a new sense of her body. She began to notice a different sense of herself between sessions, feeling more substantial in herself with her thoughts and feelings. She realized she felt angry more often. She was moving into a way of being that had captivated her in the photograph, one that had been denied to her as a daughter in the family. Language and insight followed and were informed and enriched by her bodily activity and exploration.

As diverse strands of research about babies and brains come together with clinical theory, we are beginning to recognize the force of subsymbolic and sensorimotor processes that create formative and enduring states of mind, to use Allen's (2001) phrase. In the first of these strands, contemporary neurophysiological and brain scan research is demonstrating with increasing clarity the mutually influencing interactions of the subcortical, limbic functions with cortical (symbolic/verbal) functions (Hadley 1989; LeDoux 1996; Bucci 1997a; Siegel 2001; Schore 2001). We now know that two distinct, concurrent, and lifelong modes of experience, the symbolic and the subsymbolic, the cognitive and the somatic, constantly shape psychic life. Both symbolic and subsymbolic realms of psychic experience are open to influence and alteration at any stage of life.

In a second crucial strand of research, more than two decades of direct observation of infants have dramatically altered our understanding of the nature of infancy, the infant/parent dyad, and the social construction of the human brain. From birth, human beings begin to form nonlinguistic schema of an affective and sensorimotor world that function as subcortical, precognitive templates which influence and are influenced by all subsequent cognitive and relational development. We are seeing the beginnings of a coherent theory of the somatic, affective, and nonverbal foundation of human functioning, as exemplified by Lichtenberg's (1989) description of the perceptual-affective-action mode, which operates without verbal representation or symbolic formation, and by Bucci's accounting of subsymbolic processing.

Evolving concepts in transactional analysis

It is clear that current infant and neurophysiological research reflects a range of neural developments that cannot be adequately captured in Berne's model of ego states. We shall never see an ego state light up in a PET scan in a particular area of the brain. Clarkson (1992) addressed the limits of theories of ego states in transactional analysis by introducing the language of states of self. Hargaden and Sills (2001, 2002) have extended the conceptualization of self states within the Child ego state to address the more unconscious aspects of human functioning while retaining the basic model of the Child ego state. Rath (1993) attempted to broaden the conceptualization of ego states by utilizing the idea of self-organizing systems. In a related fashion, Gilbert (1996) developed the idea of ego state networks, drawing on research models of schemas and generalized representations.

Hine (1997) carried the model of neural networks further, synthesizing neurophysiological and infant research to offer hypotheses as to the development and differentiation of ego states, describing the bridging between implicit and explicit knowing. Hine (1997), drawing on the work of Churchland (1995), Edelman (1992), Nelson & Gruendel (1981), and Stern (1985) among others, offered a theory of ego state development and organization based largely on implicit memory and learning. She emphasized the concept of generalized representations of experience, concluding that 'this fundamental neural process builds up into coherent networks of representations functioning as wholes, inter-linking each other with increasing mental complexity. Ego states appear to be an evolved example of this impressively powerful process of structuralization' (p. 278). She observed:

> Ego states exhibit several characteristics of GR (generalized representation) systems...Ego states become comparatively stable and coherent systems, as do GRs....In ego states the mental activity can be broad and can include thinking, feeling, and behaving. This is similar to the make up of a "generalized experience" as described by Moscovitch (1994)....In ego state systems the ego states have their own characteristic styles and give their own meaning to internal sensations and external perceptions. (p. 283)

Hine went on to suggest that the differing forms of mental activity characterized for each ego state reflect: 'the way each ego state system forms and how the perceptions that give rise to each system are processed and organized' (p. 284). From this perspective she has sustained a model of discrete and differentiated systems of mental activity and organization.

Allen (2001), while not directly proposing a change of terminology, suggested a change of language that points a way out of the theoretical dilemma we have inherited from Berne. Drawing on contemporary brain research, Allen writes:

> *States of mind as precursors of full ego states:* How is the activation of widely distributed neural circuits regulated? This function seems to be performed by what has been termed a 'state of mind,' the total pattern of activation in the brain at a given time. It brings together several different neural networks, any one of which can

become the dominant energy and information-processing unit of the moment....Over time, these cohesive states become more and more easily activated and coalesce into self-states. As Post and Weiss (1997) concluded, "Neurons which fire together and survive together and wire together" (p. 930)....In transactional analysis, we label the manifestations of such neural network activations "ego states." (p. 261)

Hine's and Allen's descriptions of systems of neural network activation speak more accurately, at a theoretical level, to the understanding of dynamic mental processes that is emerging in contemporary research than does our more familiar theory of ego states as psychic structures within the mind. Allen's reference to states of *mind* rather than states of *ego*, opens up the frame of reference in the accounting for the growth and change of somatic, emotional, cognitive, and behavioral organization. Allen seems to suggest that when schemas of neural organization reach the point at which 'they also include socially shared and communicable language' they may then be conceptualized as ego states rather than states of mind.

Allen's perspective also mirrors one common to body-centered therapists, many of whom are trained to differentiate evidence of differing states of mental organization, usually defined as visceral/affective, sensorimotor, and cognitive. From a developmental perspective, the visceral/affective systems of the limbic regions dominate the earliest stages of neurophysiological and interpersonal organization, facilitated and extended by sensorimotor development, and capped by the cognitive processes of the cerebral cortex. Each system is necessary for healthy functioning. While the visceral/affective and sensorimotor systems dominate early infant development, they do not then become remnants and repositories of the past but remain vital systems of mental organization coexisting with cognitive systems throughout one's life. These same subsymbolic systems are active (and hopefully utilized) in the ongoing psychotherapeutic process of linking thinking and feeling, past and present, in the midst of trying to create meaning and effectiveness in one's life.

It may well be that the most direct (and theoretically sound) means of change within the subsymbolic and affect-motor realms of experience involve systematic attention to various forms of non-verbal experience and communication, including such means of intervention as: direct work with the body, increased focus on sensory awareness, attention to the interplay of the transferential/countertransferential relationship, and exploration of unconscious fantasy. It seems increasingly clear that when we are working within these foundational realms of mental organization we are dealing with *process not structure*. While these processes (implicit, procedural, unconscious means of knowing) have definite coherence, they do not have the fixity of those states of mind we could call self or ego. We are dealing with *how things happen*, in addition to the more familiar questions of what happened and who did what. In these realms of the therapeutic process, it is the activity and experience of seeking, moving and exploring that create the therapeutic edge and the means of change.

Clinical implications

Transactional analysis psychotherapy is alive, well and growing. When we look at psychotherapy from the perspective of somatic processes and brain development, the field of the therapeutic *process* opens widely, far beyond the scope of the models of the therapeutic relationship most common in transactional analysis today. The models and metaphors of parental, patriarchal, or maternal presences have powerful draws for therapist and client alike. After all, if a client is unable to soothe himself, who better to provide the service than the therapist; if unable to understand herself, who better to provide the understanding than the therapist? Winer (1994) has challenged this parental model and its many variations in psychotherapy:

> It is too comfortable for therapist and patient to view themselves as parent and child, even seductive we might say. We all long for a wise and protective authority. The patient invests her therapist with that power and the therapist finds security in identifying with his patient's idealization of him. (p. 64)

Tronick (2001) has sought to deepen the understanding of the process of psychotherapy through the insights gained from infant studies. He has suggested the model of 'dyadically expanded states of consciousness' through which 'the collaboration of two individuals (two brains) is successful, each fulfills the fundamental system principle of increasing their coherence and complexity' (p. 193). He is cautious about simple applications of the infant/parent research that tends to turn psychotherapy into some form of parent-child relationship. I quote Tronick at length here, as his perspective raises crucial questions about our understanding of the Child ego state and our approaches as transactional analysts to the therapeutic process:

> The adult was a "being" who once had infant capacities but who no longer has (or no longer only has) infant, toddler, or child capacities….It is with these fundamentally and qualitatively different capacities that adults experience, even re-experience (interpret), their experiences….We must not apply models of mother-infant/child interaction to the therapeutic situation in a simple-minded, noncritical fashion. Infants are not patients. Mothers are not therapists….It seems to me we can learn a great deal about both by comparing and contrasting them to each other. Nonetheless, we should not confuse and confabulate mothers and infants, patients and therapists. (pp. 189-190)

Bonds-White and I (Cornell & Bonds-White 2001) examined the clinical implications of the subtle and not-so-subtle models of mother/infant and parent/child relationships that are so common in TA psychotherapy. We have suggested thinking more in terms of relatedness rather than relationship to provide a conceptualization that shifts away from the parent/child metaphors. We emphasize the establishment of a therapeutic *space* (in contrast to relationship) which allows the means to reflect, wonder, explore and move. Seen from a body-centered perspective, psychotherapy is a means through which the client discovers personal agency. In working systematically with implicit knowing, bodily activity, and sensate/motoric organization, therapy can help bring the body into the mind of the client. It is my hope as a therapist to promote a kind of bodily learning and agency which will remain in the body of the client, an implicit somatic knowing that will remain with a client outside of the office and our relationship.

What happens to our images of ourselves as psychotherapists if we cast psychotherapy into the broad fields of activity and desire, beyond those of parenting, nurturing and understanding? Psychotherapy becomes a field of uncertainty and potentiality, of play and exploration, of action and aggression, of desire and imagination. Knoblach (1996), a psychoanalyst and jazz musician, captures the flavor of somatic and interpersonal enlivening in his title *The Play and Interplay of Passionate Experience: Multiple Organizations of Desire*. I think that the conceptualization of the roles of play and desire within the therapeutic process point a way out of the long-standing binds and blind spots of transactional analysis theory, which has become imbued with variations of parenting and corrective models of therapeutic activity. 'Play and interplay' conveys the sense of mutual exploration, motoric activation, and the unconscious matrix of transference and countertransference within the therapeutic process. Play and interplay offer a therapeutic model more consistent with the emerging discoveries of research with babies and brains, rooting those babies and brains in active, moving bodies, as well as within minds and ego structures.

There is a rich, emerging literature on the place of desire and passion in psychotherapy (Davies 1994, 1998; Winer 1994; Benjamin 1995; Kloblauch 1996; Eigen 1996, 1998; Mann 1997; Dimen 1999, 2001; Billow (2000); Cornell 2001, in press) that has many implications for the issues raised in this chapter. These articles go beyond the scope of this essay but warrant the attention of those seeking to extend their thinking about the nature and purpose of psychotherapy.

Play and the creation of potential space were certainly crucial to Winnicott's (1971) understanding of both child development and the therapeutic process. Play is a complex and multifaceted phenomena. Among the contemporary brain researchers, Panksepp has worked extensively with studies of brain development in older children and has undertaken numerous studies of the role of play. Panksepp (2001) has stressed that 'young children tend to be very active a good deal of the time' and that 'all children need daily doses of rough and tumble (R&T) activities, for this may help to optimize brain development' (p. 146). Panksepp (1993) outlined the importance of play:

> Human play has been divided into a large number of categories, including exploratory/sensorimotor play, relational/functional play, constructive play, dramatic/symbolic play, games-with-rules play, and rough and tumble play. Probably this last form, rough-housing play, is presently easiest to study in animal models, but…it has received the least attention in human research. This is under-standable, for roughhousing is boisterous and often viewed as dis-ruptive and potentially dangerous by adults. Of course kids love it (it brings them "joy"), and animals readily learn instrumental responses to indulge in it.
>
> (Panksepp 1990, pp. 150-151)

In subsequent writing on the long-term psychobiological consequences of infant emotions, Panksepp (2001) names four primary and enduring emotional systems of seeking, play, lust and care. Most psychotherapeutic models (certainly transactional analysis) have the care component nailed down thoroughly. My readings of the baby and brain research strongly suggest that we, as psychotherapists, are long overdue in adding much more systematic attention to seeking, play and lust. I think we need a more rough and tough approach to the psychotherapy of adults, bringing the full range of possibilities of two adult bodies and minds to bear upon the psychotherapeutic project.

Conclusion

Am I suggesting that we throw out the concept of the Child Ego State? No, certainly not. There are certainly aspects of ego function – archaic, fixated, and defensively organized – that are very much as Berne described them in his accounts of the Child ego state and as we often seen reflected in the TA liter-ature. I would agree that these states are indeed aspects of ego function. I am, however, arguing that as transactional analysis has significantly extended its clinical reach, we have run into serious theoretical trouble as a result of the limits of ego state theory, especially in our conceptualization of the Child. I am suggesting that the Child ego state emerges from a matrix of implicit, affective, and motoric systems of subsymbolic (pre-ego) organization and motivation. These are states of mind or neural organization that precede ego development and are the unconscious and preconscious realms of mental organization. The Child ego states reflect means of functioning in reality that may sometimes contain historically rooted distortions and defenses, but at the same time involve a wealth of affective and procedural forms of knowing that enrich daily life and relatedness. We must articulate a theory of process as well as structure. I think that we are now (and this will be evident in many of the chapters of this book) seeking to evolve a clinical theory of the uncon-scious, procedural, somatic states of motivation and organization that come alive in the *process* of in-depth psychotherapy.

Consistent with the implications of contemporary research with babies and brains, we must begin to reconceptualize that level of bodily and emotional organization from that of Child ego states to that of fundamental and ongoing processes of neural activation, organization, and change. We can then conceptualize transactional analysis psychotherapy as a means and place for the activation of desires, the exploration of possibilities, and an enlivened, rough and tumble relatedness.

The author wishes to thank Jenni Hine, TSTA, Gianpiero Petriglieri, MD, Suzanne Robinson, MSW, and Robin Fryer, MSW for their careful and critical readings of an earlier versions of this manuscript.

References

Allen, J. (2000) Biology and transactional analysis: integration of a neglected area. *Transactional Analysis Journal.* 29(4)250-259

Allen, J. (2001) Biology and transactional analysis II: A status report on neurodevelopment. *Transactional Analysis Journal.* 30(4)260-268

Bauer, P.J. (1996) What do infants recall? Memory for specific events by one-to-two-year-olds. *American Psychologist.* 51: 29-41

Benjamin, J. (1995) *Like Subjects, Love Objects.* New Haven: Yale University Press

Berne, E. (1947) *The Mind in Action.* New York: Simon and Schuster

Berne, E. (1961) *Transactional Analysis in Psychotherapy.* New York: Grove Press

Berne, E. (1964) *Games People Play.* New York: Grove Press

Berne, E. (1966) *Principles of Group Treatment.* New York: Oxford University Press

Berne, E. (1968) *A Layman's Guide to Psychiatry and Psychoanalysis.* New York: Simon and Schuster

Berne, E. (1969) Standard Nomenclature. *Transactional Analysis Bulletin.* 8:111-112

Berne, E. (1972) *What Do You Say After You Say Hello?* New York: Grove Press

Berne, E. (1977) *Intuition and Ego States.* New York: Harper & Row

Billow, R.M. (2000) From countertransference to "passion." *Psychoanalytic Quarterly.* 69: 93-119

Blackstone, P. (1993) The dynamic child: Integration of second-order structure, object relations, and self psychology. *Transactional Analysis Journal.* 23: 216-234

Boadella, D. (1997) Embodiment in the therapeutic relationship: main speech at the First Congress of the World Council of Psychotherapy, Vienna, 1-5 July 1996. *International Journal of Psychotherapy.* 2: 31-43

Bollas, C. (1987) *The Shadow of the Object: Psychoanalysis of Unknown Thought.* New York: Columbia University Pres

Bucci, W. (1997a) *Psychoanalysis and Cognitive Science: A Multiple Code Theory.* New York: Guilford

Bucci, W. (1997b) Symptoms and symbols: A multiple code theory of somatization. *Psychoanalytic Inquiry.* 17: 151-172

Bucci, W. (2001) Pathways of emotional communication. *Psychoanalytic Inquiry.* 21: 40-70.

Call, J.D. (1984) From early patterns of communication to the grammar of experience and syntax in infancy. In *Frontiers of Infant Psychiatry, Vol. 2*, Call, J.D., Galenson, E. & Tyson, R.L. (Eds.), pp. 15-28. New York: Basic Books, Inc

Churchland, P.M. (1995) *The Engine of Reason, the Seat of the Soul: A philosophical Journey.* Canbridge, MA: The MIT Press

Clarkson, P. (1992) *Transactional Analysis Psychotherapy.* London: Routledge

Clarkson, P. & Gilbert, M. (1988) Berne's original model of ego states: Theoretical considerations. *Transactional Analysis Journal*. 18: 20-29

Clarkson, P. & Fish, S. (1988) Rechilding: Creating a new past in the present as a support for the future. *Transactional Analysis Journal*. 18: 51-59

Cornell, W. (2000) Transference, desire, and vulnerability in body-centered psychotherapy. *Energy & Character*. 30: 29-37

Cornell, W. (in press) The impassioned body: Erotic vitality and disturbance *Bodypsychotherapie in Theorie and Practise*. Germany

Cornell, W. & Bonds-White, F. (2001) Therapeutic relatedness in transactional analysis: The truth of love or the love of truth. *Transactional Analysis Journal* 31: 71-83

Cox, M. (1999) The relationship between ego state structure and function: A diagrammatic formulation. *Transactional Analysis Journal*. 29: 49-58

Davies, J.M. (1994) Love in the afternoon: A relational reconsideration of desire and dread in the countertransference. *Psychoanalytic Dialogues*. 4: 153-170

Davies, J.M. (1998) Between the disclosure and foreclosure of erotic transference-counter transference: Can psychoanalysis find a place for adult sexuality? *Psychoanalytic Dialogues*. 8: 747-766

DeMasio, A.R. (1999) *The Feeling of What Happens*. New York: Harcourt Brace

Dimen, M. (1999) Between lust and libido: Sex, psychoanalysis, and the moment before. *Psychoanalytic Dialogues*. 9: 415-440

Dimen, M. (2001) Perversion is us? Eight notes. *Psychoanalytic Dialogues*. 11: 825-860

Downing, G. (1996) *Korper und Wort in der Psychotherapie*. Munich: Kosel Verlag

Edelman, G.M. (1992) *Bright Air, Brilliant Fire: On the matter of the Mind*. New York: Basic Books

Eigen, M. (1996) *Psychic Deadness*. Northvale, NJ: Jason Aronson

Eigen, M. (1998) *The Psychoanalytic Mystic*. Binghamton, NY: ESF Publishers

Emde, R. (1999) Moving ahead: Integrating influences of affective processes for development and psychoanalysis. *International Journal of Psycho-Analysis*. 80: 317-339.

Erskine, R. (1988). Ego structure, intrapsychic function, and defense mechanisms: A commentary on Eric Berne's original theoretical concepts. *Transactional Analysis Journal*. 18: 15-19

Federn, P. (1952) *Ego Psychology and the Psychoses*. New York: Basic Books

Fischer, K.W. & Hogan, A.E. (1989) The big picture for infant development: Levels and variations. In *Action in Scoial Context: Perspectives on early Development*, Lockman, J.J. & Hazen, N.L. (Eds.), pp. 275-305. New York: Plenum Press

Fonagy, P. (1999) Points of contact and divergence between psychoanalytic and attachment theories: Is psychoanalytic theory truly different? *Psychoanalytic Inquiry*. 19: 448-480

Fonagy, P. (2001) *Attachment Theory and Psychoanalysis*. New York: Other Press

Frank, R. (2001) *Body of Awareness*. New York: Gestalt Institute Press

Gilbert, M. (1996) *Ego states and ego state networks*. Paper presented at the International Transactional Analysis Conference, Amsterdam, Netherlands

Giuli, M. (1985) Neurophysiological and behavioral aspects of the P-0, A-0, C-0 structures of the personality. *Transactional Analysis Journal*. 15: 260-262

Goulding, M. & Goulding, R. (1979) *Changing Lives through Redecision Therapy*. New York: Brunner/Mazel

Green, A. (2000) Science and science fiction in infant research. In *Clinical and Observational Psychoanalytic Research: Roots of a Controversy*, Sandler, J., Sandler, A-M, & Davies, R. (Eds.), pp. 41-72. Madison, CT: International Universities Press

Hadley, J.L. (1989) The neurobiology of motivational systems. In *Psychoanalysis and Motivation*, Lichtenberg, J.D., pp.337-372. Hillsdale, NJ: The Analytic Press

Hargaden, H., & Sills, C. (2001) Deconfusion of the child ego state: A relational perspective. *Transactional Analysis Journal*. 31: 55-70

Hargaden, H., & Sills, C. (2002) *Transactional Analysis: Relational Perspective*. London: Routledge

Hine, J. (1997) Mind structure and ego states. *Transactional Analysis Journal*. 27: 278-289.

Hine, J. (2001) Personal communication. October 18, 2001.

Izard, C.E. (1993) Four systems for emotion activation: Cognition and noncognitive proceses. *Psychological Review*. 100: 68-90.

Kagan, J. (1998) *Three Seductive Ideas*. Cambridge, MA: Harvard University Press.

Kihlstrom, J.F. (1990) The psychological unconscious. In *Handbook of Personality: Theory and Research*, Pervin, L.A. (Ed.), pp.445-464. New York: Guilford Press.

Knoblauch, S.H. (1996) The play and interplay of passionate experience. *Gender and Psychoanalysis*. 1: 323-344.

La Barre, F. (2000) *On Moving and Being Moved: Nonverbal Behavior in Clinical Practice*. Hillsdale, NJ: The Analytic Press.

Lachmann, F. (2001) Some contributions of empirical infant research to adult psychoanalysis: What have we learned? How can we apply it? *Psychoanalytic Dialolgues*. 11: 167-187.

Laplanche, J. & Pontalis, J.-B. (1973) *The Language of Psychoanalysis*. New York: Norton.

LeDoux, J. (1996) *The Emotional Brain*. New York: Simon & Schuster.

Levenson, R.W. (1999) The intrapersonal functions of emotions. *Cognition and Emotion*. 13: 481-504.

Levin-Landheer, P. (1982) The cycle of development. *Transactional Analysis Journal*. 12: 129-139.

Ligabue, S. (1991) The somatic component of script in early development. *Transactional Analysis Journal*. 21: 21-29.

Lichtenberg, J.D. (1989) *Psychoanalysis and Motivation*. Hillsdale, NJ: The Analytic Press.

Lyons-Ruth, K. (1998) Implicit relational knowing: Its role in development and psychoanalyic treatment. *Infant Mental Health Journal*. 19: 282-289.

Lyons-Ruth, K. (1999) The two person unconscious: intersubjective dialogue, enactive relational representation and the emergence of new forms of relational organization. *Psychoanalytic Inquiry*. 19: 576-617.

Mann, D. (1997) *Psychotherapy: An Erotic Relationship*. London: Routledge.

Marcher. L. (1996) Waking the Body Ego, Part 1: Core concepts and principles; Part 2: Psychomotor development and character structure. In *Embodying the Mind & Minding the Body*, I. Macnaughton, (Ed.), pp. 94-137. North Vancouver, BC: Integral Press.

McClelland, J.L. (1998) Complementary learning systems in the brain: A connectionist approach to explicit and implicit cognition and memory. *Annals of the New York Academy of Sciences*. 843: 153-178.

Mellor, K. (1980) Impasses: A developmental and structural understanding. *Transactional Analysis Journal*. 10: 213-221.

Milner, B., Squire, L.R., & Kandel, E.R. (1998) Cognitive neuroscience and the study of memory. *Neuron*. 20: 445-468.

Mitrani, J.L. (1996) A Framework for the Imaginary. Clinical Explorations in Primitive States of Being. Northvale, NJ: Jason Aronson.

Moscovitch, M. (1994, May) *Neurological and Cognitive Bases of Memory*. Report to Harvard Medical School Conference on Memory, Cambridge, MA.

Nelson, K., & Greundel, J. (1981) Generalized event representations: The basic building blocks of cognitive development. In *Adavnces in Developmental Psychology, Vol. 1*, Lamb, M.E. & Browns, A.L. (Eds.) Hillsdale, NJ: Lawrence Erlbaum Associates.

Ogden, T.H. (1989) *The Primitive Edge of Experience*. Northvale, NJ: Jason Aronson

Pally, R. (2000) *The Mind-Brain Relationship*. London: Karnac.

Panksepp, J. (1993). Rough and tumble play: A fundamental brain process. In *Parent-Child Play: Descriptions and Implications*. MacDonald, K. (Ed.), pp. 147-184. Albany, NY: State University of New York Press.

Panksepp, J. (2001) The long-term psychobiological consequences of infant emotions: Prescriptions for the twenty-first century. *Infant Mental Health Journal*. 22: 132-173.

Penfield, W. (1952) Memory mechanisms. *Archives of Neurology and Psychiatry*, 67: 178-198.

Post, R.M., & Weiss, S.R.B. (1997) Emergent properties of neural systems: How focal molecular neurobiological alterations can effect behavior. *Development and Psychopathology.* 9: 907-930.

Rath, I. (1993) Developing a coherent map of transactional analysis theories. *Transactional Analysis Journal,* 23: 201-215.

Rothschild, B. (2000) *The Body Remembers: The Psychophysiology of Trauma and Trauma Treatment.* New York: Norton.

Sharar-Levy, Y. (2001) The function of the human motor system in processes of storing and retrieving preverbal, primal experience. *Psychoanalytic Inquiry.* 21: 378-393.

Schiff, J.L., et. al. (1975) *Cathexis Reader: Transactional Analysis and Psychosis.* New York: Harper & Row.

Schore, A.N. (1994) *Affect Regulation and the Origin of the Self.* Hillsdale, N.J.: Lawrence Erlbaum.

Schore, A. (2001) Contributions from the decade of the brain to infant health: An overview. *Infant Mental Health Journal.* 22: 1-6.

Shapiro, S.A. (1996) The embodied analyst in the Victorian consulting room. *Gender and Psychoanalysis.* 1: 297-322.

Siegel. D.J. (2001) Toward an interpersonal neurobiology of the developing mind: Attachment relationships, "mindsight," and neural integration. *Infant Mental Health Journal.* 22: 67-94.

Steere, D. (1981) Body movement in ego states. *Transactional Analysis Journal.* 11: 335-345.

Steere, D. (1985) Protocol. *Transactional Analysis Journal.* 15: 248-259.

Stern, D.N. (1985) *The Interpersonal World of the Infant: A View from Psychoanalysis and Developmental Psychology.* New York: Basic Books.

Thelan, E. & Fogel, A. (1989) Toward an action-based theory of infant development. In *Action in Social Context: Perspectives on Early Development,* Lockman, J.J. & Hazen, N.L. (Eds.), pp.23-63. New York: Plenum Press.

Thelan, E. & Smith, L.B. (1998) *A Dynamic Systems Approach to the Development of Cognition and Action.* Cambridge, MA: The MIT Press.

Tronick, E. (1998) Dyadically expended states of consciousness and the process of therapeutic change. *Infant Mental Health Journal.* 19: 290-299.

Tronick, E. (2001) Emotional connections and dyadic consciousness in infant-mother and patient-therapist interactions: Commentary on paper by Frank M. Lachmann. *Psychoanalytic Dialogues.* 11: 187-194.

Tulving, E., Kapur, S., Craik, F.I.M., Moscovitch, M., & Houle, S. (1994) Hemispheric encoding/retrieval asymmetry in episodic memory: Positron emission tomography findings. *Proceedings of the National Academy of Sciences.* 91: 2016-2020.

Waldekranz-Piselli, K.C. (1999) What do we do before we say hello? The body as the stage setting for the script. *Transactional Analysis Journal.* 29: 31-48.

Winer, R. (1994) *Close Encounters.* Northvale, NJ: Jason Aronson.

Winnicott. D.W. (1971) *Playing and Reality.* London: Tavistock Publications.

Chapter 3

HOW ARE YOU? AND HOW AM I?
Ego states and inner motivators
Fanita English

Editors' note: English's 'concentric circles' model of the Child ego state and her stages of child development first appeared in 1977. They have and continue to be heuristically satisfying as working models for TA practitioners. Over and over again, we have found that this is the model that trainees respond to and on which they can build their own thinking (for example, Wood 1997). For this reason, we asked Fanita to up-date and re-introduce her model in the light of her more recent work on unconscious motivators. Readers can study the original model in detail in 'What Shall I do Tomorrow' in Graham Barnes' *Transactional Analysis after Eric Berne* (1977). Her work on Scripts can be found in the *Transactional Analysis Journal* (1987, 1988, 1992, 1994, 1998, 1999), and on motivators in the videotape, *The Forces Within Us*.

In this chapter, I shall re-view my earlier model of ego states – and the Child ego state in particular – in the light of more than twenty years further experience and scientific discovery. I will begin by describing the notion of age-related Child sub-systems, and link them to therapeutic practice. I will then briefly overview the three motivators (first described as drives in 1987), and explore how they dynamically animate the structure of the person. I conclude with some 'treatment pointers'.

Nature/nurture and development
How, exactly, does the structure of our personality evolve, and how do we integrate memories and conclusions that later affect us functionally?

Fifty years ago Watson and Crick discovered DNA, the depository of hereditary instructions in the cell. Differences in DNA sequences make each person's heredity unique, in addition to which, every person's experience in growing up is unique. Nevertheless, fortunately for therapists, there are plenty of common denominators among human beings, so it is worthwhile learning all we can about development and behaviour.

The human body is thought to contain around a 100 trillion cells, and, since June 2000 when the decoding of the human genome sequence was formally announced, a flurry of new studies are being undertaken about the plasticity of 'that maestro of the genome, the human cell, which at every instant is reading off hundreds of thousands of genes on a scale of activity that has until now been far too complex to track' (Wade 2001 p.8). Messages from both neighbouring and far away cells continually arrive at the cell's surface, bearing instructions that the receptor proteins convey to the interior. Then genes are turned on or off by various proteins which are constantly interacting with one another.

This is true also for cells of the human brain, which, at the last count, has eleven billion neurons that can each make up to 50,000 synapses (Gazzanica 1992, p.50)

However, as stated by Nicholas Wade, in *Life Script* (2001), (the title refers to the assumption of biologists that human "scripts" can be determined biologically), 'the interpretation of the genomic script is likely to prove as hard as the sequencing,...doubtless because of biologists' still substantial ignorance as to how the genome works.' (p. 68) He adds that, according to new research, 'the human genome seems to be 3.1 billion bases in length in the DNA. The rest of the terrain (in each cell) '.. is a graveyard of fossilized DNA, evolutionary experiments that didn't work, and dead genes on the road to extinction'.

Given the astronomical number of potential interactions on the cellular level, let alone those on the total biological and psychosomatic levels of each individual, we can certainly assume that we are affected in significant ways during formative periods of life and even later; but the ways in which we are affected may be as complex as the biological influences. The psychobiologist, Robert Orenstein, (1993, p.10) states it well: 'Contemporary neuroscientists are just beginning to peer into the complex connections among brain, behaviour and personality. This interaction begins before birth and, perhaps most surprisingly, continues throughout life. He adds: "there is a kind of 'co-development' that takes place based on the interaction between biological inheritance and the environment in which we live." Or, as Allen (2001) has put it, because of environment-dependent gene expression, 'nurture can be considered to become nature' (p. 260).

Until such time as such interactions can be traced more specifically, we must still depend on accumulated empirical and clinical knowledge to conceptualize structural development and functional processes. Empirically, it is clear that development proceeds in predetermined stages, and that a dynamic process of "co-development" takes place all the time.

So for example - nobody can teach a child to walk before he/she is ready. Yet at a certain predictable stage, a child is "motivated" by internal forces to stand, take some steps, walk, then, later, run and further experiment with jumping, climbing, and so on. What precedes walking are many efforts; from stretching helplessly to reach something, to ignominiously crawling and perhaps even being pulled away by a Major Power - a caretaker. (Why did they take away that lovely vase just as I wanted to pull it down?) But there are also positive strokes, for achieving first steps for instance.

Similarly no one ever made a child utter his/her first words, nor later struggle with speech. The mysterious forces that motivated us to walk and connect physically with our environment, differently to simply being passively handled by others, also motivated us to struggle to express ourselves in more ways than by cries that could only be understood by our caretakers. Language then becomes an important tool for communicating with others. However, while the infant brain is capable of hearing, learning and reproducing any sound in any language, in fact the only languages that can be fluently learned by a particular child are the ones spoken around him/her, be they English, Spanish or Chinese. This shows the importance of the fit between our physiological readiness and our interpersonal and affective relationships. Progress in the process of communication, all the way to becoming able to articulate in words what began as nebulous inchoate impressions or feelings, illustrates the "co-development" mentioned above.

Structure of the Child

Present-day studies with imaging of the brain show that, unlike most other organs, the brain maintains many of its archaic structures. Although it is still not possible to show effectively how thoughts and complex emotional reactions combine to affect different areas of the total brain, Berne's view that 'childhood states exist as relics in the grown-up' (Berne, 1961 p.30) was prescient, and led him to develop his original structural and functional models of three ego states as distinctive systems of thoughts, feelings and potential behaviour. He also indicated *that each ego state has its own system for thinking, feeling and behaving.*

However, I believe it is insufficient to think of just one childhood 'relic' as making up the Child ego-state. Rather, the Child contains successive 'relics' – or sub-systems, as I prefer to call them, by analogy to Berne's use of the word 'system' for each distinct ego state. He did suggest a second-order structure, but I find its details unsatisfactory. Before he was five years old, little Johnny did not exist as a C-1 Demon or as a P-1 Electrode. But he did exist as a fully-fledged baby, then a one-year old, two year-old, and so on, with particular characteristics for each age.

Therefore I prefer to conceptualize the Child with 'subsystems' that correspond to sequential chronological stages of development, and to emphasize *that each sub-system of the Child has its own system for thinking, feeling and behaving, according to the equivalent chronological age.* Thus, in working with clients, it is important to be aware that there is a vast difference between the typical thoughts and feelings of, say, a five-year old, and a one-year old. This means that functionally, in the 'now', a person will transact differently from a one-year old Child sub-system than from, say, a five-year old Child sub-system. Allen & Allen (2002) also refer to layered levels of transference and the transpersonal consequence.

Furthermore, at the time they were internalized, similar messages from caretakers and the environment got interpreted differently at different times, according to the level of maturity. Therefore, each of these layered operational sub-systems, composed of neural networks (Allen 2001), contains a large number of 'conclusions' based on messages and memories of experiences, *most of which are useful in the formation of the person's personality,* although some may be dysfunctional. It is these archaic conclusions and consequent behavioural patterns that cause difficulties in the client's current life, and it is these that must be worked with. It does not mean aiming to cancel the whole script. That would be trying to throw out the baby with the bathwater. For example, Tom, who had a new boss, became overly scared whenever this boss came into his office. Tom kept feeling an impulse to hide under his desk at such times. Why? This problem had not existed with his old boss. Yet the new boss was not more demanding than the previous one; on the contrary, he was more supportive.

When Tom brought up his dilemma in group, he realized a connection; this new boss usually allowed the door to slam behind him whenever he walked into Tom's office, even if it was to praise him. Hearing the door slam brought on a survival 'conclusion' for Tom that he was in danger, and must hide. As a child, Tom had taught himself that when he heard the entrance door slam, it meant that his father had come home drunk and violent, and Tom must hide. Most other times, his father was loving and supportive of him.

Neurophysiologically we might say that Tom's early experience with his father had sensitized that part of the brain responsible for alarm, (Allen and Pfefferbaum, 2001) and caused the conclusion that demanded hiding. Such conclusions are maintained in what Allen, (2000) following Squire et al (1993) and Gildebrand (in this volume), suggest is implicit memory, rather than in the explicit memory system which is associated with a conscious act of remembering. Nevertheless, after Tom recognized the cause of his symptom, he was no longer bound to the semi-automatic behavioral reaction of that conclusion. He still occasionally felt a slight twinge whenever his boss slammed the door, for conclusions do not necessarily disappear without a trace. They remain in the implicit memory system. But Tom learned to relax about it, and could also lightly ask his boss to avoid startling him this way, thus further reducing the number of occasions of the door being slammed, and the subsequent discomfort.

Tom's conclusion, as a three-year old, about hiding under the bed on hearing the door slam, was good for his situation at that time, but of course it was potentially harmful in his office. In general, Tom's script led to enthusiasm, achievement and good relationships. It would have been a mistake to assume, from the one scary unconscious conclusion, that Tom's total script was harmful, or even that he had undue fear of authority figures. Even harmful conclusions are not in themselves representative of someone's total script, although, along with ingrained memories of childhood messages and experiences, damaging conclusions may indeed affect some of the thoughts, feelings or behaviors of a grown individual, and thus loosely connect to his/her script. Other conclusions may continue to be important throughout life, and still others may be out-dated but innocuous, just causing some "quirks" or eccentricities in a person without doing harm.

Accordingly, for a structural model to represent the Child ego state, I like to think of the formation of that Child as a system with sub-systems that correspond to successive stages of development layered sequentially, as within a tree.

A cross-section of a cut tree reveals sequential rings, each of which corresponds to previous years, with scars at points that correspond to occurrences at particular years. Some scars extend over several rings, sometimes all the way to the bark, while others are diminished in successive rings, or even disappear beyond marking just one or two rings. The rings are uneven; at some periods, the tree grew comfortably, and the ring corresponding to that period is wider; at other periods it is narrower, or crooked.

So, on Fig.1 hereunder, I draw sub-systems of the Child of a given person in circular fashion, representing the layered stages of development which persist in the Child ego state, each with its own conclusions. Particular memories or conclusions can be indicated by referring to their location in the subsystem that corresponds to the age when they originated.

Certain conclusions may be reinforced by being repeated at subsequent stages, or they may be offset by other conclusions at other stages, and thereby lose power. In the course of life, many may also be discarded into the "graveyard of fossilized DNA."

Berne assumed that the Child ego state gets fixated at around age five to seven years, and it does seem that an initial outline of a person's script gets formed then. But clinical evidence shows that the Child ego keeps developing and changing past that age, though perhaps not as radically as before; and so does the script.

A valid argument can be made to add circles, as I have done, to represent stages beyond the first seven years of the Child systems, and to see them as representing developmental stages of the Parent, for our Parent ego state also grows and changes, though at a far slower rate than the Child. It does appear, however, that past age seven, the Parent ego state operates as a distinct system with which one or another of the Child subsystems may dialogue internally, often verbally, while previous inner communication among Child subsystems is non-verbal and hard to recognize consciously. After about age five to seven, the equivalent to what I call 'conclusions' within Child subsystems may be remembered as conscious decisions. They can be verbalized, and may be in the Child or the Parent.

Some such decisions may reinforce certain conclusions in a Child sub-system, or may offset - but not necessarily cancel - some early conclusions. This applies particularly to persons who have had successively different parents and environments, as when parents were divorced, and when a child consciously chose a particular model for himself, as Bill Clinton did with John Kennedy. Such remembered decisions do then contribute to a person's script, to reinforce certain aspects, or to divert them.

And then there is the Adult. According to Jean Piaget (1952), it is only past age twelve that a child has the capacity for abstract thought. This corresponds to the development of the Adult in Transactional Analysis. For the model I describe, the Adult can be thought of as the outer bark of the tree, which connects the inner part to daily reality, like rain or wind or sunshine, or being pecked by birds. This analogy holds also because our daily 'reality' changes constantly as time goes by. What is Adult information today may be superceding beliefs in a prejudiced Parent, but may itself generate out-dated data for the Parent of tomorrow.

At adolescence, along with the effect of tremendous hormonal influences plus resulting new complicated social interactions, various aspects of Child sub-systems are revived, and there are new ways in which the script is fashioned all over again.

Figure 1 is intended to help the reader imagine the sub-systems mentioned above. By drawing the layers of development in circular fashion, we can visualize how different stages of development persist in the Child ego state, or perhaps even in the Parent as sub-systems, each with its own conclusions.

Of course, even though we can better illustrate the sub-systems of the Child by means of a structural diagram by using the analogy to a tree's cross-section, as shown below, for practical purposes the standard first-order PAC diagram (Parent, Adult, Child) may still be drawn as a functional diagram to illustrate transactions.

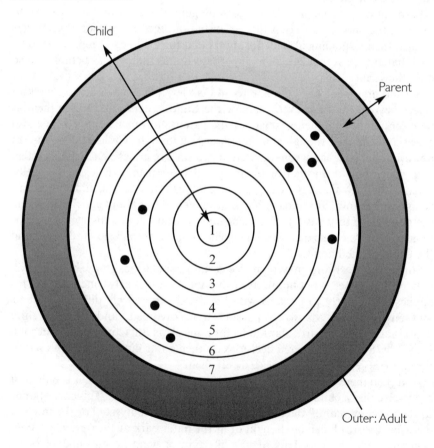

Fig. 1: A cross-sectional model of Child ego state developement

The inner core in Fig. 1 represents infancy, and subsequent rings represent separately identifiable sub-systems that are added on each year. Each number identifies a separate sub-system, and, in formal script and ego state analysis, can be used to index, on a separate sheet, descriptive references of that stage, and conclusions of that period for each person in treatment. Some conclusions may exist in only one ring, and be relatively less potent, others in several rings, reinforcing each other.

For instance in the example of Tom, given previously, the conclusion that led him to want to hide when the door slams did not appear in infancy, but did at ages two, three and four. His arousal system was sensitized specifically to that kind of signal, as a threat calling for a particular behavioral reaction. By the time Tom was over five, he had developed other ways to cope with his father than hide under the bed; but the literal pressure to react to 'door-slamming by father-figure' still persisted in his implicit memory. However, it did not get symbolized to the extent of significantly affecting his script, for there were other compensatory memories.

Here I am tempted to add a personal example. I went to an English school, starting with Kindergarten aged four and a half. We were taught always to stand up whenever we heard the British national anthem. Recently, in bed, I watched a BBC programme on TV. When I suddenly heard - "God save our gracious Queen", my whole body strained with the impulse to get up and stand! Here I was, born in a different culture, now in the U.S., at my advanced age, yet feeling powerfully pushed, semi-automatically, by an old conclusion resulting from what I was probably taught in Kindergarten, although I don't consciously remember how or when.

Obviously this conclusion is not my script, yet it certainly almost automatically commanded a specific reaction - to stand to attention. However, when we can translate an implicit, unremembered conclusion into its conscious verbal equivalent, we can choose to obey it or not, as I did, by resisting the impulse to get out of bed on listening to the anthem.

The earlier the conclusion, the harder it is to resist, because it sits in implicit memory; so it is helpful to infer the period of its origin by using any other available data to do so. In this case, I know it could not predate Kindergarten. Had the conclusion existed in an earlier sub-system, at age two or three for example, it would have been harder to resist the impulse to stand up.

Identifying and working with early conclusions

Since implicit conclusions can become a part of the Child's structure, how is a therapist to work with harmful conclusions in a grown person? It is helpful if a therapist is very familiar with child development, and has experience with actual children at different ages. This is because when a disturbing symptom is being discussed in the treatment session, the corresponding conclusion will be stimulated; the client is likely to functionally enter, albeit briefly, into the Child sub-system that corresponds to the age of onset of that conclusion. Recognizing this facilitates identifying the conclusion. Experience with typical differences among various ages also helps to recognize shifts from one sub-system to another, or to Parent, which happens frequently for defensive reasons.

Nancy, a former client, whom I knew to be a successful college teacher, came to consult me about nightmares and panic attacks following a negative evaluation by a student. As she described her symptoms, interjecting that she knew her panic was irrational, for the negative evaluation was the only one out of twenty-nine highly positive ones, she blushed, fidgeted, and looked down at her hands, the image of a shame-faced two-year old.

Knowing that it is around the age of two that being shamed sets up certain conclusions, I asked whether she knew of something very embarrassing that happened at that age. Though she could not remember it herself, she recalled her mother telling her about how she had memorized a ditty at that age, but much to the mother's embarrassment (she had bragged about this), little Nancy had failed to recite it when her father brought guests home.

After Nancy told that story, we found the connection to her panic. It was not the evaluation itself, but that an unexpected visitor had happened to visit her class just when the negative evaluation was being read, and had left before hearing the other, excellent evaluations. A conclusion had been triggered, which we might put into words as - "Terrible danger to fail in public". This caused her subsequent nightmares and fears of impending doom.

As a side effect of dealing with this particular panic, Nancy also saw that this conclusion led her to be too perfectionist for fear of 'goofing', and she gradually became more relaxed in teaching.

In 1977, I rather arbitrarily defined seven sub-systems that correspond to seven stages of child development: infant (alive or withdrawing from life); baby (from omnipotence to impotence); exploring toddler (the power of mobility); 'walky-talky' (determination and imitation); contro (control and controversy); exister (formation of the defensive existential position); scripter (what's past and future). These are described in detail in *What Shall I do Tomorrow* (English 1977). In developing these seven sub-systems, I took into account research by Rene Spitz (1957, 1963) on infants, Erik Erikson (1963) and his followers on emotional development, Jean Piaget (1952a and b) and his many followers on differences in thinking at different stages regardless of intelligence, and Melanie Klein (1963), on therapy with children, in addition to many others on child development. Finally, there was also accumulated physiological data on particular 'sensitive periods' for onset and/or development of skills like walking and talking. However, overall, distinctions are based more on my own previous experience of years doing child therapy, and subsequent experience as a Transactional Analyst, rather than on scientifically verifiable material. They have proven to be heuristically useful and I continue to find them satisfying and helpful. However, the reader may prefer to use Stern (1985) or any other system that makes sense for them.

For therapists who lack practical training with children and have no access to young children at home, the best way to develop empathetic intuition about ages is to frequently observe actual children (at the playground, on airplanes, or wherever), note their age on observing their behavior, allow such experience to sink in, and then, for instance at parties or social gatherings, note similarities and differences in grown-ups at different moments.

There is a recognizable difference in appearance and manner if a client is crying from, say, helpless 'Infant Child' or, say, from what I call a 'Contro', (the equivalent to a two-year old seeking to control with a temper tantrum,) or from a seven-year old incipient Parent. You would communicate differently with a one-year old and a five-year old, wouldn't you? This applies also to communicating with a client in one sub-system or another.

The therapist can then steer questions about the client's circumstances at that age and develop a working hypothesis about the origin of a disturbing symptom. Then, while still maintaining her own Adult, she can modulate her own body language, tone of voice and vocabulary according to the age she is dealing with, and then seek to enlist the client's Adult to define a dysfunctional conclusion consciously and decide about changing it.

Dynamic motivation forces

So far we have focussed on the structure of the Child and its subsystems. The standard functional model is useful to illustrate transactions between people and among our own ego states, in an elementary way. However, for treatment purposes, we must conceptualize a three-dimensional model to account for underlying unconscious forces that influence us perpetually through any one of our Child systems, our Parent and also, occasionally, our Adult.

As stated by Richard Restak, (2002) 'Researchers now regard the brain not as a shell, but as an active, dynamic, supremely plastic structure that changes from moment to moment'. This must be reflected in how we view functioning ego states.

Sadly, Berne did not live long enough to expand on what he called the 'three hungers'; namely, recognition, structure and stimulation. He focussed primarily on the need for strokes ('recognition hunger') as the principal motivating factor for the way we function, and he probably saw script formation as related to structure hunger. But he did not sufficiently allow for the underlying dynamic processes that motivate the establishment of conclusions, and activate responses to inner and outer stimuli.

To show these processes, which operate constantly, unconsciously most of the time, we must conceptualise a dynamic three-dimensional model with constantly moving parts whereby three motivating drives, or Motivators, as I now call them, *take turns in affecting us unconsciously all the time, and how their influence is manifested functionally through our ego states.*

The three Motivators

Our psychic energy is distributed among three Motivating Forces, ('Motivators'), that are active from birth to death to promote our growth, development, and interaction with our environment, including script formation and implementation. They oversee the process whereby we integrate implicit and explicit memories and 'conclusions' into our developing organism, and subsequently, they influence us accordingly. They affect our personality through successive stages from birth to adulthood to death, and simultaneously they affect us functionally all the time in response to internal and external stimuli. Each one of these three Motivators affects us differently, for evolution has promoted different activities for each. The three Motivators are:

Survival, Expressive and Quiescence
• The Survival Motivator operates for the survival of the individual.
• The Expressive Motivator operates for the survival of the species.
• The Quiescence Motivator relates us to the Cosmos, or spirituality.

The Survival Motivator

The influence of this Motivator can be noted from the very beginning of life, in the infant's ability to breathe, suck at the breast or bottle, and signify pain and fear; as well as in the ability to register reassuring strokes. It is because of the Survival Motivator that children intuitively sense they cannot survive without help and must influence caretakers, and/or adapt to them for basic needs. Strokes represent reassurance that these will be provided, and allay recognition hunger. Eventually, as Berne correctly emphasized, stroke exchanges evolve symbolically as transactions, and thus set preferred patterns for communicating and relating with others.

Thus the Survival Motivator not only supports awareness of an attribute like hunger or thirst, for instance, to generate manifestations, (crying, then sucking by Infant Child, in this example) to affect the 'environment' (caretakers) so they offer the needed nourishment for survival, but it also supports the development of whatever patterns of behaviour brought literal or symbolic satisfaction to meet the need. In a grown-up, the same attribute (hunger, or the memory thereof, literally or symbolically) will motivate a person to seek food, literally or symbolically, and, by extension motivate to work for literal or symbolic food, like strokes or money.

The Survival Motivator also promotes the development of a basic existential position at the Exister stage, and this in turn leads to character type, as described previously.

Survival conclusions

As indicated previously, the Child ego state contains a large number of conclusions that are integrated into successive sub-systems. Each of the three Motivators has the ability to set conclusions; however, it is the Survival Motivator which sets most of them in response to caretakers' messages, (understood or misunderstood), especially when connected to strokes or shaming.

The function of Survival Conclusions is to supplement survival instincts (that animals have to a greater extent than humans), and to generate appropriate fear and caution in certain situations. For instance, a child must learn to be careful of fire, and the Survival Motivator will register strokes (whether positive or negative) that establish the necessary survival conclusions and consequent 'automatic' caution about fire.

Unfortunately, the same mechanism operates also with experiences or ancient parental messages or models that may cease to be useful, and can be downright damaging to the grown individual. Yet the Survival Motivator will keep pushing to bring on responses based on old conclusions, whether useful or not, with their related reactive behaviours or inhibitions. This was illustrated with the example of Tom, given above, who felt like cringing under his desk when his boss slammed the door.

The example of Nancy, also given above, who became terrified when her Survival Motivator activated the fear of her two-year old Child for "failing" after a visitor heard a negative evaluation about her, is another example of how archaic conclusions can be brought to life by the Survival Motivator, with corresponding manifestations (fear, shame, and anxiety in this instance), that are no longer appropriate to the present situation.

The Survival Motivator also plays an important part in the development of the Parent ego state and activates it to develop, and seek to enforce, a variety of conscious or pre-conscious instructions, for better or worse. All such instructions are for the intended purpose of the survival of the individual, although they may turn out to be out-dated and counter-productive to a person's present-day life.

I need not elaborate further on the Survival Motivator, for essentially all that is said in Transactional Analysis about the importance and effect of strokes applies to this Motivator.

The Expressive Motivator

Although the importance of the Survival Motivator is implicitly acknowledged in Transactional Analysis, with its emphasis on strokes, the equivalent importance of the Expressive Motivator is largely ignored. Perhaps this is because the Expressive Motivator manifests itself under diverse guises, like Berne's 'stimulus hunger'. Terms like 'Free Child', 'Natural Child', or 'Little Professor' are misnomers, in my opinion; for they refer to structure rather than dynamic function, which occurs when the Expressive Motivator manifests through one or another Child system. (Note that the Expressive Motivator can also manifest through Parent, as when a teacher is excited by something a student has done.)

Manifestations of this drive are often mistakenly assumed to be manipulative and covertly related to strokes. But the *Expressive Motivator functions in response to inner stimuli, not strokes, urging action totally outside the stroke economy.* Such inner pressures are due to evolution, and have served for the survival of our species rather than that of particular individuals. So the Expressive Motivator will often induce behaviour with total disregard for immediate potential consequences, for its goals are beyond those of individual survival.

In other creatures, lion cubs, for instance, playfulness is limited to practicing skills for future survival. Playfulness ends when maturity is achieved. Not so with humans, where the Child persists throughout life, and, with it, childlike qualities of playfulness, tendencies to risk-taking, and quest for excitement, (Berne's 'stimulus hunger').

Relentless, insatiable curiosity, the propensity to adventure, experimentation, the constant quest for new ways to do things, the capacity for passionate investment in activities regardless of strokes or personal rewards, (though these may then come incidentally), have led humans through the ages to intrepid exploration, discoveries, innovation and social change, often at the cost of the lives of the very individuals thus motivated. Unlike other creatures, it is not only through procreation that humans survived. Mankind would have been killed off eons ago by more powerful creatures, had not the discoveries and creative inventions of our forebears, along with many other attributes of the Expressive Motivator, like imagination and the craving for free self-expression, turned our species into the most successful one on earth.

Expressive conclusions

Like the Survival Motivator, the Expressive Motivator sets conclusions in the structure of the Child. Most of these conclusions are set as a result of particular experiences of discovery, freedom or exhilaration during childhood, or by condensed memories of pleasure, often acquired dangerously and against dictates of individual survival. While these conclusions create some longing to repeat exciting experiences, for instance in the sexual arena, or in the course of exploration, they are not as numerous or as imperative in daily life as are Survival conclusions, since they are not reinforced by strokes. In general, the Expressive Motivator pushes for new experiences rather than reproducing old ones.

There are also many inner struggles between the dictates of the Expressive Motivator and the controls of Survival conclusions or Adult reality. This is how a famous painter describes them:

> I am always between two currents of thought - first the material difficulties of turning round and round to make a living; and second the study of colour. I am always hoping to make a discovery here, to express the feelings of two lovers by marriage of two complementary colors - to express hope by some star, the eagerness of a soul by a secret sunset glow.....
>
> Vincent Van Gogh, from a letter to his brother, 1888

The Quiescence Motivator

This Motivator encourages us to "let go" of daily preoccupations, to meditate, listen to music, or to sleep. This has many positive values, but may also lead to excessive passivity.

The task of the Quiescence Motivator is to connect us with the universe beyond our immediate environment. It supports appreciation of music, art, and diverse forms of spirituality. Ultimately, when the time is right, it might facilitate a peaceful death, but this does not correspond to Freud's concept of a death drive, since Quiescence motivates to peacefulness rather than aggression.

Quiescence often intervenes helpfully when there is a conflict between the Survival and Expressive Motivators, for instance by bringing on breathing pauses, which allow space for broader perspectives than conflict.

Quiescence conclusion
These support peacefulness, inaction, nostalgia, feelings of identity with Nature and the Universe, broad-mindedness, tolerance and appreciation of sleep; but like Expressive conclusions, they are not as numerous or as powerful as Survival conclusions. They are often experienced as religious feelings or yearnings.

Inner dynamic activity

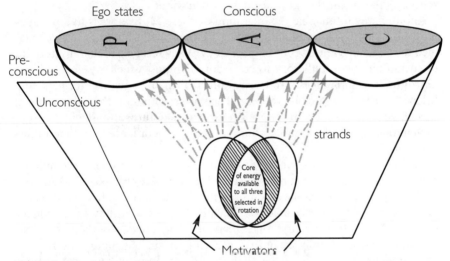

Fig. 2: The motivating of ego states

To imagine how these Motivators operate through our ego states, think of our ego states as being on the surface of consciousness, and Motivators beneath them (or above), each with many strands like a puppeteer's wires connecting to each of our ego states. According to internal or external stimuli any one of the three Motivators may activate one or another strand, which corresponds to one or more of its attributes. This will manifest as a feeling, thought or an impulse to behaviour for one or another ego state, while other strands remain dormant.

We can imagine the unconscious activity of our Motivators by visualizing a three-dimensional model, and we can note the influence of one or another

Motivator by whatever attributes manifest in our thoughts, feelings or behaviors.

Since I don't have a video or a puppeteer's stage here, I can only offer you the diagram above to illustrate what I mean.

The above schema shows the three Motivators as distinct from one another, but with overlapping areas, since they represent the same source of life-energy. So there is a continuous flow of interchanging (and often combining or competing) influence from each Motivator to our ego states.

Rather than circles, functional ego states are shown as ovals above the schema of drives to convey the idea that this diagram must be seen three-dimensionally, with ego states on the surface of consciousness and with pre-conscious potential, while Motivators, as such, are unconscious.

Each of the three Motivators may be active or inactive at any given moment, with two combining very frequently in the course of being active. Each Motivator has numerous particular attributes (the puppeteer's strands in the analogy above). These may establish any number or connections to influence any one of our ego states, usually a Child system or Parent, by manifesting as particular thoughts, feelings or behaviours.

Another way to imagine the operation of these Motivators is to anthropomorphize them as three dancing goddesses, the way the ancient Greeks imagined the effect of various gods or goddesses. They recognized that mysterious, often mutually contradictory forces from Olympus, which we now call the Unconscious, sometimes arbitrarily affected their thoughts, feelings and behaviors beyond conscious volition. Then, even without a three-dimensional model, you can visualize three goddesses that take turns in influencing us at each moment, as well as throughout our lives, in accordance with their different goals.

At a given moment only one Motivator may be active; then a second one may join and thus there can be a transition to where the second Motivator becomes primary, sometimes then bringing on the third Motivator while the first becomes temporarily inactive. Ideally, there is a healthy fluid balance between Motivators as first one, then another, comes to the fore. No Motivator can be totally excluded on a daily basis, but more time may be spent under the influence of one than the others. In many instances, there is a tug-of-war between the Survival and Expressive Motivators, or between one of these two and Quiescence. At other times, they work in conjunction. The Expressive Motivator may cooperate with the Survival Motivator in some areas, as in learning to talk and walk for a child, or being very excited by a project on the job.

Even though relatively smooth rotation among our Motivators is essential to daily function, in the course of our lives we are likely to go for preferences. So a particular individual, like Einstein, might function more of the time with one Motivator (Expressive), or a combination of two (Expressive and Quiescence), rather than the third; as long as two Motivators do not combine so tightly that they collude to consistently exclude the third, for then eventually the excluded Motivator is likely to push through in a harmful way. However, presumably Einstein also depended on his Survival drive for daily routines, and it also influenced him in writing a famous anti-war letter he sent President Roosevelt.

Some thoughts about treatment
I will end with some personal reflections about working therapeutically with the client's Child conclusions, in conjunction with his/her Motivators.

When working as a psychotherapist, I like to imagine a little video screen above each client's head, on which I see him or her in scenes at different young ages; I try to figure out, from problems presented and behaviour in the treatment group, what may have been this or that conclusion in one scene or another.

To change the impact of one or more damaging conclusions, they must be:
1 identified
2 connected to corresponding childhood experiences or messages, understood or misunderstood
3 translated from their non-verbal personal code into verbal formulations that can be dealt with cognitively (many conclusions are inchoate; they are only in implicit memory in very young Child sub-systems, and need to be "translated" into explicit vocabulary)
4 discussed openly with the patient's Adult, comparing the survival value these conclusions may have had in the past with problems they cause now.

I look at bodily reactions when a client's symptom is referred to, or, sometimes, while another client in the group brings up something. At what point does the client show fear, or shame, or secret pleasure?

At the back of my mind is also the question; What is the client's type? Is it Undersure, if the client adapts perhaps a little too readily to me or to the group? If so, I must make sure the client does not buy into an interpretation that may be inaccurate. Mild challenges to elicit more independence can be useful. Or is the client Oversure, assertive, likely to take on perhaps too much leadership in the group? If so, I must avoid direct challenges that risk turning into a power struggle. Some admissions of pain or helplessness may be good signs here, and require warm support.

In general, I am alert to changes of appearance or behaviour in what I call the "Super-now"; by that I mean that suddenly there is a 'flash' - or a fleeting moment of insight, often followed by a switch from one Child sub-system to another, or, defensively, to Parent. Such switches can be indications that we are on the right track; but also, that there is stress, and the client's Survival Motivator feels too threatened by a frontal confrontation about an archaic survival conclusion, so I must back down temporarily.

Throughout, it is useful to think three-dimensionally about how the client's Motivators are operating. In most instances, Survival conclusions cause the symptoms for which a client seeks treatment. They may have been developed, at one stage of childhood or another, to inhibit behavior stimulated by the Expressive or Quiescence Motivators. Behavior patterns that may have seemed too rash or too passive at a previous time, and appropriately brought on cautions or challenges in that environment, may now need to be revised in the light of the client's present reality.

Particularly if there is much resistance to positive change, I ask myself:

a is it a Motivator which is causing the present difficulty by maintaining the client in an unbalanced condition?

b which Motivator is it?

c is it because this Motivator is having *too much* influence, and is in conflict with the two others, or –

d because this Motivator does not have *enough* influence, and the two other drives are colluding to suppress the appropriate use of this drive?

e what value systems are involved? Motivators are a-moral. They influence us in ways that are evaluated as 'good' or 'bad' according to personal value systems. Do my value systems correspond to those of the client's Adult, in evaluating 'good' and 'bad'? If not, has the discrepancy been acknowledged and allowed for in the treatment contract?

Some trial and error interpretations, or hypotheses about unremembered past situations, may be offered. Doing so within group treatment is particularly helpful, because group members can contribute intuitive insights, and this also offsets the danger of undue suggestion by the therapist in terms of her own values. If there is empathetic rapport with the client, I may use a variety of treatment techniques, like Permission (Crossman, 1966) in order to modify a harmful conclusion or to reinforce other conclusions that offset the harmful one. Sometimes Gestalt 'hot seat' work is useful, to identify possible causes for implicit, unremembered, hurtful conclusions. It can lead to educated insights and, often, to reducing the force of harmful conclusions. I admit that I proceed from the premise that it is crucial to favour clients' expressive needs, which may include the expression of anger at the therapist, because manifestations of the Expressive Motivator may have been frequently discounted by caretakers when the client was growing up, in the name of safety or cultural dictates. As I see it, a client's passions require space, even if they are dormant. Appropriate outlets are important, lest the Expressive Motivator 'revenge' with truly harmful reactions to frustration. Here, however, is a caveat; certain psychotic or borderline patients, adolescents and children, may need more inner controls, rather than less. So here the therapist must be very careful not to give permissions without safeguards.

I have also found it useful to draw on the client's Quiescence Motivator, to help the client re-establish balance when too immersed in emotional pain. By that, I mean that I teach short meditation or breathing techniques, and encourage clients to use them at moments of crisis. This has a way of disengaging a stranglehold from the Survival or Expressive Motivators, whenever one or the other pushes too hard for priority and instant action.

Ultimately, it must be the client's Adult who determines what it is he/she no longer needs or wants, or, rather, what it is he/she now *wants* in order to drop an unwelcome pattern of behavior. There may still be some short-lived discomfort for so doing, with an old threat and survival conclusion still coming up in a nightmare, for instance, the way an amputee continues to 'feel' the amputated limb for a while, until adjusting to its absence. This also applies to emotional rackets, where it is important to support new awareness of suppressed feelings so they blossom forth, although old racketeering patterns may still persist for a while. Finally, I know the client is going to manage very well without me when it appears that her/his Motivators are rotating pretty smoothly, and that he/she can comfortably maintain or reinstate dynamic inner balance.

For inner balance is not static; nor are joy and happiness. As in sailing, our boat may keel to one side, and we may need to tug on a sail so it leans the other way, making sure, each time, that our little boat does not keel over so far as to capsize. It is this process that gives zest to sailing – and to fully living life itself.

The author gratefully acknowledges much help from Dr. James R. Allen and Deirdre English in revising this chapter.

References

Allen, J. R. (2000). Biology and transactional analysis II: A status report on Neurodevelopment. *Transactional Analysis Journal.* 30(4): 260-269.

Allen, J. R. (2001). *Biological Transactional Analysis* San Francisco: Trans Pubs.

Allen, J.R. (2003) Introduction to the section on Neurology in Allen, J.R. & Allen, B.A. *Therapeutic Journey: Practice and Life.* Oakland, CA: TA Press

Allen, J. R., Pfefferbaum, B., et all: (2001) Trauma and development: a reciprocal relationship in: Allan, J. R. & Allan, B.A. *Therapeutic Journey* San Francisco: T.A. Pubs

Barnes, G. L. & Brown, M. (1977) *Transactional Analysis After Eric Berne, Teachings and Practices of Three TA Schools,* New York, London: Harper & Row

Berne, E. (1961) *Transactional Analysis in Psychoanalysis: A systematic individual and social psychiatry.* New York: Grove Press.

Crossman, Patricia (1966) Permission and protection *Transactional Analysis Bulletin,* San Francisco

English, F. (1969) Episcript and the hot potato game *Transactional Analysis Bulletin.* 8(32): 77-82

English, F. (1971) The substitution factor *Transactional Analysis Journal* 1(1):225-230

English, F. (1975) Shame and social control *Transactional Analysis Journal* 5(1): 24-28

English, F. (1976) (a) The fifth position in H. Grayson *New Directions in Psychotherapy* New York: Human Science Press

English, F. (1976)(b) Racketeering *Transactional Analysis Journal* 6(1): 78-81

English, F. (1977) What should I do tomorrow? Reconceptualizing transactional analysis. pp. 287-327 in G. Barnes (ed). *Transactional Analysis After Eric Berne* New York: Harper's College Press

English, F. (1987) Power, mental energy and inertia *Transactional Analysis Journal* 17(3): 91-98

English, F. (1988) Whiter scripts? *Transactional Analysis Journal* 18(4): 29-40

English, F. (1992) My time is more precious than your strokes: *Transactional Analysis Journal* 22(1): 32-42

English, F. (1994) Shame and social control revisited *Transactional Analysis Journal* 24(2): 109-120

English, F. (1998) Hot potato transmission and episcripts *Transactional Analysis Journal* 28(1): 10-15

English, F. (1999) Two racketeering patterns: "I love you, so gimme!" and "Darling, you owe me!". *Transactional Analysis Journal* 29(2) 130-132

Erikson, E.H. (1963) *Childhood and Society*, New York: W.W. Norton

Gazzanica, M. (1992) *Nature's Mind*, New York: Basic Books & Harper

Greenspan, S. (1989) *The Development of the Ego*, Madison: International Universities Press

Klein, M. (1963) *Our Adult World and its Roots in Childhood*, London: Heinemann

Lieberman, A. F. (1991) *The Emotional Life of the Toddler*, New York: Free Press

Orenstein, R. (1993) *The Roots of the Self*, New York: Harper Collins

Piaget, J. (1952a) *Judgement and Reasoning in the Child*, New Jersey: Adams & Co.

Piaget, J. (1952b) *The Origins of Intelligence in Children*, New York: International Universities Press

Restak, R. (2002) *The Secret Life of the Brain* as summarized in 'Modern Maturity' magazine, Jan-Feb. 2002

Stern, D. (1985) *The Interpersonal World of the Infant*, New York: Basic Books

Spitz, R. (1965) *The First Year of Life*, New York: International Universities Press

Spitz, R. (1957) *No and Yes*, New York: International Universities Press

Squire, L. R. Knowlton, B., & Mussen, G. (1993) The structure and organization of memory in *Annual review of Psychology*. 44:453-495

Tart, C.T. (1987) *Waking up - Overcoming the Obstacles to Human Potential*, Boston: New Science Library Shambala

Wade, N. (2001) *Life Script*, New York: Simon & Shuster

Wood, J. (1997) Diagnostic and treatment planning wheel (after English 1976) in MSc/CTA dissertation examination (unpublished)

Chapter 4

THE MIRROR EXERCISE:
creating new ego states now –
a constructivist approach
Adrienne Lee

"Do not assume
that she who made the appointment
is the one who says goodbye"

The traditional view of ego states sees Parent and Child as being formed in the past (usually during childhood) by introjection and fixation respectively. The thesis in this chapter is a Constructivist one that sees the Parent and Child, as well as the Adult, being created or co-created anew each day. I present and analyse a specific therapeutic exercise that facilitates a new configuration of ego states. A technique of positive dissociation allows, in the process of the exercise, a dialogue between the grown-up and the child as though they were in an intimate interpersonal relationship. The relationship is then introjected and integrated into the structure of the personality, and can continue to develop and change ego states according to here-and-now life experiences.

A central thesis of the Constructivist approach is that the person's view of 'reality' is co-constructed anew each day in the narratives she uses to 'make sense of' the world. When this principle is applied to the concept of ego states it implies that the ego states are literally reconstructed each day. People generally agree that Parent and Child ego states relate to the person's past; Adult ego-states, by contrast, belong in the present. But when we consider this in the light of the Constructivist analysis, the distinction falls down; it is obvious instead that Parent *and* Child *and* Adult ego states are *all* experienced in the present (Stewart & Lee 1997). This has important implications for the theory and practice of TA psychotherapy and for the role of the therapist in inviting autonomy.

Although the Constructivist approach itself is a comparatively new component of TA thinking, it finds links to established theory in the concept of *orthriogenesis*, which Berne (1961) adopted from Federn (1952). Here, the person is indeed seen as re-creating her ego states anew each day, as part of the process of awakening. The new day's experience then forms the next 'ego unit', which is assimilated that night during dreaming.

> Psychic life may be thought of as a...continuum, with a single ego
> state which is modified from moment to moment in an abrupt or
> plastic way...Ordinarily the psyche is bombarded during the day
> with internal and external stimuli, not all of which can be assimi-
> lated at the time. The ensuing state of sleep offers an opportunity
> for this assimilation. Thus a day may be taken as an 'ego unit'.
>
> (Berne 1961, p. 48)

Since this process is largely outside of awareness (preconscious), the therapeutic process is to facilitate the client to retrieve this preconscious narrative
and to re-write it for herself in a way that fully accounts for her growth and
autonomy. It is clear that many existing therapeutic techniques in TA already
serve this purpose. For example, 'two chair work' emerges as a direct, dramatic way in which the client re-writes those parts of her script story that are
held as internal dialogue. A lasting change is made if the dialogue is 'written
differently' at Child level. The Gouldings acknowledge this dynamic quality
of the Child ego state:

> We see the Child as ever growing and ever developing, as the sum
> total of experience that he has had and is having in the present"
>
> (Goulding & Goulding 1979, p. 20)

'Early scene work' is in fact work with the client's present emotional experience of a past recalled scene. Therapeutic change will only be achieved if the
person re-casts that *present* experience by bringing some of her here-and-now
present resources, including the contactful therapeutic relationship, into her
recalled experience of the past. Inevitably, as the client makes changes in the
present, the 'past', which is dynamically a part of present experience, changes
too. The ego states have been reconstructed. I agree with Allen & Allen
(1997):

> In traditional transactional analysis we usually accept the idea that
> the past determines the present and the present the future.
> However, it is equally possible - and clinically it is often obvious -
> that the present can colour our memories of the past.....The past is
> not a fixed, immutable, monolithic structure.
>
> (p. 92)

The purpose of The Mirror Exercise is to enable a reconstruction or reconfiguration of the ego states. I created this exercise in 1972 and have been using
it consistently in therapy and training; the format and the clinical observations are well tested. The exercise involves a new here-and-now dialogue
between a cathected Child ego state and the Adult ego state of the person by
means of guided fantasy. The aim is to bring a past ego state from childhood
into the present, in a way that fully engages with the person as a grown-up

today, in order to heal a 'disruption of contact' (Erskine and Trautmann 1996), a deficit from childhood, or permit an exchange of permissions and resources that enable the person to grow and change. The resources and experiences in one ego state can be given to another ego state. The results of the exercise in clinical practice show that one of the ego states is primarily the major resource for the other. In most cases, the Adult, as a grown-up in the here-and-now, is a powerful resource for protection and permission for the Child, and is usually incorporated as a new Parent ego state; often the Child is a resource of energy, vitality, fun and spontaneity for the grown up. What is important in the exercise is that all three ego states are co-created and reconstructed in the present. The exercise can be repeated at different stages in the therapeutic process, and significant changes in the ego states are usually very apparent.

One of the assumptions that underpins this exercise is that major therapeutic change can take place in a fully contactful relationship of attunement and involvement (Erskine & Trautmann 1996). It is through the disruptions of contact in childhood and adulthood that script is established and reinforced. For example, if a child expects and wants a parent to celebrate her new dance and instead receives criticism or disinterest, the child may decide "I am not important", or "I am bad". The experience of shame and/or an early life decision that becomes a defence against the pain may be heightened. This disruption of contact may also reinforce an early primal wound (Lee in Tilney 1998) of abandonment, engulfment, hurt or non-involvement. The healing of the disruptions in contact are possibly available in the therapeutic relationship; however, this is by no means certain and may take years to develop. In the mirror exercise, interpersonal contact between dramatised ego states becomes intrapsychic contact and attachment. I believe that it is intrapsychic attachment and contact that repairs, builds and strengthens the sense of Self. The grown-up self can provide the only trustworthy 'corrective parenting' for the Child's primal wounds; that is, the 'grown-up' in the exercise can say with absolute integrity "I will never abandon you!" and the Child knows that this is true and has to relinquish any denial defences. Similarly, the grown-up can promise not to hurt or engulf the little one, and to remain in real, contactful relationship with her. The power in the exercise lies in the fact that this new configuration or structure is achieved through contact and attachment, a vital developmental and relational need. The contact and attachment is moreover between parts of the client's own self. The exercise enables this attachment to be both "interpersonal", in the externalised dialogue and meeting, as well as intrapsychic, when the two parts are integrated.

The Adult ego state of the person creates a 'stage', or frame, where the 'grown-up' of today and the child of yesterday can be dramatised in the present. The 'grown-up' is usually seen as a parent figure by the child, and so Parent to Child dialogue takes place. The intrapsychic relationship is dramatised through the Adult as though it were an external or interpsychic one (Fig. 1).

Fig. I: Adult dramatisation of the grown-up and archaic child relationship

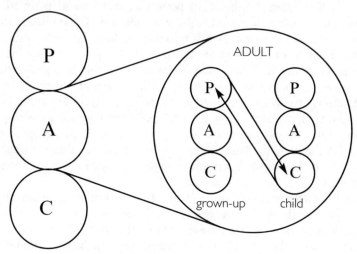

When, in the exercise, the dramatised interpersonal relationship is integrated intrapsychically, the 'grown-up' is usually incorporated as a new Parent ego state and the 'child' becomes a new Child ego state who has received contactful new parenting (Fig. 2).

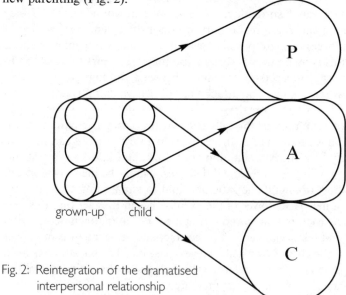

Fig. 2: Reintegration of the dramatised
    interpersonal relationship

A new internal dialogue can now take place. The intimacy and attachment that have been shared between the 'grown-up' and the 'child' are transposed into the content and structure of the ego states with the same relationship of intimacy and contact. The new internal dialogue is hence one of healthy attachment (Fig. 3).

Fig. 3: New configuration of ego states and new internal dialogue

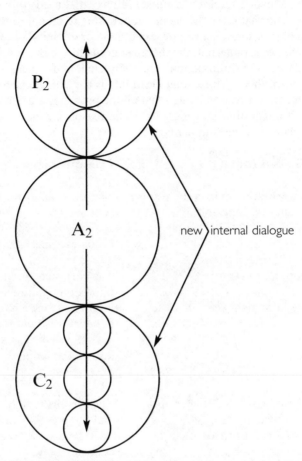

The phenomenological experience of the client is that of having a new Child ego state, which is now capable of being cathected at different ages and can continue to be self-created and self-reparented. The client also reports a phenomenological change in their Parent ego state, that now has the relevant current resources. There is an argument for giving these 'new' ego states different numbers to differentiate them from 'old' ego states, but this is not necessary if the hypothesis is accepted that we continue to recreate our ego states each day. This constructivist approach gives a new meaning to self reparenting (James 1974) and rechilding (Clarkson & Fish 1988). New resources and experiences can be developed in the Parent and Child ego states.

> Providing new parenting and rechilding experiences enables the integrated Adult ego state to draw on these positive experiences under stress and so achieve greater stability.
>
> (Clarkson & Fish 1988, p.59)

The Mirror Exercise

The Mirror Exercise is a guided fantasy that needs to be led by the therapist at a rate that gives the client enough time to complete the transactions. The client may speak her responses out loud or do the whole exercise internally. If the latter is preferred, the therapist needs to watch for body language clues to indicate when transactions are completed, and if necessary ask the client to confirm this. Whilst some flexibility is sometimes appropriate in this guided fantasy, it is recommended that all the processes are completed, especially the final integration and merging. The reason for each part of the process is explained in the commentary.

Guided Fantasy	Commentary
Imagine that in front of you is a full length mirror.	The use of a mirror provides a distinct concrete frame or boundary to put around the experience. This later becomes a special time frame.
Into that mirror put a reflection of yourself as a seven or eight year old child. (Another age may be used if relevant)	The client may need to be told to use a photograph in order to access the visual memory. The use of reflection in the mirror is important. The client sees herself reflected as a child in the mirror and is simultaneously the observer.
What does that little girl/boy look like? What is s/he wearing? Hair style? Expression on her/his face? How is s/he standing? What is s/he doing with hands? Carrying anything? etc.	The use of the third person singular and the present tense of the verb invites a distance that enables time distortion, and puts the archaic Child ego state behaviourally into the 'present' without the feelings that are attached to the past childhood experience. The specificity of the visual detail is important to anchor the Child in the present.
Next to the image of the little girl/boy, bring the reflection of the grown-up you are today, so that the two are side by side.	Now the here-and-now adult is included in the reflection - this frees both ego states from time-bound restrictions to exist simultaneously in the 'time-free' mirror frame. However, the self as observer is still present outside the mirror.

Now let the two turn and look at each other. What does the big one think of the little one? What does the little one think of the big one?	Both parts of the self are dramatised in the same time frame. The client is invited to move rapidly from one to the other and from internal experience to external awareness. The client is also outside the mirror and in the therapy room, doing the exercise. A higher, or meta self, outside the old ego states and the Script, is elicited.
What does the little one say to the big one? What does the big one say to the little one?	Contactful dialogue is encouraged
What does the little one want the big one to know? What does the big one want the little one to know?	The secrets can be told. The wisdom can be shared. This is an opportunity to intimately and honestly reveal the child's truth and also allow the future grown-up 'security' and resources to be given to the Child ego state. Sometimes the positive resource is with the Child, who can enliven the grown-up who has lost contact with the source of their energy and vitality
What has the little one got too much of? What has the little one got too little of? What has the big one got too much of? What has the big one got too little of?	These questions to the meta self invite a critical distance, at a stage where the affect may be too intense and potentially break the trance. It is pre-supposed that the intensities of the qualities noted can be increased or decreased.
What does the little one want from the big one? What does the big one want from the little one?	The presupposition here is that each have positive resources that the other can use. The awareness is both at the meta level as well as in the grown-up and the child.
What do they need to say to each other?	This can go on as long as necessary to complete the dialogue.

Let each talk and let the other listen and show that they have heard.	The therapist can facilitate in order to ensure that this dialogue is contactful and attuned.
Do they make any physical contact with each other?	If this hasn't already been experienced, then the question will invite some contact. It may be important to wait long enough for intimacy to be established before inviting the physical contact.
Is there some gift that the big one wants the little one to have? Is there some gift that the little one wants the big one to have?	The gift exchange allows opportunity for the unconscious mind to provide a symbol for the new attachment. The gift can later be realised and decoded to anchor the experience.
Now, when you are ready, find a way of enabling the two images to merge together..... ...and when you have done this OPEN YOUR EYES ...and come back out of the mirror to the here-and-now in this room.	The merging of the two selves is vitally important for the integration and reconfiguration process. If the client has difficulty doing this then the therapist can suggest how this may be done, e.g. "Let the big one open her/his arms and take in the little one to her/his heart, now merge the two."

Case study

Gerald is a client who lacks self esteem, and even though he appears successful in the world in terms of his marriage, home and career, he feels insecure and is constantly threatened by internal Parental criticism. His belief is that however successful he is, he will still not be good enough, and he will be rejected and abandoned. In the Mirror, Gerald sees a little boy in his school uniform. He looks neat and tidy, and his hair is cut trimly, but a bit sticks out above his ears. One of his socks is down and one of his hands clutches the side of his shorts. He is smiling for the camera (Gerald has used an actual remembered photograph to find the image of his eight year old) but the smile soon fades and his face changes into a worried frown. When Gerald brings his present grown-up self into the mirror frame and lets the two images look at each other, he is aware that the tall man looking down on the boy feels threatening to the boy (in the way that his father was experienced as threatening); this also feels uncomfortable for the grown-up. He bends down and goes on one knee, so that he is the same height as little boy Gerald. Already a therapeutic shift has occurred, as the child experiences the grown-up responding immediately to his discomfort. Of course, because Gerald is simultaneously the grown-up and the child, he can experience both perspectives.

The little boy likes the grown-up and is confused because the grown-up appears to be genuinely interested in him. This is a new experience of safety in a contactful relationship with a parent figure. As the grown-up, Gerald feels very compassionate towards the little boy and wants to reassure him. In the ensuing dialogue, he tells the boy that he is OK and that everything will be OK. He wants the little boy to know that even though he sometimes has a hard time at school, and even though he feels very frightened and lonely, nothing terrible will happen, and that the little one will be successful and go to University and even have his own business one day.

The little one is amazed. He wants to know if grown-up Gerald has friends. He also wants grown-up Gerald to help him "get things right". The grown-up takes the little boy into his arms and tells him that he doesn't have to get everything right, he is OK just as he is, and he can go and play instead of worrying about his homework. The little one has too much fear and too little confidence; the grown-up has too much responsibility and not enough fun. However, they are able to give permissions to each other to be unconditionally loved and OK, and to enjoy. The little one wants the grown-up to play with him and talk to him. The grown-up wants this too. In the dialogue, the little one tells of his fears one by one, and the grown-up is able to tell him unequivocally (because he already knows the future, of course) that what the little one fears will not really hurt him so much, and that the fantasies will not come true. He can tell him kindly what is true and what isn't.

He is also able to promise the little one unequivocally that he will never abandon him, that he will always be there for him. The child experiences the reality of this and lets himself trust his grown-up self to be with him and care for him. His warm smile is now very different from the 'camera smile'. The grown-up's gift to the little boy is a secret badge that says - "I'm Gerald, and I'm good enough". The child gives the grown-up a football. They laugh because they both want to play straightaway.

This client was able to find appropriate resources to give his child contactful appropriate parenting that was very different from that which he had received from his actual father. He had created a new Parent ego state from his grown-up self in relation to his own child that was now integrated as well as a new Child ego state that 'experienced' contactful parenting and new permissions. The old, criticising parent is diminished, or may even disappear, and Gerald can experience the confidence and ease that goes with being 'good enough' as he is.

In some cases, the therapist, together with the 'observing self' of the client, needs to coach the grown-up or the child to ensure a therapeutic outcome; in this case, it was not necessary. On rare occasions it is necessary to abort the exercise, because something potentially non-therapeutic or damaging is evoked, and healthy reconfiguration does not seem viable. One client pictured his little boy without clothes on and brought the grown-up next to him also without clothes. I asked him to create new images of them both dressed, and the client could not or would not do this. I then said that it is not safe and OK for grown-ups to meet children without clothes and ended the exercise. The therapist here becomes the boundary setting 'Parent' for both the grown-up and the child.

The process of the exercise invites the client to be both in the mirror, in the reflections that experience the intimacy of the dialogue, and simultaneously at a meta level, outside the mirror, like a disinterested observer or co-facilitator. In this objective or dissociated position, that I think accesses the Higher Self of the client, the client can be free of any negative or archaic emotion, and be 'outside time'. She is effectively in the position of an author who can create new ego states and a new narrative, even while simultaneously being the characters in the dialogue. A new configuration and transformation takes place. This is spontaneity; this is intimacy; this is autonomy.

"The present transfigures history.
the faces and the places and the self
that did its best to love them,
dissolve.
I make a new story."

References

Allen, J., & Allen, B. (1991) Towards a constructivist TA. *The Stamford Papers: selections from the 29th ITAA Conference*, 1-22

Allen, J., & Allen, B. (1997) A new type of transactional analysis and one version of script work with a constructivist sensibility. *Transactional Analysis Journal*, 27: 89-98

Berne, E. (1961) *Transactional Analysis in Psychotherapy*, New York: Grove Press

Clarkson, P. & Fish, S. (1988) Rechilding: creating a new past in the present as a support for the future, *Transactional Analysis Journal*, 18(1) : 51-59

Erskine, R. & Trautmann, R. (1996) Methods of an integrative psychotherapy, *Transactional Analysis Journal*, 26(4): 316-328

Federn, P. (1952) *Ego Psychology and the Psychoses*, New York: Basic Books

James, M. (1974) Self reparenting: theory and process, *Transactional Analysis Journal*, 4(3): 32-39

Goulding, M., & Goulding, R. (1979) *Changing Lives Through Redecision Therapy.* New York: Brunner/Mazel

Lee, A. (1996) The mirror exercise and reconfiguration of ego states. *ITA News*, 45,47-50.

Stewart, I. (1992) *Eric Berne*. London: Sage

Stewart, I., & Lee, A. (1997) Reconfiguring: the art and practice of autonomy. *Aspiration and Autonomy 1997 EATA Conference Papers*, Paper 33

Tilney, T. (1998) *Dictionary of Transactional Analysis*. London: Whurr

Chapter 5

INTROJECTION, PSYCHIC PRESENCE AND PARENT EGO STATES:
considerations for psychotherapy
Richard G. Erskine

In a memorial tribute to Eric Berne, Franklin Ernst (1971) declared that Berne's most significant contribution to the profession of psychotherapy was in identifying Parent ego states and differentiating them from Adult or Child ego states. This significant differentiation provides a theoretical framework for clinical Transactional Analysis that suggests a psychotherapeutic focus, which may relieve many manifestations of anxiety, depression, and low self-esteem stemming from intrapsychic conflict. Yet, most of the clinical Transactional Analysis literature has either focused on freeing the Child ego states from a compulsion to adapt, strengthening Adult ego state control, replacing a lethal introjected message with a benevolent introjected message or making behavioral changes that facilitate Adult to Adult 'ego state' trans-actions. A few articles or books have emphasized an in-depth psychotherapy of Child ego states. Very little has been written on the treatment of Parent ego states and the resolution of intrapsychic conflict. The purpose of this chapter is to clarify and elucidate the intrapsychic functions of Parent ego states and to outline methods of an in-depth, integrative Transactional Analysis psychotherapy of introjected Parent ego states. The chapter that fol-lows, 'Resolving Intrapsychic Conflict: Psychotherapy of Parent Ego States', is co-authored with Rebecca Trautmann; it includes a verbatim transcript of an actual psychotherapy session along with my annotated comments about the process of the psychotherapy.

Prior to Berne's writings on ego states (1957, 1961) previous psychoanalytic writers had identified the distinction between adult-like and child-like 'per-sonalities', 'conditions', or 'states,' and had developed the analytic methods of free association, non-gratification and interpretation as a means of both pro-viding understanding and alleviating internal distress. Much has been written on the psychological effects of 'parental influence', or Superego. However, the psychoanalytic literature lacks an adequate description of the treatment of the Superego, whether it is called internalized object, parental influence, anti-libidinal ego, introjected other or unconscious fantasy.

In 1895, Josef Breuer and Sigmund Freud wrote in *Studies in Hysteria* about Anna O's 'two entirely separate states of consciousness', which alternated frequently and spontaneously – one relatively normal and a keen observer, the other child-like and naughty. In the case they presented of Emmy von N., Breuer and Freud described how she alternated 'states of consciousness' between describing her primal experiences, and making comments to Freud about how he was conducting the analysis (1950).

In *Ego Psychology and the Psychosis*, Paul Federn (1953) observed that his patients exhibited a current ego that both identifies with internal sensations and at the same time, identifies with or discriminates from environmental stimuli. In addition, this ego manifests a feeling of identity and a response to the environment which is like that of a young child. He described these different manifestations as subdivisions or *states* of the ego, i.e., different identities. In addition, he referred to the internalization of parental figures in his patients as 'acquired ego attitudes' and related this constant psychic presence to the psychoanalytic concept of the superego. Federn's views on the ego and states of the ego significantly differed from those of other ego psychologists within the psychoanalytic movement, such as Hartmann (1939, 1964), Kris (1951, 1979), and Rappoport (1967). Although using somewhat different terminology, Federn influenced the theories of Guntrip (1961), Berne (1957, 1961), Jacobson (1964), Kernberg (1976), Kohut (1977), Watkins (1978), and Winnicott (1965).

John Watkins, like Eric Berne, also studied with Federn, but developed his ideas of ego states without an awareness that Berne was developing similar concepts. John and Helen Watkins' book, *Ego States: Theory and Therapy* (Watkins & Watkins 1997) defines an ego state as 'an organized system of behavior and experience whose elements are bound together by some common principle, and which is separated from other such states by a boundary that is more or less permeable' (p. 25). They describe both a 'core ego' as that which the person and others perceive as 'self', and 'other ego states' as 'segments of self' that are 'differentiated for adoptive purposes'. These consist of either 'introjects of significant others', or ego states 'split off from the core ego because of trauma' (p. 26).

In *An Outline of Psychoanalysis*, Freud described the development of the Superego as occurring in the long period of childhood, during which the growing human being lives in dependence upon his parents. This dependency forms within the child's ego a special agency in which this parental influence is prolonged. The parents' influence includes not merely the personalities of the parents themselves, but also the racial, national, and family traditions handed on through them (1949). In essence, because of the child's dependency, internalized elements of the parents' personality influence the ego (the person's sense of 'me') and cause the person to psychologically function differently, and under stress.

In the development of psychoanalytic object-relations theory, Fairbairn (1954) and Guntrip (1961, 1968) dispensed with Freud's concept of Superego. Instead, they theorized that in the presence of fear, a child may split off parts of him or herself, and form an ego state that is a combination of an internalized parental control, and a child's fearful compliance with that control. They termed this state the 'anti-libidinal ego' to emphasize how it suppresses and controls the 'libidinal ego' – an ego state that has the remnants of what would have been the natural nature of the person. They describe this conflict as occurring intrapsychically for the purpose of maintaining a semblance of relationship with the caretakers, by keeping the natural nature of the person suppressed. Their 'central ego' is the state which functions in the external world, and may serve as a cover for intrapsychic conflict.

Edoardo Weiss prefers the term internalization, since to him it refers to an 'inclusion within the ego' of an identification with aspects of the other's personality (1950, p. 76).

> Internalization is complete when it *substitutes*, within one's own ego, the bodily and mental aspects of a person. This substitution may be an autoplastic egotized duplication or only the egotized imagination of the physical and mental features of another personality. (1950, p. 95)

In 1912, 'Ferenczi introduced the term *introjection*, as a synonym for 'incorporation', to indicate the egotization of the autoplastic duplication of the object' (Weiss p. 76). Weiss does not like the term 'introjection' because in his way of thinking, it does not adequately describe how the person is both changed by the other, and how the internalization is also not exactly the same as the other.

In Gestalt Therapy the concept of psychological introjection - the internalization of elements of another person - is central to understanding the core theory of the need for internal and external contact. Introjection is defined as an unconscious defensive identification with another. The maintenance of an introjection prohibits full contact with both self and others (Perls, Hefferline & Goodman 1951).

The concept of the Parent ego state may indeed be Berne's great innovative gift to our profession. In 1957 Berne quoted Freud's description of Superego, and added that both Superego and Parent imply that a portion of the external world has become an integral part of the internal world; hence both are in origin exteropsychic. Berne often uses the term exteropsyche interchangeably with Parent ego states. Berne states that the idea of an exteropsyche has interesting neurological connotations, but he does not say what they are (Berne, 1957). Forthcoming research in neurobiology may map the basic circuits and identify the brain's defensive identifications with others, or their psychic presence, and perhaps even identify second and third levels of exteropsychic material.

Berne (1961, chapter 16) described theoretically the second and third order of the Child and Parent ego states. He referred to the second and third order Parent ego states as containing 'genealogical material'. It is my opinion that this influencing material can be brought to the client's awareness through a respectful and attuned therapeutic relationship, and a phenomenological inquiry that facilitates the client's discovering their experiences, fantasies, ideas and meaning making about their present lives. This is accomplished through an analysis of the transference and is often the prerequisite to an in-depth theory of a Parent ego state. Berne's 'particular interest' in working with characterological problems was in 'the persistent stringency' of a Parent ego state, specifically 'the Child segments of the Parent and the Adult parts of the Child' (1961, pp. 196-197).

The Latin origins imply that the word introjection means 'thrown inside'. However, neither the Latin nor the Greek 'exteropsyche' – outside the soul or mind – explain *how* it happens. In *Integrative Psychotherapy* (Erskine & Moursund 1988; Erskine, Moursund & Trautmann 1999), the following definition is used as an operational definition based on child development literature and clinical observations: *Introjection occurs in the absence of relational needs being met; it is a defensive unaware identification with elements of the personality of the other as compensation for unmet relational needs.* All introjections, because of their defensive nature, are dysfunctional in meeting today's relational needs, even though the content may sometimes be nurturing or effective. When external behavior or interpsychic influence is the result of introjection, it is the manifestation of a defensive internalization of a foreign object and is an impediment to full internal and external contact (Gobes & Erskine 1995).

Eric Berne (1961) extended psychoanalytic thought with his elaboration and application of Paul Federn's (1953) concept of states of the ego. Berne's contribution to the theory of ego states produced the possibility for a dramatic change in the practice of psychotherapy, and pre-dated by several years the more recent changes in psychoanalytic theory and practice (Bollas 1979; Greenberg & Mitchell 1983; Guntrip 1968; Kernberg 1976; Kohut 1971, 1977; Masterson 1976, 1981; Miller 1981; Stolorow, Brandchaft & Atwood 1987).

In the popularization of Transactional Analysis that has occurred since Berne's death in 1970, many of his original theoretical concepts have been presented simplistically. Often Berne's examples and explanations have been used as definitions of ego states, and the therapeutic richness and depth of his original concept of ego states has been overlooked.

In this chapter, we will begin by returning to Berne's original conceptualization of ego states as the theoretical base for the psychotherapy of the contact-interrupting, defensive process of introjection and the resolution of the resulting intrapsychic distress.

The ego and states of the ego

In *Ego Psychology and the Psychoses,* Paul Federn (1953) described the ego as a real, experienced state of feeling and not simply a theoretical construct. The Latin word 'ego,' as used in the English translation of early psychoanalytic writings, replaced Freud's 'Das Ich' – 'the I.' The ego is the identifying and alienating aspect of the self; it is our sense of "This is me" and "That is not me." The ego discriminates and segregates internal sensations from those originating outside the organism. The ego is our identity – the "I am hungry," "I am a psychotherapist," or "I am not a bus driver, although I can drive a bus."

Berne assumed throughout his early writing (pre-1966) that the reader was familiar with a working definition of ego; he described a state of the ego '...phenomenologically, as a coherent system of feelings related to a given subject, and operationally, as a set of coherent behavior patterns' (Berne 1961, p. 17).

Berne further used a colloquial description of ego states (Parent, Child and Adult) to refer to phenomenological *manifestations* of the psychic organs (exteropsyche, archaeopsyche and neopsyche), whose function it is to organize internal and external stimuli. Exteropsyche, archaeopsyche and neopsyche refer to the aspect of the mind taken from an external source, the early mind from a previous developmental period, and the current mind. Throughout *Transactional Analysis in Psychotherapy* (1961), Berne used the psychic organ terms interchangeably with the term 'ego state'. to 'denote states of mind and their related patterns of behavior' (p. 30).

Berne (1961) stated, 'The Adult ego state is characterized by an autonomous set of feelings, attitudes and behavior patterns which are adapted to the current reality' (p. 76). In this description, Berne's use of the term 'autonomous' refers to the neopsychic ego functioning without intrapsychic control by an introjected or archaic ego state. When in the Adult ego, a person is in full contact with what is occurring in a manner appropriate to that developmental age. This neopsychic (current mind) function of the ego accounts for and integrates: 1) what is occurring moment-by-moment internally and externally, 2) past experiences and their resulting effects, and 3) the psychological influences and identifications with other significant people in one's life. This Adult ego consists of current age-related motor behavior; emotional, cognitive and moral development; the ability to be creative; and the capacity for full contactful engagement in meaningful relationships. Berne (1961, p. 195) emphasized these aspects through the use of the Greek terms Ethos and Pathos – to which I add Logos, the ability to use logic and abstract reasoning, and Technos, the ability to create – to describe the full neopsychic capacity of the Adult ego to integrate values, process information, respond to emotions and sensations, and be creative and contactful (Erskine 1988).

The term 'Adult ego' is used in Integrative Transactional Analysis theory rather than the more popular 'Adult ego state', to denote that it is not a state of the ego but symbolizes the full neopsychic capacities of an individual without the intrapsychic control of introjected parent or archaic child ego states. Parent and child ego states are non-integrated fixations of unresolved previous experiences, that drain psychic energy and distract an individual from spontaneity and flexibility in problem solving, health maintenance or intimate relationships with people. Through corrective life experiences or an effective healing psychotherapy, Child and Parent ego states can be fully integrated into the adult's ego. With integration, the past experiences of childhood and the introjected experiences of significant others are now in one's awareness, are de-energized as separate entities, and no longer serve their defensive functions. They can now function like a valuable resource library, rather than as separate states of the ego that influence, control, and produce intrapsychic conflict.

The neopsychic ego was contrasted by Berne with archaic ego states, which consist of fixations at earlier developmental stages. In Berne's (1961) words, 'The Child ego state is a set of feelings, attitudes, and behavior patterns which are relics of the individual's own childhood' (p. 77). When in a Child ego state, the person perceives the external world and internal needs and sensations as he or she did in an earlier developmental stage. Although the person may appear to be relating to current reality, he or she is actually experiencing what is happening with the intellectual, social, and emotional capacities of a child at the developmental age of unresolved neglect, trauma, or confusion, i.e., a psychological fixation.

It should be noted that using the term Child ego state in the singular form is somewhat misleading. A child develops through a number of phases and stages (Erikson 1950; Mahler 1968; Mahler, Pine & Bergman 1975; Piaget 1936/1952; Stern 1985), and repression and fixation may occur at any of them. Under the influence of one set of stressors, we may think, feel, and act much as we did when we were six years old; under another we may perceive ourselves or the world around us as we did as infants.

The archaeopsychic state of the ego is much more complex than implied by various writers who use simple examples of spontaneity, intuition, compliance, or emotive capacity to describe the Child ego states. The Child or archaic states of the ego are the *entire personality* of a person *as he was in a previous developmental period of time.* This includes the needs, desires, urges, and sensations: the defense mechanisms: and the thought processes, perceptions, feelings, and behaviors of the developmental phase where fixation occurred.

The archaic state of the ego is the result of developmental arrest which occurred when critical early childhood needs for contact were not met. The child's defenses against the discomfort of the unmet needs became egotized – fixated; the experience cannot be fully integrated into the Adult ego until these defense mechanisms are dissolved.

Berne (1961) also explored Federn's observations that in many of his clients, there was a constant psychic presence of parental figures influencing their behavior. This parental influence is from real people who, years before, interacted with and had responsibility for this particular individual when he or she was a child. This parental presence is more tangible than the Freudian construct of 'superego' ('Uber-Ich'). Through historical investigation, it is possible to trace what was actually said or done, by whom, and at what time during the person's childhood. Through introjection (an unaware defensive identification and internalization), the child made the parental person part of the self, i.e., ego.

Berne (1961) concluded that the introjected parents also became a state of the ego which he defined as 'a set of feelings, attitudes, and behavior patterns which resemble those of a parental figure' (p. 75). However, the phrase 'resemble those of a parental figure' is somewhat misleading. From Berne's examples and descriptions in *Transactional Analysis in Psychotherapy* (1961), and from my own clinical observations, it is apparent that Parent ego states are an actual historical internalization of the personality of one's own parents or other significant parental figures, as *perceived* by the child at the time of introjection. Berne emphasized this point:

> The patient whose (mother) Parent, habitually or at a given moment, is not acting *as though* her mother 'observes, orders, corrects, and threatens,' but instead is acting *just like* her mother did, perhaps even with the same gestures and intonations. She is not acting with one eye on her Mother, so to speak [which is likely to be Child ego state]; she is reproducing her mother's total behavior, including her inhibitions, her reasoning, and (this is a crucial factor) her impulses. (1957, p. 300)

Parent ego state contents are taken in, i.e., introjected, from parenting figures in early childhood – and, to a lesser degree, throughout life; and, if not re-examined in the process of later development, remain unassimilated or not integrated into the neo-functioning ego of an adult. Since the child's perceptions of the caretaker's reactions, emotions, and thought processes will differ at various stages of development, so also will the actual content and intrapsychic function of the Parent ego state vary in relation to the developmental age when the introjection occurred.

Introjection is an unconscious defense mechanism (involving disavowal, denial, and repression) frequently used when there is a lack of full psychological contact between the child and the caretakers responsible for his or her psychological needs. The significant other is made part of the self (ego), and the conflict resulting from the lack of need fulfillment is internalized so the conflict can seemingly be managed more easily (Perls 1978).

In addition to the various physical needs of childhood (Maslow 1970), a child's relational-needs require the attuned involvement of parents or significant others. (Erskine, 1998; Erskine, Moursund & Trautmann 1999). These relational needs include:

1 security within a relationship – a physical closeness and the freedom from humiliation and physical violence;
2 validation of the child's feelings, thoughts, fantasies and various needs;
3 being in the presence of someone on whom the child can rely for protection, support and guidance;
4 having a shared experience such as playing and learning together;

5 self definition within the relationship;

6 making an impact – influencing the other, at least some of the time to respond in accordance with the child's wishes;

7 having the other initiate – to anticipate the child's needs or desires and respond accordingly; and

8 the expression of gratitude and love to the caretaker – the manifestation of bonding and loyalty.

When these relational-needs are not acknowledged, validated and normalized by significant others there is a rupture in interpersonal contact – the bond between child and caretaker is disrupted and a conflict ensues between the caretaker's mis-attunement, invalidation, emotional neglect, or physical abuse and the child's desperate attempts to have his or her relational-needs satisfied.

As a biological imperative, children require both a physical and psychological attachment to maintain psychological health (Bowlby, 1969, 1973, 1980). When needs are not met, the resulting anxiety stimulates an unconscious defensive identification with the other. The external conflict is solved by internalizing the other and disavowing one's own needs; thereby the child can stay attached, bonded and loyal. This is often accompanied by a sense of resignation, and the formation of a compensating script belief such as "If I can't get my needs met, then I don't need". The external conflict of relational-needs not-met becomes internal, where it is handled within the individual rather than continue the external relational conflict. Metaphorically, the conflict of needs-not-met is as though there was a psychological vacuum in the relationship. That psychological vacuum – the absence of interpersonal contact – is filled by unconsciously identifying with the significant other.

Brown says:

> Introjection allows a person to avoid her painful feelings associated with the loss of a person, place, or event, by creating within herself an image of the lost object. Her unconscious fantasies maintain her association with the lost object, and prevent her from working through the painful emotions connected to the loss.
>
> (1977, p. 5)

Introjected elements may remain as a kind of foreign body within the personality, often unaffected by later learning or development, but continuing to influence behavior and perceptions. They constitute an alien chunk of personality, embedded within the ego and experienced phenomenologically as if they were one's own; but, in reality, they form a borrowed personality (Erskine 1988, 1997).

Ego state determinants

Berne said, 'Transactional Analysis consists of determining which ego state is active at a given moment in the exhibition of a transactional stimulus by the agent, and which ego state is active in the response given by the respondent'

(1966, p. 223). Verification of which ego state is cathected is only possible with a four-part correlation of the behavioral, social, historical, and phenomenological determinants of ego states. *'The complete diagnosis of an ego state requires that all four of these aspects be available for consideration, and the final validity of such a diagnosis is not established until all four have been correlated'* (italics mine), (Berne 1961, p. 75).

Berne (1961 p. 74-76) described the four diagnostic determinants of ego states in the order he saw them in psychotherapy; behavioral, social, historical, and phenomenological. From a perspective of facilitating an integration of the fragmentation of the ego, I have additionally defined the identifying criteria and listed them in the following order of clinical significance (Erskine & Moursund 1988/1998):

1 The identifying criterion of the phenomenological determinant is the subjective experience of the person. It includes the sensations, desires and needs, feelings, and beliefs that shape the person's perspectives – the *how* and *what* it is like to live in his or her experience. Included in the phenomenological criteria are the physiological, emotional, and cognitive associations of significant life events and the times when elements of the personality of another were introjected. Also included is the subjective experience of the internal defense mechanisms fixated at times of neglect, traumatic experience, or cumulative devaluation.

2 The historical determinant is gleaned primarily from memories of the dynamic events between oneself and others, or the relationship between mother and father or other important family members. These can provide essential information regarding early conflicts. The *who* and *when* of early life may reveal memories of similar feelings and behavior in childhood, or memories of the parental person who offered the prototype behavior. Included is an inquiry into the distinction between the person's own fixated childhood defenses and the defense mechanisms possibly introjected from significant others.

3 The behavioral determinant involves a *developmental* focus (Berne 1961, p. 154) on gestures, posture, vocabulary, tone of voice, or other mannerisms, and the content of what is communicated. The assessment of the person's current observable behavior is compared with information about human development regarding early mother-child interaction; motor and language development; emotional, cognitive, and social development; defense mechanisms; moral development, and adult life transitions. All of this comparative information provides a background of data to assist in determining the stage of development at which emotions, behaviors, or interactions have become fixated. Behavior that is not congruent with the current context may have been normal and appropriate for a child at a specific developmental age, or may be an indication of how the patient defended himself or herself in a traumatic situation. Childlike behavior may be an indication of the person's own active Child

ego state, or just as likely, an indication of the Child ego state of an introjected parent. Interweaving the developmental assessment with the historical or phenomenological may be necessary to determine if a specific defensive reaction, behavioral pattern, or emotion is the manifestation of an exteropsychic ego state or of an archaeopsychic fixation.

4 The fourth determinant in verifying ego state cathexis is the social or *transactional*. The analysis of transactions provides data to indicate which ego state is active, the nature of the intrapsychic dynamics, and what stimulus from the psychotherapist served to trigger the cathexis. The intrapsychic dynamics include the influence of the introjected Parent ego state and Child ego state's need for a contactful relationship. Transactions between the person and psychotherapist, or, in group or family psychotherapy, between any two people, may reflect a transference either from an exteropsychic or archaeopsychic ego state. These transferences may take the form of 'roles' such as child-like 'compliance,' 'impertinence,' or 'rebelliousness'; adult-like roles of 'problem solver' or information exchange, or parental roles of 'comforting' or 'controlling' (Berne 1961, p. 93-96). It is essential in diagnosing ego state cathexis and intrapsychic conflict to evaluate these transactional roles or social entities within the context of a correlated phenomenological, historical, and developmental (behavioral) assessment. *It is only through the careful and systematic use of the four-part correlated diagnosis that it is possible to verify which ego states are influencing and which are cathected, and to proceed with the appropriate psychotherapeutic interventions* (Erskine 1991/1997).

The functions of influencing and active parent ego states

An introjected Parent ego state may be either *active* or *intrapsychically influencing.* An active Parent ego state communicates with the outside world while an influencing parent ego state operates internally. Berne (1961) described the *active* Parent ego state as reproducing the feelings, attitudes, and behavior of the introjected parent or other significant persons in actual trans-actions with people. The psychological function of an active Parent ego state is that the person diminishes anxiety and experiences some interpsychic relief from the internal influence of the introjection. For example, a mother may scream at and criticize her children in the same way her father screamed at and criticized her when she was young. She is able to feel some temporary relief from the pressure and anxiety of father's psychic presence and internal criticism by externalizing the verbal abuse. Others in her life, such as her children, may suffer the effects of the rage and criticism that is an expression of an active Parent ego state. She most likely remains unaware that the quality of her contact both with self and others is under the dominance and control of a Parent ego state. Clients seldom describe this externalization as a problem except to report their discomfort regarding what others say about their behavior. Family members may complain how "mother acts just like or even worse than grandfather."

In psychotherapy, it is much more typical that the client will describe the phenomenological experience of self-doubt, a constant sense of being controlled, the loss of knowing what one desires, and/or chronic anxiety, and/or depression. The phenomenological experience of some clients is as if they were criticizing themselves or under an internal control. Other clients may be aware of the presence of an influencing introjection or psychic presence of another person; they hear another voice that is criticizing, warning, or rulemaking. Berne referred to the influencing Parent ego state as 'the voice of an actual person' that the client may mis-identify as a hallucination (1961, p.32).

'The Parental *influence* can be inferred when the individual manifests an attitude of child-like compliance' (Berne 1961, p. 76) and/or may make use of childhood defenses such as avoidance, freezing, or fighting (Fraiberg 1982/1983); ego splitting (Fairbairn 1954); transformation of affect and reversal of aggression (Fraiberg 1982/1983), and archaic fantasy (Erskine 1988/1997, Erskine & Moursund 1988/1998). The 'child-like compliance' resulting from parental influence may be evidenced in the reactions of shame:

- a sadness at not being accepted *as one is* with one's own urges, desires, needs, feelings, and behaviors;
- the fear of abandonment because of *who one is;*
- a diminished self-concept, a lowering of one's self-worth in *compliance* with introjected criticism, and
- a sense of "something's wrong with me".

Shame is often an internal expression of an intrapsychic conflict between a reactive Child ego state and an influencing Parent ego state (Erskine 1994/1997). *When a Child ego state is either active or internally cathected (either behaviourally observable or subjectively reportable), by theoretical inference, a Parent ego state is cathected and intrapsychically influencing.* Berne (1961) described the intrapsychic dynamics of ego states as representing 'the relics of the infant who once actually existed, in a struggle with the relics of the parents who once actually existed', for it 're-duplicates the actual childhood fights for survival between real people, or at least that is the way the patient experiences it' (p. 66).

The intrapsychic conflict emerges from a child's need for relationship (Fairbairn 1954), attachment (Bowlby 1969), or contact (Erskine 1989/1997). When those needs are repeatedly not satisfied, a child may defend against full awareness of contact, attachment, and relationship needs and the resulting psychological discomfort. These needs are evident in a Child ego state's *psychological loyalty* to an intrapsychically influencing Parent ego state (Erskine 1988/1997, 1991/1997). The loyalty is in the defensive avoidance of the realization "My psychological needs were unmet", or in the unconscious fantasy, "If I'm good enough, I'll be accepted and loved" (Stolorow & Atwood 1989). The interpsychic functions of forming Parent ego states is to lessen the external conflict and have a semblance of relationship – at least an illusion of being accepted and loved – but the price of the internalization of the conflict is a loss of valuable aspects of self – a loss of spontaneity, flexibility and intimacy. The psychic presence or Parent ego state is maintained over the years because, like script beliefs and obsessions, the intrapsychic conflict functions to provide a sense of predictability, identity, continuity, and emotional stability (Erskine 2001).

Theory into practice
Berne stated that:

> ...the ultimate aim of transactional analysis is structural readjustment and reorganization... Reorganization generally features reclamation of the Child, with emendation or replacement of the Parent. Following this dynamic phase of reorganization, there is a secondary analytic phase which is an attempt to deconfuse the Child.   (1961, p. 224)

Most of Berne's descriptions of psychotherapy emphasize his first phase, the decontamination of the Adult ego from Child or Parent ego states. Berne (1966) defined eight therapeutic operations; six are interventions used to facilitate decontamination and strengthen ego boundaries – the structural readjustment of phase one. Only one therapeutic operation, psychoanalytic interpretation, is used to 'decode and detoxify' the Child ego states' past experiences, 'rectify distortions, and help the patient regroup the experiences' (Berne 1966, p. 242-243).

It is primarily through his clinical examples that one can infer Berne's use of a second analytic phase, a therapeutic deconfusion of the Child ego states. In the chapter on 'Regression Analysis' Berne rather poetically says:

> when a previously buried archaic ego state is revived in its full vividness in the waking state, it is then permanently at the disposal of the patient and therapist for detailed examination. Not only do 'abreaction' and 'working through' take place, but the ego state can be treated like an actual child. It can be nurtured carefully, even tenderly, until it unfolds like a flower, revealing all the complexities of its internal structure.   (1961, p. 226)

The reader is left to assume that Berne is applying psychoanalytic methods in this 'secondary analytic phase'. Yet he also experimented with and encouraged an active psychotherapy: 'The optimal situation for the readjustment and reintegration of the total personality requires an emotional statement from the Child in the presence of the Adult and Parent' (1961, p. 224). Other Transactional Analysis writers have developed or described active treatment methods effective in deconfusing child ego states (Goulding & Goulding 1979; Clark 1991; Clarkson & Fish 1988; Cornell & Olio 1992; Erskine 1974/1997, 1993/1997; Erskine & Moursund 1988/1998, Erskine, Moursund & Trautmann 1999; Hargaden & Sills 2001).

In all of Berne's writing, he says surprisingly little about therapeutic methods. He does not adequately describe a course of treatment for the Parent ego states. He writes about an 'emendation' – an alteration designed to correct or improve – 'or replacement of the Parent' (Berne 1961, p. 224). But no guidelines for an in-depth and integrating treatment are suggested. It is as if Berne, like many in both the psychoanalytic and Gestalt therapy traditions, did not know what to do with the pain, fear, anger, and defensive strategies of an influencing Parent ego state, and the intrapsychic pressure and distress it causes in the client. He primarily follows the psychoanalytic tradition of identifying the interpsychic influence, and then goes a bit further with therapeutic operations such as confrontation and explanation aimed at decontaminating the Adult ego. He also suggests the use of a therapeutic interposition such as illustration or confrontation, 'an attempt by the therapist to interpose something between the patient's Adult and his other ego states in order to stabilize his Adult and make it more difficult for him to slide into Parent or Child activity' (Berne 1966, p. 237). In Berne's writings the theory of Parent ego states is not sufficiently related to or correlated with therapeutic methods that decommission the influence of an introjection.

For Transactional Analysis to be a comprehensive theory of personality and methods, it is essential to integrate the theories of personality with a theory of methods. The development of an in-depth therapy of Parent ego states would be one example of the further refinement in the congruence of methods and theory in Transactional Analysis. To this end, I would like to propose an addition to the quotation from Berne used earlier about 'the ultimate aim of Transactional Analysis': *following, or in some cases concurrent with, a deconfusion of the Child ego states, there may be an additional psychotherapeutic phase which decommissions a Parent ego state for the purpose of eliminating its toxic influencing effect on Child ego states, and eventually integrating it into the Adult ego as a memory and historical resource.*

The decommissioning of a Parent ego state may be described by paraphrasing Berne's (1961, p. 226) poetic comment on the treatment of Child ego states: *when a previously introjected exteropsychic ego state is revived in its full vividness and made conscious, it is then available to the client's full awareness and to the therapist for either an in-depth therapy of the Parent ego state or at least an effective interposition. The Parent ego state can be treated like an actual client – even a client in regression. It can be nurtured carefully, or confronted or guided in how to adequately parent in accordance with his or her actual child's needs.* This is one aspect of a comprehensive theory of methods (Erskine 1997/1998) for an active, in-depth psychotherapy 'for the readjustment and reintegration of the total personality' (Berne 1961, p. 224).

I think that the 'replacement of the Parent', as Berne (1961, p. 224) phrased it, with another introjection, is *not therapeutic*. This would be akin to replacing one toxic introjection with another somewhat more benign introjection – but it is still a contact interrupting introjection. Rather, I would like to augment Berne's (1961, p. 224) previous statement about an in-depth psychotherapy of

Child ego states: 'the optimal situation for readjustment and reintegration of the total personality requires' in addition to 'the emotional statement from the Child in the presence of the Adult and Parent', *an emotional statement from a Parent ego state that either apologizes to or deconfuses Child ego states.* This allows egotized and fixated identifications - introjections - to be externalized, decommissioned, and integrated into an Adult ego. An in-depth psychotherapy for 'reintegration' of the total personality includes relaxing the Child ego states' defenses, allowing the natural inclination of the client to be expressed, decommissioning the introjections, resolving the intrapsychic conflicts, and facilitating an awareness and integration in the client of his other need-fulfilling experience with parents.

I have been using parents in this text, but the reader is to be aware that parents may not be the only ones introjected; teachers, clergy, aunts, uncles, grandparents, older siblings, anyone in authority, even other teenagers, may be introjected in the absence of need-fulfilling contact. The chapter, 'Robert: Challenging a Cultural Script' in *Integrative Psychotherapy in Action* (Erskine & Moursund 1988/1998) is a detailed example of a psychotherapy for an introjection of a culturally imposed value.

Experiential and written background

In 1974, I was conducting a weekend therapy marathon with another therapist. He informed me that one of the women in the group was severely depressed and she was convinced that she was possessed by the devil. Halfway through the evening the woman began to snarl and growl at me and then in a harsh low voice threatened to kill "her". At first both group members and I were shocked! I then remembered hearing a similar voice before at a Pentecostal religious-healing service I attended as a child on the Southside of Chicago. One of the evangelists was well known for 'casting out devils'. I had watched with child-like awe as a person was brought in restraints, snarling, growling, threatening. The evangelist 'called out the devil' and proceeded to 'pray over him'.

The memory of the healing-evangelist's active encounter with the 'devil' person was swirling in my mind. At the same time, I was also thinking about how to make sense of the client's bizarre behavior. I wondered if this 'devil' person was a manifestation of the Gestalt therapy concept of introjection and Berne's concept of Parent ego states as representing the personality of another. I began to talk to the 'devil' voice. He continued to curse at me, repeatedly threatened to kill me or "her", hissed, growled, and raged. He refused to talk to a 'crazy therapist'. I continued to talk to 'him', inquiring about his message and purpose.

During the next half hour, the voice gradually became that of an angry, drunken man – a man with a secret. He had threatened to kill his daughter if she ever revealed the incestuous rape and choking he had inflicted on her. After about two hours of a combination of both empathetic and confrontative therapy the 'father' began to apologize to his 'daughter'. Subsequently, that confession and apology stimulated in the women client, over the next few months, several memories that had previously been repressed. The active therapy directly with a Parent ego state opened the door for the client to do some intense regressive therapy, both in individual sessions and subsequent weekend marathons. The Child ego state regressions were accompanied by the slower, ongoing work at resolving her experiences of distrust and a lack of protection, as it emerged both in the transferential transactions and the absence of interpersonally contactful transactions.

This serendipitous therapy experience with the 'devil', who was a manifestation of the psychic presence of the client's father, opened a whole new perspective for me in doing psychotherapy. I no longer saw a Parent ego state only as a depository of injunctions. Nor could I any longer see the resolution of serious intrapsychic conflict as occurring in a twenty or thirty minute two-chair dialogue alternating between the client's Child and Parent ego states. Rather, I became increasingly aware of the possible complexity of psychic presence or introjections; to include not only the attitudes and thoughts of significant others, but also their emotions, defensive processes, physiological reactions, age regression, and relational needs. This can all be internalized by a child through an unconscious defensive identification when there is an absence of need-fulfilling contact, and the child's dependency is such that the other is introjected as a way to have a semblance of relationship.

The Transactional Analysis literature provides a few theoretical articles on Parent ego state problems, but there is not much written about an in-depth therapy. Bill Holloway described theoretically the 'crazy child in the Parent' and related the harshness, frequency, and consistency of the parent's 'craziness' to the formation of hamartic life scripts (1972, p. 128). In 1976, John McNeel published *The Parent Interview* which described a two-chair therapy with a Parent ego state, wherein the therapist elicits feelings and experiences of a Parent ego state in response to requests made by a son or daughter. 'In this way, the therapist demonstrates to the client how his wants or behavior were once threatening to the parental figure. This investigation is based on the belief that the original parent did not act with malice' (p. 66). McNeel designed the Parent Interview to be part of the final stage of psychotherapy, where the individual becomes aware of the internal conflicts of the internalized Parent and, through understanding him or her, achieves some level of forgiveness and acceptance of that person. McNeel warned that if the client's introjected other was 'crazy' then the therapist should not engage in a parent interview.

Dashiell (1978) also described therapy with a Parent ego state. She wrote about 'minimal resolution' wherein the therapist provides permission or reparenting to a Parent ego state that allows for an introjection to be disconnected. Such interventions free Child ego states for further therapy. 'Maximum resolution' included working with a Parent ego state to resolve archaic events in the parent's life, the release of stored feelings in the Parent ego state, or challenging the crazy or hostile Parent ego states while not abandoning the client's Child ego states. Concurrently, (1978/1997) I wrote a theoretical synopsis about the necessity of doing Parent ego states therapy, in which I describe the 'Fourth Degree Impasse' as representing the confusion within the client between the feeling introjected and forming a Parent ego state, and the person's own feelings in a Child ego state.

Mellor and Andrewartha (1980) expanded on working with the emotions in a Parent ego state and gave several short examples. Their focus, like Dashiell's, was also on reparenting – providing a new program for a Parent ego state. They also advocate making direct interventions with the internalized parent; confronting, supporting, and giving permission as necessary, to facilitate a redecision being made by the client. This was seen by Mellor and Andrewartha as especially important when a Parent ego state was experienced as having the power to sabotage or exert a harmful influence on the individual who was about to change his or her life decisions, usually decisions which maintained the family system or protected the parent. Unlike McNeel, who warns against working with a 'crazy' Parent ego state, they suggest that the technique works well when the Parent ego state is -

> ...disoriented, confused, and/or 'crazy' ... the 'craziness' goes when the needs, feelings and wants stimulating apparently incoherent or bizarre responses are identified and are accounted, when the 'craziness' is affirmed as the person's best effort to deal with these feelings, needs and wants, and when new methods, experienced as effective, are provided and tried.
>
> (Mellor & Andrewartha, 1980, p.201)

Bruce Loria, in his careful review of Berne's writings, made a plea for clinicians to remain consistent with Berne's original 'core concepts' (1988, p. 39), and to be mindful of the interpsychic complexity of both Child and Parent ego states. Loria summarizes:

> Berne is stating that a person takes into their Parent ego state the complete personalities of significant parental figures, *including their level of pathology (contamination)*. Therapists working to decontaminate the Adult ego state are likely to succeed only after they have assessed fully the extent of the introjected parental figures. Concomitantly, specific treatment strategies are needed for resolving the *contaminations of the introjected Parent and archaic Child in the Parent ego state* in the offspring. (1988, p. 41)

In writing about the therapy of relationship problems, Landy Gobes identified that the treatment of abandonment or engulfment issues involve an evaluation of 'the form and the degree of pathology in the Parent ego state' and then possibly 'therapy with the Parent ego states of the client' (1985, p. 217). In describing how she does Parent ego state therapy, Gobes says:

> The therapist can proceed as though the entire personality of mother or father were in the person's body and can ask the person to sit in another chair and be mother or father ... A client who *is* her mother seems to experience greater depths of mother's thoughts and feelings than one who role-plays her mother.
>
> (1990, p. 164)

In *Beyond Empathy: A Therapy of Contact-in-Relationship*, the methods of an in-depth psychotherapy of both Child and Parent ego states are provided in detail (Erskine, Moursund & Trautmann 1999). The client's gaining an awareness and appreciation of the psychological function of introjection is essential to the process of an in-depth psychotherapy of Parent ego states. Fred Clark identified an intrapsychic function of introjection:

> What is internalized is the thinking, feeling and behaviors of significant others (Parent ego state) as a defense against the loss of relationship with those persons. This concept, common to object relations theory, differs from psychoanalytic theory where defenses are used in service of protecting against Id drives. In relationship therapy, defenses are understood to be used in service of avoiding the pain or loss of contact (neglect) or painful contact (abuse), both being disturbances in relationship.   (1990, p. 42)

The fantasy Parent
As a normal developmental process in early childhood, children will often create an *imago*, a fantasy figure or self-generated Parent, as a way to provide controls, structure, nurturing, or whatever that young person experienced as missing or inadequate (Erskine & Moursund 1988/1998). Some children create their own personal 'bogeyman,' a frightening creature who threatens them with dire consequences for minor misdeeds. Investing the 'fantasy parent' with all the bad and scary aspects of being parented, allows them to keep Mom and Dad as perfectly good and loving.

Throughout his elementary and junior high school years, Richard was haunted by the bogeyman. As he developed into a teenager, the bogeyman ceased to be a concern; however, there was always the possibility of a stern teacher or policeman who could punish him if he got out of line. In his late twenties, Richard's grandmother died and he helped the family clean out her house. As he cleaned under her bed and in her closet, he felt extremely anxious. He anticipated some terrible punishment and, although he told himself that his thoughts were not rational, he kept expecting to find the remains of the bogeyman. Working with his therapist, Richard began to remember that as a young child he thought the bogeyman 'lived' in grandmother's bedroom, and that he also had the capacity to follow Richard to school or at play. If Richard misbehaved, the bogeyman was sure to punish him. In the process of therapy, Richard began to remember a spanking at age four, which was administered by his mother, in grandmother's bedroom, during a family party. Shortly after the spanking, Richard developed his belief in the bogeyman and could then turn to his mother for comfort, protection, and reassurance. The fantasy of the bogeyman helped the four-year-old Richard remain adapted to external parental controls, and, at the same time experience his mother as all loving and fully tolerant of his behavior.

Others may create a fairy godmother sort of fantasy parent, who loves and nurtures them even when the real parents are cold or absent or abusive. This created image serves as a buffer between the actual parental figures and the desires, needs, and feelings of the young child. The inevitable discomforts of growing up in an imperfect world are more tolerable because the fantasy figure provides what was missing with the real parents.

Anne-Marie, for example, had periods of depression in which she would eat a large amount of food. During this time, she would long for her dead grandmother, whom she described, during her therapy, as affectionate, understanding, and consoling, and who she said used to bring her wonderful food to eat. The therapist, out of curiosity, asked how old Anne-Marie had been when her grandmother died; she replied, "Fourteen months". A fourteen-month-old infant was not likely to have the experiences with a grandmother that Anne-Marie reported. As the therapist began to explore the discrepancy between Anne-Marie's longing for her grandmother and the fact that the grandmother had been dead since Anne-Marie's infancy, the client began to remember experiences from childhood that had been lost from memory for many years. Anne-Marie had repeatedly been abused by both mother and father and had often been locked in the wine cellar for days at a time without food. Anne-Marie related how the grandmother would 'appear' to her after the beatings or in the dark wine cellar to comfort her, to encourage her, and to promise her wonderful meals. By creating these images of grandmother, Anne-Marie was able to satisfy, in fantasy, some of the needs for appropriate nurturing that were drastically lacking in her parents' behavior toward her.

As they mature to later developmental phases, children often let go of their self-generated images. But when the child represses his or her awareness of needs, feelings, and memories in order to survive in the family, the self-created image is fixated, and does not become integrated with later developmental learning. Whatever the characteristics of the fixated self-created Parent, over the years it comes to operate similarly to the Parent ego state described by Berne. It functions like an introjected personality; however, it is often more demanding and illogical and unreasonable than the actual parent was (after all, it had its origin in a small child's fantasy). The self-created parent, made from fantasized images, provides and encapsulates a non-integrated package of thoughts and feelings and behaviors, to which the person responds as if they were truly internalizations from the big people of early childhood.

Treatment planning
Psychotherapy of an introjected ego state or a self-generated parental fantasy

may become part of the psychotherapist's treatment plan, after much therapeutic work has been done on the various Child ego states. Such Child ego
state therapy may include the use of a wide variety of methods to facilitate the
client's:
- relaxing of habitual defenses;
- increased awareness and perhaps expression of feelings and needs that were
  repressed, and
- resolution of both specific or cumulative traumatic experiences.

   Although some of this Child ego state therapy may include active methods,
such as redecision work or the dramatic expression of sadness or anger, much
of the therapy occurs by working within the client-therapist relationship. By
working with the unconscious process of the client's transferences, the developmentally aware and affectively attuned psychotherapist can help the client
identify the archaic interruptions to either internal or interpersonal contact.
These minute interruptions to contact and their related images and fantasies
constitute the subtle dynamics of transference.
   Transference is a constant attempt by the client to reparatively enact fixated childhood experiences, by simultaneously repeating both archaic defenses
and developmental needs in a current relationship. These subtle unconscious
enactments are an expression of an intrapsychic conflict between elements of
an influencing Parent ego state, and the developmental needs thwarted and
fixated in Child ego states (Erskine 1991/1997).
   The intrapsychic conflict between Parent and Child ego states continues
years later, because of a child's biologically-driven needs for relationship and
the resulting, though often unconscious, loyalty to his or her parents or
significant others. Therefore, it is essential to establish a solid therapeutic
relationship with any client prior to therapeutically engaging Parent ego
states: the psychotherapist must be fully protective of the Child ego states'
vulnerabilities. The effectiveness of a therapeutic relationship is built upon
the therapist's:
- attunement to the client's affect and psychological rhythms;
- sensitivity and responsiveness to both various Child and Adult ego state
  needs;
- a constant inquiry into the client's phenomenological experience;
- facilitating the client's appreciation of his or her style of coping, as well as,
- honoring of the vulnerabilities of both childhood and adulthood.
   Much of this is accomplished by working within the transference, and by
the therapist not personalizing the client's defensive reactions.
   Just as effective psychotherapy of Child ego states produces major reorganization of psychological processes, experiences, and meaning making, so also
psychotherapy of a Parent ego state produces major psychological reorganization. The client's Child ego states have been loyal to the intrapsychic influence of Parent ego states because of children's natural need for contact,
attachment, and relationship. This biological imperative for relationship must

be accounted for and respected by the therapist and, in most situations, a sufficient therapy relationship established prior to the treatment of Parent ego states or a self-generated fantasy. It is generally advised to only engage in decommissioning a Parent ego state when the client has an ongoing experience of "this therapist is there for my welfare". If therapists engage in an indepth psychotherapy that decommissions Parent ego states without such an involved relationship, then the Child ego states may be without a significant other to whom they feel a sense of protection and attachment. Metaphorically, it is akin to creating an orphan, and may result in increased anxiety or depression. In some clients, the intrapsychic relationship disrupted by a premature intervention may result in increased clinging to the intrapsychically influencing Parent ego state, or self-generated fantasy, out of a desperate need for attachment. The quality of the therapeutic relationship, as experienced by the client, is a central factor in determining when to proceed with treatment of either a self-generated fantasy or a Parent ego state. The therapist's phenomenological inquiry, throughout the duration of the therapy, and the constant investigation and repair of breaches in the therapeutic relationship, are two of the best monitors for both identifying the subtle transferences and determining the degree to which the client can rely on and draw emotional support from the therapist.

In the 'devil' example at the beginning of the previous section, I actively intervened with a Parent ego state prior to developing a consistent and reliable therapeutic relationship. This is a rare situation where neither my colleague nor I, during the early hours of the therapy-marathon, could establish a therapeutic alliance with the client's Child ego states. Her Parent ego state was interfering with the psychotherapy, primarily through intrapsychic influence and then in the marathon group, by externalization - the active cathexis of the 'devil voice'. The client had been in therapy with my colleague for the treatment of her depression and she had gained a trust in him and, by association, a degree of trust in me. This was coupled with an idealized hope for 'therapy magic'; such idealization is often an expression of the relational need to be in the presence of someone who is both protective of the Child ego states' vulnerabilities and potent enough to stop interpsychic abuse.

The therapy of her depressed Child ego states had reached an impasse. In the process of witnessing other people's therapy in the marathon the psychic presence or influencing Parent ego state became externalized. It was an opportune moment to actively engage the Parent ego state: to keep it externalized rather than allow it to retreat to a position of interpsychic abuse, and to provide psychotherapy to that psychic presence, just as I would with an actual client. This instant intervention with an active Parent ego state is particularly helpful when the influencing Parent ego state is interfering with the psychotherapy, psychologically beating up on a Child ego state; or is so controlling that the Child ego states cannot express or even sense feelings or needs. In most clinical situations, psychotherapy with a Parent ego state is initiated only after a protective therapeutic alliance is established with various

Child ego states.

In some situations, a Parent ego state may become threatened by or envious of the blossoming relationship between the client's Child ego states, and the psychotherapist's reliable, consistent, and dependable involvement. This may result in an increase in anxiety, the activation of internal voices, or self-criticism that interferes with Child ego state therapy. It may then be effective to identify the internal criticism through the interweaving of a phenomenological, transferential, and historical inquiry. Such a detailed inquiry is to determine if the internal voice or criticism is either that of a specific other person, a self-generated Parent-like ego state based on a child's fantasy, or a self-criticism that pre-empts another's criticism. Such identification and differentiation of these possibilities, along with a well-timed explanation, may provide the client with cognitive awareness of the source of the internal conflict and anxiety, and thereby some temporary respite. A description of the treatment of self-generated Parent-like ego states or self criticism that pre-empts another's criticism is beyond the scope of this chapter. However, a differential diagnosis may be useful before proceeding with Parent ego state therapy. Sometimes the self-generated fantasy is clearly evident after the Parent ego state therapy is successfully completed. The Child ego states hold on to a fantasy as an expression of attachment. Preemptive self criticisms are related to shame and self-righteousness (Erskine 1994/1997).

Sometimes a Parent ego state is continually or even increasingly influencing, particularly following regressive therapy, a redecision, or the resolution of a transferential expression of conflict and needs. I have found it more effective to address the criticizing voice on behalf of a Child ego state by speaking as though the actual parent were sitting next to the client. An example of what I have said with one woman's father is: "Stop talking to her like that; I will not let you berate her. Don't punish her for having normal child needs; let her be natural. I know life is hard for you, but you cannot solve your problems by taking it out on her. Be quiet now; later you and I can talk." This is but one of many examples of an *interposition*, wherein the therapist protectively interposes him or herself between the client's Parent and Child ego states. This often provides a large measure of relief from the intrapsychic influence, particularly if the therapeutic relationship is well developed. The client's sense is often one of the therapist being fully protective.

It is essential that the therapist make such a confrontation caringly and with respect. After all, this influencing voice represents the client's parents or significant others, and any disrespectful comment or arrogant tone may threaten the client's loyalty and thereby reinforce the Child ego state's attachment to a Parent ego state. When making an interposition I often silently paraphrase for myself an old cliché: 'blood is thicker than therapy'. With this cliché in mind, I remain respectful of the Parent ego state, even when I may feel disgusted by or ferociously angry at his or her behavior. For the sake of the child, I'm often both firm and empathic with the Parent ego state.

The interposition has two purposes: to temporarily stop the intrapsychic conflict until such time when an in-depth psychotherapy of the Parent ego state is both possible and therapeutically prudent; and, primarily, to create an opportunity to further establish the therapeutic relationship so that the client's experience is: "This therapist is thoroughly invested in my welfare."

Once deconfusion of Child ego states is accomplished, survival reactions relaxed, and script beliefs relinquished, then it may be essential to engage in treating the Parent ego states. There are also times when the client experiences not being able to change; they are still depressed, anxious, or oppressed in response to the intransigent and destructive nature of a Parent ego state. In either of these situations, it may become necessary to actively treat the Parent ego state and later engage in further treatment of Child ego states.

In conducting Parent ego state therapy, the client is invited to cathect the relevant Parent ego state, in essence to 'be' mother or father and to engage in conversation with the therapist as mother or father might. This involves the client in taking on the body posture, the facial expression, the attitude, the feelings, and the style of relating of that particular parent. In essence, the internalized parent becomes externalized. The therapist first establishes a safe and accepting emotional climate, which allows the internalized other to begin to open up and become more revealing. This is often accomplished by realistic, straight talk in the Parent ego state's frame of reference. The quality of the interaction gradually begins to shift to a more therapeutic focus. Because the therapist already has a previous knowledge about the actual parent and some of the family dynamics, he or she is able to make very personal and pointed interventions which reveal areas of conflict or emotional difficulty in the introjected parent. The Parent ego state is then invited to work through those issues with the therapist.

As stated earlier in this chapter, the replacement of a Parent ego state with another introjection is *not therapeutic.* Rather, this chapter describes both the theoretical necessity and the practical considerations of an in-depth psychotherapy of introjections, for the purpose of relieving intrapsychic conflict in our clients. In my clinical experience, I have found that an empathetic, relationally-oriented psychotherapy, aimed at dissolving defenses, honest expression of attitudes and feelings, and therapeutic respect for the individual's desires, frustrations, and conflicts, provides for the decommissioning of Parent ego states, the end of intrapsychic conflict, and the opportunity for the person to engage life with awareness, spontaneity and intimacy.

The same methods of inquiry, attunement, and involvement that are used with many clients may be used to treat a Parent ego state, including regression therapy; and even, sometimes, treatment of the parent's Parent ego states. Examples of in-depth therapy of a Parent ego states include: 1) psychotherapy for a frustrated and angry 35 year old mother dealing with an alcoholic husband and blaming her kids for her plight, 2) facilitating a regression to a father's childhood experiences, and working through memories of early physical abuse, 3) using the variety of methods suitable for deconfusion or redecision, and 4) psychotherapy for the Grandparent or Great-grandparent ego states – 3rd and 4th generational therapy. If the Parent ego state is unwilling to engage in this process and continues to be destructive, the therapist may then continue to relate with that ego state in order to advocate for the client's Child ego state. This is often experienced by the Child ego states, especially in situations of child abuse, as a kind of protection the child never had and can be a very powerful experience that brings about change.

The historical accuracy of the portrayal is not particularly relevant. What is important is the parent-as-experienced by the client. A person introjects not so much what his or her parents 'actually' thought and felt and did, as what he or she experienced them thinking and feeling and believing about the child, about themselves, and about the world. As the Parent ego state begins to respond to the therapeutic challenges to his or her life script, the introject loses its compulsive, entrenched position and the client begins to experience that it doesn't have to be this way.

> The thinking process, attitudes, emotional responses, defense mechanisms, and behavioral patterns that were introjected from significant others no longer remain as an unassimilated or exteropsychic (Parent) state of the ego, but are decommissioned as a separate ego state and become integrated into an aware neopsychic (Adult) ego.   (Erskine & Moursund 1988/1998)

Conclusion

The experience of treating a Parent ego state feels very real: to the therapist, to observers, and most especially to the client. It is not an 'as if' experience once the person gets fully involved. Therefore certain precautions are suggested:

It is essential that the client experience a therapeutic alliance with the therapist first. As a client's Child ego states, though not active, observe the understanding, sometimes empathic interaction between therapist and Parent ego state, he or she may experience that the therapist is taking the parent's 'side' and has effectively abandoned the child. For this reason, it is also imperative that the therapist come back to both Child ego states and the Adult ego of the client before the work is completed, in order to re-establish the relationship. It also re-affirms that the purpose of the procedure is only for the client's benefit (although benefits to the actual physical parents have been reported as a consequence of this experience).

After the therapeutic work with Parent ego states, make sure that the client, whether in Adult ego or Child ego states, has an opportunity to respond to the Parent ego state. This strengthens the sense of self as separate from the parent, and allows for meaningful, interpersonal contact that may have been interrupted or perhaps never present. Failure to do so sometimes results in headaches or a sense of confusion and disorientation.

Keep in mind the loyalty of a child towards its parent, no matter how abusive that parent may be or have been. Even if a client is angry at or ambivalent about a parent, if the therapist confronts too strongly or is in any way disrespectful to the parent the client is likely to feel a pull to protect the parent.

Treating a Parent ego state can take place in one session, an extended session, or over a number of sessions. After a successful process, the client generally feels a combination of feelings; relief and freedom, yet often a deep sadness as a result of knowing the parent's experience so closely and having it responded to empathetically by the therapist. Often anger is stimulated and is best dealt with immediately by having the client address a Parent ego state, as in Gestalt two-chair work. People usually need plenty of time to process the experience, express any residual feelings, and talk about the meaning they have derived from it.

In the process of treating a Parent ego state, the conflict with that significant person is claimed, experienced, and dealt with (albeit in fantasy, since the real parent is not actually present). The result is that the client regains the self that was lost in the process of avoiding the external conflict by internalizing it instead. They are less likely to act out their Parent ego states towards others and, without the internal influence, will also be in a Child ego state less. In addition, as the content of the Parent ego state becomes integrated with the Adult ego the client now has the possibility of dealing with the real person of the parent differently. Therapists may also find that previously unresolved transference issues with the therapist are now more easily resolved. I believe that in-depth, reintegrating psychotherapy of Parent ego states is Transactional Analysis' most significant contribution to the profession of psychotherapy.

References

Berne, E. (1957). Ego states in Psychotherapy. *American Journal of Psychotherapy,* 11, 293 -309

Berne, E. (1961). *Transactional Analysis in Psychotherapy: A Systematic Individual and Social Psychiatry.* New York: Grove Press

Berne, E. (1966). *Principles of Group Treatment.* New York: Grove Press

Bollas, C. (1979). The transferential object. *International Journal of Psychoanalysis,* 60, 97-107.

Bowlby, J. (1969). *Attachment. Vol. 1 of Attachment and Loss.* New York. Basic Books.

Bowlby, J. (1973). *Separation: Anxiety and Anger. Vol. 2 of Attachment and Loss.* New York. Basic Books.

Bowlby, J. (1980). *Loss: Sadness and Depression. Vol. 3 of Attachment and Loss.* New York: Basic Books.

Breuer, J. & Freud, S. (1950). *Studies in Hysteria.* New York: Nervous and Mental Disease Publishing Co., (Trans. by A. A. Brill).

Brown, M. (1977). *Psychodiagnosis in Brief.* Ann Arbor: Huron Valley Institute.

Clark, B.D. (1991). Empathic transactions in the deconfusion of child ego states. *Transactional Analysis Journal,* 21, 92-98.

Clark, F. (1990). The intrapsychic function of introjects. B. Loria (Ed.). *Couples: Theory, Treatment and Enrichment:* Conference Proceedings of the Eastern regional transactional analysis conference, April 18-21, 1990. Madison, WI: Omni Press.

Clarkson, P. & Fish, S. (1988). Rechilding: Creating a new past in the present as a support for the future. *Transactional Analysis Journal,* 18, 51-59.

Cornell, W.F. & Olio, K.A. (1992). Consequences of childhood bodily abuse: A clinical model for affective interventions. *Transactional Analysis Journal,* 22, 131-143.

Dashiell, S.R. (1978) The parent resolution process: Reprogramming psychic incorporations in the parent. *Transactional Analysis Journal* 8, 289-294.

Erikson, E. (1950). *Childhood and Society.* New York: Norton & Co.

Ernst, F. (1971). The diagrammed parent: Eric Berne's most significant contribution. *Transactional Analysis Journal,* 1, 49-48.

Erskine, R.G. (1997). The works cited below are all published in: *Theories and Methods of an Integrative Transactional Analysis: A Volume of Selected Articles.* San Francisco, Transactional Analysis Press.
- Therapeutic intervention: Disconnecting the rubberband (pp. 172-173). (Original work published in *Transactional Analysis Journal,* 1974, 4, 7-8.)
- Fourth-degree impasse (pp.147-148). (Original work published in C. Moiso (Ed.), *Transactional Analysis in Europe,* 1978, Geneva, Switzerland: European Association for Transactional Analysis.)
- Ego structure, intrapsychic function, and defense mechanisms (109-115). (Original work published in *Transactional Analysis Journal,* 1988, 18, 15-19).
- A relationship therapy: Developmental perspectives (75-95). (Original work published in B.R. Loria (Ed.), *Developmental theories and the clinical process: Conference proceedings of the Eastern Regional Transactional Analysis Association Conference,* 1989, Madison, WI: Omni Press.)
- Transference and transactions: Critique from an intrapsychic and integrative perspective (pp. 129-146). (Original work published in the *Transactional Analysis Journal,* 1991, 21, 63-76.)
- Inquiry, attunement and involvement in the psychotherapy of dissociation (pp. 37-45). (Original work published in the *Transactional Analysis Journal,* 1993, 23, 184-190.)
- Shame and self-righteousness: Transactional Analysis perspectives (pp.46-67). (Original work published in the *Transactional Analysis Journal,* 1994, 24, 86-102.)
- The therapeutic relationship: Integrating motivation and personality theories (pp. 7-19). (Original work published in the *Transactional Analysis Journal,* 1998, 28, 132-141.)

Erskine, R.G. (1998). Attunement and involvement: therapeutic responses to relational needs. *International Journal of Psychotherapy,* 3, 235-244.

Erskine, R.G. (2001). Psychological function, relational needs and transferential resolution: The psychotherapy of an obsession. *Transactional Analysis Journal* (in press).

Erskine, R.G. & Moursund, J.P. (1988). *Integrative Psychotherapy in Action.* Newbury Park, CA. & London: Sage Publications. (Reprinted in paperback 1998, Gestalt Journal Press, Highland, NY.)

Erskine, R.G., Moursund, J.P. & Trautmann, R.L. (1999). *Beyond Empathy: A Therapy of Contact-in-Relationship.* Philadelphia, PA & London: Brunner/Mazel

Fairbairn, W.R.D. (1952). *An Object-Relations Theory of the Personality.* New York: Basic Books

Fairbairn, W.R.D. (1954). *Psychoanalytic Studies of the Personality.* New York: Basic Books

Federn, P. (1953). *Ego Psychology and the Psychosis.* London: Image Publishers

Fraiberg, S. (1983, Fall). Pathological defenses in infancy. *Dialogue: A Journal of Psychoanalytic Perspectives,* (65-75). (Original work published in *Psychoanalytic Quarterly,* 51, 612-635, 1982.)

Freud, S. (1949). *An Outline of Psychoanalysis.* New York: W.W. Norton & Company

Gobes, L. (1985). Abandonment and engulfment: Issues in relationship therapy. *Transactional Analysis Journal,* 15, 216-219

Gobes, L. (1990). Ego states – Metaphor or reality? *Transactional Analysis Journal,* 20, 163-165.

Gobes, L. & Erskine, R. (1995). Letters to the editor. *Transactional Analysis Journal,* 25, 192-194

Goulding, M.M., & Goulding, R.L. (1979). *Changing Lives Through Redecision Therapy.* New York: Brunner/Mazel

Greenberg, J.R. & Mitchell, S.A. (1983). *Object Relations in Psychoanalytic Theory.* Cambridge, MA: Harvard University Press

Guntrip, H. (1961). *Personality Structure and Human Interaction.* London: Hogarth

Guntrip, H. (1968). *Schizoid Phenomena, Object Relations and the Self.* London: Hogarth

Hargaden, H. & Sills, C. (2001) Deconfusion of the Child ego state, *Transactional Analysis Journal* 31(1) 55-70

Hartmann, H. (1939). *Ego Psychology and the Problems of Adaptation.* New York: International Universities Press.

Hartmann, H. (1964). *Essays on Ego Psychology: Selected Problems in Psychoanalytic Theory* New York: International Universities Press

Holloway, W.H. (1972). The crazy child in the parent. *Transactional Analysis Journal, 2,* 128-130.

Jacobson, E. (1964). *The Self and the Object World.* New York: International University Press.

Kernberg, O. (1976). *Object Relations Theory and Clinical Psychoanalysis.* New York: Jason Aronson

Kohut, H. (1971). *The Analysis of the Self.* New York: International Universities Press

Kohut, H. (1977). *The Restoration of the Self: A systematic Approach to the Psychoanalytic Treatment of Narcissistic Personality Disorder.* New York: International Universities Press

Kris, E. (1951). *Ego Psychology and Interpretation in Psychoanalytic Therapy.* Psychoanalytic Quarterly, 20, 15-31

Kris, E. (1979). *The Selected Papers of Ernest Kris.* New Haven: Yale University

Loria, B.R. (1988). The parent ego state: Theoretical foundations and alterations. *Transactional Analysis Journal, 18, 39-46*

Mahler, M.S. (1968). *On Human Symbiosis and the Vicissitudes of Individuation.* New York: International Universities Press

Mahler, M.S., Pine, F. & Bergman, A. (1975). *The Psychological Birth of the Human Infant: Symbiosis and Individuation.* New York: Basic Books

Maslow, A. (1970). *Motivation and Personality* (Rev. edn.). New York: Harper & Row

Masterson, J.F. (1976) *Psychotherapy of the Borderline Adult: a Developmental Approach.* New York: Brunner/Mazel

Masterson, J.F. (1981) *The Narcissistic and Borderline Disorders: An Integrated Developmental Approach.* New York: Brunner/Mazel

McNeel, J.R. (1976) The parent interview. *Transactional Analysis Journal* 6, 61-68.

Mellor, K. & Andrewartha, G. (1980). Reparenting the parent in support of redecisions. *Transactional Analysis Journal, 10, 197-203*

Miller, A. (1981) *The Drama of the Gifted Child: The Search for the True Self.* (R. Ward, Trans.) New York: Basic Books

Perls, F., Hefferline, R. & Goodman, P. (1951). *Gestalt Therapy: Excitement and Growth in the Human Personality.* New York: Julian Press

Perls, L. (1978, Winter). An oral history of Gestalt therapy. Part I: A conversation with Laura Perls, by Edward Rosenfeld. *The Gestalt Journal, 1, 8-31*

Piaget, J. (1952). *The Origins of Intelligence in Children.* (M. Cook, Trans.). New York: International Universities Press. (Original French edition published 1936)

Rappoport, D. (1967). *The Collected Papers of David Rappoport.* (M. Gill, Ed.) New York: Basic Books

Stern, D. (1985). *The Interpersonal World of the Infant: A View from Psychoanalysis and Developmental Psychology.* New York: Basic Books

Stolorow, R., Brandchaft, B., & Atwood, G. (1987). *Psychoanalytic Treatment: An Intersubjective Approach.* Hillsdale, NJ: The Analytic Press

Stolorow, R. D. & Atwood, G.E. (1989). The unconscious and unconscious fantasy: An intersubjective developmental perspective. *Psychoanalytic Inquiry, 9,* 364-374

Watkins, J.G. (1978). *The Therapeutic Self.* New York: Human Sciences

Watkins, J. G. & Watkins, H. H. (1997). *Ego states: Theory and Therapy.* New York: W.W. Norton & Co.

Winnicott, D.W. (1965). *The Maturational Process and the Facilitating Environment.* New York: International Universities Press

Weiss, E. (1950). *Principles of Psychodynamics.* New York: Grune & Stratton

Chapter 6

RESOLVING INTRAPSYCHIC CONFLICT:
psychotherapy of Parent ego states
Richard G. Erskine and Rebecca L. Trautmann

Anna was a competent, attractive 50-year-old insurance company executive. She was divorced for 20 years, with two adult children who had recently moved to their own homes. Her presenting problem was that she was becoming depressed, was becoming increasingly withdrawn from social contacts, afraid she would never find a man who would love her, and was considering dropping out of the university where she was studying part-time for a master's degree in business administration. Anna identified her depression as caused, in part, by her children no longer living in her home where she could "shower them with all the love I never got".

Much of the first year and a half of therapy was spent establishing Anna's sense of trust and developing a working therapeutic relationship with both her Adult ego and various Child ego states. By working with the here-and-now interruptions to interpersonal contact between Anna and me, we were able to identify how childhood fears, expectations and script beliefs were transferred into our therapy relationship. The major script beliefs that shaped Anna's life were: "I'm a nothing"; "I won't get what I want"; "I'm all alone"; "It's all my fault"; "People can't be trusted"; and "It (life) doesn't matter".

In analyzing the transferential transactions, we were able to uncover many childhood memories that she had often cried over alone but had never told anyone. She repeatedly talked about how she felt oppressed by both her mother's and father's criticisms, and how she learned to be quiet, without needs, helpful with household chores, and to withdraw into her own private and safe world. My therapeutic attunement to Anna's affect and psychological rhythms, to child developmental levels of functioning, and to relational needs (both current and archaic) created the security for Anna to recall early childhood experiences and to regress to early Child ego states. The regressions provided the opportunity for me to assist Anna in her archaic expression of feelings and needs. The result of those therapeutic regressions was a deconfusion of her Child ego states. In the weekend therapy marathons, body therapy helped her to kick, scratch, and scream out much of the anger at her parents for having neglected her childhood needs. Such disconnecting of the childhood rubber bands and resulting redecisions resulted in lessening the effect of the script beliefs in shaping Anna's behaviors, fantasies, and catastrophic expectations.

The following example of therapy took place in a weekend therapy marathon. At the time of this example, Anna had been in weekly therapy for two and a half years and had attended three other weekend therapy marathons. During the summer recess in our therapy sessions, many of the script beliefs started to be active in her life again. Prior to the summer, these script beliefs had previously ceased to be operative because of the transferential work, deconfusion therapy, and redecisions that resulted in a reorganization of her psychological processes.

I explored the possibility of a rupture in our therapy relationship caused by the summer break in our weekly schedule. This lead to revisiting her memories of her childhood experiences where she again got clarity on her original script conclusions. She was increasingly able to differentiate her childhood construction of meaning from that of her adult perspective. Yet, the script beliefs were periodically active, particularly when she was home alone. She identified that she was lonely, and we explored how the script beliefs might function to either distract her from feelings and/or to keep her psychologically attached to another person – specifically to her mother and/or father, who were the important people when the script beliefs were originally formed.

In the few weeks prior to the therapy marathon, I increasingly wondered if the return of the script beliefs was the result of psychological homeostasis, or due to her childhood dependence on her family, or if the beliefs were also those of one of her parents. From what I had already learned from her memories of her parents' frequent fights, I hypothesized that her mother may have some of the same script beliefs. I know from clinical experience that frequently parents do not inform children of optional meanings, or confront beliefs if the child's beliefs are similar to the parent's own script beliefs. I began the therapy marathon with these hypotheses in mind. Rebecca Trautmann was co-therapist at the marathon.

Richard: Anna, ready to work?
Anna: I feel like you forgot about me. *(her shoulders are slumped)*
Richard: No, I was waiting for Rebecca to come back; she said she wanted to be with you when you work.
Anna: I know that, but it feels like I'm nothing. Like I didn't matter. *(cries)* I won't get what I want. *(cries)*
Richard: *(pause)* So are you saying that you're not going to get what you want or what you need? *(short pause)* So how are you going to deal with it?
Anna: I'll just take care of myself. *(she curls up)*
Richard: Take care of yourself. And deep inside?
Anna: Can't give up hope.
Richard: Tell me about the hope.
Anna: *(sobs)* I keep hoping that something will change before I give up.
Richard: *(Pause)* "Something" or is it somebody will change? Perhaps somebody will have to change so you don't give up.
Anna: I'm closing down.... *(pause)*

Richard: Was I off-target saying somebody will have to change?
Anna: That's too hard to feel.
Richard: "Too hard to feel." *(pause)* Feel what, Anna?
Anna: You're a nothing. Then I say "nothing matters"

Prior to this sequence of transactions, Rebecca, my co-therapist in the marathon, had left the room temporarily. Anna was disappointed and relied on archaic script beliefs "I'm a nothing", "I don't matter" and "I won't get what I want" to make sense of her disappointment. Anna's physiological reaction, voice tone, and crying are all an expression of her unconscious attempt to convey the disappointments of her childhood and her developmental needs via her transferential reaction to Rebecca's leaving. Her enactments are an out-of-awareness attempt to express an intrapsychic conflict and to seek a reparative relationship. Much of the individual therapy time over the previous two months had been spent in unravelling similar transferential enactments. I wondered if the increase in transferential transactions and the reactivation of her script beliefs was an expression of an intrapsychic conflict between Child and Parent ego states.

Richard: Rebecca, I'm wondering if this is one of those situations where the mother in her head is so controlling of her that we're not going to get anywhere with the child in her until we take care of the mother.
Rebecca: Since you see her regularly, and I don't, I have to say that I was more following your lead. And trying to match where she is here in the moment.
Richard: An argument against doing Parent ego state work is that I think Anna's been reaching out to you for the last two days. But I think her mother keeps getting in the way between me and her.
Richard: *(to Anna)* What do you think?
Anna: Makes sense. And scares the hell out of me.
Richard: I'd love to get all that "hell" out of you. Any way to get the "hell" out of you would just be fine with me.
Anna: I was glad that Rebecca was here, but I was afraid if I connected with her then I would lose you.
Richard: Lose me…?
Anna: I was my father's favorite, but my mother really hated me for it. So I had to distance from him to have a relationship with her.
Rebecca: So is it your sense that we need to work with your mother first? That she's the one who's controlling this whole show?
Anna: Yeah.
Rebecca: Would you like us to talk to her?
Richard: But only if you get some guarantees along the way.
Anna: What?
Richard: Oh, like Rebecca would let you be close to me. Not only let, but that she might take pleasure in your being close to me. Would you like that

kind of guarantee?

Anna: You mean, she won't get mad at me?

Richard: Yes. And that you could also go and be with her, and there'd be no fighting from me.

Rebecca: That'd be good.

Anna: I might even help you fold the laundry. *(Rebecca had been absent earlier because she had to take towels out of the dryer.)*

Rebecca: *(laugh) (pause)* I enjoy your being close to Richard. It's no problem.

Richard: Why, in that case ... *(Richard moves closer to Anna)*

Rebecca: So do you think we should leave you with Richard, while I talk to your mother, or does he need to talk to your mother while you stay with me?

Richard: Or, who would your mother be most affected by? A man or a woman talking with her?

Anna: I don't know; she'd just crumble.

Richard: I doubt it. I know that's really scary for you ...

Rebecca: We're good with mothers...

Richard: This is not a fragile woman we're talking about. She has her ways of getting what she wants. So I'm not so concerned about her crumbling. I hear you; she may present that way ... we'll take care of her. This is not about beating up your mom.

Anna: I wanted to take care of her.

Richard: That's the other side of it. You were always taking care of her.

Anna: *(cries)*

Richard: *(pause)* So one thing is you're scared of mama crumbling. The other is, it's your job to take care of her. Yet she made your life hell for being you're dad's favorite.

Anna: Um-hm.

Richard: Were you supposed to repair their marriage as well?

Anna: *(nods a yes)*

Richard: That's an impossible job.

Anna: *(nods a yes)*

Rebecca: Do you want one of us to talk to your mother?

Anna: Yes, that might be good.

Rebecca: Do you want a voice in choosing who will talk to your mother?

Anna: You decide.

These previous few transactions contain the development of a therapeutic contract. This is not a contract for a behavioral outcome – none of us can predict what will emerge in Parent ego state therapy – but rather the beginning of an ongoing negotiation to engage in a therapeutic process. When repressed or unconscious material is involved a person cannot contract for a predetermined outcome. The process of the therapy is often a discovery of something new to each person involved. The possibility of working with two therapists has rekindled the emotional fires of childhood – Anna is re-living her desire for being with both parents and her fear of the possible conflict between them. One of her childhood tasks was to take care of mother. Now one of the therapists will assume this responsibility while the other will be available for Anna's Child ego states.

Richard: Rebecca, will you talk to her mom? I like being there for her kid.
Rebecca: Okay... Richard's right here for you; let's find a chair for your mom. *(A straight arm chair is brought up for Anna to sit on; Rebecca stays on the mat. After things are rearranged, the work resumes...)*
Rebecca: Sit the same way your mom would sit ...just close your eyes. Let your body get right into her posture. See if you can put the same expression on your face that reflects what mom feels. *(pause)* What is your name, Mom?

The experiencing of physiological cues such as body posture and facial expression help to facilitate an externalization of Parent ego state feelings, attitudes, and experience. This is *being* mom, not merely playing a role, and what may emerge is often a surprise to the client. It is important to help the client stay in the Parent ego state. This is accomplished in part by the therapist's repeated use of the name associated with that particular ego state. In the next several transactions, Rebecca uses the name Debra several times to facilitate Anna staying in the Debra ego state – to feel and externalize that psychic presence that is internally causing conflict. Often in the first few transactions, or when emotional material in-and-of itself is confrontative, the person will switch out of a Parent ego state. The therapist directs the person to 'be' the other – to get into his or her skin, affect and experience. The therapist then talks to the 'other' as though he or she were an actual client.

Anna: Debra.
Rebecca: Debra. You can call me Rebecca ... *(pause)* What do you think about being here, Debra?
Anna (as Debra): I don't like it.
Rebecca: You don't like it? Why, Debra?
Debra: Why do I need to be here?
Rebecca: Well mostly so that I can get to know you Debra... Ultimately, it's to help Anna. And for Anna to understand how important you are in her life.
Debra: Important to her? *(emphatically)*
Rebecca: Debra, are you saying that you don't know that you're important in her life? Hmmm. How would *you* describe yourself in her life, Debra?
Debra: She doesn't need me.
Rebecca: Hm. How long have you thought that?
Debra: Always.
Rebecca: You always felt that, Debra? That she didn't need you? Debra, help me to understand how you came to believe that ... Even from when Anna was tiny?

Rebecca's series of questions is designed to get Debra, the client's Parent ego state, to tell the story from the beginning of Anna's life. Perhaps there is much earlier material in Debra's life going back to her own childhood, but starting with Anna's infancy will make a good beginning. Perhaps later in the therapy it will be evident that Debra is in a Child ego state and that regressive therapy with Debra would be most effective. For now the focus is on the adult Debra. In the following sequence of transactions, watch how Rebecca is using a therapeutic inquiry, both historical and phenomenological, to heighten Debra's awareness of her experience and emotions.

Debra: She always cried.
Rebecca: And what did you think when she always cried?
Debra: She wanted something.
Rebecca: And then?
Debra: And then what I did wouldn't help.
Rebecca: Hmmm. How did you feel then?
Debra: That I couldn't help her. Couldn't do anything.
Rebecca: "Couldn't do anything."
Debra: I had my other children too. I had my son.
Rebecca: Uh-huh. So how did you start responding to Anna then? If you thought there was nothing you could do.
Debra: I didn't know what to do. So I ignored her.
Rebecca: But somehow there was the opinion that she didn't need you. How did that happen?
Debra: She had her father.
Rebecca: Was he able to make her stop crying?
Debra: Yeah.
Rebecca: Oooh. Did it make you wonder about being a good mother?
Debra: Mmm.
Rebecca: Do you want to tell me about that?
Debra: I couldn't do it all. *(Softly, her head is looking down)*.
Rebecca: "Couldn't do it all." Is that what you said, Debra?
Debra: I had two others.
Rebecca: Debra, did you feel like you were a good mother to them?
Debra: I tried.
Rebecca: Did they seem to prefer him too?
Debra: No.
Rebecca: So you could make them feel good.
Debra: Um-hm.
Rebecca: But something about this little girl, you couldn't be a good mother to her?
Debra: No.
Rebecca: What was that like Debra? To feel that?
Debra: *(pause)* It made me feel like I was a bad mother – a nothing.
Rebecca: You look as if you're feeling really sad now. Do you want to tell

me about those feelings?

"Do you want to tell me about those feelings" is an example of both a phenomenological inquiry and a process contract. It is an opportunity for Anna as Debra to have a choice both in continuing with the therapy and in expressing what has until now been unexpressed. Each of Rebecca's sentences is an inquiry into Debra's subjective experience, even when her words are not questions but merely a repeat of what Debra has just said: "Couldn't do anything." Each inquiry is to deepen the client's experiences, for her to discover aspects of herself as Debra-in-Anna, not necessarily to gather information. Each inquiry is accompanied by the therapist's genuine interest in hearing her feelings, acknowledgement of what was said and a validation that Debra's emotions and psychological process are significant.

Debra: It was hard to get everything right all the time. It was never enough.
Rebecca: Yeah…
Debra: And having two other children …
Rebecca: Three. All little?
Debra: Yeah. And he was always working. So I was alone with the kids. There was nobody around.
Rebecca: Um-hm. "Nobody around"… That's a lot of stress. *(silence)* Keep going, Debra. I'm really interested in what this was like for you.
Debra: *(breathing heavily; long pause)* But I had to do it all, alone.
Rebecca: So Debra, you tried to be strong, even though you were feeling so sad and alone?
Debra: Yeah. I tried to make the kids behave, so he wouldn't be upset. So he wouldn't yell.
Rebecca: Mmm. What happens when he starts yelling?
Debra: He hollers and screams. And he hits.
Rebecca: Hits?
Debra: My son.
Rebecca: How do you feel about that, Debra?
Debra: Like I can't do anything. I can't stop him…
Rebecca: Why not?
Debra: Cause he'll hit me.
Rebecca: Did he ever hit you, Debra?
Debra: He just threatened.
Rebecca: But you were scared that he would hit you.
Debra: Yeah.
Rebecca: So you let him hit your son…
Debra: *(Begins to cry. Nods a yes.)*
Rebecca: Keep going, Debra, I'm listening. What do you need to say about that?
Debra: *(crying)* I felt bad that I couldn't do anything *(sobs loudly)*
Rebecca: That phrase is really important; "I couldn't do anything." There's

a lot behind that, isn't there, Debra? *(pause)* What couldn't you do?

Debra: I couldn't be a wife, and I couldn't be a mom.

Rebecca: Was he mad at you for not being a good enough wife?

Debra: Always. He'd make fun of me, too.

Rebecca: About what, Debra?

Debra: *(sigh)* How I'd have to get undressed in the dark, in another room. I was shy. I was embarrassed. *(Hangs her head down)*

Rebecca: So Debra, you wanted to undress in the other room?

Debra: I didn't like sex. *(sigh)*

Rebecca: Do you want to say more about that? *(silence)* Did you like sex before you had children?

Debra: No. Never! Never.

Rebecca: Do you know what you didn't like about it?

Debra: *(shakes her head in a no gesture)*

Rebecca: But you knew you didn't like sex ... and is that what became an issue between you and your husband? And is that what made you feel like you couldn't be a wife?

Debra: Um-hm. He said so.

Rebecca: So no matter how much you did and what a good job you did with the children, and keeping the house, and all of that, basically in your mind you were a failure and "couldn't do anything?" Is that about right?

Debra: Oh, he always made me feel like I was a failure. Whatever I did was wrong, no matter what. *(Her words are now clipped and her face muscles tight)*

Rebecca: Debra, I have to ask you – were you angry at him?

Debra: *(pause)* Yeah. *(pause)* Yeah – all the time.

Rebecca: Can you tell me about that anger, Debra?

Rebecca introduces an idea in the therapy: "Were you angry at him?" Usually it is not the best choice for the psychotherapist to introduce an idea into the therapy, lest he or she lead the client in an erroneous direction or, even more problematic, prematurely introduce an experience. Rebecca's quotation of Debra's helpless statement "I couldn't do anything" is designed to inquire about Debra's resignation and possible anger - a rather natural human reaction to such ridicule. Is it possible that Debra's feelings are not acknowledged or expressed, and therefore the affect finds a sublimated form of release, as in anger at the father being directed to a child? Further phenomenological inquiry will reveal if the therapist's idea about the anger is significant, or if another area of investigation is more appropriate. When the therapist does introduce an idea or chart a direction, it is essential that the client's sense of agency - the human needs for self-definition and to make an impact - be supported through the therapist creating an opportunity for, and even encouraging the client's saying, "no, that's not right for me." This is often done by the therapist raising a genuine question about the introduced idea or direction: "Were you angry at him?"

Debra: I couldn't really get mad. I could maybe slam a pot.

Rebecca: Right. There's always the threat he's going to hit you. So tell me about the feelings of anger that you did have. Even though you couldn't really get angry.

Debra: *(sigh)* I'd get angry at her.

Rebecca: You'd get angry at Anna? Oh, you mean instead of being angry at him?

Debra: Yeah, he would talk to her all the time.

Rebecca: And what did that feel like to you?

Debra: Like I didn't matter. I was just to have babies and clean and cook.

Rebecca: Mmmm. Ouch. So you believe that you don't matter. You didn't matter to him.

Debra: Yeah, I'm a nothing to him. He was interested in Anna.

Rebecca: So did you feel jealous of Anna? Or were you just angry at him, for giving to her what you needed from him?

Debra: I'd get jealous. Then I'd get angry if he did things for her. *(sigh)* And he would take it out on my son.

Rebecca: Well, was there something Anna did that made it like this? *(silence)* What are you thinking, Debra?

Debra: She wouldn't listen to me. She wouldn't help me enough. And he'd be nice to her but then he wouldn't be so angry.

Rebecca: What I imagine is that it must have been pretty tough on Anna to try to be taking care of both parents at the same time. Keep her father happy and also help her mom out.

Debra: She did all of it.

Rebecca: She probably tried her best. But we've got to get something straight here. Debra, was it Anna's fault? Or is the person you're angry with really your husband?

Debra: *(long pause)* I think it's both.

Rebecca: Tell me? *(pause)* How is it both?

Debra: Cause she really enjoyed being with him, that's her fault.

Rebecca: Um-hm.

Debra: She wanted to be with him.

Rebecca: Sure. Especially if he was nice to her. Why not?

Debra: He wasn't always nice to her.

Rebecca: He wasn't? Oh, I thought you said he was nice to her.

Debra: Sometimes. But later as a teen, he criticized her a lot. And she stayed away from him.

Rebecca: How come you weren't nice to her?

Debra: I didn't like her.

Rebecca: Why, Debra?

Debra: *(sigh)* I just didn't like her. She made me feel inadequate.

Through Rebecca's therapeutic inquiry, Debra is revealing her disappointments in her relationship with her husband and her jealousy of her daughter.

It seems that from infancy onward, Anna did not satisfy some important relational need of Debra's as implied in the comments, "'didn't like her"; "She wouldn't listen to me"; "She made me feel inadequate." Three factors seem to emerge: Debra's anger at her husband is directed to Anna; Debra is jealous of the relationship between her husband and daughter; and Debra does not experience Anna as providing important interpersonal psychological functions such as making an impact, experiencing security through the relationship, or receiving validation of her uniqueness, vulnerabilities and experiences. Debra's "I don't matter" and "I'm a nothing'" sound very similar to some of Anna's script beliefs. Are Anna's beliefs an expression of Debra's, are they the result of Anna's childhood conclusions and decisions, or both? When the same script beliefs are present in both a Parent ego state and a Child ego state, the synergy between them creates an even stronger resistance to dissolving, reorganizing and updating one's perspective. As this transcript continues, Rebecca's involvement, and later Richard's, is aimed at dissolving script beliefs in both Parent and Child ego states.

Rebecca: Because she made you feel inadequate? *(silence)* Go ahead, Debra, let me know what's going on inside. *(Her face has become increasingly tense)*. Something's really moving inside. Will you let me know?
Debra: *(breathing hard)* I *was* inadequate.
Rebecca: You were?
Debra: Yeah.
Rebecca: What do you mean by that? *(silence; Anna breathes heavily)* Let it come Debra. Don't hold that all inside … In some ways you sound like you're ready to explode in there. It's ok if you want to explode out here; I'm going to make sure no one hurts you.
Debra: *(long pause)* Not supposed to say anything.
Rebecca: *(whispering)* I want to hear!
Debra: Not supposed to say anything. Just be quiet, nice …
Rebecca: Yeah, I know. But I want to hear. I want to hear those unsaid things. Those feelings, those thoughts. What do you mean, you were inadequate?
Debra: I didn't know how to love my kids. How to show them *(begins to sob)*. I'd just get mad at them all the time. They wouldn't listen. I'd just tell them it was their fault. *(Crying continues)*
Rebecca: Because inside you were feeling …
Debra: I couldn't do it; I was bad – a nothing.
Rebecca: You were bad?
Debra: Um-hm.
Rebecca: Debra, did you feel loved by your parents?
Debra: *(pause)* I don't think so. *(pause)* My mother worked hard.
Rebecca: Yeah… Did she tell you you were inadequate, too? *(pause)*
Debra: Yeah.

Now there is an opening of a new theme – Debra's lack of feeling loved. The therapist has an opportunity to work with both Debra's experience of her early relationship with her parents, and how Debra made sense out of her mother's message that she was inadequate. The therapist can either cognitively explore Debra's early childhood, or support a therapeutic regression that leads to a corrective experience, redecision, and the dissolving of script beliefs. The therapist decides instead to explore how the experience of being unloved is relived and reinforced in Debra's marriage; this time-frame and marital relationship may be most pertinent to Anna's therapy. Perhaps later regressive therapy with Debra may be necessary, but for now the work has already been about Debra's anger at her husband, and the displacement of that anger onto Anna. By focusing on the difficulties in Debra's marriage, the source of Debra's jealousy may emerge. If focusing on Debra's experience of feeling unloved by her husband is not useful, then the therapist can return to early childhood experiences in Debra's life that may be the source of her jealousy, and that have shaped her script beliefs.

Rebecca: Did you hope to get some of that loving in your marriage?
Debra: Yeah. *(with a mournful sound.)*
Rebecca: Oh boy, I heard that. What was the disappointment there?
Debra: Didn't get it. No, just cook and clean and sex. Take care of the kids.
Rebecca: "Cook and clean and sex." *(pause)* "Take care of the kids."
Debra: And he'd flirt with other women.
Rebecca: Ooh. Did he tell you how inadequate you were?
Debra: Mmmm. That I was cold.
Rebecca: Even in bed?
Debra: Yeah, he said I was cold…that I wasn't sexual.
Rebecca: Um-hm. What do you feel when he says that?
Debra: Garbage.
Rebecca: And yet you don't say anything, just keep going along. But you were – you were angry, weren't you? And the only way you could let that loose just a little bit was at Anna. Am I right?
Debra: *(nods a yes)*
Rebecca: *(pause)* I'm going to ask you to do something that's probably never been possible for you before. I want you to imagine that your husband is here in this chair right in front of you, and say to him the things that you're angry about. And I'll make sure he doesn't hit you. Would you do that? *(pause)*
Debra: *(nods a yes)*
Rebecca: Just imagine him right here …what's his name?
Debra: Jason

Rebecca establishes the possibility for two-chair work where Debra will talk to her husband. Such therapeutic experiments allow an opportunity for the contact that may have been interrupted or never made, to be finally made, at least in fantasy. The person can say what has been inhibited, and, in imagining the other person present, affect, attitudes, hopes and disappointments can finally be expressed. Debra nods agreement, part of the ongoing nature of a process contract, that signals her willingness to experiment with expressing what has been pent-up inside her.

Anna has, most likely, introjected Debra's anger, resentment, hurts, and fears along with her script beliefs and psychological defenses. An opportunity for Debra to express what has been inhibited, yet unconsciously introjected by Anna, may provide a great relief of the intrapsychic conflict that Anna experiences day-to-day.

Rebecca: Just imagine Jason is right here. He's sitting in a chair across from you. What would you say to him if you knew you could say anything that was in your heart?

Debra: Hmmm *(sigh; long pause)* Nothing was ever right. Couldn't you ever just be pleased, or appreciate anything? Why was it always wrong?

Rebecca: Now a little louder, Debra. Make your questions into your own statements. A little more forcefully. I'm angry that …

Debra: It was never enough. Never right. Never right what I did.

Rebecca: Keep going Debra.

Debra: And it was always my fault. Always, everything. Everything everybody did was my fault.

Rebecca: You're doing great, Debra. Just raise your voice a little bit more so you can let that energy out. "My fault!"

Debra: *(sigh)* My fault. *(sigh)*

Rebecca: "And what I want to say to you, Jason, is …"

Debra: It's not my fault!

Rebecca: Hey, good! Let me hear more!

Debra: It was your fault.

Rebecca: Tell him how it was his fault.

Debra: Because he was always angry, always yelling, and he wanted more.

Rebecca: Say it to him: "*You* wanted more! *You* yelled. *You* were the angry one." Keep going Debra!

Debra: Everybody was afraid of you. Nobody wanted to be near you. Everybody ran away from you *(sigh)*.

Rebecca: Keep going. Tell him all you've held inside.

Debra: You were rotten. You were cruel!

Rebecca: Keep going. Feel that anger in those fists. *(hands were clenched.)*

Debra: You were miserable. You made everybody around you miserable. *(sigh)*

Rebecca: "And I feel …"

Debra: Like nothing. Like you didn't care. *(sigh)*

Rebecca: Keep going, Debra. Tell him how you feel about his making you feel like a nothing.

Debra: Mmm, I get tired.

Rebecca: Right, but that may be in order not to feel angry. Keep going, Debra. You've got lots of energy inside you.

Debra: *(sigh)* I showed you when I got my driver's license!

Rebecca: Ah, some spunk too. Good.

Debra: He tried to teach me.

Rebecca: Keep talking to him. "You ..."

Debra: You tried to teach me to drive; all you did was yell at me and make me cry. I felt like showing you. I went and I got lessons and passed the driving examination myself. *(She is pushing on the arm of the chair with both hands.)*

Rebecca: Yeah. Feel the power in that, Debra. I bet you'd like to use those hands. Right? Those hands...they've got energy in them.

Debra: He'd smash me back.

Rebecca: We're not going to let him do that. Would you like to smash him?

Debra: I'd like to pound on him.

Rebecca: Tell that to him. "I'd like to ..."

Debra: Pound on you. I'd like to smack you. Like you smacked my son. You smacked David!

Rebecca: Yeah, tell him.

Debra: You smacked David. You crushed him. Over and over again until he gave up *(crying)*. And you blamed me! Over and over again, you hit your son. He's your son!

Rebecca: Now tell him all that you feel, Debra.

Debra: He's your son, too; and you did it.

Rebecca: And tell him how enraged you are at what he did to your son. Your mutual son.

Debra: I hate you for it.

Rebecca: Again - louder, Debra.

Debra: I hate you for it.

Rebecca: Again! Louder!

Debra: I hate you.

Rebecca: Again! Keep going!

Debra: I hate you for what you did. What you had to do was just love him. That's all he wanted from you *(crying)*. You made everybody hate him, and everybody leave him.

Rebecca: Say the whole thing, Debra. All those feelings, to Jason ... Don't shut down. What you're saying is really important.

Debra: Why didn't you love us? Why didn't you show us that you loved us? Not by buying things...

Rebecca: "What I needed was..."

Debra: For you to be kind, and gentle, and loving, and caring *(sigh)*. Not to be hateful.

Rebecca has been directing the process in several distinct ways while attempting not to direct the content. Debra has retroflected her feelings, complaints, and physical reactions and now needs a cheerleader, someone to encourage the free expression of what has been inhibited. Rebecca begins by directing Debra to turn her go-nowhere questions such as "Couldn't you ever just be pleased?" into direct statements: "It was always my fault". She then encourages Debra to be louder. There is no magic in volume, but there is often a greater expression of pent-up emotions and thoughts as the person gets louder. As a result of expressing what has been retroflected, the client gains increased awareness of his or her own defenses, inhibited reactions, unfulfilled desires and script conclusions. Rebecca then 'primes the pump,' a further encouragement for Debra to express what may be held back. Priming the pump refers to the therapist's open-ended prompts that allow room for the client to finish the sentence with their own self- expression: "And what I want to say to you, Jason, is ..."; "What I needed was..."; or "I'd like to...". Debra attempted to talk to Rebecca about Jason; Rebecca directed her back to communicating with the image of Jason with, " *You* wanted more! *You* yelled. *You* were the angry one." Another type of prompt is used when Rebecca encourages Debra to address Jason with, "Keep talking to him." This is often used when the person is either becoming quiet and retroflecting what needs to be said, or is attempting to address the therapist instead of talking to the significant other.

Rebecca: I'm going to ask you to go one step more now. Debra, talk to Jason about him and Anna.
Debra: *(sigh)*
Rebecca: Look at Jason *(silence)* It's hard, isn't it? Because it's all mixed up.
Debra: Um-hm.
Rebecca: Start with what you can. "What I feel toward you, Jason, ... about you and Anna, is ..."
Debra: *(pause, very softly)* You're too close. It's not right.
Rebecca: Keep going, Debra. Say the whole thing ... It's important, Debra, to say what you need to say to Jason. *(pause)* Debra, you need to say it. This is definitely not one of those times you should be quiet and keep it inside.
Debra: *(sigh)* It's not right the way you look at her.
Rebecca: Tell him what you mean.
Debra: I can see it in his eyes - sexual.
Rebecca: Tell him what you see, Debra. Be very specific ... I know this is hard. You're doing great. But you've got to say it all.
Debra: Mmmm. *(sigh)* You shouldn't be looking at her that way; it's not right. You're confusing her.

Rebecca's prompt, "Tell him what you see... be very specific" may have provided effective support for Debra to express what she has inhibited. Debra has finally made a corrective comment to her husband, "You shouldn't be looking at her that way; it's not right. You're confusing her." Such a statement from mother to father is part of setting psychologically healthy boundaries within this family, and providing protection for the daughter, Anna. This is a mere beginning of the Parent (Debra) ego state's task of deconfusing Anna's Child ego states. One of the possible therapeutic benefits of an in-depth Parent ego state therapy is in the internalized other's truth telling, and the resulting deconfusion of the Child ego states that are listening.

Rebecca: That's good, Debra. Keep going … say what you mean, Debra. "You're confusing her … you shouldn't be looking at her that way …"
Hang in there, Debra. You've made a really good start. There's much more to say.
Debra: I can't say more.
Rebecca: You need to, Debra.
Debra: *(quietly)* It's not my place.
Rebecca: It is absolutely your place. You are her mother! Now talk to Jason about what he's doing!
Debra: He won't listen to me. *(head and eyes down)*
Rebecca: He will now! Now come on. I'll back you up! *(pause)* *(Rebecca puts her hand on Anna's-cum-Debra's back)* "You shouldn't be looking at her that way! You're confusing her!" *(pause)* What does that mean, Debra? Tell him the whole thing. Tell him what he's doing to her.
Debra: He knows. He has ideas.
Rebecca: You say it.
Debra: He knows they're his fantasies.
Rebecca: Debra, he can be lying to himself, even if he knows. You need to say it, Debra. Say it for your sake as well as Anna's. *(pause)* Do you want me to try to say it first?
Debra: I don't know how to say it.
Rebecca: Will you tell me if I'm saying it right or not?
Debra: *(nods a yes)*
Rebecca: *(pause)* "Don't look at her as a sexual object? Don't look at her like you're having fantasies of what sex with her would be like?" *(pause)* Is that close, Debra?
Debra: Um-hm. *(pause)* Yes.
Rebecca: You keep going, Debra. Say it your own way.
Debra: *(breathing hard, shaking)*

Following Debra's, "You shouldn't be looking at her that way," Rebecca's prompt of "Keep going … there's much more to say," came too soon to have a lasting supportive effect. At that moment, attunement to Debra's difficulty in telling her truth may have been far more supportive than encouraging her to express what has been retroflected. Debra gives up: "It's not my place." Attunement and empathetic understanding of Debra's reticence to talk freely to Jason may have taken the therapy in a different direction – perhaps in the direction of Debra's need for security and validation. Instead, Rebecca confronts her with, "It is absolutely your place. You are her mother!" Such confrontation has three purposes: first, the therapist takes the stance of a child advocate confronting for the sake of the child; second, it is aimed at correcting the distortions and possible script beliefs in the Parent ego state; and third, it begins the process of deconfusing the Child ego states.

Even if such a confrontation does not impact Debra, Anna's Child ego states are listening to Rebecca's message, and perhaps this will be empathetic for Anna and an opening to new possibilities for her. Debra becomes confused. She is both afraid of Jason and is in a conflict between denial, "I don't know," and maternal protection for her daughter. As a result she shuts down, rather than correct her husband. Rebecca models for Debra how to correct Jason and protect Anna: "Don't look at her as a sexual object?" Yet, Rebecca does so with a questioning attitude, "Will you tell me if I'm saying it right or not?" and "Is that close?" This is another example of the process of ongoing contracting between client and therapist; frequent use of such questions provides a constant guide to ensure that the therapist is congruent with the client's experience - an important element is ensuring that the therapist is following the client, and not programming or even suggesting the client's experience.

Rebecca: *(whispering)* Debra, you need to do this ... You know something about this so well – There's something in this story that's very important. And there's something that's happening between Jason and Anna that really confuses you. I imagine that you don't know what to do about it. Is that right?
Debra: I hate her... *(long pause – she seems to shut down)*.
Rebecca: Anna is not the problem! She is only a child. The real problem has got to be talked about straightforwardly, Debra. What is the story here?
Debra: I don't know the story.
Rebecca: Will you tell Jason what is happening in your relationship? Will you tell Jason about him and Anna?
Debra: It's wrong – the way he is with her.
Rebecca: *(long pause; whispering)* Debra... What's happening? What are you doing inside?
Debra: Just going blank.
Rebecca: Will you talk directly to me, Debra? What got scary just now? Why do you need to go away?

When Rebecca states one possible hypothesis about what Debra is not saying, "Don't look at her as a sexual object" and then continues with "...there's something happening between Jason and Anna that really confuses you." Debra is back to: "I hate her". She shuts down emotionally and physically. Rebecca urges Debra to tell her story, and Debra answers 'I don't know the story." Is Debra denying what happened? Is she so afraid of Jason that she cannot express what she knows? Or is the therapist's hypothesis taking the story in a direction that is not consistent with Debra's experience? These are all questions that the therapist must rapidly assess before making the next intervention. Rebecca's answers to each of those questions about Debra's behavior and internal process will determine how Rebecca will respond. When Debra continues to avoid facing Jason, Rebecca establishes the communication between Debra and herself with "Will you talk directly to me?" Transactions with Rebecca may be easier for Debra to manage than talking to Jason, and may clarify the direction of this therapy. But even this communication is too difficult for Debra so she returns to blaming Anna.

Debra: *(pause)* I don't know. *(pause)* I just can't say anything. *(pause)* But I know.
Rebecca: You know what?
Debra: It's familiar, but I can't think. It's just that the feeling is very familiar when I see him with her.
Rebecca: *(pause)* Okay, then let's you and I talk about what may actually be more important. What happened between you and Anna? *(pause)* You said, "I hate her." Can you tell me about that? *(long pause)* Are you with me, Debra?
Debra: Trying to get to it.
Rebecca: Okay, I'll be patient. *(silence)* But you're feeling something, Debra *(her head and shoulder are slumped)*. Is that right? Can you tell me?
Debra: It's her; she's doing it. That's what is familiar.
Rebecca: "It's her?" "She's doing it?" She's doing what, Debra? *(silence)* Are you talking about Anna?
Debra: Yes, Anna.
Rebecca: What is Anna doing?
Debra: It's her fault.
Rebecca: What is her fault?
Debra: Everything is her fault. She's bad.
Rebecca: What makes Anna "bad"? What is it she does that's "bad"?
Debra: She's a girl.
Rebecca: Because she's a girl. It's her fault because she's a girl?
Debra: She's bad – because she's female.
Rebecca: Are you bad because you're female?
Debra: Um-hm.
Rebecca: Am I?
Debra: *(pause)* I don't know.
Rebecca: Say more about how you and Anna are both bad or at fault for being female. *(silence)* Are you thinking about that? *(silence)* Debra, is that what you end up believing when you dare not think about how Jason treated you and Anna? - that it's your fault and Anna's fault just because you were born girls? I wonder if it blocks out something else.

Earlier Rebecca provided an opening to explore the hypothesis that Debra's emotional reaction to Anna was related to the possibility of Jason having sexual fantasies about Anna. This exploration is met by Debra "going blank." Is this resistance? Is the hypothesis wrong or even worse, premature? Or, is the relationship between Debra and Anna more significant to Anna's welfare at this time? Here again, Rebecca is making a therapeutic assessment regarding the direction of her next interventions. Experienced therapists are constantly observing the client's behavior and selecting from a variety of hypotheses. It is not so important that the therapist always have the correct hypothesis, but it is essential that the client be active in confirming or disconfirming what the therapist imagines to be going on inside the client.

Since the therapy is ultimately for Anna's sake, and the primary contract for this therapy is for the resolution of intrapsychic conflict between Anna's Child ego states and her Parent (Debra) ego state, Rebecca then shifts the focus: "Let's you and I talk about what may actually be more important. What happened between you and Anna?"

The therapist then asks Debra to explore the psychological function of her beliefs that females are bad or at fault: "... is that what you end up believing when you dare not think about how Jason treated you and Anna?" Such beliefs may function as a distraction from feeling and knowing about traumatic experiences. It is essential to an in-depth Parent ego state therapy to facilitate the internalized other in unravelling his or her own story – the story of how the parent's script beliefs were formed, how they were maintained and reinforced during the client's childhood, and importantly, how they may have been introjected by and/or adopted by a child.

Debra's script beliefs and defensive process have become part of Anna's life script. For Anna to have maximum benefits from this work, the therapist will focus on helping Debra to acknowledge her defenses and her underlying feelings and needs. A few transactions later, Rebecca crystallizes the therapeutic session by summarizing the effect of Debra's script beliefs on both her, and more importantly, on Anna. Yet this is not enough; another confrontation ensues – a confrontation that is both respectful and valuing of Debra's and Anna's human worth, and also challenges the script beliefs that have been passed from mother to daughter.

Debra: My mind is … it's real dizzy, and it hurts.
Rebecca: You've been working really hard here, I know that … you can blame her and you can blame yourself. Maybe instead of …
Debra: Blaming somebody else?
Rebecca: That sounds possible?
Debra: It's possible.
Rebecca: Well, I would like to tell you something.
Debra: *(nods yes)*
Rebecca: The effect of it on you and on her is exactly the sort of thing you were telling me at the very beginning. Which are things like: There's nothing you can do; There's nothing you can do right; You're at fault because you're

female; You're not worthwhile; You don't matter. *(pause)* Am I right, am I on track so far?

Debra: She wants something from me and I don't want to give it to her.

Rebecca: Why, Debra? What does she want and why don't you want to give it to her? *(silence)* What does she want?

Debra: She wanted me to take care of her, and I don't want to.

Rebecca: Umm. *(silence)* Debra, what does Anna need from you?

Debra: *(sigh)* She wants me to love her. I don't know how.

Rebecca: I believe you. I really believe you. If you think so badly about yourself, and especially if it's just because you're a woman, how can you love a child who's the same, a female? And in essence, to tell her she's special to you *(pause)*. Am I right?

Debra: I didn't get the last part.

Rebecca: Tell her she's good and special to you.

Debra: Because I know she's a nothing.

Rebecca: Well, I disagree with you. I don't think she's a nothing. And I don't think you are either. But I think you got some very mixed up ideas about being female, and what that means about your own self-worth, what that means about your relationship with men, and what that means about your role in life. You didn't know what to do with a girl child, except to put on her all those feelings that you have about yourself.

Debra: I didn't know what to do with anybody.

Rebecca: Yeah. *(pause)* In your heart of hearts, do you think she's a nothing?

Debra: *(reluctantly shakes head 'no')* All mixed up *(pause)*. She got big and she helped me.

Rebecca: Yeah. Then you got some of what you needed.

Debra: Um-hm. Yeah.

Rebecca: What you waited so long for.

Debra: Um-hm. *(crying, pause)*

Rebecca: Yeah.

Debra: She helped me.

Rebecca: Um-hm. That was really nice of her *(pause)*. I'll tell you, it's left some real big holes in her. She really needed to be special to you and loved by you from the day she was born. Instead, you passed on your story of the low worth of women and your beliefs "I won't get what I want," "I'm a nothing," and your sense of being all alone.

Rebecca has made a confrontation to Debra about her statement, "She's a nothing", and then continues with a therapeutic opinion, "I don't think you are either!" This is followed by an interpretation based on what Debra had previously declared – that she gave Anna the same message as her own script beliefs. Then a therapeutic challenge: "Do you think she is a nothing?" The confrontation is followed by crystallizing statements from the therapist that are a short analysis of both Debra's and Anna's life script: "I won't get what

I want", "I'm a nothing", and the sense of being all alone. Rebecca says to Debra, "You were angry at your husband... and instead you hated her and that damaged her." These therapeutic operations are aimed at both Parent and Child ego states – deconfusing for both Anna's Child ego states and her introjected mother, and therefore part of resolving intrapsychic conflict.

Debra: I didn't mean to *(crying)*.
Rebecca: I know. You were really quite mixed up. And stressed. And angry with your husband. And alone. All those things? And instead you hated her and that damaged her.
Debra: Yeah. I didn't mean to. *(Crying again)*
Rebecca: Anna needs a chance to talk about what it was like, living with you. Even though we understand that you didn't mean to, and we understand that you were mixed up, and we understand that in your heart of hearts you don't think she's a nothing; still she's left with a lot of the garbage of you blaming her, she is mixed-up. And she needs to be able to talk about that without feeling that she's hurting you, or that you're going to get angry at her, or hate her. Do you think we can allow her to do that? Is that okay with you?
Debra: *(sobs)*
Rebecca: Tell me about those tears?
Debra: It's nice to talk to you.
Rebecca: You know, I wish I had been in your life many years ago listening to you. It all could have been so different, perhaps getting what you wanted instead of deciding you were a nothing and at fault.
Debra: Then I would have known how.
Rebecca: Yeah. Yeah. *(pause)* Well, Debra, I really appreciate your coming and talking. And being as honest as you were able to be. Now we need to listen to Anna. Okay? Let her talk, and not get in the way, okay? *(pause)* When you're ready you can come back another time *(long pause)*. Anna, Richard is right next to you, ready to support you. Do you want to turn to him?

Even at the end of the piece of therapy with Debra, Rebecca continues to engage her in a process contract; the little agreements between client and therapist that both provide the client with a sense of being in charge and making an impact, and also provide a continual feedback to the therapist about the client's willingness to proceed with the therapy. Rebecca has been doing the therapy with Anna's Parent ego state, while Richard has been on reserve for Anna's Child ego states. Now it is time for Richard to provide the support to Anna, for her to express her own feelings, thoughts, and needs. It is essential in most situations of Parent ego state therapy to provide a supportive relationship for the Child ego states.

When the client has an opportunity to respond to the Parent ego state, a cycle of interpersonal agency and efficacy is established that may have been ruptured or perhaps never existed. This allows for the Child ego state to define her or himself and to make an impact – self-expressions that may have been inhibited or prohibited in the original relationship with the parent. To make an impact within a relationship, and to define one's self within a relationship, are two essential relational needs.

Anna: Dizzy…*(as she gets out of the chair and sits on the therapy mat)*.
Richard: Yeah, but you've been listening to your mom. All those angry words. Now it's time to address mom. Try saying to mom, "I'm dizzy listening to you, Mom."
Anna: I am dizzy. I'm tired.
Richard: Tell her what you're reacting to. What you heard.
Anna: *(pause)* It was hard for her.
Richard: She made it hard on you as well. That's what I heard. Life with him must have been hell.
Anna: Yeah *(sighs)* Life with him was hell. For her and me!
Richard: Talk to Mom. Just talk directly to her as though she's right there in that chair.
Anna: *(turns to empty chair)* I didn't want to listen to him; that was your job.
Richard: Keep going, Anna. Say it again. "I didn't want to listen to him…"
Anna: I didn't want to have to be there.
Richard: "It was *your* job to …"
Anna: I didn't want you hating me. Because I was doing your job! *(angrily)*
Richard: "I was doing your job, and you were hating me!"
Anna: Sucked!
Richard: Keep going!
Anna: He could get angry at me, too.
Richard: "And you didn't…."
Anna: You didn't protect me; you didn't love me. You even told me if I did something wrong, it was all my fault so he would get angry at me.
Richard: "And I don't like …"
Anna: I don't like your dirty looks.
Richard: "And I don't like …"
Anna: I don't like you hiding inside.
Richard: "And I don't like…"

Richard is intentionally slow in directing Anna to talk to Debra a second time. She appears to need contact with Richard first. Then a few sentences later, he again directs her to make verbal contact with the internalized mother, who has been externalized by Anna's imagining her in the empty chair. The therapist is 'priming the pump' – giving the client an open-ended phrase, that if completed by the client, may be an expression of what has been inhibited and needs to be said. It is important that the therapist carefully follow the client's body clues, emotional charge and the contextual material so as not to program the client's words. The therapist's 'priming the pump' may help the client to overcome his or her inertia of self-expression; for example, when Richard says to Anna, "And you didn't ..."; "And I don't like..."; "I need...."

The expression of Anna's "I don't like..." is a form of contact-making anger, rather than the contact-disrupting rage or withdrawal that she learned in her family. This is a new form of expression, a making of contact with the internalized mother that was both prohibited in childhood and then inhibited for more than forty years. Anna is re-experiencing the feelings of childhood, but instead of re-living them, which is reinforcing of inhibition and repression, she is doing something new – an undoing of retroflections – and the old pattern of script related behavior is altered.

Anna: I don't like you not loving me. And making me feel it was all my fault.
Richard: "Because I need..."
Anna: I need your love. I need you to be there.
Richard: Tell her about her being worried about you being a sexual object to him.
Anna: Us.
Richard: Say that to her.
Anna: Us.
Richard: Tell her what the word 'us' means.
Anna: Me and him. He paid attention to me. But then I got nervous...*(pause)*
Richard: Yeah, tell Mom about your nervousness.
Anna: Yeah, but she knew. She knew something was wrong. She knew.
Richard: Tell it to mom.
Anna: You didn't say anything, you'd just sit there.
Richard: "And I needed..."
Anna: *(crying)* I needed you to do something...
Richard: Keep talking. "Mom, I needed..." *(pause)* You needed her to "do something" Try saying: "Mom, I needed..."
Anna: *(pause)* I needed you to take care of me, and I needed you to protect me. *(angrily)*
Richard: That movement of your arm is saying something. *(silence)* Anna, mom's right there. She told you some important things, and now it's your turn. Tell her what your arm is saying *(long pause)*.

Anna has been responding to the therapist's encouragement for her to express her pent-up emotions and words. Anna's right arm is cocked as though she were preparing to either hit, grab or push. Richard directs her to express what her arm is saying. This is too much; Anna shuts down. Rebecca, suspecting that Anna's Parent ego state is again internally influencing Anna, addresses Debra. Rebecca's following remarks are an interposition – imposing herself between the influencing Parent ego state and the Child ego states who are subject to the influence: "Just because you couldn't talk about it doesn't mean that Anna can't either. Debra, let Anna do what you need to do – to say what she thinks and to be angry. You also needed to make an impact." This is permission giving to both Debra and Anna and protective of Anna.

Rebecca: Debra, just because you couldn't talk about it doesn't mean Anna can't either.
Richard: Tell her, Anna, what you mean when you say "I needed you to protect me."
Rebecca: Debra, let Anna do what you needed to do – to say what she thinks and to be angry. You also needed to make an impact.
Anna: I couldn't talk to you, Mom *(sigh)* You weren't even around; you didn't want to listen.
Richard: Talk to her now, Anna.
Anna: *(pause)* She'll get angry at me.
Rebecca: Debra, you said you were going to let Anna do what she needed to do.
Anna: She'll blame me, she'll get mad at me, and she'll only hate me more.
Rebecca: Not anymore, Anna. I'm keeping her out of the way. You're not going to get any more from her by holding back. You know that not speaking up is a dead end. Go ahead and do what *you* need to do.
Anna: *(pause)* I needed you to protect me.
Richard: From?
Anna: How he looked at me. The way he made me feel.
Richard: Name it.
Anna: Dirty.
Richard: Keep going. "He made me feel dirty…" *(pause)* So tell the whole thing: "I needed you to…"
Anna: To protect me.
Richard: From feeling …
Anna: Dirty. That it was my fault. It was not my fault! You fix it *(She again slams her fist on the mat)*. You fix your marriage or get the fuck out of it! *(said very loudly)*
Richard: Hm. Tell her why you chose those words. "Get the fuck out of it."
Anna: *(to Richard)* I didn't want to be in the middle of it! You fix it *(she again slams her fist on the mat)*.
Richard: Tell her what you've been holding back from saying.
Anna: I didn't want to be in the middle, mom. It's your marriage. I don't want to hear it. What you are doing and not doing. It's not my business! Your marriage is not my business, your sex life is not my business, your problems are not my business, your kids are not my business. Your whole fucking world is yours, not mine.

Anna has made a powerful statement about her needs within the family system: "I don't want to be in the middle." Rebecca makes another interposition and confrontation of Debra on behalf of Anna. Such an interposition and confrontation often deconfuses a Child ego state. Anna no longer slumps, she continues with, "Your marriage is not my business," etc.

Richard: Is there anything else you want to say to her?
Anna: Yeah. I don't want to fix it – the fucking craziness in your marriage is your business not mine.
Richard: Then resign from the job, Anna. *(pause)* You could send your mother to ongoing therapy with Rebecca.
Anna: Permanently? She needs it.
Richard: Do you like that?
Anna: Um-hm. Definitely. *(pause)* I was kind of waiting for my father to die so she could live. She needed therapy to get out of her marriage just like I did. But, she died first.
Richard: Did she ever get what she needed?
Anna: *(crying)* No…*(pause while crying)* But, I will from now on. I'm going to have the life I want.
Richard: Anna, let's not let the same thing happen to you. Your time is *now* – your future has lots of possibilities.
Anna: Yeah… *(pause)* *(big sighs and eye contact with both Richard and Rebecca)*

This therapy session ends with Anna's declaration of emancipation, "I'm going to have the life I want." This following Anna's expression of her anger at her mother for failure to protect her from the conflicts of the parents' marriage. The dynamics of a discordant family system, and Anna's early childhood relationship with her mother, influenced the formation of Anna's life script – a script that is both the result of many of Anna's childhood conclusions and the introjection of mother's script beliefs: "I'm a nothing"; "I won't get what I want"; "I'm all alone"; "It's all my fault"; "People can't be trusted"; and "It (life) doesn't matter."

Anna's reaction to the dynamics of her parent's marriage and the accompanying anger had been retroflected for years. The therapist's protection, encouragement and prompting opened an opportunity for Anna to begin to express what had been pent-up for so long. The undoing of retroflections is an essential part of script cure. It is through physiological constriction that vital aspects of self-expression are contained and reinforced. Retroflections maintain life long script patterns of beliefs, behaviors, and physiological restrictions learned or decided upon in the original family. Although Anna's mother had been dead for several years, Anna's Child ego states remained loyal to the intrapsychically influencing Parent (Debra) ego state. The loyalty of children cannot be overemphasized – children naturally bond to parents and may remain attached to the memories (often unconscious) of the parent's psychological dynamics – their feelings, attitudes, psychological and interpersonal defenses, behavioral patterns and messages of attribution and injunction. Psychotherapy includes making the unconscious memories conscious; that includes the memories of one's own childhood experience, affect, decisions and defenses that are fixated in Child ego states, as well as the script beliefs, feelings, and defenses introjected from parents.

Many of Anna's script beliefs were both in Parent and Child ego states. Mother's influence and Anna's loyalty were both so strong that Anna's childhood experiences and conclusions were similar to her mother's. The defensive fixations of Anna's Child ego states clustered around the formation of script beliefs, the loss of awareness of her needs, and the retroflection of her natural expressions.

In the absence of need-satisfying contact with mother, Anna used a common defense. She disavowed her own needs and feelings, and, instead, identified with the feelings, thoughts, beliefs, and coping style of mother. Mother's script beliefs also become Anna's, via introjection. It is through the unconscious defensive identification with a significant other, in the absence of relational needs being satisfied, that Parent ego states are formed.

Introjections are maintained years later, because they provide a pseudo sense of attachment to significant others, and an archaic sense of identity and familiarity. Introjections are analogous to the invasion of foreign bacteria in the human body; they produce disease. The dis-ease of intrapsychic conflict between Parent and Child ego states is manifested as a loss of knowing what one desires, chronic anxiety, depression, a sense of constant self doubt, or internal criticism. An in-depth psychotherapy includes identifying and externalizing what has been internalized. The methods are similar to those used with a variety of clients to allow the opportunity for the defensive processes to be relaxed: phenomenological and historical inquiry, affective attunement, validation of relational needs, and caring confrontation. Then regressive therapy, redecisions, corrective explanations or therapeutic interpretations may be used, to deconfuse the Child ego states in an introjected Parent ego state. The therapist's caring involvement with a Parent ego state is like an antibiotic to the diseased body; it lessens the internal distress and facilitates a natural healing process. The goal of Parent ego state therapy is the alleviation of intrapsychic conflict.

In the first two-and-a-half years of therapy, Anna had made a number of significant changes that included no longer being depressed, the relinquishing of childhood script beliefs, increased job satisfaction, and a beginning interest in wanting a permanent love relationship. Anna's loneliness was triggered by a combination of the summer recess in our therapeutic relationship, the end of her busy schedule pursuing a master's degree, and a loss of hope in having a significant relationship. In reaction to the loneliness, Anna intrapsychically activated the introjected script beliefs of her mother – now she was not alone. Mother's psychic presence was always available. Mother's script beliefs provided a primitive sense of attachment and meaning.

Following this piece of Parent ego state therapy, Anna remained in individual therapy another year-and-a-half and attended three other weekend marathons. We continued to address her emotional reaction to her mother, her profound sadness about her family dynamics, and her sense of a lack of love throughout her life. Later, a significant aspect of her therapy was the resolution of her confused relationship with her father.

Her self-esteem continued to grow; she was in script less and less. There were some occasions, often accompanying disappointments in relationships, that the script beliefs would be active for a couple of hours. With continued therapeutic focus on both the Child and Parent ego states origin of those beliefs, the exploration of new meanings for life's events, and the discovery of current options, her life script has ceased to be operative. She is now free to live her own life without intrapsychic conflict. Recently she has fallen in love with a partner who cherishes her.

Chapter 7

EGO STATES:
a personal reflection
Diana Shmukler

The beginning of the new century is an opportune time to evaluate the relevance of TA and particularly one of Berne's central and original contributions: the notion of ego states. This chapter will address this question in the light of the current thinking in the field and the changes that have taken place. I will consider a number of instances and examples where I have found the ego state model valuable. Further, I will take a critical view and discuss the limitations as I understand them. What I am aiming for is a picture of strengths and weaknesses across both orientations and contexts. Thus, I will begin with a contextualisation both in terms of culture, orientation and perspective. I will argue the case through the inclusion of a broad theoretical frame in addition to examples and applications from my experience. I am concerned with relevance, applications and clinical implications – though not necessarily in any specific order.

Since this is a subjective perspective, I need to introduce the work with some biographical and personal details so that I can establish a context for my thinking. I was born in South Africa to European parents, who emigrated there shortly before the Second World War. The reason why this is important is that I grew up, was educated, and received much of my professional experience in a highly politicised – and also culturally diverse and racially defined – society. These factors both colour and inform my perspective on life, on the work and on my ideas.

South Africa is a country that has recently been through a massive upheaval and change, managing to transform itself politically against all predictions. Although the transformation has brought in its wake a lot of turmoil and insecurity, it points to a situation of radical change and suggests the possibility of encompassing diversity and difference. The 'Truth and Reconciliation Commission' has won international acclaim and recognition for its extraordinary attempt to develop a shared history. This endeavour helps lay the ground for enabling South Africans to create a multiracial society and come to terms with a violent and difficult past.

How then is this background connected to ego states? Early in my academic career as a young member of staff on a highly politicised and radical campus, I was confronted with questions of relevance. What is the relevance of academic Western Psychology when the problems facing the country are of such an urgent and extreme nature? I was hard put to find answers. What

was, however, clear to me even then was that if we cannot solve:
- the one-on-one problems,
- the nature and meaning of prejudice and racial hatred, and
- the extreme position that people are willing to adopt in the service of preserving cultural identity and cultural integrity,

then all the political rhetoric in the world leads to a transfer of power, but no real change in the society.

I see social sciences, particularly psychology and even more specifically psychotherapy, as one of the most relevant disciplines at this moment in history. In the hundred years or so since Freud's groundbreaking work, we have come some way in terms of individual psychology. We know something about internal processes and also about interpersonal dialogue. The challenge for the new century is to develop a better understanding and a powerful psychology of large groups, systems, organisations and institutions. Linked to these ideas is the need for an understanding of the impact of cultural identity and diversity on the individual personality.

When we turn to the intrapsychic and interpersonal psychology, TA in general and ego states in particular have a contribution to make across fairly broad contexts. So this is my first point. TA, and the language of ego states, has an immediate intuitive appeal, providing accessible psychological know-ledge to people without a presupposition of education, academic background or even a western orientation to life. Certainly in South Africa notions such as Parent, Adult and Child, with their universal and readily grasped meaning, made it possible to describe complex psychological ideas for most South Africans, irrespective of their backgrounds or levels of education.

My experience of working in South Africa across very diverse situations, population groups and contexts was that teaching people some basic TA, particularly the theory and practical applications of ego state models, provides a shared language within which one can work psychologically, with access to peoples' inner and outer worlds. Furthermore, in any developmental work, the flexibility and richness of the model of ego states makes it possible to keep working at ever-increasing levels of depth and complexity. This says a great deal about the relevance and universality of the ideas.

I turn now to the theoretical frames. As a student, I was educated in a behavioural approach to psychology. Such an approach was and remains widely used in many schools, creating a particular legacy of experimental and behaviourally based psychology. I was also left – as were many of my con-temporaries – with little understanding of how this approach to people, mind, consciousness, and particularly to psychotherapy, was helpful or especially relevant. Many of the institutions, including mental hospitals, adolescent units and prisons, also based their approaches to treatment almost entirely on behaviourally oriented programmes. Undoubtedly, addressing behaviour is sometimes not only necessary, but critical, in illnesses such as eating problems as well as many other severe forms of behavioural disturbance. Nevertheless, as broad-based solutions to complex situations such as I have described, these programmes are severely limited.

In the absence of psychoanalytical thinking to inform their work, South African therapists in the '60s and '70s had to rely on the alternatives available at the time. Beyond the behavioural tradition, humanistic and existential attitudes were gradually introduced. Carl Rogers visited South Africa twice, and his ideas had a powerful impact on a generation of mental-health professionals.

The person-centred approach is particularly useful and relevant in training counsellors and others in listening skills which, of course, form the basis for many useful and effective psychological processes. However, there is a limitation to how far one can move people without the core understandings of how a developmental process will shape the adult personality. When TA was introduced it filled this deficit for many mental health professionals by providing a built-in developmental model. TA thus provided both the developmental model and the possibility of working within a therapeutic relationship, thereby allowing for work with the transference and countertransference dynamic.

I see TA as a highly flexible approach to therapy, counselling and many other fields of interpersonal or intrapsychic work. As such, it provides a good entry point. However it naturally also has limitations in complex situations. Where the limitations are apparent, I believe that there is a need for models that allow for explanation of unconscious processes. In the discussion below I will repeatedly come back to this point and illustrate it as I consider the various contexts.

Political contexts

I feel an ever-increasing sense of urgency for social scientists of all persuasions to address the larger issues confronting us as a species at this time. It seems to me that time, energy and resources should be committed to developing models and understanding beyond interpersonal and intrapsychic functioning, to that of larger systems and groups. After September 11th, this sense of urgency can only increase. We desperately need to understand the forces at play that create such a need for violence and vengeance. Our present explanations are extremely limited.

The conceptualisation offered below does not address or offer the kind of explanation that I believe is necessary, but is merely a preliminary and superficial step. My belief is that an understanding of the unconscious processes in groups, systems and organisations is required. This thinking is complex and sophisticated and needs to be developed with a good understanding of unconscious processes as well as systems thinking. To date, the people working in the group relations field have the best contribution to make in the development of meaningful models (see, for example, the Tavistock Model as developed by A.K. Rice and others from Bion's earlier ideas (Miller & Rice, in Colman & Bexton 1975)). It is also necessary to consider issues of identity and identity formation and how these issues are related to group membership and culture. The discourse that encompasses such thinking has little connection to ego state theory. Although one could make some connection, the value of doing so is questionable.

I illustrate this point with an experience I had some years ago at a group relations conference in England that was attended by participants from many countries. At some point during the two-week period we were invited to form ourselves into small groups in a very short space of time. This process usually happens without much conscious discussion or awareness. There were about 70 participants in total in the large conference, but I had spent most of my time until that point in a smaller group. Barely knowing the other participants, I 'found' myself in a group of about fourteen people, eleven of whom were South Africans, ex-South Africans or Jewish. This was a powerful illustration based on personal experience of how people intuitively form themselves into like groups in terms of identity, cultural background and even the less obvious characteristics of race, through the unconscious processes in a group. This phenomenon cannot be explained by ego state theory.

There are other ways, however, in which the notion of ego states can be useful in this arena. Although clearly a simplification of complicated historical and political dynamics, the notion of Parent, Adult and Child as an entry point is helpful in understanding and describing power relationships and dynamics. Further, the difference between a parental transaction, whether controlling or protective, and an adult relationship, is a powerful and important distinction to make; in South Africa, where the family structures are primarily paternalistic and authoritarian, this comparison is powerfully evident.

As I have elaborated elsewhere (Shmukler 2001) the strength and weakness of TA lie in the language and the accessibility of the concepts. The introduction of TA into the field in the early '70s was met with excitement and enthusiasm. It was instantly recognised as a highly useful and potentially relevant way to lead people into psychological understandings in numerous settings and with a number of different problems. By providing an intuitive map, it proved to be readily accepted and widely used in many mental health settings.

In an early unpublished paper relating TA to the political situation in South Africa under a white government, I described how clear it was to us that the whites were in the parent position and all other races were in some sort of child position. Each of the significant racial groups could be seen as occupying a sub-system, and these would be related to the whole as the ego states are connected to each other. A powerful example would be the so-called 'coloured' race which, in the South African nomenclature then prevailing, referred to a mixed-race person, i.e., neither African nor European. They readily saw themselves as the stepchildren of the white government, disadvantaged in not being classified with the white group although identifying themselves with the [white] Afrikaners in terms of both language and religion. The most pertinent aspect of this conceptualisation for people was the clear lack of adult-to-adult relating or a space for such contact to occur.

There remain many situations in the current climate in South Africa in which I find the use of the language of ego states helpful in people's understanding of situations. In most contexts that involve authority and power, an explanation that includes Parent/Child is readily grasped and enables people to consider their options. Specifically, they recognise that they can call on an adult structure and negotiate a different relationship, rather than automatically accepting a child position. Providing people with an ego state model is experienced as empowering and helpful.

Organisational contexts
Organisational contexts are among those in which the ego state model is both helpful and effective in promoting understanding and providing a language for psychological awareness, in terms of individual dynamics and interpersonal situations. Where authority, power and conflict are involved as described above, an ego state model has immediate and intuitive appeal. The challenge for facilitators of processes is to cathect and maintain Adult functioning in these situations. This involves encouraging dialogue and creative problem-solving and the use of script, or racket system, to promote self-understanding. Feedback, performance reviews, other performance-related indicators and task- and work-related functions are all relevant to invoking adult behaviour and responses. While the ego state model is not sufficient to explain all unconscious organisational systems, it can certainly be enormously and immediately useful in contexts where there is a major demand for Adult functioning, while many situations are evoking either Parent or Child responses. The ego state model that is usually taught and used in organisations tends to be a simplified one, such as the functional model. The usefulness of this model is that it is related to behaviour. However, use of Berne's (1961) original model of ego states, which is a more phenomenological model, allows for the possibility of greater understanding and insight. Intuitively, people will respond to the notion that we have introjected or internalised the real person of our parents, and that we can slip into their behaviour and responses outside our awareness.

I have found in organisational systems that a consideration of the Parent ego state, from many different aspects, is highly relevant. It seems that people bring their Parent ego state – and particularly their experience and views of their fathers – to bear in the work situation. Working with leaders of organisations to help them recognise how Parent ego state functions (both positive and negative) are being attributed to them while, at the same time, how they are inclined to adopt Parent ego state characteristics and attitudes, proves extremely fruitful. It is especially interesting to see how not just men's, but also women's behaviour at work, seems to be very influenced by their fathers. Women who had good relationships with their fathers when growing up, and in many ways were 'daddy's little girl', are able to handle powerful men at work with an ease and comfort that women growing up with an experience of distant and intimidating fathers, are not. Where their fathers were absent, authoritarian, distant or otherwise frightening, even highly competent and powerful women often lose their adult functioning in the face of their male bosses and counterparts.

Clinical applications

As I consider ego states in psychotherapy, it is clear that Berne's (1961) original understanding of ego states provides a powerful umbrella description of the most usually occurring dynamic in the therapeutic relationship. The parent/child dialogue forms much of the ongoing nature of clinical process. Many of the examples described below can readily be conceptualised in this frame. On the other hand, although this description fits, the second order structure, working with Child or Parent ego state, and many of the recent approaches to a developmental relational TA (for example Moiso 1985, Moiso & Novellino 2000, Novellino 1984, 1985, Hargaden & Sills 2001, 2002), encompass a greater sophistication of detail, allowing for a refined analysis. However, generally there is a lack of model that enables one to talk about unconscious processes, which leaves a problem in providing a fuller and sometimes essential understanding. Berne himself, being psycho-analytically trained and having himself had two very experienced analysts as his own therapists, clearly used an understanding of unconscious dynamics and assumed that future TA therapists/analysts would be as well grounded as he was in basic psycho-analytical theory (see Novellino, pp. 149-168 in this volume). Unfortunately, as we well know, many TA practitioners are not well versed in psycho-analytic thinking, often have not done enough personal work and are not sufficiently in touch with their own issues. In other words, they would not be sufficiently aware – and not trained well enough – to consider what they may be needing to act out or project into the therapeutic situation.

One of the most worrying examples of this problem is when a therapist projects their own unresolved issues into/onto the client and then proceeds to try and cure it in the other. I suspect that this dynamic is widespread. This problem could be lessened where there is an awareness of the tendency, and a serious attempt to work with it in supervision. Such awareness presupposes an understanding and recognition of such an easily occurring potentiality. Here too there is a distinction between work that can productively be pursued using an ego state model, and that demanding greater complexity and work with unconscious dynamics.

Brief-term work, many counselling and supportive relationships, some couples work, coaching and mentoring, can all benefit from the use of an ego state model. Clients often find both the language and the conceptualisation helpful. Again, where one wishes to deepen the insight and understanding, listening for the unconscious messages becomes imperative. Although Berne (1961, 1966/1994) recognised and described the covert levels of communication (for example, game theory is a particularly powerful use of the notion of projective identification), the more general use of TA does not have an easy access to these processes.

As described above, I have used and found TA in general, and its two most significant and original contributions, i.e., that of ego states and the other of script, to be extremely useful. In my early days as a clinician, these notions helped me move my clinical work forward and provided me with a map that was both elegant and powerful. I was able to think developmentally and systemically, and also work both intrapsychically as well as interpersonally with these ideas as a theoretical backdrop.

Further, I found that the combination of TA and the trauma and crisis work that I was doing in South Africa had made me willing and able to work with high levels of affect. I am very willing to invite affective responses and do not back off from them. In fact, I felt not only encouraged, but confident, that the way forward clinically was to evoke and support affective reactions. I do not feel any of this is wrong or inappropriate today, but rather that clinical work is more complex than striving for catharsis even with concurrent insight.

My own understanding and clinical work has changed irrevocably since I have had the opportunity to integrate psychoanalytic theory into my practice. As I have understood the subtle and complex effects of the transference-countertransference context within which we always work, I experience an ego state model as limited.

In considering the limitations, it would be useful for me to examine the way I have moved in my own understanding of psychotherapy. Using a broad definition of therapy as a helping relationship, and seeing that the therapeutic aspects lie very directly in the relationship, increasingly I have found that attention needs to be paid to the unconscious dimensions. Berne, with his psycho-analytic background, never lost sight of this understanding; explicitly or implicitly, he would have taken into account the unconscious as well as the conscious elements of his therapeutic relationships.

TA can open up and provide a base for some work into people's psyches, and be very useful in providing insight and understanding to individuals about their internal processes. The notion of scripts and the patterns that we create - and how we bring our past into influencing the present - speaks to these insights that TA provides. Nonetheless, the loss of the rigour of working with and understanding unconscious relationship elements - particularly one's own countertransference reactions - leads to an impoverished work and understanding.

Of course, many situations do not demand the sophisticated reading of the unspoken and implicit communications that lie between people. However, I believe that when we embark on intensive long-term, in-depth psychotherapy, it becomes impossible not to work with the unconscious dynamic and, as a therapist, one's own unconscious contributions to the relationship. The problem with an approach to clinical work that does not begin from this frame is that it becomes increasingly difficult to introduce it later on. Also, much valuable insight and understanding is lost. Where we create a therapeutic situation in which the therapist conducts or facilitates the understanding and/or growth of the patient, but neglects the unconscious relationship, the opportunity is available for all kinds of acting out processes, as described below.

I do not wish to suggest that psychoanalytic treatment is the 'cure-all' of therapies. Many of the patients I have worked with or heard about in supervision would not have been able to have worked psycho-analytically; or they would not have stayed in psycho-analysis; or they may have in fact experienced some psycho-analytic treatment, and though helped somewhat, still needed some other form of treatment. So there are clear limitations in psychoanalytic approaches over and above the lengthy and expensive form of treatment.

On the other hand, I can be equally critical of humanistic approaches in general, and TA approaches in particular. By not addressing or fully working with and understanding the unconscious aspects of the transference dynamic, many enactments - and acting out of unconscious processes, particularly those of the therapist - occur. Conflict can be avoided, and the therapist can maintain a picture of themselves as, for example, nurturing or indispensable.

There is an explicit as well as an implicit need, and often a mandatory requirement, for therapists to do their own therapy and understand their issues. In terms of ego states, it is here that although a Parent/Child description can be used, it does not capture the complexity and subtlety of these projective phenomena. Casement (1985) says:

> Working in the transference is demanding and complex. It stresses the need to deal with conscious and unconscious processes. That which is unconscious is by definition, out of awareness. This can be true with countertransference as well as transference...close supervision is required if the therapist is to become aware of what he or she may unconsciously be communicating to patients.
>
> (in Shmukler 2001, p. 98)

Relational psychotherapy
In the remainder of this chapter, I shall describe some of the key elements of an effective relational psychotherapy, that both contain and transcend the original concept of ego states. I would describe the essence of relational therapy as demanding a full engagement in the relationship, in the present, while at the same time being aware of the unconscious meaning of the interaction. This demands an understanding from the therapist about who he/she becomes in the mind of the patient. Usually, this is some parent figure and an aspect of the Parent ego state. At the same time, it can be a shifting transference, that will, at times, require the therapist to take up the child position, in order for the patient to communicate something about the experience of their early childhood; an experience that is out of their awareness, and one which they cannot communicate in words.

Becoming 'someone who...'
Interventions of this nature, i.e., "who do I become in your mind?" which I

would conceptualise as working with the transference, requires the therapist to be working at two levels, at least, at the same time. First, the therapist steps into the projection, taking it as some reflection of what is going on in the here-and-now between her/him and the patient. Simultaneously, the therapist must understand that there is an influence from the past at play here. By working in this way, I find it is possible to maximise the use of the self and the relationship – and, at the same time – to include the understanding of those powerful notions of projection, projective identification, etc. This conceptu-alisation does not rest on the notion of ego states.

I have found that working in this way enables me to hold in mind or work with both the conscious and unconscious processes. Somehow, although who I become is often clearly a manifestation of a Parent ego state, I have found that that interpretation is not sufficient in and of itself. I do not necessarily experience myself as parental, but have a much more complex counter-transference. In fact, I often avoid making interpretations about specific parents; for example, I become "someone who...", as in, 'someone who might criticise you/reject you/judge you etc".

On being organised by the patient

Being organised by the patient is a way I describe what I am striving to do in sessions. By this, I mean I work towards creating the space in the room to allow the patient to organise me, and then understand that organisation in terms of what it means for the relationship. For example, a patient recently said to me, quite critically, that I spoke a lot in a particular session. In fact, she went on to say, since working with me she found she was talking more to her own patients. The next week she commented that I seemed to have spoken much less. I reflected on the two sessions, and found there was not a marked difference in my own mind about how I had interacted with her. What was clear to me, however, was that if I had indeed been less active in the second session, this had been in direct response to what was being mobilised in me at that time.

I would extend this notion further and say that more and more I allow the process or the situation to organise me in some way, and then read my reactions or responses as relevant to the situation. For me, this is close to Bion's (1978) 'beyond memory or desire'. It is something about being in an open state of mind on entering into a situation, in order to be as fully present in the here and now as possible; a place that is difficult to reach and hold. Further, it involves paying attention to my inner process and thoughts, in other words, seeking a state of free association or reverie. I do not find it particularly useful to attempt to describe work of this nature in ego state terms.

Conspiring to act out an unconscious need

As soon as one changes any boundary condition in the therapeutic contract, the way is laid open for an enactment or acting-out situation. It is not necessary to deliberately create such situations in therapy. The ordinary vicissitudes of the work will allow for such contingencies to occur. All one needs to do is be alert to the possibility and optimise it as it arises. For example, when I was teaching at a large University, a client of mine who had a great fear of exposure and humiliation, would, nonetheless, walk into one of my classes when she was not registered for that course. I pointed out to her that by doing so, she was inviting me to stop the class, ask her to leave, and thereby become an agent of great humiliation to her.

Meeting the need and not responding to the want

In many instances, the patient's need is for the boundary to be firmly held even as they wish to have their wants responded to. Developmentally, many parents and children confuse needs and wants. An often-unrecognised need, that contradicts the child's felt want, is the case where the child needs firm boundaries and the parents need to risk their anger in the holding of these. The same can be true of the patient in the therapeutic relationship.

One of the ways I have managed the need to provide a holding environment, practising weekly sessions, is to offer various forms of telephone contact. Changing boundaries and the way one practises opens new opportunities or possibilities for acting-out, as well as understanding and being able to access and work with a transference dynamic.

On one occasion, I had agreed that a patient could phone me for brief moments of support, with the understanding that my mobile phone might not always be switched on. This arrangement had proved satisfactory and worked well in the past, as the issue was about being able to feel the connection, but not necessarily for lengthy contact. On this occasion, I had given the patient times during which I would be able to talk. I was about to start work with another patient, when the phone rang; I had forgotten to turn off my phone and the patient had called exactly on the time boundary. Between us, we had created the situation for the patient to experience me as abrupt and unresponsive; in fact to be treated exactly like a 'patient'. Of course, the patient *is* a patient, but in the room a patient is often unaware of how they may be seen from the outside.

Painful as this experience proved to be for both patient and therapist, it also proved to be very important. The patient was unconsciously pushing to experience the boundary and have a therapist hold them while also managing the emotional reaction (i.e., the anger and the experience of frustration). This example had very much to do with meeting the need rather than the want. It could be thought of in terms of a failure in empathy and thus a transmuting internalisation of recognition of the failure and responding to it. Of course, it can be described in ego state terms; for example, the need of the Child ego state to experience a clear and boundaried parental figure. Some therapists may find it correspondingly containing to understand this experience theoretically. However, I feel that such a description neither furthers the work nor encapsulates the experience in the conceptualisation.

Sounds like TA ... but is it?
There is naturally a great variety of therapeutic contexts in which, one way or another, the therapist will be seen or experienced as a parent - usually, a critical or controlling parent. What I have come to in my work is to not make an immediate or obvious transference interpretation or other direct allusion to this, but rather to stay with the understanding that I have become, and may even feel, like a critical parent in those moments. Naturally, therefore, the patient is most likely to respond as a child and would certainly be in a regressed state of mind. The clinical challenge for the therapist is to work with their own feelings of criticism and not act them out in some way.

One of the most significant clinical examples that I can offer, to illustrate how my own thinking and work has changed as a therapist, comes from a very long therapy during which I had changed considerably in my style of work. Previously, I was working in what could be described as a blend of humanistic/developmental TA, which had an element of re-parenting and a strong emphasis on working with the regressed Child ego state. Gradually, I began to realise the limitations and problems associated with this way of working. I became aware of the invitation to further acting out, of an almost addictive quality to the client's need for nurturing. I also began to see the danger of the therapist acting out their own unconscious agenda in the situation. I began to shift in style to a therapist who was not practising a physically holding and/or touching style of therapy.

At one point in the treatment, my patient had wanted to go to a workshop run by a therapist who included a lot of re-parenting style therapy, with physical holding of adult clients in regressed states, a style of TA very popular in the '80s and '90s. We discussed the meaning of her attending this particular workshop at length. In my view, going to this workshop would be a direct attack on our work, and I made this interpretation directly and clearly. In her next session she asked me if I had changed my mind. I commented that this sounded exactly as if she were asking my permission, whereas I had made an interpretation based on my understanding and, therefore, that was still how I understood the situation. Now, of course this can sound like a parent/child transaction, and that is how the client read it. However, simply explaining it that way misses something of the confrontation being made to me and to the therapy, particularly as earlier in my practise I may have worked that way myself. This specific struggle between us, in which I remained firm and clear, proved to be one of those significant moments in our work together.

Working in the here-and-now; "getting it into the room"
As I am being experienced as the real person who is doing something real in the relationship, I also am aware that the work is happening in the relationship - in the room, and in the here-and-now. Usually this process occurs by projective identification or unconscious communication. The most powerful moments in therapy are those moments when the transference experience becomes real between therapist and patient. I am talking of those moments

when, as therapist, you actually do let the patient down, in the classic ways of forgetting appointments, making changes etc. Mistakes made in accounts, around names and biographical details, are all ways in which therapists are capable of getting it wrong even when they work very hard to get it right

Thus, I see a significant clinical challenge as 'getting the process into the room'. Every year I go to South Africa during the European winter. This is a time of year when therapists do not traditionally take a break. Over a number of winters, we had tried different ways for a particular long-term patient to manage this difficult break in the work. In the first year, the patient went back to a previous therapist. In a subsequent year, she tried someone from a different orientation, and then the following year an art therapist. Each of these excursions led both to productive work, and to problems.

By the fourth year, I was aware that one of the crucial elements to the work needed to be how to get the process/state of mind experienced in my absence, into the room and between us, rather than expressed to caretaker therapists or via mail. At about this time in the work, I had begun shifting in my approach (as described above), and had made a decision in my own mind to extract myself from any form of physically holding patients. In order to implement this decision, I moved across the room into a separate chair; previously the patient and I had sat side by side on a couch, an arrangement that had been experienced by the patient as creating a powerful connection between us. By my moving across the room into an independent seat, I had suddenly, and unexpectedly, created the experience in the patient's mind of being very far away.

When the patient said to me "I feel as if you are thousands of miles away" - while, in reality, I was just a few yards across the room, I realised that, fortunately, I had managed to re-create the psychological experience of my being a long way away *in that moment*. Once that objective had been achieved, it was possible to work directly with the separation/abandonment experience between us, rather than one that was being reported to me on my return and after the event.

Couples therapy

Early stages of couples work and brief work with couples can be fruitfully conceptualised in ego state terms. Many cognitive behavioural approaches (including contracts, describing Parent/Child interactions and so on) to this work rest on some notion of ego states. However, when one needs to work in more depth with the dynamics in the couple's relationship, it again becomes necessary to think about the underlying dynamics and beyond an ego state model.

People form partnerships for powerful conscious and unconscious reasons. Where relationships run into problems, these reflect that peculiar paradoxical element that the positive choice of a mate, in the sense of freeing a person from the script, often also contains the script-reinforcing elements. In these instances, the use of TA, the notions of ego states and scripts, and similar understandings of self-perpetuating repeating patterns are extremely relevant and helpful. However, sometimes the relationship dynamic has to do with one partner *carrying feelings on behalf of the couple*. I find it simpler to conceptualise in these terms, rather than in ego state terminology, because of the latter's tendency to lock the patient into an unnecessary mind-set of a parent-child dynamic.

For example, a couple came in to therapy because the man had contacted me with the request that I see his partner, whom he described as very insecure. Something about the way he tried to make the appointment for her prompted me to suggest that they come together. Undoubtedly she was insecure - and partly for good reason. He had been attempting to create a contract with her whereby it would be perfectly permissible for him to have other relationships, since an 'open relationship' would be agreed up-front. She was reluctantly trying to make sense of this arrangement, when she happened to meet and go out with another man. When her husband became greatly distressed by this reversal, it became clear that she had been carrying and holding the insecurity of infidelity for both of them. Certainly one can describe this situation in ego state terms and talk about the switching Parent/Child positions. It was simpler and clinically clearer for me, however, to think about the powerful projective processes between them.

Summary and conclusions
In this chapter I have taken a wide-angled perspective on the notion of ego states. By being one of the first relational theorists, Eric Berne provided us with a theory and a language that has found wide application and relevance. In addition, his model carries an implicit and explicit developmental base that enhances its clinical strength. Certainly, through the second half of the last century, his original and in many ways unique and powerful conceptualisation has contributed to and found applications in many areas of interpersonal and intrapsychic work. I have briefly touched on different applications and provided examples from my own experience. Although this discussion is highly personal, I have been privileged and fortunate to work across many contexts and cultures, and in different roles. In all these situations, I have found myself at times greatly helped by my knowledge and understanding of TA. On the other hand, I would also have been limited if this were the sole means at my disposal. Consequently, I have presented strengths and weaknesses, advantages and limitations, in order to produce as rounded a perspective as possible.

In conclusion, I would sum up by saying that the greatest strength of the notion of ego states lies in its being an initial approach - a way of opening up the work and leading people into a psychological understanding of themselves and others. The idea of separate and independent states of the ego that co-exist in all of our inner worlds is hugely powerful, clinically useful and eminently practical. As is well known, there is nothing as practical as a good theory. The theory of ego states qualifies for this statement. Further, through its roots in psychoanalysis, TA marries well with many contemporary approaches and integrates into most modern relational/developmental views of human relationships and dynamics. However, as we work towards greater complexity and depth, and we are impelled to address issues of race, colour, politics, large group behaviour and violence, new and different ideas, theories, and even paradigms, become essential.

References:

Berne, E. (1961) *Transactional Analysis in Psychotherapy,* New York: Random House

Berne, E. (1994) *Principles of Group Treatment.* Menlo Park, Ca: Shea Books. (First Published. 1966)

Bion, W. (1978) *Second Thoughts.* London: Heineman

Hargaden, H. and Sills, C (2001) Deconfusion of the Child: a relational perspective *Transactional Analysis Journal* 31(1) 55-70

Hargaden, H. & Sills, C (2002) *Transactional Analysis - A Relational Perspective,* London: Routledge.

Moiso, C.M. (1985) Ego states and transference. *Transactional Analysis Journal* 15(3) 194-201

Moiso, M. & Novellino, M. (2000) An overview of the psychodynamic school of transactional analysis and its epistemological foundations. *Transactional Analysis Journal* 30(3) 182-187

Novellino, M. (1984) Self-analysis of countertransference. *Transactional Analysis Journal* 14(1) 63-67

Novellino, M. (1985). Redecision analysis of transference: a TA approach to transference neurosis. *Transactional Analysis Journal,* 15(3) 202-206

Shmukler, D. (2001) Reflections on Transactional Analysis in the context of contemporary relational approaches. *Transactional Analysis Journal,* 31(2) 94-102

Chapter 8

ON CLOSER ANALYSIS
Unconscious communication in the Adult ego state and a revision of the rules of communication within the framework of Transactional Psychoanalysis

Michele Novellino

Transactional analysis, like all the other schools of psychotherapy, has been going through significant changes - particularly in the last decade. The January 2001 issue of *Transactional Analysis Journal* (Daellenbach 2001) on schizoid personality, for example, is full of psychoanalytic references; names like Fairbairn, Stern, Kohut and others recur. I find this gratifying, as my approach to transactional analysis has leant this way since the beginning (Novellino 1982).

Nevertheless, a closer examination of the psychoanalytic movement reveals more than just a *comparison*. Instead, we can increasingly recognise how deep the psychoanalytic roots of Berne's work have always been. Freud (1905) considered that the distinctive elements of psychoanalytic treatment were the centrality of transference and resistance. Today, both of these terms have evolved, but if we pay close attention to what Freud actually said, we have no difficulty in placing transactional analysis within the category of psychoanalytic therapy. Furthermore, Berne, in different sections of his work, highlights the central importance of transference phenomena (1961, 1966, 1972), and defines the transactional analyst as a *para-freudian* (1972). In fact, I would argue that transactional analysis should be described as one of the derivations of contemporary psychoanalysis. As such, it needs the articulation of another form of transaction that is central to psychotherapy.

Bateman and Holmes (1995) have identified a fundamental element shared by the various schools of psychoanalysis – namely the central importance of the interaction between patient and therapist. In other words, the phenomena that form Sandler's (1994) so-called 'present unconscious' and which are also described by G. Klein's (1976) 'clinical theory'. As transactional analysts, we are familiar with Berne's methodology firmly focusing on the transactions that occur in the therapeutic setting, whether it be group (Berne 1961, 1966) or individual (Novellino 1998). For this reason, transactional analysis clearly demonstrates that fundamental element described by Bateman and Holmes.

Berne identifies three fundamental types of transactions (complementary, crossed and ulterior), all of which can be identified within the therapeutic relationship. Crossed transactions involve transference and countertransference. Type I transaction is called 'transference'. The patient reacts to the Adult-Adult stimulus, offered by the psychotherapist, with a Child-Parent response. That is, he or she behaves as if he or she had perceived the stimulus as originating from the therapist's Parent Ego state. Berne defines this type of crossed transaction as essential to describe many of the existing conflicts inside relationships. He also introduces the Type II crossed transaction, called 'countertransference'. To an Adult-Adult stimulus offered by the patient, the psychotherapist, in his or her turn, answers from Parent-Child, as if he had perceived the patient in the Child Ego state. In other words these transactions are seen as script driven and leading to 'pay-off'. Similarly, ulterior transactions are seen as the script-laden messages underlying the social level of transaction, and leading to script reinforcement.

Berne however, while addressing the problem of transference in various chapters in his work, in fact limits his theory, in terms of transactional analysis proper, to these simplified concepts. In particular, there is no explicit mention of transference when he deals with the rules of communication (the first rule in 1963, the second and the third in 1966). The first rule is applied to complementary transactions, and establishes that a communication based upon them can proceed indefinitely; the second rule is applied to crossed transactions and establishes that a communication based upon them comes to a stop or interruption; the third rule affirms that a communication based upon ulterior transactions has a behavioural outcome defined mainly at the psychological level.

In 1964, Berne, referring to these rules, maintains that they are independent of the transaction's *nature* and *content*, and that hence they are based upon the *vector direction*. I consider this clarification to be enlightening. Berne seems to ignore the importance that those excluded factors may have to the outcome of the communication, thereby giving the vector direction an exclusive meaning, and, inevitably therefore, a reductive one as well.

McCormick (1977) has already highlighted how it is possible to hypothesise as many as seven types of complementary transactions, and even seventy-two types of crossed transactions. Referring to this data, Massey (1991) maintains that Berne considered only one type of crossed transaction (the one defined as Type I) to illustrate the transference phenomenon transactionally, while every type of crossed transaction, except the ones which involve the neo-psychic Ego state, should be seen as transference sequences. Undoubtedly Berne, with the two types of crossed transactions, which he called transference and countertransference, opened the way for an important interpersonal process of therapeutic communication. It is now up to us to widen, update, and render it consistent with the initial formulation of transference theory - the psychoanalytical one. I have already devoted years of theoretical research in this direction (Novellino 1984, 1985, 1987, 1990), and I believe that we can develop a psychodynamic theory of therapeutic communication.

The transactional analyst is familiar with the notion of the 'contaminated' transaction – one that conveys, outside awareness, the Child or Parent transference message and which invites the therapist into a game. However, to explain all unconscious transactions simply in terms of transference regression to Child, is to ignore the reality of the here-and-now, co-created relationship between therapist and client and its unconscious processes. I propose therefore, another level of unconscious psychological level transaction, which is located in the Adult ego state. Its aim is not to further script but to convey to the therapist the patient's experience of him or her in a way that reveals script but does not act on it. This invites the therapist into a different way of working and inevitably calls for a psychodynamic revision of the rules of communication. This chapter aims to examine the use of the rules of communication in the light of transference theory, referring particularly to the theory of unconscious communication within the Adult ego state.

Transactional psychoanalysis?

I start here with a review of TA as a contemporary psychoanalysis in order to differentiate it from other approaches using the theory. To illustrate, I offer a 'virtual' therapeutic example to illustrate the main differences and similarities between current schools of transactional analysis, as well as the inevitable idiosyncrasies of the therapist's style, and the patient's clinical situation.

The patient, at the beginning of the session, says: "Listen...I really can't do the things that you tell me to do....you told me to pay attention to what happens between my wife and me when we argue, but I really can't think after we argue... I'm starting to think that this therapy isn't right for me... months have passed and nothing has really changed..."

Let us try to imagine how therapists from different schools might respond to this situation. A *classical school* therapist would probably invite the patient to consider the ego state from which he/she is communicating (in the above example, it is the Adapted Child), either in order to encourage a cathexis of the Adult ego state, or perhaps to analyse the psychological games that the patient is presenting to the therapist (in this case 'Wooden Leg'). A *redecision school* therapist, and also one from the *integrative-eclectic school*, might first invite the patient to change his/her "I can't" to "I don't want to", to recover his/her own personal power. Then he might move into contractual regressive work that invites the patient into a Child ego state, recalling a childhood scene where the patient may have decided to give up his/her ability to think. The injunction, (either Don't Think, or another one to which the patient responded by deciding not to think) presumed intrapsychically to be in P_1, would be 'personified' in a remembered character.

A *re-parenting school* therapist might identify or confront discounting (of personal abilities in the above example) and passivity (doing nothing), using ego states in the analysis of the symbiotic consequences that are implicit in the situation.

A *psychodynamic school* therapist will focus his/her intervention on transference and countertransference mechanisms that are inferred from the patient's assertions. The central theme will be the deeper meaning within the analytical relationship, of what the patient is saying. For example, the attempt to project onto the therapist, his/her feelings of devaluation and distrust of changing. This way of thinking and working differs from other approaches to transactional analysis and is wholly compatible with the thinking of contemporary psychoanalysis.

A number of facts support this statement:

1 Psychoanalysis, from a theory based on instinct has, since Klein (1948) and especially Sullivan (1964), moved towards understanding psychopathology in terms of interpersonal concepts of development. Its emphasis has therefore focused increasingly on the therapeutic relationship.

2 Transference and resistance remain the unifying clinical areas of the psychoanalyst's and the psychoanalytically-oriented psychotherapist's interventions.

3 'Interpretation', which was originally understood to be based on the 'logic' of the therapist, is seen today as more based on intuition and empathy.

4 The unconscious is 'something' that is always present during therapeutic interaction and cannot be eliminated.

The major misunderstanding of transactional analysis is that it is a 'humanistic psychotherapy' and thus different from the psychoanalytic and behavioural movements (Clarkson, 1992). I believe that there has always been confusion on this issue (Novellino, 1990). Humanistic psychology (Rogers, May, Maslow, etc.) is a 'movement' of ideology and values in relation to the nature of the individual and to the psychologist's role. This ideology goes beyond any metapsychological or methodological positions. To place transactional analysis in this movement is to undermine the depth of the Bernean theoretical foundation, and, paradoxically, to impoverish its revolutionary nature. It is necessary to separate the philosophical level (humanistic-existential) from the theoretical-methodological level (psycho-analytical) of the approach.

Within the psychodynamic school, all of Berne's work can be read as a continuous attempt to revise Freudian literature. Right up until his death in 1972, Berne asserted that transactional analysts are 'para-freudian'. They work through analysis of childhood experiences and script which have become unconscious, and lead the individual to follow repetitive and predictable interpersonal behaviour patterns. The ego remains at the centre of reflection within transactional-analytical theory and follows in the footsteps of the first ego psychologists (Federn and Weiss, co-founders of the Italian Psychoanalytic Society). On the other hand, the other two poles of the Freudian triad, Super-Ego and Id, have been relegated to an abstract and secondary dimension. The result of Berne's choice is that he places himself, on the one hand, in the tradition of ego psychology, and on the other hand, near to developments in object relations theory. It is important to remember that even Fairbairn (1952) offers a tripartite theory of Ego, describing a libidinal Ego tending towards the gratifying object, an antilibidinal Ego, a sort of internal persecuting object, and an observing central Ego. Berne thus anticipates many of the positions of object relations theory and of self psychology, moving from an instinctual theory to an interpersonal motivational theory. Briefly, it seems to me that Berne ends up placing his work at a sort of cross-roads where, in fact, contemporary psychoanalysis now finds itself, as a result of being confronted by theoretical and clinical research.

This classifies transactional analysis as a psychotherapy characterized by phenomenological research into personality, meant in a distinctly interpersonal sense.

The Bernean ego

The Bernean ego is a Freudian ego because it mediates internal and external energies. It manages the individual's homeostasis with respect to the world, and to his or her personal history. Berne attempts to place the ego at the centre of three essential psychological themes:

- awareness of self;
- individual destiny;
- social behaviour.

The ego is conceived of as resulting from a series of events of a relational nature, where the environmental vicissitudes of the 'transactional' child are seen within their dynamic experiences, both real and fantasized. Child-Parent transactions lead to the construction of intrapsychic 'deposits' that repeat, at the internal dialogue and interpersonal behaviour levels, the same transactions. The Child ego state is the sum of meaningful experiences that the child has had during his interactions with parental figures, and how these experiences have been fixated at the cognitive and emotional levels. The Parent ego state is seen as the sum of the parent images, including both cognitive and emotional aspects, that the child has introjected. These images remain in dynamic relation with the Child's systems, both in their inhibitory attitudes and in those that facilitate personality functions.

Based on Child-Parent interactions, repetitions of the dynamic exchanges that really occurred within the individual's history, there is also the development of mental faculties that progressively lead the individual to develop the ability to analyse here-and-now contact (Adult ego state).

Motivation

The model offers, therefore, three systems of ego organization, all tied to the primary function of Ego adaptation. Within these, an ulterior aspect characterising Berne's work is the concept of *motivation*. Here, Berne moves away from classical Freudian thought in seeing the main human motivation as not sexual or aggressive, but rather what he calls 'recognition hunger'; an innate and primary need to receive environmental stimuli. Berne sees this 'hunger' as central to Child-Parent interactions. Recognition hunger leads the child, as a matter of survival, to engage in various interactions with parental figures. How this happens will determine the positions that the child assumes in respect to the self and to reality.

In the Freudian model, human motivation is explained as the need of the psyche to mediate, through a complex defensive system, the primary sexual and aggressive instincts; the endogenous pressure that derives from these instincts pushes the psychic apparatus to resolve conflicts with the environment, through a secondary internalization of the interpersonal world.

In identifying the centrality of recognition hunger as a need for relationship, Berne is again separating himself from Freud by seeing attachment as a primary need and not a secondary one. In this, he places himself in a similar frame to Bowlby (1969), another psychoanalyst who develops the centrality of the concept of relationship and thus moves away from the original Freudian concept of drive.

Self awareness, individual destiny and social behaviour

Berne sees individual destiny as the dynamic effect of two psychological positions, autonomy and script. Autonomy is conceived of as the result of full awareness and understanding of ego states leading to the possibility of realistic choices. Script is the repetition in the here-and-now of archaic decisions, that the child made in order to protect and fulfill his/her need for recognition. Thus, the concept of psychological script has its roots in both intrapsychic and relational perspectives. At the intrapsychic level, it is the 'descendant' of repetition compulsion and transference neurosis; at the relational level, it can be understood to be the sum of internalized Child-Parent transactions that lead to here-and-now transactions and games. This notion is wholly in keeping with Sullivan's (1964) work on interpersonal psychiatry.

It is at this relational level, that ego states and script offer the most innovative and characteristic aspect of Bernean work. Ego states are conceived of as phenomena which, activated by different ego images, determine the emergence of different states of self-awareness, leading to observable behaviour. Ego states and script are analyzable both inductively and deductively, and therefore may originate both from the subject's present and childhood history. Depending on the individual's transactional styles, he can be recognized within his life experiences.

Thus, Berne's theoretical-methodological apparatus places the relational event at the centre, both as a new *ego metapsychology* and as an analytic methodology. A consequence of all of Berne's original work is to place transactional analysis directly within the modern psychoanalytic movement. His departure from exclusively Freudian positions, while remaining anchored within a strategy of interpretation, renders transactional analysis a *neo-psychoanalytic psychotherapy*. I therefore assert that Bernean theory is a true *transactional psychoanalysis* (Novellino 1996, 2002).

Mitchell's (1988) important work reviewing recent developments in psychoanalysis, describes the relational movement as a 'selective integration' within psychoanalysis. The relational movement offers a way to overcome the apparent opposition between the intrapsychic and interpersonal, while still considering psychodynamic phenomena within a *relational matrix*. Relationships should not simply be understood as pure acting-out of internal object relations, but as the result of the mind's primary requirement of inter-personal self-regulation. Particularly relevant is the way Mitchell writes about *interpersonal transactions* (1988), which confirms the legitimate presence of Bernean theory within the relational psychoanalytic movement; therefore, the re-naming of Bernean psychotherapy as a true transactional psychoanalysis, is anything but metaphorical, but is indeed accurate.

Berne's model corresponds completely to the epistemological criteria described by Mitchell:

1 Berne starts from the Freudian model, respecting the presuppositions linked to the Freudian idea of structure. These are identifiable in the concepts of ego states and unconscious dynamics, which are present in the theory of psychological games and script. He surpasses his roots in a revolutionary manner by proposing unequivocally, as behaviour's primary motivation, the psychological need known as stroke hunger.
2 Intrapsychic and interpersonal dynamics are seen as two sides of a coin. Internal dialogue and interpersonal communication are the reciprocal mirrors of the individual's activity within his interpersonal context.
3 Archaic models of interpersonal relations influence present ones in a reciprocal dynamism; what has occurred with primary parental figures partly explains here-and-now transactional styles, but these later ones, for example the psychotherapeutic relationship, lead to a continuous elaboration of the early ones. The vicissitudes of contact are the consequence of a continuous interaction between past and present;
4 The Bernean mind is a dyadic type, both within actual communication analysis (the internal dialogue between ego states is reflected within the different possible transactions), and in the analysis of psychopathology, through game and script analysis.

All the material presented in this chapter expresses this relational charac-teristic as the essence of Berne's intuition. Now we can move on to the ana-lysis, within a transactional psychoanalytic framework, of a specific area of Bernean theory - namely communication.

The fourth rule and Type II transference transaction

Berne (1961) established that the aim of 'Transactional Analysis Proper' is to identify the ego states that interact during each single interpersonal sequence. In this way, he established the foundation of so-called Social Psychiatry, and through the three rules of communication, the principles of interpersonal dynamic that the transactional analyst needs to follow in order to establish an effective therapeutic alliance. Recent neopsychoanalytical developments of transactional analysis require an update of these three rules in order to meet the methodological requirements related to transference and countertransference phenomena; in other words the transactional vicissitudes mentioned above. I suggest that transactional analysis frames the concept of transference transaction within a theory of unconscious communication, which includes a psychological level of communication within the Adult ego state. This leads to a need to update Berne's work on the rules of communication.

Debate within the TA community

The TA scientific community has dealt widely with the topic of transference in transactional analysis, especially in the April and July 1991 issues of the *Transactional Analysis Journal:* for example in the papers by Erskine, Allen and Allen, Clark, Clarkson, Jaoui, Shmukler, Karpman, Matze, Massey, and Joines. Overall, it seems to me that all these works have an interesting intrapsychic perspective - although many are less interested in a thorough transactional examination of the issue of transference. For such an exploration, it is necessary to go to my own work (1984, 1985, 1987) and to that of Moiso (1985).

Erskine (1991) offers a useful definition of transference transactions, seeing them as an interpersonal expression of intrapsychic conflicts within the extereopsychic and archeopsychic Ego states. Within this view, he separates therapeutic communications into transference transactions (originating from the Adapted Child or the active Parent) and non-transference transactions (originating from the neopsychic Ego state). He also analyses transference phenomena in terms of scripts and defense mechanisms. Therefore, although his work is of fundamental importance, I consider that he uses the term 'transaction' improperly, because it does not analyse the phenomenon in terms of stimulus-response. Clarkson (1991, 1992), who studied the topic of transference in original and thorough ways, amplifies Berne's concept of the tranference transaction, clarifying that when there is an Adult-Adult stimulus activated by the psychotherapist, the patient may respond either with a Child Ego state or with a Parent ego state. This accords with what was said by Erskine (1991) and Massey (1991). Clarkson (1992) goes so far as to introduce a further clarification of the Bernean concept of the transference transaction, when she says that this may also occur if there is a Child-Parent stimulus originating from the patient, where the psychotherapist responds from Adult-Adult. My understanding of Clarkson's assertion is that this transaction would be what Berne has called 'exasperating' (1961).

Allen & Allen (1991) suggest an interesting classification of the types of transference. The first two types originate from a projection onto the therapist of aspects of early conflict; the first corresponding to Berne's transference transaction, the second to Moiso's split transference (1985). The third type originates from the projection of early developmental fixations (Clark 1991 and Shmukler 1991); and the fourth type originates from the projection of early non-pathological aspects.

Hargaden & Sills (2001), in describing their three types of transference, come nearest to articulating the transference communication within the therapeutic relationship, although they do not differentiate their ideas clearly enough from the three traditional types of transactions, and therefore miss the opportunity to fully explore the blend of past and present interaction in the unconscious level of Adult communication.

Karpman's (1991) work suggests one of the few attempts to approach transference from a transactional point of view. He hypothesizes a IB type of tranference transaction, in which the patient's response does not originate from Child but from Adult contaminated by Child. What I believe Karpman is actually offering is an analysis of the Type I transference transaction from a structural rather than a functional point of view.

In summary, while the literature is rich with discussion about the phenomenon of transference there is a lack of direct analysis of the elements of the transference transaction – the unconscious communication from the patient to the therapist.

Unconscious communication

In 1987 and 1990, I developed the theme of psychodynamic transactional analysis (Novellino & Moiso 1990) by examining the unconscious themes in transactional analysis. I propose to further examine the issue of transference from a transactional point of view, with the introduction of the concept of *unconscious communication* from the Adult ego state, which consists of a message that the patient sends to the psychotherapist where the following characteristics exist:

1 the communication occurs out of awareness and is not accessible to consciousness; in other words it occurs at the unconscious level, and it is therefore accessible only through interpretative work;
2 the message is communicated through a narrative that is centred on facts, events, and people outside the therapy situation (*social level of the transaction*);
3 the *psychological level* arises via *associative* links; the topic concerns the therapeutic relationship and particularly the way the patient experiences the psychotherapist;
4 the aim of the psychological level is *not* a script pay-off, i.e. it is not a psychological game;
5 the aim, on the contrary, consists of communicating to the psychotherapist emotional experiences which are unacceptable to conscious reason.

Clinical example (one):
R. is a woman in her early forties who entered psychotherapy after a depressive episode following her separation from her husband. Her initial goal was to re-kindle her joy of living, to establish new social and meaningful relationships, and to understand the reason for her enormous difficulty in accepting separations. In the therapy, she goes through the important work of decontamination and deconfusion, where she recognises the importance to her development of an

absent and distant father, and of a basically depressed mother. Her mood grad-
ually improves, her social relationships grow, and above all, she gets involved
with another man who is available and affectionate. At a certain point during the
therapy, R. starts affirming more often that she feels better and is free from her
problems. She begins to consider the possibility of leaving therapy. Soon after-
wards, the following interchange occurs during a particular session:

R I wanted to tell you something that happened to me the other day. I went
to see my old uncle…you know how important he was to me. He was the only
person who used to play with me. He used to tell me fairytales and I was able
to sleep peacefully only when he was at home. It's been some time since I've
seen him, even though I've known very well that he's been ill. I left his home
feeling very sad. I think it's the first time since I've been well that I've felt
anything similar to depression again.

The therapist, while he listens to the story, feels a strong discomfort in which
he notices some sense of guilt, the nature of which is not yet clear to him. So he
asks the patient:

T What do you think caused your sadness?
R I've asked myself that …*(her expression, while speaking, seems to be visibly*
depressed) I said to myself that maybe I thought that my uncle was about to
die, that I would've lost the only person who I felt protected by when I was
little.
T This seems like a very understandable reaction, knowing your past history.

The therapist feels his discomfort increasing and that he is somehow directly
involved with what the patient is expressing. At this point, he has an intuition
and to verify it, he asks her:

T Have you noticed anything different in your uncle's behaviour lately?
R Thinking about it…yes I think so. It's been a long time since he's called me
on the phone - to ask after me…But really it's obvious that he's sick…maybe
it's right that I should be the one to take care of him…

After this response, the therapist starts understanding that his intuition was
probably right. In the past month he has twice had to ask the patient to post-
pone her session because of serious family circumstances. His son had recently
undergone an operation, which the patient did not know about. This had led, for
the first time, to a change in the therapy setting, initiated by the therapist instead
of the patient. The setting was a weekly appointment and always at the same
time and day. This change had occurred whilst the patient was considering ending
her therapy. The therapist suggests his hypothesis to the patient:

T I have the impression that this meeting with your uncle may mean

something else within our relationship.
R I don't understand...in what way?

Whilst the patient's words indicate surprise and non-comprehension, the therapist notices that her face is beginning to redden.

T Do you remember that I've had to ask you to postpone two of our sessions this month?
R Yes, it's true, but I had completely forgotten...
T Exactly. I have the impression that this forgetfulness of yours is important, and I realise that we haven't talked about your feelings about it. It was the first time that it had happened, and, if you think about it, it all happened during an important time for you...
R. You're referring to the fact that I mentioned that I was starting to feel ready to finish therapy?
T I think that you are spot on. Now do you understand what you've been trying to tell me through your sad meeting with your uncle?
R I'm not sure, but it could be that it seemed to me that the moment I felt grown-up, you started distancing yourself from me, it's like I can't depend on you any longer.
T I was thinking something similar. I'd also think that we both know something else from your past history that can be of help in understanding your feelings of sadness. Remember how many times we worked on the fact that when you used to ask your mother if you could go out on a date, you would see her become sad. Usually you started feeling guilty and ended up staying with her?
R It's true...I feel this as the heart of it... it's as if I've felt you asking me to postpone our sessions as a demand to take care of you, while...*(starts crying deeply)*, actually while I finally fell in love with another man.

Comment

This vignette illustrates the important methodological principles of psycho-dynamic transactional analysis. The first is that the therapist asks himself about the *meaning* of what the patient is telling him. While the patient starts telling her story, he asks himself about the meaning of the patient's choice of topic. He wonders about the patient's aim in telling him that episode and her feelings about it. The second principle involves the therapist paying attention to his own emotional participation in the patient's telling of her story; the *countertransference analysis* guides the therapist towards understanding the psychological levels of the communication.

Having recognised some countertransferential response, a third aspect is the therapist's attempt to place the story within the context of the therapeutic relationship; the *context* is fundamental in order to understand what R. is trying to say to the therapist with her story.

To analyze the context means to pay attention to what is happening in the wider field. R. feels ready to leave therapy and this is an extremely important phase of the therapeutic relationship - particularly if considered in terms of transference and countertransference.

In the elaboration of this theoretical material, I have especially made use of Langs' work (1973-4), whose interpersonal evolution of the Freudian theories is fundamental in to integration of psychoanalysis and transactional analysis.

Two types of transaction

In the light of this, I found it useful to distinguish two types of transactions (1990):

1 *monological* transactions are characterised by univocal messages, resulting from secondary process which is produced at the conscious or pre-conscious level. They correspond to complementary and crossed transactions and the first and the second rules of communication apply to them.

2 *bilogical* transactions are characterized by a manifest social level, which is the result of secondary process, and by a psychological level, which is the result of primary process. They aim to send 'coded' messages within the therapeutic relationship. They are an ulterior type of transaction, but due to their characteristics, they *do not* fall within the third rule of communication. They send an unconscious message about how the patient experiences the relationship with the psychotherapist, and they accomplish it through narratives concerning people and events which are apparently external to the setting, manifesting an *internal* experience in relation to the therapeutic relationship. The problem consists of understanding what the patient is saying to the therapist with her 'narratives'. The therapist gathers intuitively with his A1 that maybe what the patient says in relation to other people might actually concern him.

In the above example, he will take into consideration at least two things:
- the person cited within the narration is a 'parental' type: for R. it concerns her uncle;
- the content of the patient's communication is linked to her experiences, or maybe also to unmet desires; R.'s uncle did not call her during the time that she was beginning to be happier in her life.

The psychotherapist then has the option of exploring the emotional implication in the therapeutic relationship. In R.'s case, it is as if the patient is complaining to the therapist both of abandoning her and of leaving her the task of commenting on what happened. This was true, because the therapist had neglected to discuss with the patient how she might have reacted to his postponing the sessions. As conveying this in a conscious and intentional way was unacceptable to her, R. resorted to a coded message.

A methodological approach, such as the one described, furnishes the transactional analyst with a new possible view of the patient-therapist communication. It is one that corresponds with a process proposed notably by both Langs and Malan (1979) and also Woods (1995), who used Langs' material to analyse transference and countertransference.

In order to address and understand this type of unconscious communication, and therefore the coded messages sent by it, two principal means are to be considered: countertransference analysis and defence mechanism analysis (Novellino 1984,). Countertransference analysis uses the perception of one's own experiences and is fundamental to understanding intuitively the fact of being the object of the patient's narrative (once any possible projective or paranoid interferences on the therapist's part are excluded). Defence mechanism analysis is based on the recognition of the two mechanisms that the patient activates simultaneously within the unconscious communication: *displacement* and *symbolization*.

The example clearly illustrates that the message sent by the patient can belong to two different areas. Firstly, it can refer to unconscious script material, particularly to the protocol. In this sense, the patient colours the therapeutic relationship with her early childhood experiences and the dramas that are linked to the script decision. It is hence a transference process in a narrow sense, equivalent to Erskine's transference transaction (1991), and also to the first three transference types of Allen & Allen (1991). In ego state terms, the ulterior transaction emanates from Child. According to the psychodynamic approach to TA, the appropriate operation (Berne 1966) is interpretation (Novellino 1990).

Secondly, the unconscious communication can express the patient's here-and-now experience of the therapeutic relationship. For instance, the therapist has genuinely been inattentive, and this is experienced by the patient. The patient cannot express her feelings due to archaic script experiences ("I cannot criticize Dad"), but conveys them nevertheless. It is necessary to identify this second transactional process, because the content of the experience is current and Adult; only the defence is archaic. Therefore, this level will then be interpreted as transference (Child ego state), while the experience in itself is not transferential. We find ourselves therefore, within the area of Erskine's non-transference transactions (1991) and Allen & Allen's fourth type of transference (1991).

In summary, bilogical transactions manifest, through coded narratives, archaic or current experiences which the patient has towards the therapeutic relationship, and that he or she cannot express consciously because of script defences.

The previous clinical vignette (Patient R.) was an example of unconscious communication, which consisted of a message sent by the patient concerning her here-and-now emotional experience of the therapeutic relationship. Let us now consider an example that illustrates the other possible aim of the unconscious communication; in other words, that of leading the therapist towards the experience analogous to the protocol, with the aim of helping the therapist to understand it, rather than to play out a Game.

Clinical example (two)

L. is a man in his early thirties, who has been in therapy for one year for problems caused by borderline personality disturbances: high aggressiveness, chaotic sexual experiences, difficulty in carrying through projects, alcoholism. He has already gone through various psychotherapies, all abruptly terminated. The contract was for two individual sessions per week. During the phase under discussion, after a period of committed regular attendance, the patient starts missing a few sessions, inducing frustration and concern within the therapist. During one of the sessions, following two missed ones, the patient starts talking about some events of the past week.

L I've been feeling confused lately. I haven't felt like working, so I took a few days vacation. I went around nightclubs after sleeping all day. One evening I saw an old University professor of mine together with his young girlfriend. A good-looking girl...I don't know why, but I couldn't stop myself from trying to pick her up, and thinking about it now it's as if I felt a sadistic need to embarrass him even though he was visibly annoyed...

T Were you aware of what you were thinking about at the time?

L I was fantasising about taking her to bed with me, of leaving him there all alone like a stupid fool, and I was also ready to get into a physical fight with him. I would've made him bleed!

T So you imagined all this without him giving you any reason to feel angry towards him...

The therapist uses Specification and Confrontation with the patient.

L His presence just upset me. He presented himself suddenly, with a beautiful girl next to him, while I was alone and sad...I felt so - so angry!

T So you're giving him the responsibility for your behaviour and anger.

L Now that I'm talking about it no, but then yes, I was mad at him!

The therapist experiences an increasing irritation with the patient while he highlights the incongruity of his behaviour. In the meantime he also feels a vague fear within himself, and reflects upon the fact that maybe L's anger is intended for him. He remembers the last no-shows of the patient, and starts formulating a hypothesis concerning what the patient is actually trying to tell him with his narrative.

T Your tone sounds irritated to me...do you agree?

L *(after a long silence)*... I don't know why, but I feel very annoyed. Why do you think I feel this way?

T You see, now you're asking me to think, and I think that this is exactly what was happening between us and why you ended-up feeling irritated. You were describing an episode which I asked you to reflect upon. I think there's something in that story which I should just listen to. Something you prefer that we don't think about together. Does this make sense to you?

L I think that we already talked about this...there are some emotions that I don't want to think about.

T Do you want to now? *(L. nods)* You told me about a period when you didn't feel like doing anything, you felt depressed, you didn't go to work...

L So...?

T Maybe it's a coincidence, but you told me this after missing a few sessions.

L Yeah...it's true... *(his tone of voice lowers and the expression becomes interested).*

T Let's try to consider your story as a sort of a metaphor. You miss the sessions...you continue now...substituting the characters of the story with both of us instead...

L I find myself all alone, depressed, and...I imagine that you're well, maybe with your wife or your daughter, in fact your family...*(starts crying)*...I usually felt this way during school, I was envious of the other kids. They all seemed to have a beautiful and normal family that would wait for them at home while when I went back...no one was ever home. So then I hated everything and everybody. I wanted to destroy the world. Sometimes I was so mad that I couldn't go to school because of the fear of hurting someone...

T I think it's very important that you're reliving this part of your life...We have to work on the envy that you felt and that has made you escape from relationships. The envy that you might feel towards me is also very important because it brings back an archaic emotion for you... Only now you're not alone to take care of it.

Comment

In this example, the therapist asks himself about the meaning of the patient's narrative and why it is told only after the missed sessions. He utilizes his own countertransference reaction to ask himself how the narrative might relate to him in some way; and so invites the patient to reflect upon what he is communicating.

In this example, the unconscious communication includes:

1 A psychological level transmitted by the patient analogically through a narrative, which, in code, sends the therapist a transference type of experience. In other words, envy managed through an old defense mechanism of avoidance. The therapist understands the psychological level and recognises his own reaction of fear towards the patient's anger (countertransference analysis).

2 Recognition by the therapist of the unconscious level of the narrative.

3 The therapist responds to the patient's stimulus by guiding him towards an interpretation.

4 The emotion directed towards the therapist originates from the patient's protocol. In other words, from a childhood envy towards anyone who had anything that he could not receive.

Thus we have a transference transaction carried out through an unconscious communication. As I have previously stated, I believe that this type of transaction, a particular type of ulterior transaction, does not respect the third rule of communication. This rule refers to the 'classical' ulterior transactions that describe a social level and a psychological level, which is different and recognizable from the patient's non-verbal process: the tone of voice, posture, language and so on. I consider this as mainly belonging to the *pre-conscious* dimension. The typical example that Berne gives for this type of transaction is supplied by psychological games (1964); their behavioural outcome is given by the psychological level itself.

What is it then that characterises the third rule?

I believe that two aspects are involved; the first highlights the existence of messages which go 'against' the Adult control of communication, and the second focuses upon the behavioural result of the communication. Psychological games fully represent these two aspects, especially if we apply them to the therapeutic relationship. If a game occurs, the evolution of the therapeutic alliance will take different directions from the conscious intentions; the psychotherapist who would like to understand and explain, in other words activate the Adult of the patient, will find himself with destructive pay-offs.

In unconscious communication and in the bilogical transactions manifesting it, we find ourselves with two aspects not included in the traditional concept of ulterior transaction:

1 the psychological level meets the aim of the therapeutic relationship, since its purpose is that of supplying new material to be understood;
2 the possible result, even if determined by the psychological level, is not of a behavioural type, but instead a cognitive one.

For these reasons, I locate the source of the unconscious level of transaction within the Adult ego state.

A fourth rule of communication

In view of what I have proposed so far, as an extension of Berne's communication theory, I believe it is useful to hypothesise a fourth rule of communication specifically in relation to unconscious communication and related bilogical transactions.

- A bilogical transaction should be understood as an exchange organized as follows (see Fig. 1 below):
- a *stimulus* arising from the patient, consisting of a social and psychological level, which is superimposed and which originates functionally from the Adult of the patient who 'narrates' something that relates to his/her own extra-analytic life; the same narration expresses metaphorically, in code, an emotional experience about the therapeutic relationship;
- the psychotherapist, who has intuited the metaphorical level, helps the patient to understand the hidden experience, i.e. his or her *response* consists of an interpretation.

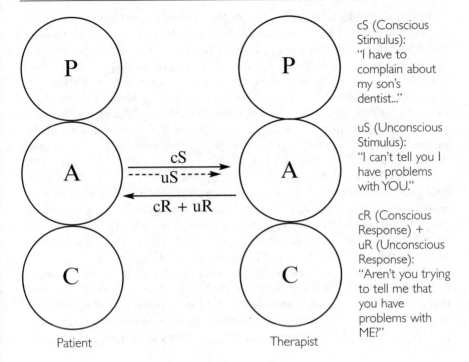

cS (Conscious Stimulus): "I have to complain about my son's dentist..."

uS (Unconscious Stimulus): "I can't tell you I have problems with YOU."

cR (Conscious Response) + uR (Unconscious Response): "Aren't you trying to tell me that you have problems with ME?"

Fig. 1: The Adult unconscious communication

This type of transaction does not belong within any of Berne's three rules:

1 The first rule deals only with non-ulterior transactions and therefore is inadequate, since the communication proceeds without difficulties; not because the two (psychotherapist and patient) go on talking at the overt (Social) level of communication, but, on the contrary, because the psychological level is made clear.

2 The second rule is insufficient, since the communication proceeds precisely because the psychotherapist answers at a different level from the one that the patient socially expects.

3 The third rule deals with a behavioural level and not a cognitive one; the Adult becomes 'decathected' to produce a destructive script pay-off *that blocks the therapeutic alliance.* In the ulterior transactions described by Berne, the result of the communication tends towards excluding Adult, and therefore blocking the understanding of what is going on in the therapeutic relationship. In bilogical ulterior transactions, the purpose of the unconscious communication is that of opening new channels of connection, i.e. to improve the therapeutic alliance.

A fourth rule of communication relies on three elements. First, it recognises and organises the specifics of the therapeutic relationship in a way that allows for everything that the patient tells the psychotherapist to be considered to be a message about the relationship. Then, the psychotherapist has to be capable of grasping the patient's unconscious messages, dividing them into transferential and non-transferential ones. As a result of this, the progress of the therapeutic alliance is influenced, and hence the psychotherapy.

The fourth rule can therefore be defined as: *The outcome of an unconscious communication depends on the psychotherapist's capacity to intuit the symbolic psychological level of the transaction* (Novellino, 1996). If the psychotherapist understands the patient's coded message, this will lead to a correct interpretation and therefore to progress in the psychotherapy; if this is not the case, the therapeutic alliance will come to a stop.

The concept of intuition is very present in Berne's work (1977). He considered it to be at the root of the psychotherapist's diagnostic ability. I believe it useful to apply the concept of intuition to transactional analysis proper, which Berne himself in some ways over-simplified, reducing the rules of communication to a functional descriptive approach that limits the understanding of the deep dynamics existing in the therapeutic relationship.

An inevitable consequence of introducing a fourth rule of communication, one that is specific to the therapeutic relationship, is to revise the current taxonomy of transference transactions. As I have previously illustrated, we actually find in the TA literature much writing on transference as an intrapsychic phenomenon (ego states, defences), and very little from a truly transactional point of view.

My proposal is to consider at least two types of transference transactions:
1 the first type is the one that corresponds to the rules of communication described by Berne. In particular, I would distinguish a *Type IA* transaction, as described by Berne (which corresponds to the second communication rule), and a *Type IB* transaction, i.e. the one that corresponds to the third rule of communication and concerns psychological games. Both of these involve the Parent or Child ego states.
2 I would define the other transference transaction as *Type II*. This is linked to unconscious communication and can be seen as originally emanating from the Adult ego state. It corresponds to the fourth rule of communication.

Again, I believe that intuition can be used to better distinguish the two types of transactions which both contain an ulterior message; that is, Types IB and II. I believe that in the case of a psychological game (transaction IB), the therapist's intuition will be tuned towards grasping the game's psychological level (the preconscious level), while in the Type II transaction, the intuition must recognise the message's code at an *unconscious* level. This calls for a subtle level of receptivity on the part of the therapist. The work of the transactional analyst is to refine and develop his or her intuition and imagination.

Conclusion
In this chapter I have addressed a topic that readers may consider current

within the advanced debate on modern transactional analysis. I am aware that I am also proposing a view that needs further examination and subsequent refinements. What I have endeavoured to make explicit here will need to be further discussed, improved, and amplified. The recent work of transactional analysts (for example in the *TAJ* January 2001) suggests that this is an area which is rich in possibilities as practitioners develop their understanding through their work. It is my hope that I have opened a door.

With thanks to Charlotte Sills for her assistance with this chapter.

References

Allen, J.R. & Allen, B.A. (1991) Concepts of transference: a critique, a typology, an alternative hypothesis and some proposals, *Transactional Analysis Journal*, 21(2) 77-92

Bateman, A. & Holmes, J. (1995) *Introduction to Psychoanalysis. Contemporary Theory and Practice.* London: Routledge

Berne, E. (1961) *Transactional Analysis in Psychotherapy: A Systematic Approach to Individual and Social Psychiatry.* New York: Grove Press

Berne, E. (1963) *The Structure and Dynamics of Organizations and Groups* New York: Grove Press

Berne, E. (1964) *Games People Play.* New York: Grove Press

Berne, E. (1966) *Principles of Group Treatment.* New York: Grove Press

Berne, E. (1972) *What Do You Say After You Say Hello?* New York: Bantam Books

Berne, E. (1977) *Intuition and Ego States.* San Francisco: TA Press

Bowlby, J. (1969) *Attachment and Loss, Vol. I: Attachment.* London: Hogarth Press.

Clark, B.D. (1991) Emphatic transactions in the deconfusion of Child ego states' *Transactional Analysis Journal* 21(2) 92-98

Clarkson, P. (1991) Through the looking glass: explorations of transference and countertransference, *Transactional Analysis Journal*, 21(2) 99-107

Clarkson, P. (1992) *Transactional Analysis Psychotherapy.* London/New York: Tavistock/Routledge

Daellenbach, D. (ed.) (2001) Theme Issue: The schizoid process. *Transactional Analysis Journal* 31(1)

Erskine, R.G. (1991. Transference and transactions: critique from an intrapsychic and integrative perspective, *Transactional Analysis Journal* 21(2) 3-76

Erskine, R.G. & Zalcman, M. (1979) The racket system: a model for racket analysis, *Transactional Analysis Journal* 9(1) 51-59

Fairbairn, W.R.D. (1952) *Psychoanalytic Studies of the Personality.* London: Tavistock Publications & Routledge & Kegan Paul

Freud, S. (1905) On psychotherapy. in: (1953-66) *Standard Edition of the Complete Psychological Works of Sigmund Freud.* London: Hogarth Press

Hargaden, H. and Sills, C. (2001) Deconfusion of the Child ego state, *Transactional Analysis Journal* 31(1) 55-70

Jaoui, G. (1991) Transference process and transactional process. *Transactional Analysis Journal* 21(2) 108-111.

Joines, V. (1991) Transference and transactions: some additional comments, *Transactional Analysis Journal* 21(2) 171-173.

Karpman, S. (1991) Notes on the transference papers. *Transactional Analysis Journal* 21(2) 136-140.

Klein, G.S. (1976) *Psychoanalytic Theory: an Exploration of Essentials.* New York: International University Press.

Klein, M. (1948) *Contributions to Psychoanalysis 1921-25.* London: Hogarth Press.

Langs, R. (1973-4) *The Technique of Psychoanalytic Psychotherapy.* New York: Jason and Aronson.

Malan, D.H. (1979) *Individual Psychotherapy and the Science of Psychodynamics.* London: Butterworth & Company

Massey, R.F. (1991) The evolution of perspectives on transference in relation to analysis. *Transactional Analysis Journal* 21(3) 155-169

Matze, M.G. (1991) Commentary on transactions in the context of transference. *Transactional Analysis Journal* 21(3) 141-143

McCormick, P. (1977) *Social Transactions.* San Francisco: TA Press

Mitchell, S.A. (1988) *Relational Concepts in Psychoanalysis: An Integration.* Cambridge-London: Harvard University Press

Moiso, C.M. (1985) Ego states and transference. *Transactional Analysis Journal* 15(3) 194-201

Moiso, M. & Novellino, M. (2000) An overview of the psychodynamic school of transactional analysis and its epistemological foundations. *Transactional Analysis Journal* 30(3) 182-187

Novellino, M. (1982) *Un approccio triadico alla resistenza in psicoterapia.* Atti Ià Conv. Naz. Di AT., Roma

Novellino, M. (1984) Self-analysis of countertransference. *Transactional Analysis Journal* 14 (1) 63-67

Novellino, M. (1985) Redecision analysis of transference: a TA approach to transference neurosis. *Transactional Analysis Journal* 15(3) 202-206

Novellino, M. (1987) Redecision analysis of transference: the unconscious dimension, *Transactional Analysis Journal* 17(1) 271-276

Novellino, M. (1990) *Conflitto Intrapsichico e Ridecisione.* Roma: Città Nuova ed.

Novellino, M. (1990) Unconscious communication and interpretation, *Transactional Analysis Journal* 20(3) 168-172

Novellino, M. (1996) A psychodynamic review of Berne's rules of communication, in: *TA papers.* Bisceglie: Don Uva ed.

Novellino, M. (1998) *L'Approccio Clinico all'Analisi Transazionale.* Milano: Franco Angeli ed.

Novellino, M. & Moiso, C.M. (1990) The psychodynamic approach to TA, *Transactional Analysis Journal* 20(3) 187-192

Rappoport, D. (1951) The conceptual model of psychoanalysis. in: Knight, R.P. – Friedman, C.R., *Psychoanalytic, Clinical and Theoretical Papers.* New York: International University Press

Sandler, J. & Sandler, A.M. (1986) The past unconscious, the present unconscious and the interpretation of transference, *Journal of Psychoanalytic Inquiry* 4:367-99

Sandler, J. & Sandler, A.M. (1994) The past unconscious and the present unconscious: a contribution to a technical frame of reference. *Psychoanalytic study of the child,* 49: 278-292

Schmid, A. (1990) Intuition of the possible and transactional creation of realities, *Transactional Analysis Journal* 20(3) 144-154

Shmukler, D. (1991) Transference and transactions: perspectives from development theory, object relations, and transformational processes. *Transactional Analysis Journal* 21(3) 127-135

Spence, D. (1987) *The Freudian Metaphor: Toward Paradigm Change in Psychoanalysis.* New York: Norton

Sullivan, H. (1964) *The Fusion of Psychiatry and Social Science.* New York: Norton.

Wallerstein, R., ed. (1992). *The Common Ground of Psychoanalysis.* New York: Jason Aronson

Woods, K. (1995). The indirect analysis of manifestation of transference and countertransference. *Transactional Analysis Journal* 25(3) 245-249

Chapter 9

THE PSYCHODYNAMICS OF RACE AND CULTURE:
an analysis of cultural scripting and ego state transference

Suhith Shivanath and Mita Hiremath

The focus of this chapter is on ego states, race (and racism), culture, and their impact on intra- and inter-psychic processes for both client and psychotherapist. It is accepted in TA to think of racism and prejudice as Child and Parent contaminations of the Adult. Here we offer additional frameworks which focus on the Child ego state. We use Berne's (1961) model of structural ego states, Moiso's (1985) ideas on ego states and transference, and the Schiffian (1975) concept of symbiosis. In addition, we have developed and enlarged Steiner's original script matrix (1974) into a three-layered model which takes into account a person's individual script influences, the scripting through their religion and culture, and the scripting through the wider white society in which they live. For the purposes of this chapter we will look at the effects of being visually different, i.e. black in a majority white society, and the survival issues involved, and we will define what we mean by culture. Eric Berne (1983) states it is the psychiatrist's task to 'evaluate the possible psychodynamic effects of a given store of lore' (p. 261). We will expand on this by looking at the meanings attributed to 'black' and 'white' and their impact for both Black and white clients and therapists.

We will outline our experience of working with Asian women clients, as well as the implications of the dynamics of race and culture when working with Asian, African-Caribbean and white clients.

The function of culture is a means of group survival through developing a sense of group 'self' versus 'the other.' A sense of self through belonging to a group is imparted through religion, social mores, rituals, festivals, language, modes of dress etc., and part of this includes being able to identify what other people look like. Felipe Garcia (quoted in Roberts 1975) argues that:

> Cultural Scripting...can be a much greater influence to overcome than personal scripting because it is reinforced everywhere in society. A cultural script is reinforced by major institutions and sub-cultures in the society such as schools, churches, governments, the medical, educational and legal professions, the media and so forth. (p. 183)

'Race' is defined as 'one of many subdivisions of mankind distinguished by physical characteristics' (Penguin English Dictionary). Robert Carter (in Thompson and Carter 1997) states that:

> Race applies to all people not just Black people. Therefore, it is essential that theories take into account race as it affects all people. That is, theories and models of psychological treatment must be racially inclusive. (p. 97)

When we meet a person, the colour of their skin usually leads us to make assumptions about them and their culture. So this separation of race from culture is an artificial one. However, doing this enabled us to peg our arguments on to existing TA tools, and to develop them to include issues of race and culture.

Managing differences

Culturally, children in Britain are brought up not to stare or point and to believe that it is rude and impolite to name what is noticeable in another person. We know that children break this rule when they are being cruel to one another by name calling. (White therapists talk of their Free Child curiosity about differences, wanting to ask questions, to touch, and stare, but quickly learning that this is 'rude behaviour', and to not notice, or mention differences). Most Black children growing up in the UK also learn to conform to this norm. Additionally, white children in the West grow up being part of the dominant race and culture, and their skin colour is mirrored back to them. For Black children this is very much not the case. The point is made eloquently by Andrea Levy (2000) an African-Caribbean woman who writes of her childhood :

> I was educated to be English. Alongside me...were white children.
> But those white children would never have to grow up to question
> whether they are English or not.

This indicates the level of adaptation that is continuously being processed in order that a Black person may 'survive'. Scripting may involve minimising their differences in the face of white dominance. In our experience of working with Black clients, the theme of not belonging, and whether to, or not to, or how much to adapt, forms part of everyday conversation. Challenging mainstream culture 'means going against the awesome tide of institutional resistance'. (White & White 1975, p. 179). This may mean (1) drawing negative attention on to yourself, and (2) rejecting some of the niches in society where black people are accepted e.g. sport and music for African-Caribbean people, and administration and commerce for Asians.

Given that we live in 'multicultural Britain', issues relating to racial and cultural identity as they arise in the therapeutic relationship can no longer be considered irrelevant. Transferential and counter-transferential responses stem from frames of reference that include who we are racially, culturally and individually. It is important for all therapists to have an understanding and awareness of all their ego state responses so that we become aware of our impact on a client who may represent the 'other.' This includes having an awareness of our own racial identity, prejudices and biases.

Kohlrieser (1999) quotes E.T. Hall who states: 'Culture hides more than what it reveals, and strangely enough what it hides, it hides most effectively from its own participants' (p. 2). In other words, like out-of-awareness individual script beliefs, cultural mores and norms are taken for granted, and we are unaware of how they influence our individual frames of reference. White & White (1975) talk of cultural scripting serving the purpose of 'cultural institutions', and that children learn to develop survival scripts first through the family, and then to modify, give up, and develop new aspects in response to wider society. James and Jongeward (1971) describe cultural scripting as '..accepted and dramatic patterns that occur within a society. They are determined by the spoken and unspoken assumptions believed by the majority of the people within the group.' (p. 70). They further suggest that cultural scripts reflect what is thought of as the 'national character.'

Denton Roberts (1975) argues that the treatment of cultural scripting is not a matter of simply clearing up a Parent contamination, as Berne suggested, but rather that it involves a re-decision affecting all ego-states.

Cultural scripting

When working with white groups, we invite them to name some symbols that highlight their culture. It is often our experience that most British white people have been unable to say very much about their culture. Their common response is that they represent the norm. Valerie Batts (2000), at a recent conference, used the phrase "the fish don't know it's in water" to highlight this point. Individual white people commonly make choices about belonging to specific groups, but are not accustomed to identifying them as their communities. They are seen and see themselves as individuals. Most Black people on the other hand, partly because of the difference in skin colour, are associated with their racial and cultural group before they are seen as individuals.

This difference can originate from the specific minority culture, and takes on new meanings when living in the context of race and racism. For instance, in many Muslim Asian and African cultures, there is an important concept called, 'izzat' which is an Arabic word roughly meaning 'family honour.' It is a concept closely linked with gender, sex, respect for elders and respect for the community. A woman's 'honour' prior to marriage belongs to her father, and on marrying it belongs to her husband. This honour extends from her to her whole family. If a woman were to leave her husband, she would be bringing dishonour on her whole family. This in effect means that her family would be shamed in the community and in wider society. Although 'izzat' mainly applies to the Muslim communities, in our experience, the concept also has meaning for women in the Sikh and Hindu communities.

Generally, community has a prominent significance in many Black cultures. Living in a community with an acceptance of their traditions, values and religion, is an important source of support. These communities can be a safe haven from both the conscious and unconscious racism that exists in the larger white society. Additionally, a seemingly obvious point to make is that there are enormous differences within the Black cultures. For example, there are significant differences between people from the north and the south of India based on history, religion, culture and language, among others. Sometimes these differences are lost when living in a dominant white society.

The model

We have developed a culturally inclusive model in order to account for these complexities. We have developed and enlarged on Steiner's original script matrix (1974), creating a three-layered model which takes into account a person's individual script influences, the scripting of the religion and culture within which they have been brought up, and lastly, the scripting of the dominant white society in which they live. By doing this it is possible to acknowledge the multiple layers of influences on a person. It allows us to consider both the intrapsychic processes and the social, cultural and political context in which an individual lives. The model also enables the therapist to look at their own influences and acknowledge similarities and differences.

We initially draw up the client's individual script matrix, based on the messages transmitted from their parents and the decisions they made as a child in response to them. Alongside this we draw up their cultural script matrix. It is through the cultural script that messages of a particular culture, its social norms and its gender roles are transmitted. Much of this is communicated through the extended and joint family and also the community, as represented by community elders, leaders, and the temple, mosque or church. Lastly, we draw up a third layer of scripting, which is from the predominantly white society. In our experience, this third layer of scripting has a direct impact on the child's development (as shown in the diagram below), and messages are transmitted from the major institutions in this society such as schools, the government and the media. This will include beliefs about self and other in terms of race, colour, self-worth, and sense of belonging. This third layer of scripting also has an impact on the cultural script matrix as represented by the client's own community, religion and culture.

Asian women clients

In our experience, we have found that many Asian women clients present with issues related to abuse at home. Some of the women have been clearly told by their family and community members that, if they leave, then they will be "disowned." This means that they will cease to exist as far as their families and community are concerned. In the process of therapy, the women often come to an impasse where they consider the implications of leaving their husband/family. The parents' and community's roles are similar in terms of guiding, educating, and supporting a person throughout life. For many of our clients, living in an abusive situation in their own community is a better option than being cast out of that community into the wider white society, which they experience as hostile and unsafe. For some the losses involved would be too great.

Therapists' parallel dilemmas

In cases such as these it is important that we remain deeply respectful of our clients' decisions, whatever our Child and Parent feelings might be. As psychotherapists working with different cultures and communities, we need to work on both an intrapsychic level and at a level which addresses their cultural scripts. To ignore a person's cultural script, and the scripting from the wider white society, would be to deny the impact of culture, race and racism on their everyday lives. Unless we do this, we run the risk of pathologising our clients.

We have been challenged in taking such issues to our white supervisors, for fear that our communities will be judged or seen through some racial stereotype. Acknowledging this dilemma to ourselves offers us a sense of the client's sense of shame, or risk-taking, and a sharp reminder of the experience of representing 'the other' within wider society. The felt knowledge, of the importance of acceptance by community, has helped us process our own Child ego state anxieties and fears about a woman who chooses to leave her family despite her family's threats, or a woman who decides to stay in an abusive situation, because the loss of family and community is too great.

Yasmin is a Muslim Pakistani woman. Her family history was that she was the youngest of 7 sisters and brothers. She had been physically abused by her father since she was a young child. She was also disabled and walked with a limp. Her family believed she was stupid, due to her disability. She recalled her mother saying, "I wish I had strangled you at birth." So, among the injunctions she received from her mother were, Don't exist, Don't be a Girl and Don't be You.

At school the children made fun of her because of her disability and her race. Many of the children refused to play with her because she was "the colour of mud." Yasmin learnt at school that Jesus was the only way to go to God, and that other religions were wrong, or even immoral.

We used the model illustrated below (see Fig. 1) to identify her script messages on the three different levels (family, cultural and wider white society). The following diagram illustrates the influence on Yasmin of her individual script, her Sikh cultural script and the scripting of the wider white society in which she lives.

Fig. 1: Cultural script matrix

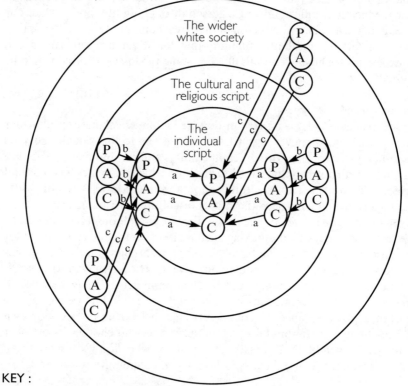

Adapted from Steiner's (1974) Script Matrix

KEY :

a. Yasmin's Individual script

Mother: P to P - Please me, Try hard, Be compliant

A to A - Hide your feelings, Give up your needs

C to C - Don't exist, Don't be a girl, Don't be You,

Father: P to P - Be good and compliant

A to A - Work hard and deny your own needs

C to C - Don't think, Don't have needs, Don't be a girl

b. Yasmin's religious and cultural script

P to P - Please others, Sacrifice for others, Men matter more

A to A - Hide your feelings. Here's how to prioritise, family
community and religion

C to C - Don't feel, Don't have needs, Don't be powerful

c. The wider predominantly white society

P to Yasmin's P and to Yasmin's parents P - We are superior, we
know best. Black people are dirty/dangerous, Muslims are dangerous

A to Yasmin's A and to Yasmin's parents A - Here's how to exclude

C to Yasmin's Child and Yasmin's parents Child - Don't be you,
Don't be the colour you are, Don't be powerful

Transference and countertransference
The symbolism attached to 'Black' and 'White'
Eric Berne (*The Mythology of Dark and Fair*, TAJ 1983) writes of the importance of paying attention to folklore as a transmitter of cultural messages. In highlighting the significance of 'dark' and 'air', he asks if:

> it is merely of academic interest, or whether it is dynamically significant in influencing human behaviour. It soon becomes evident that it has been repeatedly used as a rationalisation, if not as a driving force, for the most sinister and unbridled expressions of hostility. (p. 264)

The colour black is steeped in religious symbolism denoting evil, darkness, the devil, badness, danger and so on, while white represents all things good. These messages are carried in children's stories, through into adult images of dark versus light.

In the wake of the Stephen Lawrence enquiry, there has been much talk in the media of the need for 'colour blindness'. The ulterior message here is that it would be better if everyone is treated the same. Since human perceptions are influenced by cultural norms, and are never neutral, this begs the question 'the same as whom'?

It is not known how old a Black child has to be before s/he takes on negative attitudes and views about the colour of her or his skin. From our own experiences, and from our work with Black clients, we have observed that there are significant differences in thinking, feeling and behaviour, in response to race and racism, between those who emigrated here as adults, as opposed to those who were either born in the UK or emigrated as children. We have observed that with the former group (adult emigrants), racism is experienced from their Adult ego state, and that they do not experience this hostility from their Child ego state. The latter group (child emigrants and Black children brought up here) experience racism very much as an attack on their very being, in their Child ego state, because such attacks were a part of their early experiences.

James and Jongeward (1971) suggest that many young people, born in to a different environment from that of their parents, are rejecting earlier script themes as having little relevance to their lives today. The above authors argue that many of these young people are yet again facing the 'struggle for survival'. However, we argue that today it emerges in a different way. When Black and Asian adults come to this country, they often feel gratitude to the British for letting them come. This is despite their struggles against racism, unemployment and bad housing, amongst other issues. Their reasons for coming here range from a search for better jobs and education for themselves and their children, through to a need to escape from persecution. They do not struggle with their ethnic identity. They are Indian/Caribbean/African, etc. Growing up in their country, their race and culture was mirrored back to them by society.

In contrast, for many second and third generation immigrants, growing up as part of a racial minority group, their struggle takes a different path. They experience racism and prejudice from childhood, without experiencing the process of their race and culture being mirrored back to them by the wider society. Unlike their parents, they do not feel gratitude for being allowed to be here. As black people who are born here, they believe that they have a right to be here. However, many experience an inner struggle with their racial, cultural and ethnic identity. A result of this struggle is that some second and third generation immigrants today define themselves as 'Black British', or 'British Asian'.

The following are some examples of these dynamics.

Black client, Black therapist

Lennox Thomas suggests that feelings of 'blackness' are an inescapable part of the Black client/Black therapist dyad. The following example is reported by one of our supervisees in relation to her work with an Asian client.

> *At the beginning of our relationship, Savita spent considerable time questioning my level of training and expertise. She wanted to know why I, as an Asian woman, decided to be a therapist, as she knew very few Asian people who chose psychotherapy as a profession. I felt on some level that she was perceiving me as an Asian therapist to be inferior to a white therapist*

As Thomas says (quoted in Kareem and Littlewood 1992, p. 143), 'that a black person could aspire to and achieve professional status is, for them, a matter of questioning.' Savita also believed that all Asian women were destructive and incapable of taking care of her needs, as this had been her experience with her mother.

By using the model above, the therapist was able to appreciate that her very presence challenged her client at all three layers: (1) transference of mother (2) community's expectations of women (3) white society's stereotype of Asian women.

Lennox Thomas (quoted in Kareem and Littlewood 1992) argues that:

> in order to work effectively across cultures and with people of different colour, psychotherapists...need first to attend to their own racism, their own prejudices and their own projections on other racial and cultural groups. (p. 134)

When Poonam expressed feelings of disgust and revulsion about her looks, although the therapist felt empathic, she was also aware of a societal counter-transferential reaction, where a voice in her head said, "Why don't you put some makeup on, you'd look a lot better then." This is the cultural scripting for many Asian women which the therapist had also swallowed, which says, in her mother's voice, "An Asian woman's face is her fortune.'"

White client, Black therapist
- Positive transference: Amy deliberately sought out an Asian therapist because, as a child, she had been bullied by some of the white children at school and was befriended by the Asian kids. Her stereotype of Asian people was that they were, "reliable, honest and hard-working." She had therefore sought out an Asian G.P, an Asian secretary, and an Asian therapist!
- Negative transference: Simon is a white gay man working with a Black therapist. He reported that he was unable to talk about his sexuality with her, as he thought that Black people were more homophobic then white people.

Cultural countertransference
The next example highlights the cultural differences within the same ethnic group. Here both the therapist and client are Asian women. The therapist is an Indian woman of Hindu parentage. The client is Muslim from Pakistan. Their cultural scripts are therefore quite different. The therapist is aware not only of centuries of conflict and hostility between Hindus and Muslims in India; she is also aware that her ancestors were involved in the persecution of Muslims. She is sometimes aware of a degree of tension between herself and the client, which has felt almost tangible. She sometimes feels that the client's father is condescending and is mocking her, as if he is saying, "Who do you think you are, you Indian woman from the village?" In response, she is aware of her own Parental voice, which is saying, "I know what you Muslim men are like, always oppressing women." She is taken by surprise at the anger she has experienced, since she knows that from her Adult, she does not believe this. She sometimes feels that between them, they are bringing centuries of religious oppression into focus in the consulting room.

Lennox Thomas (quoted in Kareem and Littlewood 1992) argues that the relationship between the Black therapist and the Black client is a complex one, in that it has to deal with the effects of internalised racism. He states that a Black therapist raised in a white society will need to have developed a positive self-identity about their race, culture and self, against many obstacles. A positive self-identity will be one that resists the common negative stereotyped views of Black people. Hence, it is important for Black therapists to explore in their own personal therapy how race and racism has affected their own self-development. The degree of racism many Black people have experienced and internalised is profound.

Implications for psychotherapists
As psychotherapists it is our responsibility to explore all our ego state responses to race and racism. We accept that our parents, grandparents, and

great-grand-parents form some part of our psyche. We need to consider how these important parent figures respond to people who are different. It is equally important to know the contents of our structural Child ego state and how we respond from this place.

Orbach (1999) states: 'Racism is such an ubiquitous aspect of western life that we don't have a hope of escaping it.' (p. 120). Orbach underscores the importance for therapists to process 'the psychological fallouts of racism' (p. 121) Given the above, what are the survival strategies that might be evoked when faced with visible difference, both for the therapist and for the client? Our premise is that the processes of therapy are a mirror image of the processes contained in wider society. Thomas (1992) states that a white therapist 'raised in the confidence of their superiority of their whiteness' (p. 151) will bring this dynamic into their practice, and there is potential for this dynamic to be re-established. He quotes Curry's concept of 'pre-transference' which relates to 'what we learn about people's social or ethnic groups and ...leads us into thinking that we know individuals from those groups long before we meet them.' (p. 151). He goes on to say that racism:

> is a functional part of the ego structure and we each need to know what it acts in the service of. The practising therapist...can often find themselves derailed by these issues with the emergence of their own countertransference through conventional attitudes to their patients' race.   (p. 151)

An important task for psychotherapists is to enable the client to name the 'unsayable'. Daniel Stern (1998) talks of mirroring as representing affect attunement. For the developing child, mirroring is an important mechanism through which s/he develops a sense of self. Does this sense of self include being visually mirrored through seeing their own skin colour reflected back to them? If this is important, does the same apply to the client-therapist dyad? As Black trainees and clients it has been our experience that it is deeply impactful to have our Blackness mirrored back to us by a Black psychotherapist/trainer. Johnson (1987) states that the infant's deep wish to be special to the parent is experienced through mirroring by the parent. If this is incomplete or unavailable, the infant experiences deep shame, and buries his or her needs by mirroring others, i.e. pleasing them or excluding themselves. For Black people who grow up as a racial minority, the lack of their own race being mirrored or reflected back to them is profound. As a result, some Black clients experience a sense of not belonging, not being good enough, and from their Child ego state, they wish they were white. This is often evident in the transference and countertransference responses in the therapeutic relationship.

Perhaps it is good enough to provide a supportive therapeutic environment in which clients may externalise their internal processes. A big contribution to this, however, is the therapist's willingness to process and acknowledge their own thoughts and feelings about their race and racism. An additional factor to bear in mind is that for Black people, their racial identity is consistently present and a constant reminder that they are the 'other'.

In wondering about the client's presentation, it is sometimes very difficult to separate family issues from those stemming from survival decisions concerning racism. Self-hatred might result from mis-attunement by the family, *and* from stereotypes about black people. How do therapists process this material without looking at their own stereotyping processes? For most therapists, it would be more familiar to go with psychological explanations linked to child development within the family. Thinking about racism requires us all to honestly assess how we might collude with racial stereotyping. The term racism evokes strong feelings in Black and white people/psychotherapists. White colleagues have talked of feelings of guilt, and shame, and shutting down on their curiosity, not knowing what would be OK to say. Valerie Batts calls this a form of 'modern racism' (1998). Black colleagues talk of the pull to please, to minimise our differences, and not raise the issue of racism for fear of being disliked and/or causing upset. Frank Fanon (1952/1986), back in the 50s, wrote about black people putting on a mask in order to survive in white society. As psychotherapists we are in a unique position to understand and process the dynamic of racism. If we take a moment to ask ourselves what the term 'black' symbolises for us, and similarly what meaning the term 'white' might hold, this would enable us to surface aspects of our cultural scripting which we take as given.

Splitting in the Child ego state

Moiso's (1985) work on ego states and transference serves as an useful tool for speculating about the symbolism attached to the colours black and white, and how these serve the process of racism. From a very young age fairy tales and folklore teach us to differentiate good from bad. Eric Berne (1972) called this splitting (between good and bad) the fairy godmother and the witchmother. Moiso (1985) goes on to say that this splitting is a 'defensive division protecting the Adult (A_2) from intrapsychic conflicts' (p. 183).

The colours black (bad) and white (good) are used to separate one from the other. This split is reinforced through cultural, social and political processes and maintained through a level of discounting of here-and-now information (e.g. the significance of skin colour and/or the humanity of Black people). Our thinking is that in order for white people to view Black people as OK, their blackness needs to be negated or 'magic-ed' away ("we are all the same really") (P_{1+} transference). In the following examples we will illustrates the effects of this splitting. By and large, this is an out-of-awareness process, involving tensions within the Child ego state.

White client, Black therapist

A white client living for the first time in a multi-ethnic area of London seeks psychotherapy because of her high levels of anxiety. She is referred by her GP to an NHS service where she is seen by a black psychotherapist. On exploring with the client her fears of being amongst black people she is invited to express her thoughts and feelings about being with a Black therapist. She quickly states that that she does not see the therapist in the same way. As she talks of her upbringing in rural England, the therapist begins to understand her need to keep the therapist 'OK and safe', i.e. to become an 'honorary white person' for her. The therapist in turn needs to hold and contain her own feelings about not being seen, while her client gradually resolves her split.

Within the therapeutic relationship this client struggles with wanting and needing to relate to the therapist. The fact that the therapist is Black is enormously challenging for her. In order to feel safe, the client needs to split off the therapist's racial identity and what this might mean to her. If she did not do this, her anxiety about Black people would then also be in the therapy room; she would not be able to maintain the bond she has and needs with her therapist. Drawing on Moiso's (1985) ego states and transference diagram, we can track this process.

Fig. 2: Transference of colour

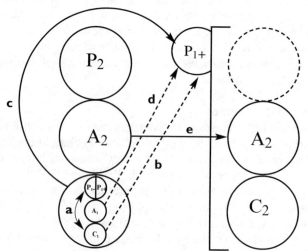

Developed from C. Moiso (1985) diagram in *Ego States ansd Transference*

a $P_{1(+\ \&\ -)} \longleftrightarrow C_1$: Black people are dangerous   *internal dialogue*
b C_1:   I need you
c C_2:   You are my fairy godmother   *splitting process*
   You will save me
d A_1 :   You are not be the same   *transference message*
   You are not like those 'other Black people'
e $A_2 \longleftrightarrow A_2$:   I don't see you as Black   (C_1: feels relief)

The other side of this process is the splitting off and projection of P_{1-} onto the Black person. Here the Black person is seen only for their blackness and what they represent in white society. Everything else about them is discounted. The Black person is not seen for who they are, but is on the receiving end of racism. The effects of this projection could be at a minimum, to avoid contact with Black people, and at its most dangerous, literally to get rid of them, as in the case of Stephen Lawrence[1]. We argue that both P_{1+} and P_{1-} projections are different forms of racism.

Black client

The effects of the above process on the Black Child ego state structure are complex and profound. One internal decision in response to this abuse is for Black people to deny their own Blackness, in the hope of belonging and being accepted. Reshma recalled a time when she was 2-3 years old; she had started wiping her hands, saying she didn't want to look dirty. She wanted to look like her friend Elizabeth who was white (and therefore clean). As a child at school she was bullied by white children, who believed she was inferior and dirty. Reshma spoke about how as an adult, sometimes her white friends and colleagues said that they did not see her as Asian or thought that she wasn't like other Asian people. Initially, Reshma was pleased by this, as she was embarrassed and ashamed of being Asian, and she did not want to be seen to be different from her white colleagues.

Structural ego state analysis and symbiosis

The above process has significant implications for the therapeutic relationships between Black and white clients and therapists. In our experience, Black clients with white therapists can hold back and minimise their 'blackness'. Second Order structural ego state diagnosis often will reveal P_2 commands to be loyal to their race and culture (*don't tell them anything about us*), C_2 feelings of shame and envy, and A_2 decision to hold back until there is some evidence that the white therapist demonstrates an awareness of the significance of race and racism. Structural ego state analysis of white people may in turn reveal guilt about their own history. This then acts as a barrier to openness and curiosity about the therapeutic relationship. The therapist's discomfort about racial difference is picked up by A_1 in the Black client. The Black Child has an instinctive need to keep 'them' (powerful people/white people) OK, at the expense of their own C_1 needs. The Schiffian (1975) model of Second Order Symbiosis helps clarify this process. The Child ego state of the Black client maintains the relationship by suppressing his/her needs in the service of the white therapist's needs. Putting a theoretical frame around this process highlights the need for all psychotherapists to process and understand the significance of their own racial identity, and how this influences their relationships with clients across all races, and other areas of inequality. Thomas (1992) suggests:

> even a Black patient who has a sophisticated understanding of racism and its effects on the inner world might have a long-held fantasy of 'white is right. (p. 142)

A supervisee reported feeling that her relationship with her white supervisor

Fig. 3: Racism discounted within the symbiosis

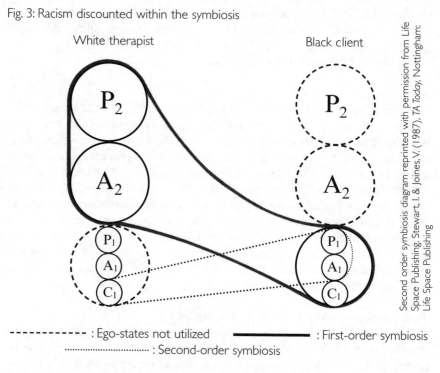

White therapist

Black client

Second order symbiosis diagram reprinted with permission from Life Space Publishing. Stewart, I. & Joines, V. (1987), *TA Today*, Nottingham: Life Space Publishing

- - - - - - - - - - : Ego-states not utilized   ━━━━━━ : First-order symbiosis
················· : Second-order symbiosis

was a good one, as she received valuable professional support from it. However, part of her also felt that she was not being seen for who she was. When she explored this in her own therapy, she realised that she felt that her supervisor had not seen or accepted the fact that she was Black. She also became aware that she had not confronted her supervisor, because she was scared that by bringing up the issue of race and racism it would threaten their relationship, and the supervisee would then not have the vital professional support she needed. So in order to maintain contact with her supervisor, she denied her race and culture and her feelings about this. Her A_1 decision in this case was "In order to keep this white teacher around it is best for me to deny my blackness." She was aware that in her C_1 she felt deeply ashamed of being Black. Her experience at school was also of having to hide her race and culture, in order to survive in a predominantly white setting.

With this new awareness and understanding she decided to bring up the issue with her supervisor. Her supervisor responded by suggesting that perhaps she had a need for a 'perfect' supervisor. Through her ulterior transaction of "You are making a fuss", the supervisee's needs were missed. The supervisee then felt bad and ashamed for 'upsetting' the supervisor and drawing attention to her blackness, i.e. her difference. She then withdrew and chose not to bring up this issue again. In doing so, she confirmed her script belief that white people needed to be protected from racism and that drawing attention to her colour was deeply shameful. It was only after exploring this issue with her Black colleagues and her therapist that she was able to decide, using her Adult, that she could either choose to continue to confront the supervisor about what was not being acknowledged in their relationship, or choose another supervisor. What she wanted to explore with the supervisor was what it meant for her as a Black woman to be with a white supervisor, and how this might impact on their relationship.

In this example, there is a first-order symbiosis between the supervisor and the supervisee, with the supervisor being in Parent and Adult. However, the supervisee, using her A_1, also picks up the supervisor's sense of defence, guilt, and shame around race and racism. Using her P_1 and A_1 she decides to take care of her supervisor's C_1 in order to keep her around.

The above also demonstrates the importance of white therapists and supervisors having an awareness and understanding of the power dynamics between Black and white people in society, and how this can be replicated in the therapeutic and supervisory relationship.

Conclusion

We have highlighted some of the issues stemming from the intra- and inter-psychic dynamics of race and culture and, in particular, their relevance to the therapeutic relationship. TA has many useful theoretical models, which offer tools for extending their application to include cultural and racial differences. Given that we now live in multi-cultural Britain we believe that, as therapists, it is imperative for us to develop skills, understanding and awareness of how we all play a part in the dynamics of race and racism. We need to actively engage all our ego states in order that we may influence and inform our work as psychotherapists and supervisors.

We are familiar with the world of psychotherapy being predominantly white and middle class, with an unstated expectation that people outside these categories need to fit in, in order to belong. It is commonly accepted that psychotherapists need to process their own vulnerabilities in order to work effectively with clients. Oppression impacts us on personal, social, cultural and political levels. The issue of the significance of culture, racial identity, the place we occupy in the world as a consequence of this identity, and the meanings we make about self and other, is no different.

Suhith Shivanath and Mita Hiremath wish to acknowledge Beverley Allwood Ellis for her part in the development of this material.

Notes

1 The Stephen Lawrence Enquiry refers to the Macpherson Report, chaired by Sir William Macpherson of Cluny and published in 1999, into the police investigation of the racially motivated murder of Black teenager Stephen Lawrence. The report makes many recommendations for the reform of the Metropolitan Police service and the UK police force as a whole, to eradicate institutional racism.

2 GP: General Practitioner, the term used for medical doctors providing a general medical service within the community
3 NHS: UK National Health Service

References

Batts, V. (1998) Modern racism: new melody for the old tunes in *EDS Occasional papers No.2*. Massachusetts: Episcopal Divinity School

Batts, V. (2000) ITA Conference, Canterbury, England

Berne, E (1961) *Transactional Analysis in Psychotherapy*. New York: Souvenir Press

Berne, E (1961) *Games People Play*. New York: Grove Press

Berne, E (1983) The mythology of dark and fair: psychiatric use of folklore *Transactional Analysis Journal* 13(3)

Carter R (1997) Race and psychotherapy: the racially inclusive model, in Thompson and Carter : *Racial Identity Theory*, New Jersey: Lawrence Erlbaum Associates

Fanon, F (1952/1986) *Black Skin, White Masks*. London: Pluto Press

James, M & Jongeward, D. (1971) *Born to Win*. New York: Signet

Johnson, S. (1987) *Humanizing the Narcissistic Style*. New York: Norton

Kareem, J. & Littlewood, R. (1992) *Intercultural Therapy*. Oxford: Blackwell Science

Kohlrieser, G. (1999) The Kosovo refugee crisis, in *The Script*, ITAA, California

Levy, A. (2000) The Guardian Newspaper, 19th February

Moiso, C (1985) Ego states and transference, *Transactional Analysis Journal* 15(3), *Volume of Selected Articles from the TAJ*, 1981-90, California

Orbach, S (1999) *The Impossibility of Sex*. London: Penguin

Roberts, D (1975) Treatment of cultural scripts. *Transactional Analysis Journal* 5(1)

Schiff, J.L., with Schiff, A.W., Mellor, K. Schiff, E., Schiff, S., Richman, D., Fishman, J., Wolz L., Fishman, C., & Momb, D. (1975) *Cathexis Reader: Transactional Analysis Treatment of Psychosis*, New York: Harper & Row

Steiner, C. (1974) *Scripts People Live* New York: Grove Press

Stern, D. N. (1998) *The Interpersonal World of the Infant*, London: Karnac Books

Thomas, L. (1992) In Kareem, J. & Littlewood, R. (1992) *Intercultural Therapy*. Oxford: Blackwell Science

White, J.D. & White, T. (1975) *Cultural Scripting. Volume of Selected articles form the Transactional Analysis Journal*, 1971- 80. California

Chapter 10

'WHO AM I FOR YOU?'
The Child ego state and transferential domains

Helena Hargaden and Charlotte Sills

In this chapter our primary focus is an analysis of the influence of the Child ego in the therapeutic/transferential relationship. In other words, we offer a model which allows for an exploration of unconscious processes. While we recognise that there are contrasting models and views on the Child ego, we write from the view that the Child ego has a literal meaning, (there was once a childhood), is of symbolic significance, and is the basis of developmental understanding in psychotherapy. For the purpose of this discussion, we draw upon our theory of self and three transferential domains (Hargaden and Sills 2002). This model allows for a diverse understanding of the Child ego as well as providing a map to chart subjective and unconscious processes. Thus we are less concerned with making a case for objective reality. Briefly restating our theoretical perspective, we give a definition of deconfusion, and under the headings of the transferential domains recount vignettes which show how the Child ego state can be a force for both good and ill in transactional analysis relational psychotherapy.

Throughout the chapter we use the words client and patient interchangeably, since we think client suggests autonomy and patient suggests depth in the work. We use the word transformation both to specify a type of transference, and also in the more usual sense of describing a process of change. Although we would normally try to avoid the reification of the Child ego state, we take poetic licence in our symbolic references to the Child.

The gift of the Child ego state
One of Berne's first definitions of an ego state was that it merely denoted, 'states of mind and their related patterns of behavior as they occur in nature.' (Berne 1961/1968 p. 30). Berne observed that patients shifted from one ego state to another. It is now well documented that Berne, drawing upon research and his own clinical observations, classified ego states into three categories, Parent, Adult and Child. In his original definitions, Berne distinguished the Child ego state by its, 'autistic thinking and archaic fears and expectations (primary process).' (ibid. p. 31). We have observed in our practices that many clients present with such traits. Although some people can disguise this internally regressed state quite well, the astute transactional analyst will soon notice signs in the therapeutic relationship that all is not as it appears.

Whilst patients may operationally be diagnosed as in their Adult ego state, phenomenological enquiry can elicit a different clinical picture.

Developing the work of Federn, (1977/1953), one of Berne's gifts to the psychotherapy community was to identify the Child ego state. This concept is readily understood by anyone, of any culture or any age. It is simple and easy to grasp. Even those patients with an excluded Child ego state understand the concept. The term Child evokes archetypal images and resonates in our unconsciousness. It conveys a straightforwardness, a humanity, a need for acceptance; it elicits a warmth in ways which the more academic and pejorative connotations suggested by those terms describing similar manifestations of regression, such as, id, object or primary process, do not. The term can also elicit other feelings, negative and dismissive ones.

Child ego as symbol and conduit for transformation

> The child motif not infrequently occurs in the field of psychopathology…. But the clearest and most significant manifestation of the child motif in the therapy of neuroses is in the maturation process of personality induced by the analysis of the unconscious, which I have termed the process of individuation.
>
> (Jung CW9, 1, p. 279)

Symbolically the Child contains within it transformative powers. After all, it was the child within us who created our self-image - a masterly work - and such other amazing devices as our scripts and rackets. This describes a paradoxical situation, for the potential for good and ill spring from the same source. Such a work of art demands at the very least an imaginative response from the therapist. We caution against a too reductive approach which may squash the life force of the Child for therein lies the spirit and soul of our client. We must avoid the castrated version of humanity that is conjured up in the use of the word 'decontamination'. The Child ego state, symbolic of transformation, offers possibilities for both therapist and client to work in tandem, to aspire for better and to allow space for the emergence of conflictual ego states and release the potential for healing. As one client in a therapy group put it: "Once I thought I would leave therapy in a blaze of glory, with certificate in hand and yet another achievement to show the world - now I am leaving because it just feels right to leave…. and for the first time in my life, allowing myself to stay until I want to go feels like a reward which I can really not put into words - I just feel a happiness inside, a loosening and a strong feeling of self love."

Child ego as negative influence in the therapy

Unfortunately, the Child ego state also evokes at times an overly sympathetic or controlling response. Whilst it is a natural countertransferential response to feel protective or directive with clients who are regressed, it is not, in the final analysis, therapeutic to work with the Child ego state in a literal way. To do so often leads to supporting a permanent regressive state rather than facilitating the move towards maturity. For instance, a supervisee offered his client an object for him to take home from the therapist's office during a break, because the client expressed fear and anxiety. Such an action makes the client feel temporarily cared for and perhaps – more to the point – makes the therapist feel effective; but ultimately most of these tokens of 'caring' do not enable the development of a mature ego. Although well intentioned, such actions contribute to an infantilisation of the client who may suspect that the therapist cannot bear his pain. It is no wonder then that some clients can develop a belief that somehow the therapist should meet their needs, that there is something almost sacred about needs and that once identified they must be met at every possible turn. Thus the therapist can become an instrument of gratification rather than one of growth.

Fig. 1: The Cohesive Self

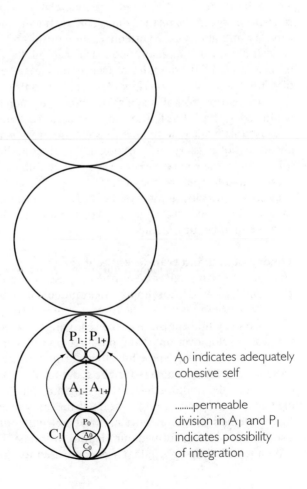

A_0 indicates adequately cohesive self

........permeable division in A_1 and P_1 indicates possibility of integration

Hargaden & Sills (2001)

The Child often has malevolent intentions which can hinder growth if not addressed. If envy, greed, contempt and lack of respect are not analysed, then the therapy can founder and be sabotaged by the unconscious. If, for example, the therapist fails to adequately mirror the hostile, nasty, perhaps envious Child, those malevolent aspects of self will not become conscious. We explore this in more detail below in the story of Tina.

Deconfusion of the Child ego state

Deconfusion is the process by which the therapist facilitates the patient to connect with her internal Child ego and bring experiences, feelings and sensations – in other words complex states of the mind – into the therapeutic relationship. It is the process by which the client is enabled to become more conscious. As the patient connects with her Child ego state, she will contact aspects of her self that as yet have remained under-developed (described as walled-off experiences and located in C_0 - Fig.1). She will also connect with aspects of her self that feel alien and other to her which we locate in P_1. Through the process of the transferential relationship, this unconscious material will emerge in the relationship. The treatment plan involves the therapist's capacity and ability to be attentive, thoughtful and skilful in understanding her countertransferential responses. The methodology for deconfusion consists of an analysis of the domains of transference together with the therapist's use of empathic transactions (Hargaden and Sills 2002). The aim of deconfusion is the transformation of unconscious processes such as archaic, dormant and conflicted aspects of self, into a more conscious, vibrant and mature dynamic. Because this work is so unique to each and every person, there is, inevitably, an element of mystery and paradox in this process. When Joanna left therapy, for example, she smiled rather ruefully. The things she had most feared and dreaded had happened, one of which was that she had lost her job. In some respects she had lost a lot – particularly her illusions and fantasies. Yet she smiled. "I have my self", she said. The therapist felt humbled and yet satisfied with the therapeutic outcome.

Theory of Self and transferential domains

Our model of the self is described fully elsewhere (Hargaden & Sills 1999, 2001, 2002) so we do not propose to examine it in depth here, only in as much as is necessary to introduce the three domains of transference.

We see the Child ego state as the self, with C_1, A_1 and P_1 as aspects of the self that develop over time from pre-birth onwards, much as Stern (1985) sees the domains of self. The Child then forms the heart of the person and is brought to every encounter - for good and for ill. We offer, in Fig. 2, a reformulation of the traditional ego state diagram, which locates the self (C_2) and the Parent (P_2) ego states at the heart of the 'present self' (A_2); as we see every Adult interaction as a manifestation of not only our here-and-now self but also the self that has formed our identity over time.

Within the Child ego state, C_1 is comprised of the primary, fundamental relationship between infant and environment (mother) – which we describe as P_0/C_0 (see Fig. 1). This relationship is contained within the Child ego and is probably best understood as an internalised model of interaction which has been described by Stern (1985), as giving rise to reactions that have been generalised. The earliest ways of being with and interacting with the 'other' lay down the foundation of what can best be understood as 'implicit relational knowing' (Tronick et al 1998). Thus, this relationship will colour the tone and shape of relationships to come. Where there has been extensive misattunement or little attunement, the experience of self remains under-developed. There is neurological evidence to suggest that this is the case; '…a number of disciplines are now converging on the centrality of the basic principle that the growth of the brain is dependent upon and influenced by the socioemotional environment' (Schore 1994, p.78). The under-developed self is therefore unable to be autonomous until certain structures in the brain are activated through the relationship which begins in utero. This suggests a type of schizoid process where a secret, internal world has never been activated, and we locate these aspects of self in the walled off parts of C_0. These primal yearnings are implicated in what we have called *introjective transference.*

Fig. 2: The Whole Self

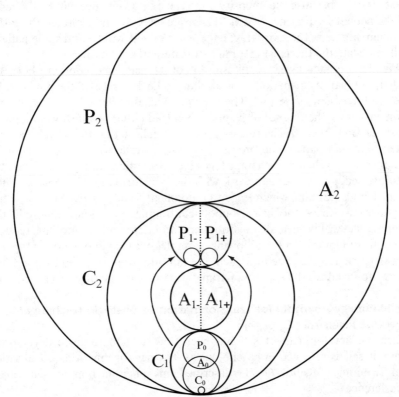

Hargaden & Sills (2001)

When the infant feels 'beside herself' – engulfed and overpowered by emotional experiences that are not contained by the mother or by the environment, then the infant represses these feelings. Such feelings are experienced as P_1 and have an 'other' feel to them. This process of 'other' emerges in what we have called the *projective transferences* (P_1). In other words, we see P_1 as the repository of rejected elements of infantile experience alongside the internalised perceptions of parental responses. We believe that every individual will have inactivated affective states, and suppressed or split off at least some aspects of her experience. The extent of this will depend on the interplay between infant and caretaker. When there has been significant cumulative trauma then there is more fragmentation; the patient will strive towards mental health using a process of projective identification, which we have called *transformational transference.*

These categories are meant as a map to enable the therapist to chart some of the complex feelings that emerge through the transference. These transferential domains are not really discrete and co-exist alongside each other in the treatment. Overall, we consider all types of transference as an unconscious attempt by the patient to co-create a series of transactions that involve the therapist in finding the appropriate emotional and cognitive response. A theoretical distinction between transferential phenomena can be supportive to the therapist, because the intensity and type of transference will be the result of the patient's experience of self. The more insecure and ruptured the earlier attachments were, the more fragile the sense of self will be and some patients will implicate the therapist in a multi-transferential relationship.

We believe that every manifestation of transference contains both the potential for transformation – the attempt to heal – and also the potential for the reinforcement of script. The therapist will find herself often in pivotal moments where her choice of response will lead either to transformational or to sterile outcomes. As as rule of thumb we believe that the more literal the interpretation of the Child process - the more sterile will be the outcome of the therapy. When the therapist is able to contain, analyse and use her intuitive self, she will able to work with the transformational energy available in the Child ego state, which leads to fundamental shifts in ego energy. When the therapist relies too heavily upon contractual guidelines and reductive analysis, she will be stranded by too literal an interpetation, and thus reduced to sterile outcomes. In the following examples, we examine the three types of transference and describe how each one can offer opportunities for the Child energy to be either the symbol of transformation, or the obstacle to change.

Child energy – symbol for transformation or obstacle to change?
Introjective transference/C_0 longings
When the development of self has been thwarted, the urge to develop the sense of self is reflected in psychological strivings for mirroring, idealisation and twinning. Kohut (1971) describes this phenomenon as self object transferences.

Introjection is both a defence and a normal developmental process; a defence because it diminishes separation anxiety, a developmental process because it renders the subject increasingly autonomous.

(Rycroft 1968)

In this type of transference the patient seeks to enter a symbiosis (Shiff et al., 1975) with the therapist in order to meet developmental needs. The patient seeks to introject the therapist as an unconscious psychological striving towards health and autonomy.

The introjective transference refers to how the patient experiences the therapist and could be described as the implicit relationship. When the introjective transference emerges, the patient feels that the therapist is benign, neutral in some way, attentive, warmly interested, engaged, perfectly attuned, capable, and even affectionate. Patients who have an unconscious need for a prolonged experience of self-immersion, such as patients who were children of overly self-involved parents, and who have not experienced an attentive environment, seem to require this transference specifically. For example, Anna went to see two therapists for an initial assessment. The first therapist offered interpretations about the issues Anna brought and she left feeling that she had been pathologised. The second therapist asked some general questions and listened carefully to her answers. She smiled at times, nodded at others, but although enquiring, was mainly quietly attentive. Midway through the session Anna smiled and her eyes widened; she looked very young, and the therapist realized that she was internally quite regressed. "I like it here - I want to come and see you." It became clear that Anna felt secure and safe and was clearly at the beginning of an idealizing transference. As this was only the first session, the therapist had little idea why this transference emerged so quickly or was so obviously needed. Indeed, at first glance, it seemed as though the patient had little or no problems of any significance. Naturally, the story became more complex, as the therapy progressed. Anna had suffered significant psychic loneliness with a mother who was defensive and self-obsessed, and who required Anna to be a mirror for her. Her father too, had required that Anna mirror his needs for her to be ineffective at sport, stereotypically 'feminine' in the misogynist sense of being physically and mentally his inferior.

The striving of the Child for the perfect sense of attunement and loving attachment that may have eluded his infanthood, or been too early abrupted in childhood, acts as a positive symbol for change.

When Bill arrived at therapy the therapist experienced him as garbled and inarticulate. One of the most defining features of his childhood had been the death of his father, when Bill was only fourteen. Bill's initial issue was that his wife had left him to have an affair with another man, thus breaking up the family they had made with their two-year-old daughter. Bill was in despair, grief, anger and pain but could not articulate it. The therapist found herself required to listen and attempt to make sense, whilst feeling quite frustrated and puzzled for many of the sessions. She invited Bill to join her therapy group and for the first time it became more clear how he was using her in the therapy. He described the therapist, to the other group members, as an 'honorary man'. He was quite taken aback when she reflected this back to him at a later stage, since he did not remember it. She interpreted his sense of her as a man as his unconscious striving to finish and complete the growing up he had never quite managed to do when his father died and he had been left feeling burdened and under developed, yet required to be the 'man of the house'. Through the process of therapy he became stronger, more decisive and less inclined to look after the women in his life to the detriment of his own needs and psychic happiness. In essence he seemed to become more masculine, taking charge and dealing with the complexities of divorce, a new relationship and the development of a new family in ways which had never been voiced as the object of the therapy. Yet the therapist was sure that the introjective transference was the domain in which they mostly worked. He used her as a sense of protection, security and attentiveness – like a good father's presence – but eschewed any attempts at transactions which may have been more penetrating. The therapist learned to go with her intuition and at the same time used empathic interpretations as the sense of the therapy became clearer to her. Bill was indeed transformed in the therapy; although nothing dramatic ever occurred and nothing very concrete or tangible ever emerged.... Bill changed, and seemed to become a man.

Within this transferential domain, however, the Child energy can sometimes block the progress of the therapy. For instance when a patient persists in idealization and requirements to merge and seems unable to move into individuation, the therapy can feel lopsided and there is a sense that something is not quite 'right'.

For instance, in Monica's therapy she presented as extremely hurt and battered from sinister and odd experiences with her adoptive mother. Monica seemed to fall in love with the therapist from the very beginning. The idealising transference began almost immediately. For several years Monica used this relationship to feel more confident and gain security in herself. She seemed to have taken in the image of the therapist as good, benevolent and kindly. Naturally the therapist wondered where the bad experiences had gone but increasingly in the therapy, Monica seemed less concerned with them and more involved in her life. At the same time the therapist felt a sense of strangeness that Monica persisted in seeing her in such an idealised fashion. There was no real sense of a mature ego but more an adoring child. The therapist began to feel that it was time to deal with some of the projective feelings, that she was sure were being denied. At the same time she hesitated about raising this. Just as the therapist started thinking about this Monica began raising the question of ending her therapy. The therapist, although still ambivalent, wondered aloud, with Monica, about the more negative influences from her past and suggested that she might be putting the therapist on a pedestal. Monica became quite indignant and argued with the therapist that she did not need to deal with her idealization and that she wanted to keep things that way for 'ever'. Monica left therapy shortly afterwards, telling the therapist that she thought she was wonderful, and would keep her in her heart forever. On reflection, it could have been that Monica was correct and that she could not have tolerated connecting with the projective aspects of her 'self' that had been kept so firmly outside the walls of the therapy room. Nevertheless the therapist knew that nothing transformational had taken place because the idealisation had persisted and not been worked through, although, of course, this may even have been right for Monica as not everyone either requires to (or perhaps should) go through the deconfusion process.

Projective transference (P_{1+}/P_{1-})/defensive and splitting transferences

These transferences occur when the patient projects P_{1+}/P_{1-} onto the therapist in order to work through unintegrated experiences. It is well known that, owing to the influence of Melanie Klein (1988), projection has been accepted as a normal developmental process. In a misattuned environment the infant splits between good and bad. 'Splitting of both ego and object tends to be linked with denial and projection, the trio constituting of a schizoid defence by which parts of the self (and internal objects) are disowned and attributed to objects in the environment.' (Rycroft 1995 p.173). The projective transference is the patient's mechanism for keeping a coherent sense of self whilst projecting repressed internal conflict onto the therapist.

We build on the work of Moiso (1985) whose article offers a clear articulation of the P_2 and P_1 transferences and the implication of these for the process of psychotherapy. We believe that in fact it is possible to project material which may be conceptualised as any of the second and third order ego states, not only the Parent ones. We see this in everyday life in such situations as when a mother turns rageful towards her toddler, when the toddler is manifesting some aspect of infanthood that had been forbidden to the mother in her past, which triggers her P_{1-}. In the psychotherapy setting, the client may invite the therapist into a Parent to Parent competitive symbiosis (Schiff et al 1975) at either the traditional P_2 level or at the P_1 level, as he projects his vulnerable A_1 outwards. Most often, however, it is the Parent ego state (P_1) - experienced as other - that is projected onto the therapist.

Elsewhere (Hargaden and Sills 2001 2002) we have described the process by which a person builds his or her identity based on the foundation of his C_1. Most people have some good experiences and some bad experiences of themselves and other people, and as time goes by they manage to integrate them well enough. Some individuals, however, have early experiences that are so painful, chaotic and unbearable that there is no coherent sense of OK self; C_1 experiences are fragmented, split off or suppressed. The sense they make of themselves in the world (A_1 and P_1), the 'story of themselves', is created in such a way as to protect them from recathecting the trauma of C_1 (see Fig. 3 where the lines delineating the split in A_1 are impermeable). Commonly this story is labelled 'narcissism' in the psychotherapy world. People with a narcissistic injury form a picture of themselves as perfect (in A_{1+}) and create a 'perfect parent' for themselves in P_{1+} who offers them the unconditional approval and admiration that they needed and did not receive as infants. Such individuals present themselves to the world as shiny and glossy. They have taught themselves not to experience discomfort and only do so in those moments when something happens to shake their vision of themselves as 'the greatest', adored by the 'perfect other'. In order to support such a defence, this person needs to have a reasonable supply of people onto whom he or she can project P_{1+}. As children they may have had adoring but uncontactful mothers whose praise and love was delivered when the child fulfilled the mother's narcissistic needs. As adults they may have jobs which carry the sort of power that ensures adulation, or at least compliance and support from others – whether out of true admiration or out of fear. This individual becomes skilled at avoiding, dismissing or derogating anyone who will not support his frame of reference.

When such a person comes for therapy, it is often because something has happened that simply cannot be redefined as positive, thus the individual feels exposed to painful feelings and a sense that his whole self is crumbling. Alternatively, he may say that everything is fine, but that life is passing and 'surely there must be something else'. He is losing his looks or his interest in making money or his excitement about controlling the world around him; basically the things that shored up his glossy successful identity are no longer working.

Moiso (1983) makes the important point that narcissistic clients are likely to start therapy by projecting their idealised (we might say idolised) P_1 onto the therapist. (Note that this is a different idealisation than the one described under Introjective transference and denotes a different psychological need.) They do this because their security and comfort is based entirely on maintaining their sense of themselves as 'the best'. Moiso warns that the therapist must consent to accept this transference and work in this unreal glow for a significant period of time, until the client feels safe and accepted enough to be able to bear a challenge to his frame of reference. To confront the idealisation too soon would result in such a loss of inner stability for the narcissistic person (to say nothing of a loss of face) that he would have to denigrate the therapist and leave the therapy. In the case of Monica above, this is exactly what happened. Even though the therapist did not confront the idealisation, Monica left, since in effect, there was nowhere else for the therapy to go unless the full projective transference emerged. Perhaps this was the very thing which Monica was avoiding. This then is an occasion for therapist abstinence, and we have talked elsewhere about the client's need to literally *use* the therapist in the symbiosis, to use her assumed power (in the three 'P's of Berne and Crossman (1966)) to support him while he dares to test the boundaries of his 'gilt-edged' self.

We have diagrammed this sort of defence as an impermeable split in A_1 and P_1, in which the individual establishes a fixed-circuit loop of A_{1+} and P_{1+} as his identity. But there is another way of creating that impermeable defence against a fragmented early C_1. People whose childhood was characterised by

Fig. 3: The Child Ego State: The undeveloped self

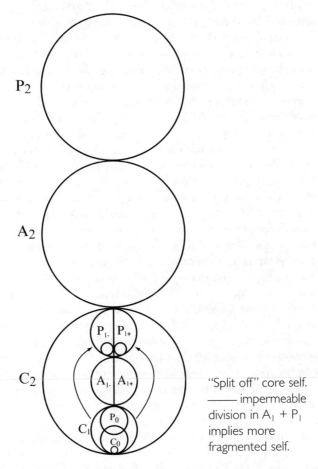

Hargaden & Sills (2001)

P_2

A_2

C_2

P_{1-} P_{1+}

A_{1-} A_{1+}

P_0

C_1

C_0

"Split off" core self.
———— impermeable
division in $A_1 + P_1$
implies more
fragmented self.

unremitting criticism and abuse, may have the same injury to the self, the same need to create for themselves an identity that avoids the early pain. But in order to be congruent with the world around them, they may create an internal loop of A_{1-} and P_{1-} that is every bit as essential to their sense of themselves in the world as the apparently more agreeable persona of the obvious narcissist. Their fundamental self-concept is as bad, miserable, and inept. They hurl insults on their own heads and seem inexplicably to be at their most congruent when they are acting out, cutting themselves, berating themselves and so on.

Fran appeared to make a positive connection with her therapist from the start. The therapist liked her and sympathised with her painful situation as Fran attempted to raise her children alone, after having eventually been abandoned by her abusing husband. She struggled with money, she found it hard to hold jobs, she was tortured by memories of her father who had abused her for years in her childhood, then killed himself when school officials began to investigate Fran's disturbed behaviour. For two years, the psychotherapy proceeded successfully, including decontamination of Fran's belief in herself as the guilty victim and the world as abusing and persecuting. She also seemed to find some relief in telling the therapist about her childhood, weeping for her young self and her father.

However, as time went by, the therapist began to notice a pattern whereby, however well the work had gone, Fran somehow reverted to her picture of herself as bad and 'useless'. Whatever changes she made in her life, some unexpected event would occur to dash her hopes - her new job would collapse, her children would attack her, or she would be turned down for income support. Again and again, she would present as defeated and hopeless, railing against the 'authorities' in some guise or another. At first the therapist empathised with her plight. He was not going to discount the existence and significance of the social and economic difficulties Fran endured and he felt very supportive of her efforts to take charge of her life. Gradually, however, he became more and more frustrated. He was also aware of feeling inadequate and ashamed. How could it be that after all this time, Fran should still have the same self-hating beliefs about herself and resentment towards the world? How could it be that he was clearly involved in a Game – where he was the unsuccessful Rescuer (the ineffectual neighbour of Fran's childhood, who had known about the abuse but had nothing to offer except sympathy)? He tried challenging her commitment to change but that was met with woeful agreement and an increase of self-criticism on Fran's part. He tried encouragement and affirmation. Fran received it with gratitude, seemed temporarily to shift, and then slipped back to the original position, as she did after numerous apparently successful pieces of redecision. The therapist felt completely defeated himself and he shared that with Fran, whose only response was to be pleased that he knew how it felt.

The therapist began to understand that this negative loop (A_{1-} and P_{1-}) was essential to Fran's functioning. This was the sense of self for which she had been recognised. Her mother, a disturbed and disturbing woman, had seen Fran as representing all that was weak, bad and useless. She hit her frequently and encouraged the other children to bully her. When her husband killed himself, rather than have his abuse exposed, she blamed Fran wholeheartedly. The therapist realised that this was not an impasse that could be redecided. Fran had no 'other self' from which to redecide. Therefore, when the psychotherapy work had come close to intimacy, to a real feeling of love or need, Fran had retreated into the negative loop. She experienced the invitation to change as a threat to her survival, a loss of her fundamental sense of self in relationship.

The therapist therefore started to do nothing. He sat with Fran and got as 'near' to her feelings as he could. He amplified her self-hatred from time to time, or simply stayed with her quietly, neither supporting nor contradicting. Metaphorically, he let himself be used as Fran's caretaker. Metaphorically, his client was the little girl who sits on the broad accepting lap of her nanny, banging her head against the unprotesting chest as she roars for her mummy. Little by little, she began to speak more directly to him and he started to feel more signif-icant to her. Fran's air of defeated victimhood deepened to grief and despair and then eventually to a sense of wholeness.

The way we make sense of what happened in this therapy is in terms of ego states and self. Fran could not cathect a different ego state, a more positive iden-tity, because of the fear of loss of self. She had no idea who she was if not the defeated victim. So instead of the therapy acting to change her script beliefs, she needed to integrate tiny pieces of positive relationship into the negative self that she knew. Over time, that 'conceivable self' began to change very slightly. Fran was able to recathect the disowned experiences of her C_1.

In our experience, this type of A_1/P_1 structure is extremely rigid and not easy to modify. A great deal of patience is needed of the therapist, who is required both to hold safe the notion of the client's potential self while prac-tising abstinence in terms of any investment in change, or betraying any inkling that the client is not completely OK as she is.

Transformational transferences C_1/P_1

The patient brings into therapy not just the content of past relationships, but also the experiences of how things were done and how events unfolded - which is why words alone are not sufficient. Stern, (1985) refers to this process as RIGs (Representations of Interactions that have been Generalized). These patterns of attachment have been co created with a past caregiver and other significant people in the patient's background. The patient knows uncon-sciously what they need but may often be unable to communicate it except on a behavioural or symbolic level. In the case of cumulative and/or traumatic experiences the inarticulate speech of such a heart can only communicate symbolically through a process of projective identification. This process is described by Ogden (1992), who proposes that the infant induces a feeling state in the other that corresponds to a state that he is unable to experience for himself. The recipient allows the induced state to reside within, and by reinternalizing this externally metabolised experience, the infant gains a change in the quality of his experience (Ogden 1992). In this transference, the therapist is required to transform the experience by making it containable and meaningful. In other words, she must hold it and model a way of managing it that is different to the client's experience. In the following vignette, we show how unarticulated aspects of the patient's archaic Child emerged into the therapy. In this instance, the Child was trying to wreck the therapy and only through a consideration of the projective identification was the therapy saved from malevolence.

When Tina decided that it was time to end her therapy, she and her therapist discussed how they would take perhaps up to a year to bring the therapy to closure. This length of time seemed right given that Tina had attended twice a week indi-vidually, and once in a group, over a lengthy period of time. Tina's history was one of turbulence. Her parents had both been severely narcissistically wounded.

They were grandiose in their lifestyle, intemperate, and apparently seemed to have very little grasp of reality. They had economically fallen from a great height and consistently struggled – and failed – to take care of their four children. Fortunately for the children, social services responded by fostering them out fairly regularly and taking care of their schooling needs. Thus Tina had survived through a combination of some excellent schooling and pockets of adequate parenting. Despite all this, she had retained an idealised relationship with her parents whom she had at times represented as artists and poets. The idealisation had kept Tina out of the dreadful despair and abandonment she had suffered throughout her life.

Throughout the therapy there had been considerable transferential processes but now it seemed that Tina had worked through these and the therapist felt satisfied that Tina was freer to live her life than she ever had been before. A year before Tina decided to leave, she had met a man who was very different from the abusive types with whom she had been involved in the early days of her therapy. This in itself testified to Tina's changed psyche and yet the therapist, whilst wanting to wholeheartedly support Tina's leaving, felt that something was not quite right. She tried to ignore it, understanding that she may be caught up in a type of perfectionism. But the feeling did not go away.

As the therapy drew to an end the therapist observed with increasing dismay and frustration that Tina was continually turning up five to ten minutes late at the group, then sitting heavy and withdrawn, seemingly unconnected to the sessions. Although the therapist enquired, hypothesised, challenged and confronted it was to no avail. Tina said that she did not know what was going on.

Eventually, one evening, Tina rang to say that she would be about ten minutes late. When the therapist put down the phone she felt a surge of anger and thought, "Why do you bother to come at all? Why not leave us alone?" Hearing her feelings, the therapist realised that she felt attacked, immobilised and impotent. Tina arrived to the group twenty-five minutes late. The therapist confronted her again. Another member of the group chimed in saying that as she had been driving towards the group session that evening, she had felt a heavy feeling of not wanting to come and declared with irritation that she was fed up with Tina and wished she would go. Another member said she felt the same since it seemed that Tina was neither engaged nor attached. Some one else spoke up to say that actually he was beginning to feel confirmed in the part of him that thought therapy was "a load of bollocks". Upon hearing these comments the therapist felt alarmed. She felt that the group and the therapy was under attack and felt a sense of destruction. The emotional tension in the room was palpable and the therapist nevertheless thought that at least, now, something was happening and Tina was at last engaged! Searching for inspiration into herself she suddenly remembered the story of how Tina's family home had been burnt to the ground, and how shortly afterwards, her father had died, alone and isolated in hospital because he had been unable to contact any of his family. She inquired of Tina how she had said goodbye to her father – and what had happened when the flat had burnt down. In the emotional atmosphere created by the group members and the therapist, Tina connected with previously repressed experience. Her passive mask collapsed and her face contorted with grief as she sobbed and recounted the story of the destruction of her home and the death of her father. She realized that she had never grieved her father's death. Nor had she dealt with the trauma of the fire which had been caused by a very disturbed member of her family. As the story unfolded, the group members felt lighter and the therapist was able to feel true compassion. The darkness and heaviness experienced by members of the group vanished as Tina sobbed. In a later session Tina interpreted the events as having happened to a different person. She recognised that she had been disassociated and too frozen to connect with the loss of her father and deal with the devastating effects of the fire in which she had lost so much. She recognised that the ending of the therapy was, in some way, similarly traumatic. She was bringing to an end a close, involved and committed relationship in which she had felt so much that had never before been expressed. She had felt so heard, met, mirrored and loved and the thought of saying goodbye brought back the painful feelings of cumulative abandonment and the final terrible betrayal of her father, who died alone, in hospital and in despair. It took enormous integrity and courage for Tina to stay connected with her feelings and her understanding.

As the therapist listened, she knew then the full extent of the destructive and envious forces that formed part of Tina's internal psychic world. They had remained unconscious until the ending had forced the archaic experiences to become more conscious, through the unconscious pressure upon group members and the therapist. The malevolent Child force had tried to destroy the goodness of the group and the therapist who had become more and more powerless just as Tina must have felt in the face of such destruction.

Through this transformational process the therapist found the possibility for empathy towards Tina. She recognised that in some ways she had missed mirroring some of the more distorted, hostile and destructive aspects of Tina's self. Now she could appreciate the extent to which contempt had played a significant and covert aspect of the therapy. For instance she recognised that she had ignored Tina's lateness quite often, whilst at the same time she had allowed Tina to reduce her fee, considerably. As she considered these aspects now, she was able to bring the contempt into awareness in the therapy in a non-punitive way which led the way towards integration. Tina became more calm and relieved, as she felt mirrored in the part of her that had been hidden in the shadows.

Conclusion

Facilitating a client to integrate non-verbal or suppressed parts of self involves the therapist in trying to find a way to hear the coded messages that express the inarticulate speech of the heart. We believe that this requires a careful analysis of the dynamics between client and therapist, which cannot take place without therapist involvement, intuition and imagination, and can be aided by an understanding of three domains of transferential and countertransferential relationship. These dynamics arise from the Child ego state, which we believe to have the potential for being both the transformational energy for growth and also the destructive saboteur of the therapy. Recognition of these potentials adds a new dimension to the therapist's understanding and practice.

References:
Berne, E. (1964) *Games People Play,* New York: Grove Press

Berne, E. (1968) *Transactional Analysis in Psychotherapy*, Souvenir Press, London. (First published 1961, Grove Press, New York.)

Crossman, P. (1966) Permission and Protection, *Transactional Analysis Bulletin:* San Francisco: TA Press

Federn, P. (1977) *Ego Psychology and the Psychoses* Maresfield Reprints (first published 1953)

Hargaden, H. and Sills, C. (1999) The Child ego state: an integrative view, *ITA News.* Spring Edition

Hargaden, H. and Sills, C. (2001) Deconfusion of the Child ego state, *Transactional Analysis Journal* 31(1)55-70

Hargaden, H. & Sills, C. (2002), *Transactional Analysis: A Relational Perspective*, Routledge Press, London

Jung, C. G. *Collected Works,* Vol.I para. 279. Edited by H. Read, M. Fordham, G. Adler & W. McGuire, (translated by R. Hull). London: Routledge & Kegan Paul

Klein, M. (1988) *Envy and Gratitude and Other Works 1946-1963.* London: Virago Books

Kohut, H. (1971) *The Analysis of the Self,* New York: International Universities Press

Moiso, C. (1985) Ego states and trandference *Transactional Analysis Journal* 15(3)194-201

Ogden, T. (1992) *Projective Identification and Psychotherapeutic Technique*, London: Karnac Books

Rycroft, C. (1968) *A Critical Dictionary of Psychoanalysis*, (Second Edition) London: Penguin.

Schore, A.N. (1994) *Affect Regulation and the Origin of the Self* , New Jersey: Lawrence Erlbaum Associates

Schiff, J.L., with Schiff, A.W., Mellor, K. Schiff, E., Schiff, S., Richman, D., Fishman, J., Wolz L., Fishman, C., & Momb, D. (1975) *Cathexis Reader: Transactional Analysis Treatment of Psychosis*, New York: Harper & Row

Stern, D.N. (1985) *The Interpersonal World of the Infant*, USA: Basic Books

Tronick, E. Z. and the Process of Change Study Group (1998) Non-interpretative mechanisms in psychoanalytic therapy: the "something more" than interpretation. *International Journal of Psychoanalysis:* 79(5)903-921

Chapter II

THE NEOPSYCHE:
the Integrating Adult ego state
Keith Tudor

In transactional analysis literature, of the three ego states the Adult ego state is the least developed. Twenty five years ago Krumper (1977) commented that 'the Adult ego state seems to get little attention in TA theory' (p. 299), an observation which is as true today as then. A survey of articles published in the *Transactional Analysis Journal* over four decades (1962-1999) reveals 18 on the Adult ego state, compared with 70 on the Parent and 27 on the Child, reflecting 16% of the total number of articles on Parent, Adult and Child ego states. In *Transactional Analysis in Psychotherapy,* Berne (1961/75a) comments on the features of the ego state model as presented in the two-dimensional medium of diagrams on paper, reflecting that 'the Parent was put at the top and the Child at the bottom intuitively' (p. 60). Assuming that Berne himself wrote that sentence 'in Adult', it is interesting that the Adult ego state appears to attract less of his intuition. Here, in Berne, as elsewhere in TA theory and practice, the Adult ego state is a residual state left over after all the elements of Child and Parent have been detected, and reduced to 'the earthly realities of objective living' (ibid., p. 60). It is as if the symptomatology of TA itself excludes the Adult from its full analysis, design or consideration.

During the course of writing this chapter I asked a number of TA practitioners what their view of the Adult ego state was. Responses included: "There's nothing in it", "It's empty", "It's separate", "Who wants to be a computer?", "Adult is boring. It just does things", "It's here today, gone tomorrow: today's Adult is tomorrow's Child", even "Does the Adult exist?" These comments and questions reflect not only the responses or reactions of particular practitioners, but also, more broadly, reflect the Adult as portrayed in TA literature. Despite more recent work developing Berne's (1961/75a) incipient notion of the Integrated Adult (such as James & Jongeward, 1971; Erskine, 1988; Erskine & Moursund, 1988, Lapworth, Sills & Fish, 1993), Berne's description of the Adult as a data-processor still haunts TA. Even the 'Integrated Adult' appears a somewhat dull and static entity. In this chapter, I aim to lay this particular ghost by describing and developing an expansive Adult ego state which characterises a pulsating personality, processing and integrating feelings, attitudes, thoughts and behaviours appropriate to the here-and-now - at all ages from conception to death. This present-centred state of the ego has the ability and capacity to act autonomously (with awareness, spontaneity and intimacy), to laugh, have fun and be silly, to learn, to develop and maintain a critical consciousness, to aspire, to express ambivalence and disappointment, to have a sense of community feeling, social justice, spirituality, and much, much more... The Integrated - or, more accurately, *Integrating* – Adult describes the individual's capacity to reflect upon and integrate their own archaic states as well as past introjects, and to draw on them in the service of present-centred relating - in life as well as in the therapeutic milieu, whether as therapist or client.

In arguing the case for this expansive and Integrating Adult, this chapter is divided, like the courses of a substantial meal (to be digested over time), into five parts. Before offering a critical review of the literature on and models of the Adult ego state from Berne (1961) onwards, I firstly locate these discussions in the context of debates about ego states in general. In doing so, I discuss the implications of the metaphor of 'ego states' and lay the theoretical foundations for the Integrating Adult by considering TA as an organismic psychology. Following this (in the third part of the chapter), I present a revised model of the Adult, based on constructivist approaches to TA and, specifically, co-creative transactional analysis (Summers & Tudor, 2000).[1] This provides a methodology for the practice of expanding the Adult ego state. Given my constructivist reading both of TA as well as the therapeutic field in general, I emphasise the social/cultural context of such theory and practice and development as well as its relation to health psychology. The chapter concludes with a reflection on the implications of an expanded notion of Adult ego states for TA itself. Whilst the chapter is written in a certain, linear and logical order, the reader, depending on their interest and appetite, may of course skip the *antipasto* (ego states) and even the *primo piatto* (on the Adult ego state in TA literature), preferring instead to address the *secondo* or main course (on the Integrating Adult) first: in other words, each part is designed to read independently – and, of course, interdependently.

Ego states

Ego states are fundamental to TA, indeed it may be said that they define TA. As Berne (1970/73) put it: 'Parent, Adult, and Child ego states were first systematically studied by transactional analysis, and they're its foundation stones and its mark. Whatever deals with ego states is transactional analysis, and whatever overlooks them is not' (p. 223). Since Berne's original work, notably Berne (1961/75a), the definitions, diagnosis, structure and function of ego states have been much debated (see particularly Novey et al., 1993 as well as other references in this and other chapters). No conceptual or clinical deconstruction, reconstruction or expansion of the Adult ego state can take place in isolation from the Parent and Child ego states and current considerations of their nature, structure and function. Thus, in this first part, I refer to some discussions on ego state theory, following which I discuss the implications of the ego state metaphor, and the value of meta perspectives on ego state theory and models.

Ego states – states of the ego
Drawing originally on a biological metaphor, Berne (1961/1975a) described aspects of human mental activity as 'organs' or, more precisely, 'psychic organs' whose function is to organise external and internal material. Drawing on Federn's (1953) work identifying states of the ego, Berne (1961/75a) defined these 'phenomenologically as a coherent system of feelings related to a given subject, and operationally as a set of coherent behaviour patterns, or pragmatically, as a system of feelings which motivates a related set of behavior patterns' (p. 17). Berne viewed the personality as a complex system, *which may be thought of as* being organised into three structures:

1 An elaborative system connected to the mental-emotional analysis of the here-and-now (the *neopsyche*)

2 A system aimed at organising introjected psychic material (the *exteropsyche*)

3 A system linked to the organisation of instinctual drives, basic needs and primary emotional experiences (the *archeopsyche*).

These systems form the basis of three discrete mental, emotional and behavioural organisations which Berne referred to as *ego states*, naming these 'psychic organs' and their activities as the Parent ego state (exteropsyche), Adult ego state (neopsyche), and the Child ego state (archeopsyche), (see Fig. 1).

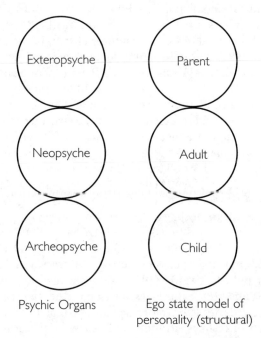

Exteropsyche

Parent

Neopsyche

Adult

Archeopsyche

Child

Psychic Organs

Ego state model of personality (structural)

Fig. 1: Psychic organs and corresponding ego states (Berne, 1961/1975a)

However, as Jacobs (2000) points out: 'the relationship between the psychic organs archaeopsyche, neopsyche, and exteropsyche...and the ego states Parent, Adult, and Child...is a distinction between an *imagined framework* and the identification and naming of behaviours into *generalized categories*' (p. 12, my emphasis). Furthermore, following Holloway (1977) and Ohlsson (1988), Jacobs argues that there are many state*s* of the ego in relation to each psychic organ, the implication of which is that the familiar structural diagram does not reflect the myriad functional manifestations of these three psychic absolutes. Whilst I agree with Jacobs on this as regards the Parent and Child - and that it is more accurate to use the terms Parent ego state*s* and Child ego state*s* - I do not agree with regard to the Adult manifestation of the neopsyche (an argument developed below.) In any case, it was unfortunate that Berne chose to represent psychic organs and ego states by means of identical diagrams which reflect and imply correspondence.

Moreover, once Berne moved beyond this original (first order) structure of the personality, matters became more complex. Indeed, Berne's (1961/75) original second order structural analysis ego diagram, in which he labelled the original ego states P_1, A_1 and C_1 and then subdivided them (to include P_2, A_2 and C_2), has subsequently been renamed P_2, A_2 and C_2 with the subdivisions - within the Child ego state only - carrying the nomenclature P_1, A_1 and C_1! A second complexity (and confusion) concerns different understandings (and ego state diagrams) about human (child and later adult) development. A number of TA authors - Levin (1974), Schiff et al. (1975), Woollams and Brown (1978), Klein (1980), Levin-Landheer (1982), Novey (in Novey et al., 1993) and Hine (1997) - propose an unfolding, epigenetic development of ego states, broadly, Child, then Adult, and then Parent. (For a comparison of the theories of Levin, Schiff et al. and Klein, see Magner, 1985). However, these views are based on a conflation and confusion of metaphors; on the one hand, ego states as an image and representation of the structure of personality and, on the other, ego states as a metaphor for stages of development. Assertions that the Adult ego state (A_2) does not begin to develop until 12 months (Levin, Schiff et al., and Woollams & Brown), 18 months (Klein) or 'a later stage of cognitive development' (Hine 1997, p. 285), are not based on a structural definition of ego states. If the Adult ego state is defined as 'characterized by an autonomous set of feelings, attitudes, and behaviour patterns which are adapted to the current reality' (Berne, 1961/75a, p. 76), it follows that the neonate has an Adult ego state (see Gobes in Novey et al., 1993) or, as Sprietsma (1982) puts it: 'a person is actually "Born Adult"' (p. 228). In the spirit of James and Jongeward's (1971) comment that 'the Adult ego state is ageless' (p. 277), and taking this logic one step further (back), I suggest that a person is conceived Adult or, more accurately, that the foetus, developing autonomous sets of feelings, attitudes and behaviour patterns, adapting to its reality *in utero*, may be thought of as having a neopsyche or an Adult ego state (- and, of course, depending on its experience in the uterine environment and that of its mother, may also develop an archeopsyche and exteropsyche with their respective Child and Parent ego states, see Fig. 4 below and Bale, 1999). This view is also consistent with developmental theorists as diverse as Lake (1980), Stern (1985) and Piontelli (1992) - and is represented in part three.

One of the great problems in discussing ego states within (let alone outside) TA is the different - and *differing* - views and models of ego states. This confusion dates back to Berne himself, who defined ego states in contradictory ways (Berne 1961/75a). Central to our current concern is the issue as to whether the Child ego state is defined as comprising fixated material only, and the Parent as comprising only introjected material; or whether both Child and Parent also 'contain' archaic experiences and introjects which are script free. As Stewart (2001) points out, one's view of cure is dependent on which of these two definitions is adopted, that is, whether the 'totally cured person' may be characterised as having only an Integrated Adult, or whether s/he has all three ego states: 'it's purely from this difference in definition that the difference between the two models arises' (Stewart 2001, p. 144). In the absence of standard nomenclature and agreed definitions (and unlike Stewart I think this is no bad thing), in the interests of open (and clear) communication, I think it *is* incumbent on authors and practitioners, supervisors and trainers to be clear about the models and definitions they use - and in this I agree with some of Stewart's (2001) 'call to action'. In using and discussing definitions, I find the 'if...then' formulation of philosophical logic consistent with constructivist philosophy, accurate and useful, thus: "*If* we define Adult in such a way, *then* we may consider this quality or experience as Adult - and, by implication, not Child or Parent".

The matter of metaphor

In referring to Berne's view of personality (above), I emphasised the phrase '*which may be thought of as*' to reflect and represent the metaphorical 'as if' nature of 'ego states'. In this I am with Loria (1990), Allen and Allen (1991, 1995), Schmid (1991) and Jacobs (2000) in viewing ego states as useful metaphors for understanding personality, rather than 'realities' in themselves. However, from Berne (1961) onwards, a number of theoreticians and practitioners within TA have argued that – and from the basis that – ego states are real (see Jacobs, 2000 for a useful review of these different traditions). However, although, following Federn (1953), Berne (1961/75a) claims that Parent, Adult and Child are 'phenomenological realities' (p. 24), he does not claim the ego state *model* as 'real'; 'hence a set of circles... *may be taken as a fair way of representing* the structure of personality' (p. 40, my emphasis).

One of the problems with ego states and the ego state model is, as Loria (1990) observes, that they (and it) have become reified:

> the concept *ego state* that was used originally by Berne in a figurative or illustrative manner has taken on the characteristics of a *thing* with its own constitution and existence – the metaphor has become reified. Like Berne's mythical "psychic organs"...an ego state cannot be abstracted from a person like a gall stone. (p. 154)

As Jacobs (2000) comments: 'at this point it is doubtful if psychic organs will ever be identified with actual neurological sites' (p. 12) - although Drego (2000) appears to find a way of squaring these particular circles by emphasising the *phenomenological* nature of psychological realities. Notwithstanding this, the general reification of ego states as absolute realities misunderstands the nature and use of metaphor.

Kopp (1971) defines metaphor 'as a way of speaking in which one thing is expressed in terms of another, whereby this bringing together throws new light on the character of what is being described' (p. 17). Thus metaphor is, as Gordon (1978) puts it, a 'novel representation' of something. It is not the reality or the referent object; neither is it the only way of representing and describing the referent (in this case human personality); and it needs re-freshing. In this sense 'ego states' and 'ego state diagrams' are merely metaphors, which may be assessed by their accuracy in offering a representative description of personality, and their usefulness in facilitating clinical (educational and organisational) practice - and social change (after all TA is a social psychiatry). In discussing the person-centred approach, a colleague said "The reason I like the [person-centred] approach is because it's got the best metaphors" (P. Sanders, personal communication, January 2001) - 'best' in this sense meaning the most useful, philosophically coherent, personally compatible, etc. In many ways choosing a particular theoretical orientation may be viewed as: "You pays your money, and you buys your metaphor"! Three implications follow from this perspective on metaphor and are briefly elaborated with regard to TA.

A metaphor is a metaphor is a metaphor

Transactional analysts, along with other therapists and practitioners involved in 'talking therapy' clearly need to mind their language, indeed, to mind about language, and to have a view about the nature of metaphor as well as the metaphors they and their clients use. Viewing and talking about the Adult as an objective data-processor clearly influences the way we think about ourselves and others, what it means to be Adult (and adult), the nature of therapy, cure, etc..

The metaphor that is the metaphor is not the metaphor

This echo of Taoist philosophy - the way that is (presented as) *the* way is not the way, encapsulated in such sayings as 'If you meet the Buddha on the road, kill him!' - reminds us to stay awake to the dangers of standardisation and regulation, whether theoretical, intellectual, professional or organisational. The reification and objectification of ego states and the ego state model itself and the over-detailed concern (even obsession) with what's 'in' particular ego states (- the answer to which is, of course, nothing -), contradicts Berne's original contribution of structural analysis as a 'systematic *phenomenology*', especially in his and its attention to detail regarding the requirements for diagnosis (Berne 1961/75a).

Metaphors are mutable

Metaphors need to be renewed in a continual process of novel re-presentation. The problem with the ego state model of transactional analysis is, in this respect, the problem of inaccurate, unhelpful and outmoded metaphors such as the data-processing, computer-like Adult. Also, as the metaphorical frameworks of therapy are influenced by the *zeitgeist* (see Sanders & Tudor 2001) - and vice versa - it is important that metaphors and the language of therapy also reflect and represent the zeitgeist and, of course, people's constructions of it:

> We prefer to think of human psychology in terms of a different, more enduring - and, for us, a more satisfactory - metaphor, namely an ecological one. The person-as-biological-system is best understood as a complex micro-system within and connected to a complex macro-system. Psycho-technology, then, is of no more use in human healing than technology has been in taming the forces of nature.   (Sanders & Tudor 2001, p. 149)

Furthermore, as Jacobs (2000) puts it: 'creating alternative metaphors will develop a more personal, *mutually constructed relationship* between helper and helped' (p. 21, my emphasis). If we argue (as I do) that the foetus has an 'Adult', this may be the point at which the Parent, Adult, Child metaphor breaks down and we need to represent new metaphors by means of new nomenclature such as 'past self' or 'fixated (experienced) self' (Child); 'other self' or 'fixated (introjected) self' (Parent); and 'present self', 'fluid self' or, if I nail my colours to an organismic mast, more accurately and simply, 'organism' (Adult).

From metaphor to metatheory

If the critiques offered in this first part of the chapter thus far may be characterised as from *within* (concerning ego state theory and models) and from *alongside* (regarding metaphor), then this section offers a critique from *above* i.e. from a metatheoretical perspective.

Pine (1990) identifies four psychologies based on four different views of human nature: drive theory, ego psychology, object relations and self psychology theory. As Sills and Hargaden point out in their introduction to this volume, this taxonomy offers a useful metatheory for understanding the different (and differing) theories and models of ego states within TA. What Pine omits, however, is organismic psychology, based on organismic motivation (see Woodworth with Sheehan 1931/65; Goldstein 1934/95; Hall & Lindzey 1978). With the exception of its influence on the person-centred approach and, to a certain extent, on gestalt psychology and psychotherapy, organismic psychology is one of the lost traditions in the history of twentieth century psychology - although, interestingly (and significantly for our present purposes), Hagehülsmann (1984) suggests that most schools or traditions within TA rest on assumptions which represent an organismic model of human nature. Taking Hall & Lindzey's (1978) summary of organismic theory, Table 1 compares this with aspects of TA as a way of setting out the theoretical foundations for a more organismic view of the neopsyche.

Organismic theory	Transactional analysis
Organismic theory is integrative 'Organismic theory emphasizes the unity, integration, consistency, and coherence of the normal personality. Organization is the natural state of the organism; disorganization is pathological and is usually brought about by the impact of an oppressive or threatening environment' (Hall & Lindzey 1978, p. 298).	There is an increasing interest in integrative TA and TA as an integrative psychotherapy (see Erskine & Moursund, 1988; Clarkson, 1992). The implications of health psychology and 'normal personality' have been explored by Cornell (1987) and Summers & Tudor (2000) amongst others. In this sense, organisation may be viewed as Integrating Adult (A_2) and 'disorganisation' as Child and Parent.
Organismic theory is holistic Thus, whilst its constituent parts may be differentiated for analysis, *any such part is not abstracted in principle from the whole.*	This argues for a more holistic view of the personality (than is generally current in TA) in which ego states are seen as a useful atomistic abstraction (or not) only in the context of the organismic, holistic organisation of such 'parts'.
Organismic theory is based on a unitary drive theory In the more general field of humanistic psychology, this is usually conceptualised as the drive of self-actualisation (see Maslow, 1967/93).	This is not prominent in TA. Berne refers only occasionally to drive theory in his writings. The influence of Freudian ideas on drive appears in Berne's references to *eros* and *mortido* (Berne, 1969/81). The nearest Berne comes to a 'drive theory' is his thinking on human hungers (Berne, 1970/73). Interestingly, Hine (1997) views ego state theory as 'an early integration of drive theory (wired-in networks), and self-schema theory (networks developed mainly in the self-other relationship)' (p. 284).

Organismic theory (cont.)	Transactional analysis (cont.)
Organismic theory emphasises the inherent potentiality of the organism for growth This refers to the actualising *tendency* to be found in all organisms and in nature itself (see Rogers, 1959, 1978, 1980).	This was recognised by Berne in his references to physis (see Berne, 1963, 1969/81, 1972/75b).
Organismic theory is all-encompassing This refers to the broad theoretical base offered by organismic theory for understanding the total organism.	TA is generally viewed by its proponents as offering a broad understanding of the total organism/person in their context, especially given its fields of application. Berne's (1961/75a) outline of the significant properties of the ego states/psychic organs involves reference to a wide-ranging multi-disciplinary knowledge base.
Organismic theory takes a holistic approach to the study of the person This follows on from the previous point and emphasises heuristic research methodology.	TA's approach to research over the years has tended to be more empirical than heuristic.

Table 1: Locating TA as an organismic psychology

Within TA and based on Berne's (1961/75a) own criteria for ego state diagnosis, Drego (2000) identifies four ego state models (actually meta models or paradigms) - the phenomenological, the historical, the behavioural and the social - which have what Drego refers to as 'socioethical aspects' which affect the quality of human life. She presents this overview of ego states from a multi-dimensional perspective on science; one in which ego states are both metaphorical and real, intrapsychic and transactional, archaic and contemporary.

Having reviewed the context or ground in which Adult ego states are located, I now turn my attention to the figure of the Adult ego state itself. In the second part/course (*primo piatto*) of the chapter, the TA literature on the Adult is reviewed; this is followed, in the third part (*secondo piatto*), by an elaboration of the Integrating Adult ego state.

The Adult ego state in TA

Whilst numerous contributions and models over the past forty years have developed the structural analysis of Parent and Child ego states at a second and even third order level, the Adult remains largely blank. This is, in part, due to Berne's (1961/75a) ambivalence about the Adult - indeed, he himself describes this as 'the most obscure area in structural analysis' (p. 195). In a short passage on the Adult in a chapter on the 'finer structure of the person-ality' (Berne 1961/75a), three important points concerning Berne's thinking about the Adult may be discerned.

Berne places 'ethos' (moral qualities) and 'pathos' (responsible feelings) within the Adult (see Fig. 2). The A_2 between ethos and pathos was later referred to as 'technics' (Kertesz & Savorgnan, cited in James & Jongeward, 1971) - and is sometimes referred to as 'logos'. In his article on ego structure, Erskine (1988) suggests that, along with ethos and pathos, logos (the ability to use logic and abstract reasoning) and technos (the ability to create) 'describe the full neopsychic capacity of the Adult ego state to integrate values, process information, respond to emotions and sensations, and be creative and con-tactful' (p. 16).

Although Berne represents these as a second order structural analysis of the Adult, it is not clear precisely what is 'second order' about this incipient and somewhat speculative analysis.

Also, it is not clear what the remaining A_2 (sic) (the Adult in the Adult) represents. Although this finer structure is sometimes referred to as Berne's embryonic 'integrated Adult', he himself acknowledges that 'the mechanism of this "integration" remains to be elucidated' (Berne 1961/1975a, p. 194). It is indeed a 'tentative formulation' (*ibid.*, p. 195).

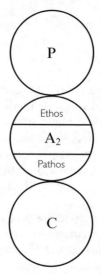

Fig. 2: Second order structure of the Adult (Berne, 1961/1975a)

Thirdly (and perhaps most importantly for our current concern), Berne does advance a view of the epigenetic origins of the Adult:

> It appears that in many cases certain child-like qualities become integrated into the Adult ego state in a manner different from the contamination process...it can be observed that certain people when functioning *qua* Adult have a charm and openness of nature which is reminiscent of that exhibited by children.   (pp. 194-5)

This is a significant passage, which hints at the integrative process (or 'mechanism') whereby qualities, attitudes, feelings, behaviours, and thoughts, which are integrated into the Adult, are uncontaminated and unproblematic. At the same it infantalises the Adult by suggesting that Adult qualities are 'child like' in origin - not only metaphorically ('as if') but structurally. This is itself a serious contamination of what it means to be Adult (also see Gobes in Novey et al 1993). Lest this be viewed as a momentary slip, a few sentences later, Berne elaborates:

> transactionally...anyone functioning as an Adult should ideally exhibit three kinds of tendencies: personal attractiveness and responsiveness, objective data processing, and ethical responsibility; representing respectively archaeopsychic, neopsychic and extero-psychic elements "integrated" into the neopsychic ego state.
>
> (p. 195)

There are two principle implications of - and objections to - this view:

1 That the Adult in the Adult is (only) an objective data processor. This view is contradicted by human Adult experience, by much subsequent thinking in TA including this present work, and by developments in neuroscience.
2 That the origins of these qualities of attractiveness and responsiveness, and ethical responsibility, lie necessarily in archaic or introjected material. Given Erikson's influence on Berne (see Stewart 1992), this view is presumably based on an epigenetic formulation of child development (e.g. Erikson 1950) and is contradicted by research in the field of child development over the past fifteen years (see, for instance, Stern 1985).

Other models of the Adult ego state in TA

The problem inherent in these implications is, again, based on a confusion of models and undeclared differences of definition, and specifically, a conflation of the structural and functional models of ego states. In the above passage from Berne, the key lies in the words, 'anyone *functioning* as an Adult...'. This is not only prescriptive and somewhat grandiose ('anyone'), it is partial, as it is concerned only with functioning.

As regards the functioning of the Adult, there has been some considerable debate over the years as to whether the Adult 'contains' feelings. Eminent transactional analysts such as Steiner, James and Harris have asserted that the Adult is 'impassionate', without feeling, unemotional, etc.. Developing the ubiquitous computer analogy, Krumper (1977) suggests that, like any other computer, the Adult may be divided into subsystems representing: the function of memory (content) (Ac) (analogous to recording tape), and the function of associative processes (Aa) (analogous to the central processor). In an attempt to complement the existing theory of the functioning of the Adult ego state, Phelan and Phelan (1978) introduce the concept of the 'fully functioning Adult', with functional subdivisions; drawing on research on the characteristics of left and right brain hemispheres, this accounts for the 'Rational Adult', and the integrated behaviour alluded to by Berne and referred to as the 'Poetic Adult', a term the authors choose to emphasise the 'non linear and creative dimension of thinking' (p. 123). In a similar vein, Kujit (1980) distinguishes between two Adult 'categories': the Analytical Adult and the Experiencing Adult.

While these terms and concepts have contributed to our understanding of the Adult ego state, they have largely done so by means of an implicit functional model of ego states. Describing particular functions of the Adult by use of terms such as the 'Poetic Adult' (a compound noun) implies a particular state of the ego. As Erskine (1988) points out, when Berne (1961/75a, 1964/68) used the terms 'adapted' and 'natural' in relation to the Child ego state, he used them as modifying adjectives, referring to manifestations of intrapsychic dynamics. Terms such as 'Free Child', 'Critical Parent', etc. are problematic, as such descriptions are nominalisations ultimately based on assumptions about the nature of social science - concerned with realism as an approach to ontology (concerning the essence of things), positivism in epistemology (concerning the grounds of knowledge), and determinism regarding human nature - all of which are at odds with a constructivist philosophy and its method of enquiry and practice. In order to elaborate this, it is now time to proceed to the main course (part 3) concerning the neopsychic Integrating Adult.

The Integrating Adult
Alf (client) C.1: *(withdrawn, sitting hunched up, head down on one side)* I'm not sure what I'm doing here. *(pauses, sighs...)* I'm not sure there's any point...if you can help...

Bea (therapist) T.1: *(sighs)* You're not sure if I can help you and if there's any point...

C.2 Alf: *(interrupting, looks up)* That's right *(said with some energy)*, I'm not worth it.

T.2 Bea: You said that with some energy.

C.3 Alf *(aggressively)***:** So?

T.3 Bea: So...you made contact with me, with some energy, when you said

"I'm not worth it". It's as if...

C.4 Alf: Yeah, well, I'm not worth it.

T.4 Bea: *(pause)* It seems that you maintain your view that you're not worth it by interrupting me.

C.5 Alf: *(head down)* I'm sorry.

T.5 Bea: I didn't say that for you to be sorry.

C.6 Alf: *(silent for some time)*

T.6 Bea: Did you get it wrong again?

C.7 Alf: *(nods)*

T.7 Bea: Well, maybe I got it wrong too.

C.8. Alf: *(looks up)* What do you mean?

T.8 Bea: Well, the way I put it, about interrupting me, may have sounded like I was blaming you.

C.9 Alf: *(nods)* Yeah.

T.9 Bea: What I was observing was that you seemed to be judging yourself ("I'm not worth it") and closing the door on what I might say.

C.10 Alf: *(long pause...begins to cry, softly, moving in and out of contact, looking up at Bea and then looking away)*

T.10 Bea: *(maintains eye contact with Alf, when he looks away)* I'm still here.

C.11 Alf: When I was naughty, my mum used to shut me in the toy cupboard. In the end I used to go there first before she could get me.

T.11 Bea: So you used to close the door before she could get you.

C.12 Alf: *(nods)*.

T.12 Bea: That sounds like a good way of protecting yourself then. *(pause)* And now, here, with me?

C.13 Alf: Well I guess I don't have to shut you out... *(continued below p. 222)*

By now it will be clear to the reader that this author favours a definition of the neopsyche as the congruent, expansive and expanding aspect of the individual's personality, which may be expressed in a number of ways. However, it is precisely because of constructivist objections to realism, positivism and determinism in social science and associated 'objectivist' methodology, that this present contribution seeks to develop a systematic *intersubjective* phenomenology of the Adult. It does not, therefore, seek to offer another 'objective' (and ultimately functional) view of the Adult ego state. In developing and describing the 'Integrating Adult', the properties of the neopsyche are explored, as is the nature of its organising principle: integration. This is followed by some concluding observations about the structure of the Adult ego state and the implications of this constructivist perspective for present-centred human development.

Properties

In an important but rarely quoted passage in *Transactional Analysis in Psychotherapy*, Berne (1961/75a) discusses the four significant properties of ego states (and psychic organs) (see Table 2).

Properties	Description	Disciplines
Executive power	'each gives rise to its own idiosyncratic patterns of organised behaviour' (Berne, 1961/75a, p. 75).	Psycho-physiology, physiology, pychopathology, neurophysiology.
Adaptability	to the immediate social situation.	Social sciences.
Biological fluidity	in the sense that responses are modified as a result of natural growth and previous experiences' (*ibid.*, p. 75).	Psychoanalysis.
Mentality	mediating the phenomena of experience.	Psychology, especially introspective, phenomenological, structural and existential psychologies.

Table 2: The properties, description and associated disciplines of psychic organs (summarised from Berne, 1961/75a)

Moreover, 'the complete diagnosis of an ego state requires that all four of these aspects are available for consideration and the final validity of such a diagnosis is not established until all four have been correlated' (p. 75). These properties are briefly elaborated here as regards the Adult ego state.

The *executive power* of the Adult has been discussed more in relation to other ego states than to and of itself, for example: 'the Adult is the only force which can effectively intervene between the Parent and Child, and all thera-peutic interventions must take account of that' (Berne 1972/75b, p. 373). From a constructivist point of view, the transactional analyst is more inter-ested in the 'power in' the client's Adult as distinct from the Adult's 'power over' other ego states or other people. This also offers an empowering Adult-Adult alternative to the Parental (Parent-Child) permission transaction which is, essentially, about 'giving power', an alternative which facilitates people's personal power (see Rogers 1978).

Adaptability to the environment (uterus, family, community, workplace, etc.) is an important feature of organismic development and of being human and, inevitably, a social being, whether child or adult - or Adult. (Again, it is important not to confuse Adult with being 'grown up'.) This is not to suggest that we simply accept, assimilate and adapt to our environment (which may be thought of in terms of passivity, discounting, symbiosis, script and game theory); it *is* to acknowledge that adaptability concerns taking account of others, of limitations and of consequences, tasks which are not only social but also existential. Given constructivist sensibilities to the *inter*subjective and to *shared* responsibility (see Summers & Tudor 2000), the emphasis here is on *inter*-adaptability.

The 'natural growth' inherent in *biological fluidity* reminds us that ongoing adult development (as with child development) includes maturation, learning and socialisation and that alongside continuity in development (from child to adult) there is also discontinuity and even a reversal of patterned interactions (see Neugarten 1968). Similarly, personality development may be continuous, discontinuous or interrupted. The notion of fluidity in growth (and personality) echoes Rogers' (1961) process conception of psychotherapy in which he proposes a movement from fixity (and rigidity) to one of fluidity, at which point 'the person becomes a unity of flow, of motion... he has become an integrated process of changingness' (p. 158).

All aspects of the human psyche mediate the phenomena of experience (*mentality*). In stating this Berne clearly defines TA as a 'systematic phenomenology' - and transactional analysts, therefore, as systematic phenomenologists. What distinguishes the current, present-centred *neo*psyche from its *archeo*psyche (archaic, experienced) and *extero*psyche (archaic, introjected) counterparts is precisely its integrated and integrating process of changingness: experiencing, reflecting, mediating and integrating.

Clarkson and Gilbert (1988) use these properties to argue that the Parent and Child (as well as Adult) are open to growth, development and change. However, whilst the properties of executive power, adaptability and mentality clearly apply to all psychic organs and ego states, it does not make sense that the exteropsyche or the archeopsyche have biological fluidity as they are precisely fixed states: how can you have a Child ego state that grows up?

Whilst these Bernean properties of psychic organs are consistent with Hall and Lindzey's (1978) summary of principles of organismic theory (see Table 1 above), they do not carry the sense of movement and aspiration inherent in the concept of *physis* (Berne 1969/81) or more elaborated in the concept of the 'actualising tendency' (Rogers 1959, 1978, 1980). The characteristics of the actualising tendency, which, like physis, is found in all forms of organic life, are that:
- It provides the sole motivation for human development and behaviour
- It is both individual and universal, holistic, ubiquitous and constant (this is similar to Drego's (2000) view of the wholeness of the Adult)
- It changes in tension
- It is a constructive, directional process which is both organisational and aspirational, towards autonomy
- It is reflective of pro-social human nature
- Reflective consciousness is its salient human channel (Brodley 1999).

Berne himself demonstrated an early interest in science and neuroscience (specifically the experimental work of the neurosurgeon Penfield) and would certainly appreciate the current interest in the pyschotherapeutic implications of research in this field (see Chapter One of this volume). Recent research in neuroscience on the architecture and evolution of the brain demonstrates that it retains features of our ancestors: reptiles, lower mammals and primates, respectively:

- The striatum (also referred to as the basal ganglia) which is responsible for motor routines, including automatic ones.
- The paleomammalian brain (or limbic system) which is associated with emotion and behaviour as well as uniquely mammalian behaviours such as nursing, parental care, play and the infant distress cry. Thus, primal yearnings, which Hargaden and Sills (2002) locate in C_0, are viewed here as age-appropriate 'properties' of the Adult/neopsyche.
- The cortex (or neomammalian brain), the greatest degree of development of which in humans is the prefontal cortex, which is responsible for planning, directed attention, delay of gratification, affect regulation, etc. (see Pally 2000).

Furthermore, and again consistent with organismic psychology, rather than these functions being located in a particular brain region, the brain operates as a dynamic integrated whole (Edelman, 1989). This research is highly significant for discussions about the neopsyche as it is clear that such brain functions are organic and organismic, integrated, Adult and present-centred. In this context, it is clearly more relevant to help people acknowledge their 'inner reptile' or 'somatic simian' than it is to help people to get in touch with their 'Inner Child'!

Having discussed the properties of the Adult ego state, we now turn to the meaning of integration and integrating - which is core to our understanding of the neopsychic Integrating Adult.

Integration, integrating

It is no coincidence that this current work has evolved in the context within the broader psychotherapeutic field of great interest in integrative psychotherapy. Such interest is itself no coincidence given that 'integration', the capacity to reflect upon and make sense of our worlds, lies at the heart of what it is to be human - and at the centre of our current concern. In her major work on concepts of mental health, Jahoda (1958) viewed integration, specifically of our attitudes towards ourselves and our style and degree of growth and development, as a key concept in mental health. Other writers view integration as criterial to psychological health and maturity. In this section I elaborate some of the features of integration - and of the neopsyche (see Fig. 3)

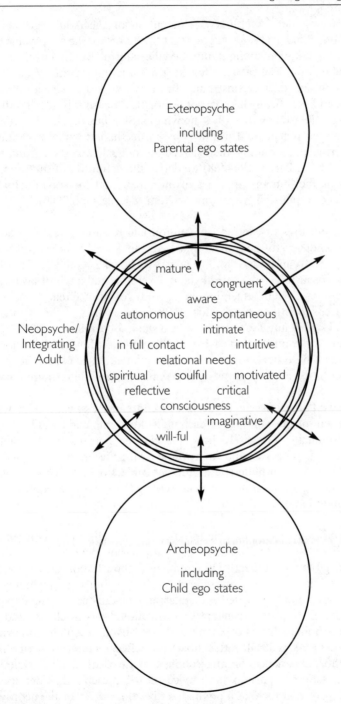

Fig. 3: The Integrating Adult in motion, showing arrows of contact and aspiration

Autonomy Citing Berne's (1961/75a) definition of the Adult ego state as 'autonomous', Erskine (1988) suggests that this refers to 'the neopsychic state of the ego functioning without intrapsychic control by an introjected or archaic ego' (p. 16). The capacity for integration requires freedom as well as separateness from external constraint. In the work of the German philosopher, Kant, and specifically his concept of practical Reason, Brady (1980) sees automony and Reason as virtually synonymous. Significantly, Jahoda's (1958) review suggested that mental health is based on the individual's relation to reality in terms of autonomy, their perception of reality, and environmental mastery, and from Berne (1964/68) we derive the definition of autonomy as the release of the human capacities of awareness and for spontaneity and intimacy - and responsibility (see van Beekum & Krijgsman 2000).

Relational needs Present-centred, age-appropriate relational needs – and the impetus or tendency to meet them and have them met – are central to the neopsyche (and to an understanding of it). Following Kohut (1971, 1977), relational needs are viewed as healthy and developmental and not necessarily pathological. Although emerging in a study of transference, the eight relational needs identified by Erskine (1998) - for security; to feel validated, affirmed and significant; for acceptance by a stable, dependable and protective other person; for confirmation of personal experience; for self-definition; to have an impact on others; to have another initiate; and to express love – as well as other 'imperatives', may also be taken as essential inter-human needs.

Consciousness The neopsyche is the seat of consciousness: experience which arises as a result of the workings of each individual brain and mind in relation to its environment. Precisely how consciousness arises as a result of particular neural processes and interactions (with the brain, body, and the world) and how we can understand different subjective states (referred to as 'qualia') is the business not only of neuroscience but also of psychology, and, indeed, transactional analysis.

Reflective consciousness Being able to reflect on oneself, on the content and process of life is an essential part of being human or 'person' (Harré 1983), and is a crucial for the 'reflective practitioner' (Schon 1983). Of course, this includes the ability to reflect on different aspects of ourselves including the past and archaic and introjected ego states: 'the healthy ego is one in which the Adult ego state, with full neopsychic functioning, is in charge and has integrated (assimiliated) archeopsychic and exteropsychic content and experiences' (Erskine 1988, p. 19). It is this capacity to reflect on ourselves and others, to spit out those experiences or introjections that are or are no longer relevant, and to assimilate the past in the service of the present, that defines the 'Integrating Adult' - which, as a noun, describes the *process* of the neopsyche (and not simply one of its functions).

Critical consciousness One of the problems with functional terms such as 'Critical Parent' and 'Rebellious Child' is they label criticality and rebellion as negative, problematic and ultimately pathological. In my view an essential quality of the 'Integrating Adult' is, precisely, a critical consciousness which is alert and which does not accept what is assumed, given or received. It is no accident that, in addition to such qualities as openness, caring, having a desire for authenticity, wholeness and intimacy, a yearning for the spiritual and, significantly, being a 'process person', Rogers' (1980) view of 'the person of tomorrow' also includes the qualities of scepticism, having an authority within, and even being anti-institutional. In expanding the Adult - and our concept of Adult and what it means to be adult - I am reclaiming critical conscious-ness, dissent and deviance. As Samuels wryly puts it:

> What interests me about the therapists is how conventional they are! They are happier with straight people. They are happier with nuclear families. It is a very odd thing that we deal so much with the unconscious - we deal with the kinky - and yet we are a very conventional group of people.   (Samuels & Williams 2001, p. 3)

Maturity and motivation The neopsyche is the mature psyche (given that maturity is age-appropriate). It is 'fully functioning' in the Rogerian sense of the concept, that is: synonymous with optimal psychological adjustment and complete congruence, and characterised by openness to and trust in experi-ence, and the ability to live attentively in the present (Rogers 1961). Sharing a unified and integrative concept of human motivation, the neopsyche is synonymous with the organism, behaving as an organised whole; interacting with perceived outer and inner realities in the service of the actualising tendency; engaging in an organismic valuing process; constantly differentiat-ing; and always in motion (as suggested by its representation in Fig. 3). As Rogers (1951) puts it: the human species (as with other species) 'has one basic tendency and striving - to actualise, maintain and enhance the experiencing organism' (p. 487). Drawing on Rank's view of will as a positive guiding organisation and integration of the self, Amundson and Parry (1979) pay attention to the will as 'the directing dimension of the personality' (p. 20).[2]

Imagination There is a sense of liberation about the neopsyche (certainly in this constructivist conceptualisation). Free from the contaminations of archaic fixated and introjected material, the mature organism/person is curious, open to contact and relationship - not only with people but also with things, through ideas, aesthetics and the arts. It/he/she is playful and sensu-al. Just as this is the ego state of pure Reason, it is also the location of sheer intuition (which some may define as extremely rapid reasoning). Alongside its[3] reflective and critical consciousness lies the state of unconsciousness, remembered through dreams and the imagination, as:

> There are more things in heaven and earth, Horatio,
> Than are dreamt of in your philosophy.
>
> (Shakespeare *Hamlet*, I.v.166)

Whilst I believe that these are key features of the neopsyche (and in this context it behoves me to advance them), of course there are others. Spirituality or spiritual aspirations may be viewed as essentially neopsychic (and, of course, depending on an ego state diagnosis, also archeopsychic or exteropsychic). The present-centred nature of the Adult is compatible, for instance, with Buddhist teaching on philosophy, psychology and practice in everyday living. It is clear, however, that any description of properties, features or qualities would not be sufficiently organismic, constructivist, co-creative, dialogic or simply comprehensive. Any qualities of an organismic, evolutionary neopsyche, as expressed by the name 'Adult ego state', must necessarily be described in relation to a particular individual in terms of a full ego state diagnosis, i.e. behavioural, social, historical and phenomenological (à la Berne 1961/75a).

Before discussing the methodology of expanding the Adult, some of the theoretical implications of the argument thus far are summarised. (Readers who are enjoying the gastronomic metaphor may consider this insertion as a sorbet before the fourth course!).

Integrating Adult - A structural summary of a state of process

A number of theoretical points follow from the arguments advanced so far:

1 As 'ego states and transactions are elicited from meaning (rather than the other way round)' (Summers & Tudor 2000, p. 24), the Adult ego state is (literally) deconstructed in favour of a process conception of the neo-psychic Integrating Adult (see Fig. 3). As a present-centred, processing state of the ego, it is not subdivided along pre-conceived or functional lines (as do Berne 1961/75a; Krumper 1977; Phelan & Phelan 1978; Kujit 1980).

2 The neopsyche/Integrating Adult is thus conceptually different from the archeopsyche and exteropsyche which are defined respectively by their archaic and introjected nature, within each of which are posited a number of distinct ego states which describe specific archaic, fixated and introjected states of the ego.

3 Physis and the 'arrow of aspiration' are conceptually located in the neopsyche/Integrating Adult and not in the Archaic Child (as Berne 1972/75b). Summers (personal communication, February 2002) distinguishes between this mature physis and 'pseudo physis' which he views as 'a narcissistic, archaic Child or Parent defence'.

4 As people are conceived Adult, Gobes' model of ego state development (in Novey et al 1993) is more consistent with the present view of the neopsyche/Integrating Adult and is thus preferred to that of other TA developmental theorists (from Schiff et al 1975 to Hine 1997).

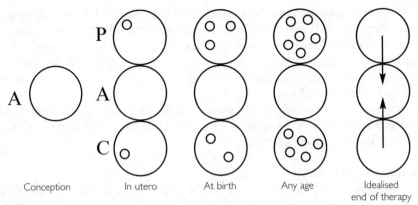

| Conception | In utero | At birth | Any age | Idealised end of therapy |

Fig. 4: Ego state development in the Integrating Adult model (developed from Gobes in Novey et al., 1993)

5 As the Adult develops from conception, the organismic processes and qualities hitherto associated with the 'Little Professor' (A_1) (such as intuition, creativity, etc.) (see, for example, Woollams & Brown 1978; Hine 1997) are conceptually relocated in the developing and evolving Integrating Adult (A_2). As the archeopsyche describes that archaic (experienced) part of the psyche which encompasses a number of archaic, fixated states, then the name 'Little Professor', or designation A_1, refers to a pseudo 'adult-in-the-Child', whose consistent patterns of behaviour and experiencing are characterised by a 'smartness' which is learned as an adaptation, and which may be distinguished from an organismic, neopsychic intelligence and intuition (Integrating Adult). (To view A_1 in developmental terms is to mix metaphors, that is, a particular description of the *structure* of personality at any one time with an epigenetic, *developmental* model of personality.) Similarly, present-centred emotions, such as C_0 yearnings (Hargaden & Sills 2002), are conceptualised as within the neopsychic Integrating Adult.

6 Functional nomenclature such as 'Critical Parent' and 'Adapted Child' are not considered helpful to a constructivist understanding of the individual or to such conceptualisations of personality and ego states. Terms which describe a 'critical Adult', 'rebellious Adult' or 'revolutionary Adult' may help both therapist and client (and theorist) in a process of *metanoia* (change), expansion and liberation. The key question is whether such qualities are *integrated* and form a present-centred sense of self - or not. In short, if, for example, nurturing and caring are integrated, then they are 'Adult' (i.e. a quality of the evolving neopsyche); if they are not, they may be understood as an Introjected Parent ego state or an Archaic Child ego state (depending on the diagnosis). In the absence of specific diagnosis, and in the endeavour of promoting a systemic phenomenology (i.e. transactional analysis), it is simply confusing to name these qualities as 'Nurturing Parent', etc.

This present work in effect criticises the reification of both Child and Parent ego states in TA theory and practice. However, the objection to reification extends to include that possibility with regard to the Integrating Adult. The difference is - and thus this danger is assuaged by the fact that - there is no end to integration; as the neopsychic Adult is in constant process, it may not be fixated either clinically or conceptually.

Having laid the conceptual and theoretical foundations of a new view of the neopsyche, it is time to turn to the methodological implications of this perspective for clinical practice.

Expanding the Adult

In this fourth part (we are now on to the sweet course or *i dolci*[4]) and with reference to clinical psychotherapeutic practice, I elaborate some of the implications of the previous theoretical discussion of the neopsychic Integrating Adult for both practice and method, beginning with a continuation of the previous vignette (from above, pp. 212-3).

C.13 Alf: Well, I guess I don't have to shut you out.
T.13 Bea: *(nodding)* Umm...and an important part of the therapy here is to play with what you're guessing and what you know about you and me.
C.14 Alf: *(smiling)* Playing sounds good...
T.14 Bea: *(smiles)*
C.15 Alf: *(pause)* You mean guessing is OK?
T.15 Bea: In the absence of knowing, guessing sounds pretty good to me.
C.16 Alf: *(throws his head back, laughs and lets out a huge breath)* What a relief. I feel lighter...better...like I'm not wrong.
T.16 Bea: So now you have the possibility of being lighter, better, right, of breathing easily.
C.17 Alf: *(sitting forward, taking big breaths)* That's right. It's like I was only seeing through a mist, having a film over my eyes. Now I can see you and see that you care, that you're not being critical, that you don't think I'm wrong and that you're not going to shut me in the cupboard, I guess.
T.17 Bea: So you're still guessing on that one!
C.18 Alf: *(smiles)* No... and I guess sometimes yes.
T.18 Bea: That's the play: the interplay between knowing here and now that you're OK and worth it and sometimes not knowing that about yourself and not knowing that about me in relation to you.
C.19 Alf: That's about it.

Assuming health (alongside illness)

This present constructivist contribution draws on a tradition of health psychology, as does its predecessor on co-creative TA (Summers & Tudor 2000). In this frame of reference, we may be ill and well at the same time; alongside our psychopathology (however we describe, define and categorise it), there is a 'psycho*sanology*'; alongside mental illness is mental health or well-being (see

Tudor, 1996). This perspective argues for the addition of a sixth 'health' axis to the current *DSM-IV* multi-axial diagnosis (see Tudor, in press). More subtly, our 'illness' may be part of a health crisis in the organism. What this means in practice is that what many clients present as illness, a crisis or a problem, is simply a part of life. In my initial transactions with a client (and supervisee or trainee), I am often concerned both to understand and to deconstruct the present 'problem', usually by means of specifying and confrontational transactions. Often I say something along the lines of "So that's the problem. What's the matter?" This both acknowledges that there is a perceived problem but that there is not necessarily anything the matter. Either it has literally little or no 'matter' (as in substance), or having a problem is *in itself* not necessarily a problem. This is informed in part by Freire's (1972) 'problem-posing' pedagogy of the oppressed which welcomes and moreover poses problems to the student, through the discussion and resolving of which learning (in Freire's context, literacy) develops. Interestingly, James and Jongeward (1971) suggest that 'raising the right question' activates - and strengthens - the Adult. In the vignette above, the therapist's assumption of health alongside pathology may be seen in her acknowledging the client's creative adaptation in the past (T.12) and in his present 'guessing' (T.13). Following phenomenological method - after all TA is a 'systematic phenomenology' (Berne 1961/75a) - the therapist also challenges the client's self judgement (in C.2).

Assuming Adult neopsychic functioning (alongside Introjected Parent and Archaic Child ego states)

One therapeutic slogan of a constructivist, co-creative TA might well be: 'Assume Adult - until proved otherwise'. Building on the assumption of health, and the co-existence of health and illness, this therapeutic assumption and attitude supports the neopsychic Integrating Adult functioning of the client. As above, some of what is presented as archaic and/or introjected may well not be and, at this stage, decontamination work is useful to clarify the phenomenological difference between archeopsyche and exteropsyche on the one hand, and the neopsyche on the other - and it is worth noting that 'decontamination' is, in effect, therapeutic work with the Adult ego state. However, the metaphor is limited in that it focuses only on dealing with contaminations - and, moreover, implies a notion of cure as a fixed, uncontaminated, de-scaled, barnacle-free Adult ego state. *Expanding* the Adult takes this process a step further in inviting the client literally to expand their consciousness, autonomy, etc.. As noted earlier, critical consciousness requires and, indeed, contributes to an evolving Adult definition of what it is to be adult. Again, more subtly, given the different nature of the neopsyche on the one hand and the archeopsyche and exteropsyche on the other (see above, pp. 29-30), it follows that we can be 'in' Adult and Child or Parent *at the same time*. Similarly, we can co-create present-centred non-transferential Adult-Adult relating at the same time as we co-create transferential (or partially transferential) relating (see Summers & Tudor 2000). In the vignette the therapist assumes Adult functioning alongside transferential relating (T.3), in acknowledging her 'mistake' (T.7), and in inviting the client to focus on present relating (T.12, T.13 onwards).

Making contact

Rogers (1957, 1959) describes contact or 'psychological contact' as the pre-condition for therapy. With the exception of Erskine's (1988, 1993) work on contact, enquiry and attunement, and some recent work (van Beekum & Krijgsman 2000; White 2001), transactional analysis, certainly compared with gestalt and person-centred psychologies and therapies, has under-emphasised this necessary condition of the therapeutic relationship. In this present work, contact is viewed as a consistent attitude and endeavour, embodied by the therapist, which conveys an acceptance of and empathy for the client. Such attitudes, of unconditional positive regard and empathic understanding, if received by the client, resonate at many levels, especially in the limbic system as well as in the imagination, and encourage the client's self acceptance and self-understanding. In expanding the Adult, such contact is present-centred, focusing on what is happening here-and-now rather than what was happening there-and-then, on what *is* happening rather than on what isn't happening - this focus and emphasis may be seen in the vignettes above. In many ways the whole piece is concerned with making and maintaining contact, including non- verbal contact (e.g. T.10), and acknowledging the break or rupture in the contact (T.4 to C.9). In this sense, transactional analysis 'proper', that is, the analysis of transactions, may be viewed and experienced as the moment-by-moment analysis of contact between therapist and client: both when contact is full and ongoing and when it is ruptured. Acknowledging and working through ruptures is an essential part of the therapeutic process, and promotes an expansive and contactful relationship. Put another way: 'ruptures in the empathic process, perceived or real, offer opportunities for the therapist to facilitate the client to integrate previously disassociated ego states' (Hargaden & Sills 2002 pp. 57-8).

Diagnosing psyche and ego states

With its plethora of diagnostic theory and formulations, TA is open to the criticism that it apes the medical model of diagnosis→treatment→cure. Steiner's (1971) caution about diagnosis as a form of alienation remains largely lost in the mists of a once radical time in TA. The word diagnosis, from the Greek, implies distinction and discernment, and in itself does not carry the more pejorative overtones of its close association with the more deleterious aspects of the (allopathic) medical model. At best, diagnosis is based on ongoing enquiry in the therapeutic relationship with a view to enhancing the understanding of both client and therapist. In terms of the accuracy of diagnosis - of ego states - Berne (1961/75a) offers a (usually) sequential outline of a clinical procedure for correlating four requirements for a full diagnosis, based on:

1 *Behavioural* diagnosis - usually made on the basis of clinical experience, taking account of demeanours, gestures, voice, vocabulary, and other characteristics (see C.2, C.5 in the vignette above).
2 *Social* or *operational* diagnosis - the response of someone else in the environment of the subject concerned (see T.4).
3 The *historical* diagnosis - the subject's internal corroboration of the original prototype for the behaviour, attitude, thinking, feeling, etc. (e.g. C.11)
4 The *phenomenological* diagnosis - based on the subject being able to re-experience in the present, 'in full intensity, with little weathering' (p. 76), the earlier, historical moment or epoch (see C.1 to C.7).

All too often, ego state diagnosis is based on the viewer's reading of the external manifestation of a particular behaviour, based on a crude classification of associations: critical (Parent), rebellious (Child), etc. Unfortunately, as noted above (p. 211), Berne (1961/75a) falls into the same trap, associating attractiveness/responsiveness with Child, and ethical responsibility with Parent. Another pitfall in clinical practice is diagnosis based on the social/operational reaction of the practitioner without sufficient reflection in terms of their own cultural frame of reference, countertransference, etc. which, if unchecked, untrained or unsupervised, can lead to defining and blaming transactions. What was radical about Berne's contribution was in giving equal weight to the internal, phenomenological experiencing of the client (the historical and phenomenological criteria), as well as providing theory which encourages the practitioner to be both thorough in checking out the *properties* of a person's ego state, as well as cautious and exploratory in offering all this to the client as (only) one way of describing and understanding themselves and their world. One of the implications of this present work is that the therapist needs to know and to be able to distinguish and discern in relation to each client what is Adult and what is not - by means of a full ego state diagnosis.

If this is the enquiring approach to diagnosis, then the necessary attunement is in how this is delivered, mediated and processed. Just as there are process contracts (see Lee 1997), so diagnosis needs to be held as a process - and, indeed, is formulated *in* the process, e.g. through analysis of the therapist's countertransference or through reflection on and acknowledgement of co-created co-transferential relating. There are several points in the vignettes above when the therapist might have been tempted to interpret what the client was saying, and to make the link to a diagnostic formulation (- note the 'the' as in 'to make *the* link', as if there is only one). Instead, she reflected on the rupture in the relationship, acknowledging the part she played in it. To paraphrase Berne's (1966) comment that 'visual observation is the basis of all good clinical work and takes precedence even over technique' (pp. 65-6); contact, enquiry and attunement are the basis of a good therapeutic relationship, and take precedence over diagnosis.

Working in relationship to support integration

The emphasis in clinical practice in expanding the Adult is on the co-creation of the therapeutic relationship, both transferential and present-centred (see Summers & Tudor 2000). Both therapist and client bring to therapy ideas, both contaminated and expansive, about what it means to be adult: "If I were really grown up, I wouldn't be feeling this hurt"; "If I were really grown up I wouldn't need to be a therapist"; "Now I'm adult I can laugh and cry, sing and weep"; "Part of being adult and having a place in the world is being a thera-pist", etc. Therapist and client, as any parties in any relationship, are always co-creating something. Therapy is attending to what we co-create. In this frame of reference, therapy is:

- Firstly, the co-creation of new (neo)psychic relational possibilities, played out, tried and tested in the therapeutic relationship and milieu (for example, the possibility of 'guessing' in the vignette above); and
- Secondly, concerned with dealing with the grief of past traumas, deficits and limitations - and in this, therapy is essentially a phenomenological and existential process.

The approach promoted in this chapter does not ignore TA therapeutic work with Archaic Child ego states (such as deconfusion) or with Introjected Parent ego states (such as the Parent interview); rather it offers a re-framing of such therapeutic work by means of its focus on the neopsychic Adult. It does generally confront an overemphasis on the 'Inner Child': it is too late to have a happy childhood; it's not too late to be happy now, and to review and reframe that unhappy childhood. Thus regressive therapy is generally eschewed in favour of strengthening present-centred Adult functioning. This is the task of a genuinely integrative psychotherapy. In similar vein, what are diagnosed as 'personality disorders' are viewed, within this present frame of reference, as personality *processes*, in response to which the work and the healing lies in the therapeutic relationship and especially the observance, maintenance and negotiation of boundaries.

Organisational implications of the Integrating Adult

In this brief concluding part, some organisational implications for TA of this present view of the neopsychic Integrating Adult are briefly considered.

If 'ego states' are reified then the structure of personality becomes reified and potentially ossified. People talk about being "in my Child" and, worse, "my Child is feeling...", etc. So too, at an organisational level, there is a danger that the structure of the 'personality' of TA in its ethos, values and organisa-tion becomes fixed, rigid, obsessive and conservative. Offering an organismic and process view of the mature and evolving personality, the theory of the Integrating Adult and the methodology of expanding the Adult, supports those transactional analysts who are reflective, critical, imaginative, and embracing of diversity, including criticism. This is particularly important as 'rebellion' (especially in clients and trainees) is often pathologised. Unlike Moiso and Novellino (2000), I do not see the 'rebellious aspect' of TA stressed at all. Far from it; the radical and critical spirit of the early years of TA has been all but lost.

The Integrating Adult brings - indeed, insists on bringing - a reflective and critical consciousness to bear on all aspects of life, including the organisation of TA and TA organisations. One of the principles which inform therapeutic communities (TCs) is that there is a 'culture of enquiry' in which 'all members...can question managerial issues, psychological processes, group and institutional dynamics...discussion is regarded as a learning experience... everything within the community is available for discussion...[and] managerial information and issues which affect the community are shared with the whole community' (Kennard & Lees 2001, p. 148). These principles, which are entirely consistent with TA's commitment to open communication, may be useful in offering support for the broader therapeutic community of TA at all levels and, within it, training institutes, to promote open communication, including criticism, and mutual learning through dialogue.

Specific concerns about the state of TA include:

- Pressure to conform to traditional views of theory, for instance, regarding contracts and escape hatch closure which, together with a "You can't quote it if it's not published" attitude to the development of theory and ideas, generally encourages conformity and discourages exploration.
- Pressure to complete training at one training institute - which may suit the trainer/institute financially and psychologically, but equally may not suit the trainee. This is particularly ironic given TA's perspective on autonomy; its history in terms of the (original) mentoring model of training whereby, before the comparatively recent advent of training institutes, student/ practitioners, attending particular workshops, events and short courses, put together their own package of training towards certification; and the fact that the current organisational structure and examination requirements within TA still allow for such a portfolio approach: all of which leaves more freedom of choice and personal power with the student.
- Certain structures and attitudes which serve to protect a professional hierarchy:
  - The accreditation of trainers within TA can appear and be experienced as a kind of pyramid selling of training which, in promoting a closed shop attitude to training, excludes and discounts the experience of others, including some trainees who are themselves experienced trainers.
  - The notion that the TA practitioner cannot say or do something publicly about TA until they are qualified, i.e. as a certified transactional analyst.

These concerns could be viewed as evidence of a heavy, institutional, 'Be Strong' and 'Be Perfect' TA Parent (with hints of 'Please Me'), which would suggest that, as a community, we need to be mindful of TA's obsessive-compulsive traits, adaptations, etc. as well as the adaptations it - and we - engender. In this sense this present contribution may be seen as an intervention (or interposition) designed to confront organisational atrophy, in support of script prevention and autonomy.

As with any good meal, taking in a number of courses over a number of hours, ending with a plate of cheeses (*i formaggi*) and preferably accompanied by a robust red wine, this chapter is offered in the spirit not only of satisfying a certain hunger, but also of stimulating the senses, to be sampled, chewed over and some even spat out, to be reflected upon with good friends, to be dissected and expanded. If this helps the reader - and, ultimately, their clients - to make more sense of themselves, others and their worlds and to be able to impact on them with a sense of social responsibility and citizenship as autonomous, conscious, imaginative and free-thinking human beings, then this chapter has been worth preparing and offering - and digesting.

Notes

1 In many ways this chapter follows on from the work developed by Graeme Summers and me in our article 'Co-creative transactional analysis', published in the *Transactional Analysis Journal* 30(1). Whilst I have written this chapter *da solo*, it has been enriched by continuing discussions with Graeme and with my friends and colleagues Helena Hargaden and Charlotte Sills, to all of whom I am grateful for their continued support, encouragement and feedback.
2 Amundson and Parry make the case that Berne brought to fruition many of Rank's proposals; interestingly, Rank also influenced Rogers.
3 The 'its' in these sentences are used for literary effect, they are not intended to reify the Adult ego state.
4 In this part/course, there is a selection of sweets; in other words, whilst some practice and methodology is presented, it is by no means comprehensive. Ultimately it is for the individual practitioner to develop their own practice and method of expanding the Adult. In Italy there is a tradition of guests bringing their own selection of sweets to a meal; it is in such sharing, sampling and experimentation that co-creative TA practice will evolve.

References

Allen, J.R., & Allen, B.A. (1991) Concepts of transference: A critique, a typology, an alternative hypothesis and some proposals. *Transactional Analysis Journal*, 21(2), 77-91.

Allen, J.R., & Allen, B.A. (1995) Narrative theory, redecision therapy, and postmodernism. *Transactional Analysis Journal*, 25(4), 327-334.

Amundson, J.K., & Parry, T.A. (1979) The willing Adult. *Transactional Analysis Journal*, 9(1), 20-5.

Bale, A. (1999) Prenatal personality formation and ego states. *Transactional Analysis Journal*, 29(1), 59-63.

Berne, E. (1963) *The Structure and Dynamics of Organizations and Groups*. New York: Grove Press

Berne, E. (1966) *Principles of Group Treatment*. New York: Grove Press

Berne, E. (1968) *Games People Play.* New York: Grove Press. (Original work published 1964)

Berne, E. (1973) *Sex in Human Loving.* Harmondsworth: Penguin. (Original work published 1970)

Berne, E. (1975a) *Transactional Analysis in Psychotherapy.* London: Souvenir Press. (Original work published 1961)

Berne, E. (1975b) *What Do You Say After You Say Hello?* London: Corgi. (Original work published 1972)

Berne, E. (1981) *A Layman's Guide to Psychiatry and Psychoanalysis.* Harmondsworth: Penguin. (Original work published 1969)

Bradey, N. (1980) Philosophical links to Transactional Analysis: Kant and the concept of reason in the Adult ego state *Transactional Analysis Journal,* 10(3)

Brodley,B.T. (1999) The actualising tendency *The Person-Centred Journal,* 6(2), 108-120

Clarkson, P. (1992) *Transactional Analysis Psychotherapy: An Integrated Approach.* London: Routledge.

Clarkson, P., & Gilbert, M. (1988) Berne's original model of ego states. *Transactional Analysis Journal,* 18(1), 20-9

Cornell, W.F. (1987) Life script theory: A critical review from a developmental perspective. *Transactional Analysis Journal,* 18(4), 270-282

Drego, P. (2000) Toward an ethic of ego states. *Transactional Analysis Journal,* 30(3), 192-206.

Edelman, G. M. (1989) *The Remembered Present,* New York: Basic Books

Erikson, E. (1950) *Childhood and Society,* New York: WW Norton

Erskine, R.G. (1988) Ego structure, intrapsychic function, and defense mechanisms: A commentary on Eric Berne's original theoretical concepts. *Transactional Analysis Journal,* 18(4), 15-19

Erskine, R.G. (1993) Inquiry, attunement and involvement in the psychotherapy of dissociation. *Transactional Analysis Journal,* 23(4), 184-190

Erskine, R.G. (1998) Attunement and involvement: Therapeutic responses to relational needs. *International Journal of Psychotherapy,* 3(3), 235-243

Erskine, R.G., & Moursund, J.P. (1988) *Integrative Psychotherapy in Action.* Newbury Park, CA: Sage

Erskine, R.G. & Trautmann, R.L. (1996) Methods of an integrative psychotherapy. *Transactional Analysis Journal,* 26(4), 316-329

Federn, P. (1952) Ego Psychology and the Psychoses. New York: Basic Books

Freire, P. (1972) *The Pedagogy of the Oppressed* (M.B. Ramos, Trans.). Harmondsworth: Penguin.

Goldstein, K. (1995) *The Organism.* New York: Zone Books. (Original work published 1934)

Gordon, D. (1978) *Therapeutic Metaphors.* Cupertino, CA: Meta Publications.

Hagehülsmann, H. (1984) The 'Menschenbild' in transactional analysis: Conceptions of human nature. In E. Stern (Ed.), *TA: The state of the art. A European contribution* (pp.39-59). Dordrecht: Foris Publications

Hall, C., & Lindzey, G. (1978) *Theories of Personality.* New York: Wiley

Hargaden, H. & Sills, C. (2002) *Transactional Analysis - a Relational Perspective,* London: Routledge

Harré, R. (1983) *Personal Being.* Oxford: Blackwell.

Hine, J. (1997) Mind structure and ego states. *Transactional Analysis Journal,* 27(4), 278-289.

Holloway, W. (1977) Transactional analysis: An integrative view. In G. Barnes (Ed.), *Transactional Analysis after Eric Berne.* New York: Harper's College Press.

Jacobs, A. (2000) Psychic organs, ego states, and visual metaphors: Speculation on Berne's integration of ego states. *Transactional Analysis Journal,* 30(1), 10-22.

Jahoda, M. (1958) *Current Concepts of Positive Mental Health.* New York: Basic Books.

James, M., & Jongeward, D. (1971) *Born to Win: Transactional Analysis with Gestalt Experiments.* Reading, MA: Addison-Wesley.

Kennard, D., & Lees, J. (2001) A checklist of standards for democratic therapeutic communities. *Therapeutic Communities,* 22(2), 143-51

Klein, M. (1980) *Lives People Live*. London: Wiley

Kohut, H. (1971) *The Analysis of the Self*. New York: International Universities Press.

Kohut, H. (1977) *The Resoration of the Self: A Systematic Approach to the Psychoanalytic Treatment of Narcissistic Personality Disorder*. New York: International Universities Press

Kopp, S. (1971) *If You Meet the Buddha on the Road, Kill Him!* London: Sheldon Books

Krumper, M. (1977) Sub-dividing the Adult: Ac and Aa. *Transactional Analysis Journal*, 7(4), 298-9

Kujit, J. (1980) Differentiation of the Adult ego state. *Transactional Analysis Journal*, 10(3), 232-7

Lake, F. (1980) *Studies in constricted confusion: Exploration of a pre-and peri-natal paradigm*. Privately circulated publication

Lapworth, P., Sills, C., & Fish, S. (1993) *Transactional Analysis Counselling*. Bicester: Winslow Press

Lee, A. (1997) Process contracts. In C. Sills (Ed.), *Contracts in Counselling* (pp.94-112). London: Sage

Levin, P. (1974) *Becoming the Way We Are: A Transactional Analysis Guide to Personal Development*. Berkeley, CA: Levin

Levin-Landheer, P. (1982) The cycle of development. *Transactional Analysis Journal*, 12(2), 129-39

Loria, B. (1990) Epistemology and the reification of metaphor in transactional analysis. *Transactional Analysis Journal*, 20(3), 152-62.

Magner, V. (1985) *Series of comparative charts of psychological theory No. 1: Child development*. Available from Metanoia Institute, 13 North Common Road, London W5.

Maslow, A.H. (1993) Self-actualization and beyond. In *The Farther Reaches of Human Nature* (pp. 40-51). London: Arkana. (Original work published 1967)

Moiso, C., & Novellino, M. (2000) An overview of the psychodynamic school of transactional analysis and its epistemological foundations. *Transactional Analysis Journal*, 30(3), 182-7.

Neugarten, B.L. (1968) *Middle Age and Ageing*. Chicago, MI: Chicago University Press.

Novey, T.B., Porter-Steele, N., Gobes, N., & Massey, R.F. (1993) Ego states and the self-concept: A panel presentation and discussion. *Transactional Analysis Journal*, 23(3), 123-38.

Ohlsson, T. (1988) A 'mandala' model of the Adult ego state *Transactional Analysis Journal*, 18(1)30-8

Pally, R. (2000) *The Mind-brain Relationship*. London: Karnac Books.

Phelan, B.N., & Phelan, P.E. (1978) The fully functioning adult. *Transactional Analysis Journal*, 8(2), 123-6

Pine, F. (1990) *Drive, Ego, Object and Self*. New York: Basic Books.

Piontelli, A. (1992) *From Foetus to Child*. London: Tavistock/Routledge

Rogers, C. R. (1951) *Client-Centered Therapy*, London: Constable

Rogers, C. R. (1957) The necessary and sufficient conditions of therapeutic personality change. *Journal of Consulting Psychology, 21*, 95-103.

Rogers, C.R. (1959) A theory of therapy, personality and interpersonal relationships, as developed in the client-centred framework. In S. Koch (Ed) *Psychology: A Study of Science, Vol. 3: Formulation of the Person and the Social Context* (pp.184-256). New York: McGraw-Hill.

Rogers, C.R. (1961) *On Becoming a Person*. London: Constable.

Rogers, C. R. (1978) *Carl Rogers on Personal Power*. London: Constable.

Rogers, C.R. (1980) *A Way of Being*. London: Constable

Samuels, A. & Williams, R. (2001) Andrew Samuels in conversation with Ruth Williams. *Transformations, 13*(Supplement)

Sanders, P., & Tudor, K. (2001) This is therapy: A person-centred critique of the contemporary psychiatric system. In C. Newnes, G. Holmes & C. Dunn (Eds.), *This is Madness Too: Critical Perspectives on Mental Health Services* (pp.147-160). Llangarron: PCCS Books

Schiff, J.L., Schiff, A.W., Mellor, K., Schiff, E., Schiff, S., Richman, D., Fishman, J., Wolz, L., Fishman, C., & Momb, D. (1975) *Cathexis Reader: Transactional Analysis Treatment of Psychosis*. New York: Harper & Row

Schmid, B. (1991) Intuition of the possible and the transactional creation of realities. *Transactional Analysis Journal, 21*(3), 144-154

Schon, D.A. (1983) *The Reflective Practitioner*, New York: Basic Books

Spinelli, E. (1989) *The Interpreted World: An Introduction to Phenomenological Psychology*. Newbury Park, CA: Sage.

Sprietsma, L.C. (1982) Adult ego state analysis with apologies to "Mr Spock". *Transactional Analysis Journal, 12*, 227-31

Steiner, C. 91971) Radical psychiatry: Principles in Agel, J. (Ed.) *The Radical Therapist* (pp. 3-7) New York: Ballantine Books

Stern, D. (1985) *The Interpersonal World of the Infant: A View from Psychoanalysis and Developmental Psychology*. New York: Basic Books

Stewart, I. (1992) *Eric Berne*. London: Sage

Stewart, I. (2001) Ego states and the theory of theory: The strange case of the Little Professor. *Transactional Analysis Journal, 31*(2)133-47.

Summers, G., & Tudor, K. (2000) Cocreative transactional analysis. *Transactional Analysis Journal, 30*(1), 23-40

Tudor, K. (1996) *Mental Health Promotion*. London: Routledge.

Tudor. K. (1997) Counselling and Psychotherapy: An issue of orientation. *ITA News No.46*, 40-42.

Tudor, K. (in press) Mental health promotion. In I. Norman & I. Rylie (Eds.), *Mental Health Nursing*. Buckingham: Open University Press.

van Beekum, S., & Krijgsman, B. (2000) From autonomy to contact. *Transactional Analayis Journal, 30*(1) 52-57.

White, T. (2001) The contact contract *Transactional Analysis Journal, 31*(3)194-8

Woodworth, R. S. with Sheehan, M.S. (1965) Contemporary Schools of Psychology (3rd edn.) London: Methuen (Original work published 1931)

Woollams, S., & Brown, M, (1978) *Transactional analysis*. Dexter, MI: Huron Valley Institute Press.

Chapter 12

EGO STATES and EGO STATE NETWORKS: some questions for the practitioner

(Developed the keynote address delivered at the TA conference in Amsterdam in the Netherlands on 15th March 1996)

Maria C. Gilbert

Basic to the practice of Transactional Analysis is the assumption that at any given moment in time, a person is in one or other ego state, which influences the individual's response to the current context. Ego states are always phenomenological experiences in the present. In Berne's words (1972), they are 'coherent systems of thought and feeling manifested by corresponding patterns of behaviour' (p. 11), which form the building blocks of a person's ongoing experience of self. An ego state embodies a person's construal of reality as he infuses his experience with meaning in the lived-in moment of the present in a particular, never-to-be-repeated context.

The currently experienced ego state will shape the person's action. An ego state can be described 'pragmatically as a system of feelings which motivates a related set of behavior patterns' (Berne 1961, p. xvii). How does the ego state that a person is currently experiencing relate to that person's history? Does the process of recalling and 're-living' in the present an episode from personal history, of itself lead to change? What can we know about accuracy of memory as this impacts on the therapeutic process? These are a few of the issues that are raised for the TA practitioner by the theory of ego states in Transactional Analysis.

The individual's phenomenological experience of a particular ego state represents her subjective sense of her own 'narrative truth' in the present. A person's experience of factors in the current context as well as fantasy may play a part in the construction of the person's narrative, but an individual's experience will be influenced heavily by their own encoded meanings of past events. Much of our work as Transactional Analysts, in working with a person's script, involves facilitating the person to change the meaning of their personal narrative in such a way that it supports them more effectively in the present. As Allen & Allen (1995) said, 'A major task of the therapist is to help develop a context that the patient can use to modify his or her old story or to develop a new one' (p. 330). The active nature of memory as a reconstruction of the past was recognised by Bartlett (1932). From his experiments, he concluded that people do not passively record material in memory; they actively reconstruct experiences in order to make sense of them, and in this process may emphasize certain features and ignore others (quoted in Baddeley, 1990). In the process of living, people are constantly modifying, building upon and reinforcing their personal narratives, and in this process reconstructing their past. The Transactional Analyst provides a safe context in which clients can embark on a re-evaluation of the meanings attached to their histories. In psychotherapy, this restructuring of a person's narrative involves working with all her ego states. Allen & Allen emphasize, as many humanistic therapists do, the importance of the present experiencing of the client: 'We live in the present. This is our lived time. We create our memories in the present and project them into the past' (Allen & Allen 1995, p. 330). So when a Transactional Analyst is working with a client in a particular ego state, she is working with the client's present experience as this has been shaped by the client's personal history and is networked in with the person's past.

Much of Berne's work involved the manner in which archaic fixated ego states, or ego states incorporating the assimilated psychic presence of another, affect the spontaneity of present behaviour. This raises several interesting and important questions for the Transactional Analyst. An ego state is not a memory, it is a vivid coherent phenomenological experience in the present; but ego states are related to memory, and draw on our accumulated experience from past developmental stages. I therefore intend to look at the relationship of ego states to memory, and then to discuss the interlinking between different ego states that creates a pattern that shapes our perception of new events. I will then raise briefly some ideas about change, and reflect on the relevance of the recovery of earlier ego states to the process of therapy.

These concerns can be distilled into the following three questions:

- How do ego states relate to a person's memory of events?

- How is the current ego state that a person is experiencing networked in with other ego states in their overall coherence of self experience?

- Does the recall and recovery of complete ego states from the past necessarily promote or even relate to the change process?

Ego states and memory
Currently the accuracy, distortion or even the possible fabrication of recovered or delayed memories is very much in the public consciousness. In flashbacks or involuntary and sometimes unwanted memories, a person relives an experience from the past in the current time. A memory from the past is brought into the present and experienced in the context of a current ego state. Much of Berne's original scientific basis for the existence of prior or archaic ego states was based on the work of Penfield and his associates (Berne 1961, p. 248). He saw this as evidence both for the existence of complete ego states and the possibility of re-experiencing these ego states in the present. In his references to Penfield's experiments, Berne makes clear that it is the person's

construal of the event at the time that is vividly recreated in the present and has intense phenomenological reality for him. Berne does not claim that this memory is autobiographically accurate.

> The subject feels again the emotion which the situation originally produced in him, and he is aware of the same interpretations, true or false, which he himself gave to the experience in the first place. Thus, evoked recollection is not the exact photographic or phonographic reproduction of past scenes and events. It is the production of what the patient saw and heard and felt and understood.
>
> (Berne 1961, p. xvii)

Of particular interest to Berne was the fact that the Adult ego state was aware of the current context and was an observer of the re-living of the past event. In such an experience, a person can evaluate, in Adult ego state, the past interpretation of events against his current evaluation of the experience(s), and reconstruct the memory in the light of present understanding. However, a person may not be able to assess in the present the historical accuracy of a re-lived ego state, from the memory of the past events. It is the meaning attributed to these events that is the subject matter of the script analyst. Fonaghy & Target (1995) state this position as follows: 'Psychotherapy neither aims to, nor is it likely to be capable of, achieving subtle resolution of historical truth of emotion and meaning' (p. 7).

Penfield's research has led many people, including some Transactional Analysts, to conclude that all experience is recorded in detail in the brain and can therefore be potentially re-accessed. Sometimes it is also assumed that the recovery and re-living of fixated Child ego states is of essence based on an accurate recording and recovery of a single historical experience. Research into memory throws doubt on both these assumptions. Clearly we do store much more information than we can retrieve at any given moment, but does this mean that all our experience is stored in our memory banks and therefore capable of being accurately retrieved? Baddeley (1990) questions the validity of such conclusions, based on the current status of research into memory. He says that there is no evidence to suggest that what was being reported by Penfield's patients, when the electric probe was applied to the brain, were indeed actual historical events. Under normal conditions, it is possible to have a clear and very detailed image of an incident you were sure you experienced, which turns out never to have occurred. In addition, amnestic patients sometimes show a disruption of the ability to judge familiarity of material. So it is possible that such a person could experience an event as familiar when this is not accurate or even part of their own experience. Criticisms of Penfield's conclusions are in themselves, of course, not conclusive. But they do caution practicing Transactional Analysts not to be too categorical in their assumptions that the storage of all memory traces (hence of Child and Parent ego state information) are retained in an intact and complete way in the person's memory, and in their assumptions about the biographical accuracy of remembered events or the recovery of complete ego states. The assumption that all memory traces are stored and hence potentially available may lead a therapist to 'pursue' these and place pressure on a client to 'recover' what may not have been retained.

Recent research into memory substantiates the viewpoint that even vivid recollection is not necessarily accurate (Baddeley, 1990). Fonaghy & Target (1995), in referring to the work of Minsky (1980,1986), point out that the perceptual qualities of memory are not of themselves indicators of accuracy, since 'vivid imagery reflects the neural structures in common between perception and memory, rather than necessarily showing authenticity of recall' (p. 2). For this reason, vivid phenomenological experiencing of sensory and emotional impressions is not of itself proof of accuracy. Nor is accuracy necessarily related to confidence in a particular memory. Neisser & Harsch (1992) exploring the phenomenon of flash-bulb memory, embarked on a study in which they demonstrated that memories of the circumstances in which individuals first heard about the Challenger disaster were experienced as vivid and detailed but were accurate in only three out of the forty subjects. Many subjects, when they were subsequently shown their own original report of the event, claimed that this had been wrong (reported by Fonaghy & Target, 1995).

Although memory for faces is impressively accurate (71 % in the Goldstein and Chance study 1971), trauma may significantly affect such accuracy (quoted in Baddeley 1990). He reports a particularly striking incident that happened to the Australian psychologist Donald Thompson who had been carrying out research on eye-witness testimony and possible distracting features that affect accurate recall. Thompson carried out a number of studies demonstrating that witnesses were likely to be strongly influenced by the clothes the criminal was wearing, and frequently tended to identify a suspect in a line-up on the basis of clothing alone. He got involved in much public discussion culminating in a live television interview. A few weeks later he was picked up by the police, placed in a line-up and picked out by a woman who claimed that she had been raped by him. It subsequently transpired that the time of the rape coincided with his appearance on live television. With some relief he pointed out that he had a very good alibi! It transpired that the unfortunate woman had actually been raped while watching his television programme; she was indeed correct in recognising Thompson's face, but not in assigning it to the rapist (Baddeley op.cit.). A similar example is quoted by Terr in her book *Unchained Memories* (1994) with regard to her client Eileen Lipsker, who recovered a memory of being raped at the age of seven or eight by "a black man with a green-tipped Afro haircut". As the memory gradually sharpened over the months, her picture of this man emerged in greater detail. Then Eileen realized that her mental representation of the rapist had come from a Jimi Hendrix poster on the rapist's wall. Her head had been pressed in that direction and this picture had become engraved in her memory. At this point, Terr goes on to report, the man who had actually raped her came to mind. He was a friend of her father's, whom she had not known very well (Terr 1994, p. 41). These are two examples quoted from personal experience of traumatic events.

In memory research, "misinformation" experiments conducted by Loftus and her associates at the University of Washington with college students show that people can be led to believe that they have perceived a false detail that is subsequently suggested to them, and reconstruct their memories to accommodate this (Quoted in Baddeley, 1990). This has led to a distinction between the overall validity of narrative autobiographical memory which seeks to accept the subjective truth of a person's narrative, whilst taking into account that biographical or historical accuracy must be relative given that multiple perspectives on the same event seldom concur. Nor are most people particularly good at recalling details of an event accurately, and can subsequently be persuaded to incorporate inaccurate details into their accounts.

However, in Baddeley's review (1990) of research on autobiographical memory, he points out that several studies by Hudson and Fivush and by Wagenaar do suggest a very high level of recall of autobiographical events, and a low level of distortion, *given adequate cueing*. Cueing refers to prompting memory such as may happen spontaneously when we revisit a childhood home, smell a familiar smell, or bump into a person from another era of our lives. Or it may result from someone else who was present at a scene or has recorded the material reminding us of details. We have probably all had many experiences of recalling memories from cueing when we meet an old friend and engage in one of those "Do you remember when we....?" or "Do you remember old so-and-so's face when....?"

Research into context-dependent and into state-dependent memory is also of interest here, since both involve a type of cueing. In his research into context-dependent memory in deep-sea divers, Godden found that material learnt underwater was best recalled underwater. A subsequent experiment conducted by Godden and Baddeley suggests that environmental cues may be helpful in locating a relevant memory trace (Baddeley, 1990). This will not be news to people who have returned to a room in their homes in order to remember what it was they had set out to look for elsewhere! In state-dependent memory, it is the person's internal state that acts as the cue. When someone is depressed, the person is more likely to recollect other depressive periods or events in their lives. Goodwin et al. found that what is learnt when drunk is best recalled when drunk. It appears that the person's internal state helps him to access the memory (reviewed in Baddeley, 1990).

However, Barclay (1988) questioned the accuracy of recall for detail in some of these prior memory experiments. He used a procedure where he embedded into an account distracter items which had many of the characteristics of a similar event that the person had in fact experienced. Under these circumstances, errors were frequent. In discussing these results, Barclay distinguishes between the 'truth' of a recollection and its 'accuracy'. Baddeley sums up Barclay's conclusions as follows: 'A recollection is true if it represents the person's general experience of the situation and his attitudes to it, in short, if it correctly conveys the gist of the experience. It would be accurate only if the detail were correctly reproduced' (Baddeley 1990, p. 309). Child ego states re-lived in the present may have much of this quality, picking up on the essential intentions of significant others and their impact on the person at the time, retaining the gist of the experience and hence the implicit truth of the event, but not reflecting accurately all the circumstantial details of the encounter(s). Neisser (1981) found that Dean's testimony in the Watergate trial (when checked against actual recordings of his conversations) fell into this category; it was accurate in broad outline, but highly inaccurate in detail (Neisser in Neisser and Hyman 2000). Baddeley concludes his discussion of the relevant research as follows:

> I would agree with Neisser that much of our autobiographical recollection of the past is reasonably free of error, provided we stick to remembering the broad outline of events. Errors begin to occur once we try to come up with detailed information from an inadequate base. This gives full rein to various sources of distortion including that of prior expectations, disruption by misleading questions, and by social factors such as the desire to please the questioner, and to present ourselves in a good light.
>
> (Baddeley 1990, p. 310)

For the Transactional Analyst working with the phenomenon of the fixated Child ego state in the present, this research is both supportive and cautions extreme care in not 'leading' the client with suggestions or interpolations. However, it does suggest that cueing related to the time of the event (for example, through the use of early photographs or the scene-setting of redecision therapy) may help clients fill out the gist of the memories of earlier ego states. A knowledge of state-dependent and context-dependent memory can also be of assistance. Apparently if a person is assisted to recreate the context in the mind's eye of a particular event, then he may gradually be able to fill in more and more detail. This technique, now used in assisting eye-witness recall of crimes, has long been successfully employed by Transactional Analysts!

Ego state networks

The theory of ego states as presented by Berne is based firmly in an interactional model of experience in that a person is 'assimilating the parental ego state' (Berne 1961, p. 67) in a relationship context, whilst in the process of responding to this parental person from a child ego state. Many of a person's ego states will be related to situations in which they are in the presence of another; it is these ego states and their networks that I particularly wish to expand upon since these form much of the focus of Transactional Analysis in practice.

Schiff, in a small booklet entitled "Ego state networks" (undated), points out the links that exist between different ego states; these networks form part of a person's memory and background of experience.

> Notice that each ego state has its own network of content messages, and that these messages are interwoven internally so that they weave a kind of spiderweb. When an external event stimulates one part of the network, vibrations are set up which will radiate outward from the point of stimulation. (p. 16)

This idea is also briefly referred to in *The Cathexis Reader* (Schiff et al., 1975) as follows:

> An individual's frame of reference is the structure of associated (conditioned) responses (neural pathways) which integrates the various ego states in response to specific stimuli. (p. 49)

The idea that Parent, Adult and Child ego states are connected 'structurally and integrated functionally into a whole which is characteristic of the overall person' (op. cit. p. 49) underpins much of Transactional Analysis therapy. These links between ego states in an individual's personal history are the result of the person's unique constellations of relationships and experience. Drego (1981), in discussing her approach to the phenomenological model of ego states writes that this model deals with 'ego states as systems'. She elaborates on the systemic nature of ego states in the following way:

> Ego states as they appear in experience are a complex of interwoven elements. The many messages, attitudes, forms of thinking and acting, feelings, ailments, ambitions, talents, aspirations that come from parental figures all intertwine to become a set, so that at any given moment the Parent ego state is a re-experience-able complex. It may be the sum total, or selected web of many moments in the past. So too the Child ego state may be a matrix of archaic scenes and experiences, put together in its own unique fashion. The active state of mind, i.e. the active ego state at any given present moment is a combination of experiences. (Drego op.cit., p. 22)

Here she is highlighting the interconnectedness of many past experiences that may be combining to create the particular experience of the Parent or Child ego state in the present context. The same could be said to be true of the Adult ego state. I find myself substantially in agreement with her. Ego states, albeit discrete and boundaried, are intimately intertwined with our past experiences and reflect the integration of many components into our current response to a situation. Berne (1961) implies, though does not explicitly state, the existence of such a networking process between ego states when he uses his metaphor of warped coins. He writes:

> The Child is a warped ego state, which has become fixated and has
> changed the direction of the whole subsequent portion of the
> continuum. More specifically, it is either a single grossly warped
> ego unit (a really bad penny), or a series of slightly warped ego
> units (a set of pennies from a poorer mould).
>
> (Berne 1961, p. 39)

He goes on to outline the difference between the traumatic neuroses and the
psychoneuroses:

> In the case of the traumatic neuroses, the Child is that confused
> ego state which was fixated on the day X of the month Y of the
> year Z in the patient's infancy. In the case of the psychoneuroses,
> it is the unhealthy ego state which recurred day after day under
> similar adverse conditions from month A to month B of the year
> C in the patient's infancy.   (Berne, op.cit. p. 39)

Although Berne made a particular point in his writing to stress the discrete
nature of an ego state and its internal coherence, this reference to the
unhealthy ego state recurring in the child's life suggests the presence of a linking effect between many such similar experiences. No ego state experience can
ever be identical to another, since context and time do not stay static in the
ever-moving flow of experience. In that sense it is unlikely that even the fixated
ego state in traumatic neuroses remains unchanged when it is relived or
re-experienced in the present.

In the course of ego state development, the person is internalizing, not
isolated subjective experiences, but a whole relationship network, which is
reflected in the links between the Adult, Parent and Child ego states. An ego
state reflects an individual's current experience of relationship, a person's
coherent constellation of meaning attributed to a particular interaction with
another person in the present time. This will inevitably be influenced by memories of past interactions. The Adult ego state is the sum total of a person's
integrated internalized relationship networks that enable the individual to
respond functionally in the present situation. I believe that the Adult ego state
incorporates the person's capacity for immediacy of sensory, affective, cognitive and behavioural experience, together with the synthesizing integrating
process involved in updating embedded schemata that govern the perception
of events. The Parent ego state is the person's experience in the present of the
perspective of the assimilated other - enabling her to see herself from the
vantage point of the other with the attendant feelings, attitudes and behaviours.
In that experience she is moving to the opposite side of the dyad - experiencing
a different view of the narrative of her life, which may enhance or disrupt her
experience of self.

Allen & Allen write:

> While it might be more accurate to conceptualize oneself as a
> group of texts (or the associated community of ego states), it
> generally is more comfortable to be in touch with only one story
> (and one ego state) at a time.   (1995, p.333)

Fixated Child ego states reflect the person's view of experience at a particular
point in history... but an interesting question for the Transactional Analyst is
the manner in which the re-living of the fixated Child ego state is related to
episodic memory and the effect of trauma on schemata embedded in implicit
memory. McNamara and Lister-Ford (1995) have pointed out how early
traumatic memories that are lost to conscious awareness may become the
antecedents to cognitive disorders, and disrupt subsequent information
processing.

The development of ego states involves the internalisation of early relationships and the effects of an individual's relationship 'maps' on subsequent
interactions. These networks of ego states provide the population of our
internal worlds. In his description of human development, Daniel Stern
(1985) talks of how the child builds up, through repeated similar experiences,
a "RIG" (Representations of Interactions that have become Generalised) of a
particular constellation of episodes with a primary carer. The generalised
representation is not a specific memory, rather an abstract distillation of a
number of specific memories that share similar components. He writes: 'It is
a structure about the likely course of events, based on average experiences.
Accordingly, it creates expectations of actions, of feelings, of sensations, and
so on that can either be met or violated' (Stern 1985, p. 97).

As early as 1932, Sir Frederic Bartlett proposed an interpretation of memory
that assumed that people remember new material in terms of existing structures which he termed schemas or schemata. He saw a schema as an organised
structure that captures our knowledge of some part of our experience, and is
influenced by our effort after meaning. In summing up Bartlett's contribution.
Baddeley writes:

> Applying a schema will typically help the subject to understand,
> since the schema encapsulates what he knows of the world.
> However, when material is presented that is not readily incorporat-
> ed into the schema, distortions will occur. Bartlett explored these
> by presenting his subjects with unfamiliar structured material, for
> example a North American Indian folk tale. When subjects
> recalled the story, they typically distorted it by omitting features
> that did not fit in with their prior expectations or schemas, and by
> distorting other features'.   (Baddeley 1990, p. 335)

This process is reflective of the script in action.

The concept of the schema seems close to Stern's (1985) concept of the RIG, and a particular schema is probably composed of a series of related RIGs. Such RIGs, built up in our interactions with others, are related to our core experiences of self in relationship, and will shape our characteristic ways of loving and relating. An example of such a RIG would be: "If I approach someone close to me for support, this is likely to be forthcoming". This will have been derived from an accumulation of achieving satisfactory outcomes of this type with people in my life. A person is unlikely to be able to recall all the individual episodes that have shaped this schema, but will have a vivid sense of the accumulated experiences collapsed into a few prototypical memories of events. Such a prototypical experience may be explicitly recalled or relived in the form of a Child ego state, or simply colour our attitudes to relationships outside of conscious awareness.

So when I vividly re-experience a 'Child ego state' in the present, this experience may actually involve a combination of individual encounters with a significant other that have collapsed into a prototypical 'episode', that draws on details from several linked experiences of a similar kind. Such a re-lived or remembered 'Child ego state' may have powerful narrative truth for me and carry the gist or truth of the original experiences in a combined form, but may not necessarily be correct or historically accurate in detail. However, the experience may still be vividly alive and sensorily rich for me as I experience the phenomenological reality of this ego state.

Some RIGs related to being with people who have significantly influenced the experience of "self" for us will have a vital influence on our subsequent relationship history, either in drawing us towards people or of injecting us with mistrust of intimacy ("I'm loving and lovable" or "I'm a nuisance and unwelcome here"). Whenever we experience a particular set of circumstances, we will recall a specific type of interaction with a 'self-regulating other' called 'evoked companions' by Stern (1985), who writes: 'The evoked companion is an experience of being with, or in the presence of, a self-regulating other, which may occur in or out of awareness' (p. 112). This is reminiscent of Berne's reference to the Parental influence that 'can be inferred when the individual manifests an attitude of childlike compliance' (Berne 1961, p. 25).

Stern (1985) likens this concept to Bowlby's concept of "working models of the mother". However, he points out that any 'working model' will be composed of a series of RIGs, which form the smaller building blocks out of which such representations are created by the child in the course of development (Stern 1985). These prototypic images are based on multiple memories of specific relationships that have evolved and changed over time. These prototypes form the basis of our relationship roles. If a person was fortunate enough to grow up in an 'average expectable environment' (Winnicott 1989, p. 195) then she is more likely to develop RIGs that will serve her well in getting her needs met in subsequent relationships.

Winnicott (1989) writes:

> For me, a good-enough mother and good-enough parents and a
> good-enough home do in fact give most babies and small children
> the experience of not having been significantly let down. In this
> way average children have the chance to build up a capacity to
> believe in themselves and the world - they build a structure on the
> accumulation of introjected reliability. They are blissfully unaware
> of their good fortune, and find it difficult to understand those of
> their companions who carry around with them for life experiences
> of unthinkable anxiety, and a deficit in the department of
> introjected reliability.   (p. 196)

There is a constant process of updating and change in internalized representations, as a person encounters new life situations and individual
differences in people. As these experiences of the other become internalised
and integrated into the Adult ego state by the growing child, the specific
events may be lost to conscious memory and the person will proceed on the
basis of working models of others that they have developed over the course of
time and experience. Such a working model is the result of networks amongst
Parent, Adult and Child ego states in a constant dynamic interactive process,
as the person responds and updates his experience in response to the current
context of his life. The central frame or schema governing our interpersonal
relationships has been named the core interpersonal schema (Beitman1992).
This is similar to the concept of the racket system (Erskine and Zalcman
1979) within Transactional Analysis.

The introjected others of childhood and adolescence, with their unique attitudes, feelings, behaviours and expressions, populate our internal world and
form the contents of the Parent ego state (Berne, 1961). At times we will
reproduce the behaviour, attitudes and feelings of such an introjected other or
'borrowed' self (Weiss 1950, p. 37) without being consciously aware of the
origins of this process. Each Parental introject will be networked in to a
specific set of experiences in Child ego state (the RIGs described by Stern),
except in rare instances where a single traumatic event may have become
indelibly fixated in memory and exerts a determining influence on subsequent
experience.

Erving Polster (1995), in his book *A Population of Selves,* describes a similar
process in his discussion of self-development in the person. He holds that a
person comprises "a multiplicity of selves" all of which form part of his being
in the world. He distinguishes between 'member selves' (the more peripheral
aspects of self) and 'essential selves' (core senses of self) in his discussion of
different experiences of self that become constellated into clusters. He maintains that people 'animate' these clusters by naming them "my angry self"
"my loving self", "my business-like self", and so on. The 'essential selves'
form part of the person's enduring core experience of self and when such a

sense of sense of 'self' is threatened in relationship, a person is likely to react strongly and protectively (Polster 1995, pp. 49-52). Polster's position is close to that of Ryle (1992) in his discussion of reciprocal roles and that of Karpman (1968) in his delineation of script drama roles. What Polster adds to the discussion is the concept of 'animating' the different facets of ourselves. In this sense he considers that Perls' original delineation of a 'topdog' and an 'underdog' in our intrapsychic structure constitutes such an animation of experience. The advantage for the therapist, in identifying the manner in which people may have 'animated' their particular self experiences, is that this then opens up the way for energizing less well-recognized dimensions or activating new ones, as Transactional Analysts do when they encourage a client to mobilize the 'Free Child'.

Our internalised network of relationship dynamics will include the 'games' we learnt to play in childhood in imitation of, and in response to our parents. We have in our internal world a record of all the roles in a particular game, and when we move into Victim we will project onto the other protagonist the role of Persecutor or Rescuer, or the reverse may apply. This relates directly to Ryle's concept of internalized reciprocal roles. The reciprocal roles that form part of our internalised experience of relationship networks subconsciously influence the manner in which we engage with new relationships (Ryle 1992). These schemata result from cumulative networking amongst ego states that is dynamic, flexible and ever-changing in the process of integrating our experience in the Adult. This integration in Adult ego state forms the basis of the organising principles that 'shape and thematize a person's experiences' (Stolorow & Attwood 1992, p. 25) contributing to the current status of the overall frame of reference.

The 'subselves' or 'reciprocal roles' may well constitute the functional ego states of Transactional Analysis. When the Transactional Analyst uses the terms Free Child, Adapted Child, Rebellious Child, Controlling Parent or Nurturing Parent, I believe we are referring to a series of ego states that are networked into a similar 'mental set' and represent a familiar prototype of our experience. A re-experienced Adapted Child ego state, for example, may be phenomenologically vivid and carry the 'truth' of our earlier experience, but can be derived from many interlinked episodes of our past, some of which may be lost to our autobiographical memory, perhaps forever. This in no way conflicts with Berne's statement that 'Parent, Adult and Child represent real people who now exist or who once existed, who have legal names and civic identities' (Berne 1961, p.13) since we are drawing on experiences that actually happened. The distinction between the 'truth' and the 'accuracy' of memory seems most applicable here. When we use the functional terms I have listed, we are not ever referring to a single episode in time or a single experience; rather we use these terms to refer to an interlinked or networked series of related episodes or complete ego states that have culminated in a repeatedly familiar experience which we choose to 'animate' as the Adapted Child. To quote Berne: 'At a certain point... she shifted into the ego state of a 'good' (prim) little girl' (Berne 1961, p. 12). When the client is this good, prim little girl she may have a phenomenologically vivid sense of herself as a younger person at a particular age adapting to parental demands, which may represent a constellation of details and similar feelings from many related episodes of that era or epoch. Such a vivid experience will have narrative autobiographical truth for the client.

Do we need to recall earlier individual episodes of our experience in order to change our schemata (our scripts)?

Our cognitive, emotional, sensory and behavioural response to a current stimulus is the result of the sum total of our accumulated ego state experiences. Our Adult ego state responses in a particular context are shaped by the network of similar related experiences that formed the relevant schema. The schemata constitute the principles that unconsciously organise a person's experiences (Stolorow, Atwood and Brandchaft, 1994). These principles would appear to be encoded in our implicit memory and shape our behaviour for the most part outside of our Adult awareness. When the Transactional Analyst encourages the client to do a 'trace-back' to an earlier experience, and to recover the phenomenological re-experiencing of an earlier complete ego state, it is with the intention of raising to the person's awareness the meaning that was once associated to this and similar experiences, resulting in the script. The vivid re-experiencing of the earlier ego may not be autobiographically accurate, but will often contain the 'truth' of the child's ongoing interactions with a significant other. Fonaghy and Target point out that -

> such constructed experiences are far more likely to be inaccurate than accurate, although undoubtedly they will contain the essence of a wide range of interpersonal experiences distilled into a configuration represented within that mental model. In that sense, the memory will be inevitably true.   (Fonaghy and Target 1995, p.8)

However, they continue to say that truth in such a case may well have been coloured by subsequently accumulated events, expectations, fantasies etc., that influence the way in which we constantly restructure our memories of past events. In the process of changing the script, the focus is on changing the meaning of events for the person in the context of a safe, holding therapeutic relationship. By supplying permission, protection and potency, the Transactional Analyst enables the client to attach a different significance to personal history whilst internalising a new 'evoked companion', to use Stern's term, that will henceforth be linked into the neural pathways associated with similar experiences in the future. The therapist's task is to assist the client to make changes in the frame of reference that will free the person to live more productively in the present. To what extent it is necessary or even possible, in the process of reworking our personal narrative, to recover in detail the record of events that have impacted on us in the past, remains an open question.

Finding the episodic routes to our schemata may or may not facilitate the process of change. Perhaps in the case of the isolated traumatic episode that has become fixated and remains unprocessed in the person's life, it may well prove essential to recover or recall such an episode in order to evaluate its meaning in Adult. Much of the work done with post-trauma victims is based on this principle. Once the event is described and re-lived in detail it still needs to be integrated into the person's narrative, involving at times a re-organization of the person's self-concept if not also of the meaning they attach to life. Where we are dealing with a network of experiences that have become con-stellated into a subself that has internal coherence (the drama roles of Karpman or the functional ego states of Transactional Analysis) then the details of individual episodes may have become subsumed or even lost to memory. What may be available to the person are prototypical scenes or occasional individual episodes that stand out. These can then be re-evoked to surface the context in which the schemata were formed, so that these are avail-able for reformulation or redecision. I quote Fonaghy and Target (1995) on the concept of psychotherapeutic change:

> Change will occur through the re-evaluation of mental models of understanding self-other representations implicitly encoded in the human mind. Change is a change of form, not of content. (p. 8)

The self-other representations of our internal world constitute the material to be worked with in therapy. Whether we can recover individual episodes from our history or not, we will be re-enacting historical (Child) ego states and assimilated (Parent) ego states in the relationship with the therapist. We not only *tell* our narrative to the therapist, we also *enact* it in the transference, thus giving expression to what may only reside in implicit memory stores. A person is many stories, from different viewpoints, some incompatible with one another and each member of a person's internal ego state population holds a story. The therapist may well ask as the client walks into the consulting room: "Who is engaging with me today?"

The concept of ego state networks provides the Transactional Analyst with a rich framework for dealing with the many 'selves' that the client brings into the consulting room. In this chapter I have also attempted to relate these manifestations to the current research into memory to support therapists in understanding their clients' stories.

References
Allen,J.R. & Allen,B.A. (1995) Narrative theory, redecision therapy and postmodernism in *Transactional Analysis Journal* 25(4)327-334

Baddeley, A. (1990) *Human Memory : Theory and Practice.* United Kingdom: Lawrence Erlbaum Associates

Beitman,B.D. (1992) Integration through fundamental similarities and differences among the schools in *Handbook of Psychotherapy Integration* (Eds) Norcross, J.C. and Goldfried, M.R. New York: Basic Books

Berne, E. (1961) *Transactional Analysis in Psychotherapy.* New York: Ballantine Books

Berne, E. (1972/1975) *What Do You Say After You Say Hello?* London: Corgi

Coleman, A. D. & Bexton, W. H. (eds) (1975) *Group Relations Reader.* San Francisco: Univ. Calif, Medical centre

Drego, P. (1981) Ego State Models. *Tasi Darshan,* 1(4)119-146

Erskine, R.G. & Zalcman, M.J. (1979) The racket system in *Transactional Analysis Journal* 9(1)51-59

Fonaghy, P. & Target, M. (1995) *Memories of Abuse : Psychological and Psychoanalytic Perspectives.* Keynote address at University Psychotherapy Association Conference in Sheffield, England

Goldstein, A. G. & Chance, J.E. (1971) Recognition of complex visual stimuli. *Perception and Psychophysics,* 9, 237-241

Goodwin, D. W., Powell, B., Bremmer, D., Hoine, H., & Stern, J. (1969) Alcohol and recall: state dependent effects in man. *Science,* 163: 1358

Karpman, S. (1968) Fairy tales and script drama analysis in *Transactional Analysis Bulletin: Selected Articles from Volume 1 through 9,* 1976, San Francisco: TA Press

McNamara, J. & Lister-Ford, C. (1991) Ego states and the psychology of memory in *Transactional Analysis Journal* 25(2), April 1995, 141-149

Minski, M. L. (1985) *The Society of Mind,* London: Heineman

Neisser, U. & Hyman, I.E. Jr. (2000) *Memory Observed* New York: Worth Publishers

Perls, S. F., (1948) Theory and technique of personality organization. *American Journal of Psychotherapy,* 2: 565-586

Polster, E.(1995) *A Population of Selves.* San Francisco: Jossey-Bass

Schiff, J.L. (undated) A Discussion of Ego States and Ego State Networks. personal publication.

Schiff, J.L., with Schiff, A. W., Mellor, K., Schiff, E., Schiff, S., Richman, D., Fishman, J., Wolz, L., Fishman, C., & Momb, D. (1975) *Cathexis Reader : Transactional Analysis Treatment of Psychosis.* New York: Harper and Row

Ryle, A. (1992) *Cognitive-Analytic Therapy: Active Participation in Change* Chichester: Wiley

Stern, D. (1985) *The Interpersonal World of the Infant.* New York: Basic Books

Stolorow, R.D. & Atwood, G.E. (1992) *Contexts of Being.* Hillsdale NJ: the Analytic Press

Stolorow, R.D., Atwood,G.E. and Brandchaft, B. (1994) *The Intersubjective Perspective.* New Jersey: Jason Aronson

Terr, L. (1994) *Unchained Memories.* New York: Basic Books

Wagenaar, W. A. (1985) My memory: a study of autobiographical memory over six years. *Cognitive Psychology,* 18, 225-252

Weiss, E. (1950) *Principles of Psychodynamics.* New York: Grune and Stratton

Winnicott, D.W. (1989) In Clare Winnicott, Ray Shepherd and Madeleine Davis (Eds), *Psycho-Analytic Explorations.* London: Karnac Books

Chapter 13

A JOURNEY TO THE HEART OF EGO STATE THEORY

Steff Oates

Knowledge is proud that he has learned so much.
Wisdom is humble that he knows no more.
William Cowper (1731 - 1800)

As my understanding and use of a variety of ego state models is an evolutionary process, I have charted my experiences as a journey. My intention in this is to emphasise three main ideas. The first is that we, as Transactional Analysts, appreciate the importance of our own and our clients' narratives (Allen & Allen 1995). Second, we use theoretical models wisely and flexibly (see quote from Cowper above). Third, our role as therapists may not be so much about *what* we know, as *who* we are willing to *be* in the co-creation of a therapeutic dyad (Summers & Tudor 2000). I use case examples throughout to illustrate my views of how theoretical concepts, such as ego states, can form a solid foundation from which we practice, and, if not used wisely, may interfere with what is important in the therapeutic process.

Interpretation

Although I didn't know it at the time, an experience I had in 1980 marked the beginning of my journey towards becoming a Transactional Analyst. I was in my first job at a residential establishment for troubled young people. My wise Officer in Charge had gently encouraged me to wonder whether some uncomfortable physical symptoms I was having at the time had their roots in my psyche. He suggested I have a quick word with our in-house consultant child psychiatrist.

After fifteen minutes with the psychiatrist I found him to be a pleasant man, but concluded (at that time) that he was completely mad. My view of my idyllic upbringing at this stage was completely ego syntonic. His questions as to my role in the family were shocking.

Twenty-one years and umpteen therapy hours later I realise now that his brief diagnosis was astoundingly accurate. As far as I can remember, I gave him very few historical details, and he certainly didn't encourage me to talk about my experience concretely, so I did not provide him with the basis of what we would know as a phenomenological diagnosis. However, I now conclude that his intuitive interpretation did come from a social and behavioural diagnosis (Berne 1969).

As I reflect on this now, his process seems to have been similar to Eric

Berne's. Berne honed his observational skills and intuitive powers in his days as an army psychiatrist. He did this by assessing, during army intake interviews, how accurately he could determine the occupation of people who sat before him for a short period of time. These experiences were part of the foundation of ego state theory that now offers a model for understanding and observing inter-personal and intrapsychic processes.

This theory has provided therapists with wonderful tools that aid in understanding, articulating and responding to client's processes and needs. When first introduced, I can imagine the excitement of everyone who discovers the powerful simplicity of the theory. At the same time, my experience has led me to realise, just as powerfully, that whilst our efficiency as therapists is greatly enhanced by these ideas, it is fundamentally dependent on how fully we are prepared to bring the whole of ourselves into the work.

These days as a Transactional Analyst psychotherapist and trainer, I value the fine theory and observational skills we are taught. I also emphasise the importance of pace, delivery and humility, and last, but by no means least, the importance of our distinct and personal experiences, in the therapeutic relationship.

Ego states

I am aware that these days there are many differing points of view about ego states, expressed with varying levels of complexity and clarity. In this context, I appreciated Ian Stewart's (2001) reminder about being clear. I value his call for us to debate, confer and continue to discuss the meaning of the theory, and that we work towards broad agreement on the terms.

In my first year of training, I remember the confusion when the trainer was teaching ego states. He said, "Of course, none of this is true, you know!" There were horrified gasps around the room from some of us. "Why teach it then?" I remember thinking. As a trainer, I now use my version of the same line. What I emphasise is that the value of any model lies in how helpful it is for any one individual and that value will vary.

I believe that psychotherapists, ideally, should maintain flexibility and humility in their approaches. I am glad of the solid foundation of theory that I have, and I want to use it and teach it in a way that keeps me and others open to a whole range of possibilities.

When I think of this range, I reflect on the variety of clients with whom I have worked. There were, for example, people like the man, whom I will call Edgar, who came to therapy because he had read *I'm OK, You're OK* (Harris 1995). Through his reading, he had been able to bring some meaning to the difficulties he was having. Our contract was clear, and he used our sessions to help identify how unhelpful experiences from the past impeded his current functioning.

It was Edgar who introduced the ego state model into our sessions. He wanted to know how he could "spend less time 'in' Child around people at work". Through the establishment of a supportive relationship with me in therapy, he was able to make the changes that he wanted. Using my training, I was able to facilitate decontamination, deconfusion, and redecision. Edgar left therapy feeling satisfied and with more options in his relationships with other people. My view of Edgar now is that his sense of being "cured" was to do with his having more energy for moving between ego states. In our work, we were able to clarify fixated material and introjects that were holding him back. In doing this, Edgar developed more here-and-now capacity to process the contributions that each of his ego states made to his life.

Then there was the woman I will call Maud, a very smart thinker who worked with me initially for twelve months, had a break of two years, and then returned. She had trained in Neuro Linguistic Programming and came at first with an urgency to "live her life!" In the first period we did some effective therapy, but her appointments were intermittent. On her return, she told me she needed to address a fear of dying that she had experienced all of her life. I emphasised that our work would need more commitment and regularity of contact. Maud agreed to this.

As we began this work, Maud still had a yearning for me to explain things theoretically so that she could understand them, yet I had a 'felt sense' that this was not the way the work should go. I sensed that each time we started analysing, although we both felt comfortable with thinking processes, there was something missing between us that needed to be addressed.

Our work became very intense as I encouraged Maud (and myself) to see what happened when we stayed with discomfort rather than moving to find 'answers'. At times, I would feel scared at my 'not knowing' what to do and worry that I was not helping Maud. At the same time, I became excited that the work would also seem to take on a life of its own. As we became accustomed to this, Maud and I became confident at waiting and holding ourselves in the unknown. Eventually Maud was able to contact deep despair and to 'use' the strength and commitment of the relationship we had developed to heal early and deep abandonment issues. On reflection, a most satisfying aspect of this work was that Maud and I developed greater capacities for openness and honesty with each other, in each moment.

Nearing the end of one very tender session, I started to give a theoretical explanation of what we had just experienced. This disrupted our process at that point. I now realise that this was probably more to reassure myself than anything else. Subsequently, I sensed that I had intervened rather clumsily, and the break in our contact had been disappointing for both of us. I asked Maud about it at the next session. Her reply was to use a line from a film she had seen, which eloquently described her experience with me. "Well Steff, last session I felt like I was drowning, and all you did at the end was describe the colour of the f.....g water!" It was a lesson well learnt.

These days, I teach psychotherapy trainees, Berne's (1961) original model of integration using three types of ego states, where the notion of 'cure' is seen as our having free access to Parent, Adult and Child. I also teach the model of Integrated Adult as postulated by Erskine (1988) and Gobes (1993), that the 'idealised' end of therapy is a fully integrated Adult ego state without interference from Parent or Child.

I am aware of considerable debate, some of which has suggested that these two models do not go together. I have heard some people trying to prove that one is wrong by using the other. I, however, experience the models both as different and compatible. Accordingly, I make sure that I teach this to my trainees. To be congruent, I state that at this stage it is Berne's model that works best for me.

Recently while I was teaching, Paul Staniland asked a very thought-provoking question. "If we can have integrated Adult, then why not integrated Child and Parent?" As we talked, we considered how integrated Child or integrated Parent might look. We reflected that this would mean uncontaminated ego states in first, second and third order structures. It would mean present centred relating from Parent, Adult and Child. As I tried to visualise the experience, I imagined myself skiing, enjoying the thrill, excitement and wonder of the glistening snow crunching under my skis. I would be moving my body freely, being alert to potential dangers and fully in the moment. Whilst others (Summers & Tudor 2000) might see all these experiences as being enjoyed in Adult, I prefer to describe it in terms of integration from three types of ego state.

Whilst I appreciate the Integrated Adult model as emphasising therapy in the here-and-now, I do recognise that in this model, Adult ego state encompasses age-related thinking, feeling, and behaviour. My preference, however, is to use Berne's original model (1961), whereby Parent and Child ego states do not necessarily imply pathology. For me, focussing on three types of ego states accounts for all that I bring to this moment, helpful or unhelpful. Using the above example, I can enjoy my current mastery of a ski slope, and remember with some fondness the past embarrassment and discomfort of those early days on the nursery slopes.

Clarkson (1992) stated:

> Berne's contribution resides in the recognition that Parent, Adult and Child ego states are three categories of existential phenomena, not theoretical contructs. The importance of establishing an uncontaminated Adult ego state in the mature personality is emphasised. It is also acknowledged that each type of ego state (whether Parent, Adult or Child), can influence any of the others in helpful or harmful ways and is modifiable over time.
>
> (Clarkson 1992, p. 53)

I agree with Clarkson in that I experience the three types of ego states phenomenologically; I disagree with her in that I see them also as theoretical constructs. I do not actually think there are three parts of me, but I use the three types of ego states to bring meaning and order to the variety of my experiences. It is in this way that I see them as something that I experience phenomenologically and as a model I use to understand myself and others.

Using this model, I see Parent and Child as historical and continually updated. An expanded Adult (Gobes, in Novey et al, 1993) does not yet honour, for me, the value of my history, both good and bad.

Using ego state theory

I find ego state theory invaluable in promoting therapeutic understanding, particularly in bringing meaning and order to what I am experiencing (as mentioned above). It also helps me to sense much more clearly what is needed to establish the mutuality for which I strive in the therapeutic relationship.

My contributions to this mutuality are fundamental. What I bring to each moment counts, and will be significantly influenced by my history. I am committed to remaining open to change whenever my past appears to bring limitations to the present, or to my capacity to relate. Just as importantly, I recognise that present events can stimulate the need for completely new learning.

I agree with Summers & Tudor (2000) that 'the past is as much affected by the present as the present is influenced by the past' (p. 27), and I like their emphasis on co-created therapeutic learning and their attention to present-centered relating:

> It is the juxtaposition of co-transferential and present-centred relating, developing in parallel, that facilitates the therapeutic emergence of transference. The duality of relating enables trans-ferential phenomena to be experienced, compassionately identified, and contained in the relationship.
>
> (Summers & Tudor 2000, p.30)

Where I differ from their position is that I consider we can have present-centred relating in all three types of ego state. This means that I can enjoy and honour the archaic in a way that may not be possible in their model. I have also found that clients and therapists can 'co-create contactful engagement in a manner that is new' from a place of integration from Parent, Adult or Child.

In *What Do You Say After You Say Hello*? (1975), Berne writes of ego states as 'coherent systems of thought and feeling manifested by corresponding patterns of behaviour' (p. 11). He also writes: 'It is important for the individual to understand his Child, not only because it is going to be with him all his life, but also because it is the most valuable part of his personality' (*ibid* p. 12).

In a model that uses three types of ego states, I see that I can bring all of myself to the therapeutic relationship and thereby invite my client to do the same with me. Each time we meet, we can consider the three types of ego states as 'work in progress'.

I find Berne's model valuable because, in any one moment, my client and I bring into our relationship echoes of the people we once were, and the potential of the people we may become. Our willingness to allow this relationship to be co-constructed freely from this mix brings endless possibilities to us both.

An important part of the process for therapists is expressed well by Ken Mellor (1980a). He writes,

> My experience of...good practitioners ... is that they have ongoing awareness of all three ego states and they use each when they think it will be helpful to do so.
>
> (Mellor 1980a, p. 330)

Regression versus progression

It is now relevant for me to consider the regressive dimension of ego states. I think one of the most powerful aspects of ego state theory is that it highlights relics of the past that influence present day functioning. Berne's approach clearly taught us, through the concept of ego states, to observe our clients re-accessing experiences that originated from younger ages.

In developing my understanding of regressive processes, I have also been influenced by Frank Staemmler (1997). In his work, he refers to Daniel Stern's (1985) developmental model of the senses of self and the domains of relatedness. I enjoy his emphasis on the creative function of the regressive process. He sees it as an opportunity for expansion to include other senses of self and domains of relatedness. He also challenges the assumption of regression being a temporal process in which the person returns to an earlier developmental phase. He asks us to consider regression more as reverting to less differentiated psychological states. As I understand it, this involves a process that restricts access to one or more domains of relatedness and does not necessarily involve reverting to earlier domains.

Staemmler suggests:

> *"A regressive process is a (transitional or lasting) restriction of a person's current possibility to realize all of her formerly acquired competencies according to her needs in a given situation. Such a restriction can relate to competencies that have been acquired both in early and in later periods of psychological development"*
>
> (Staemmler, 1997, p. 74 – original italics).

This leads me to consider whether regressive processes can occur in each type of ego state. If, as I believe, the three types of ego state are modifiable over time (Clarkson 1992), then we will acquire new competencies to use from each. From time to time, as in the example I give below with Maud, I may restrict my competencies in one area. I suggest therefore, that if we do not assume that regression is temporal, that we can experience regression to less differentiated phases of Parent, Adult or Child.

For example in my work with Maud, I can now see my ill-timed theoretical explanation of our work as partly involving a regressive process. Some observers may have seen it as an 'Adult debrief', yet the loss of contact with Maud led me to question how present I was with her in that moment. The process that she and I had been involved in was much more primitive than this transaction allowed, and I believe she was right to challenge my lack of attunement. In fact, I now realise that what I did was regressive, in that it was the way I used to respond to archaic experiences such as Maud was going through. Using Staemmler's model, I now see it as my not allowing or trusting the natural process of our relating at a level of core or emergent self. My intervention, due to my own discomfort, was an attempt to shift her prematurely to a sense of verbal self, which was not readily available or natural to her at that time.

I am reminded again here of my interview, with Ken Mellor in ITA News (1998):

> My experience is that we are more effective with people, if we practise being with ourselves. This basically means noticing what we're experiencing as deeply as possible, the whole time we are with our clients. The approach is to be with ourselves as we sit with and remain aware of our clients. While doing this, we encourage ourselves to wait before acting. In this way, the things we do will arise out of our being with the client, rather than out of some sort of cognitive structure.
>
> (Mellor in Oates 1998, p. 26)

The foundation of ego states

From my point of view, when I allow myself 'to be with' the client in the way that Mellor suggests, I am more likely to be open to my full range of competencies. I have a concern that it is sometimes assumed that all clients' difficulties can be resolved through cognitive processes. This has led me to search out other approaches and to consider the dynamic foundation from which ego states spring.

I find Jon Wagner's work on the phylon state (2001) helpful in conceptualising this concern. He considers that the phylon state is a proto-state that precedes ego state development. Wagner and I recently co-presented these ideas in a workshop entitled 'Searching for the Soul in Psychotherapy'

Wagner states:

> The difficulty in using ego state theory to trace all human development is that it obscures the radical difference in mid-brain stem processing, and does not even consider the basic temperament and instincts that are wired into individuals.
>
> (Wagner ITAA conference in Halifax, Nova Scotia 2000)

Hoewever, I can relate Wagner's work to my understanding of Mellor's model of impasses. Wagner's phylon state underlies and overlaps Mellor's understanding of third order structure.

Mellor (1980c) states that different types of primal pain (from Primal Therapy Theory) are developed in relation to brain structures. He relates these to the different considerations that are needed for resolving the three degrees of impasses. First degree impasses involve neo-cortical processes, second degree impasses involve mid-brain processes and third degree impasses involve brain stem processes.

Wagner describes phylon state as having characteristics different to ego states. In his thinking, phylon state represents our phylogenetic roots; these include a distinct bonding reflex that is responsible for building communities. He sees it as connected to the rhythms of creation, and that it operates a fundamental emergency response system. In the phylon state, thinking processes are very polarised.

Wagner then articulates what I consider to be a common mistake. The mistake is to assume that the 'stuckness' that we encounter with clients can always be explained in terms of ego states.

> A difficult diagnostic problem for professionals who promote personal growth is determining if automatic responses are derived from rigid ego structures or phylon state learning by absorption. If the Phylon State, which responds prior to us learning how to think, generates the automatic response, then putting your client into a situation that expects thinking is potentially abusive.
>
> (Wagner, ITAA conference in Halifax, Nova Scotia 2000)

For me the phylon state, combined with Mellor's understanding of third order structure, enables us to give credence to primitive processes that have not yet been explained clearly in ego state terms.

At the 2001 UKCP conference on psychotherapy and neuroscience, fascinating and highly sophisticated ways of measuring primitive brain processes in relation to feelings were demonstrated. What was also interesting was the debate between the role of the psychotherapist and that of the neuro-scientist. I was reminded of the challenge from Lewis, Amini & Lannon (2000, p. 10), that psychotherapists have 'spun an intangible castle in the air for humanity to inhabit and neuroscience has delivered a concrete hovel'. It seemed from this that ne'er the twain shall meet. Yet at the conference, I heard of the recent developments in affective neuroscience and infant research, and this helped me to anchor TA theory more firmly in the physio-logical dimension. The current research is serving to underpin our experiential work with a more sophisticated understanding of brain states. I see it as an opportunity for us as Transactional Analysts to expand our theory and make an even greater contribution to the current research.

In our contribution, however, I am aware that we could create our own 'concrete hovel' of TA theory. The foundation of TA theory is a fantastic resource and necessary to support our work with the client, but it is *not* the work itself. Our theoretical structure might lead us to work in a particular way with a client, and while it may be relevant, we need to ensure that the way we work is not more to do with the approach than it is to do with the client. Therapy is not structural analysis, for example, although some therapy may well involve structural analysis.

Winnicot (1980) advised caution with regard to technique and treatment, emphasising that treatment may be carried out with limited technique, and treatment can fail though the technique might be highly developed. When referring to his work with Piggle, he wrote of -

> the importance of my *not understanding* what she had not yet been able to give me clues for. Only she knew the answers, and when she could encompass the meaning of the fears she would make it possible for me to understand too.
>
> (Winnicot 1980, p. 48, Winnicot's emphasis)

The therapist's role

These views have major implications for the therapists role and have prompted me repeatedly to ask, "So what is our job?". Bill Cornell (ITA conference 2000), quoting from Christopher Bollas, said that the job is "to show up and pay attention and that is not always as easy as it sounds."

For me this means paying attention to our clients, to ourselves, and to the relationship as much as we are able. In my sessions, I sit in full awareness of ego state theory and full recognition of how it informs my practice, but the theory as such is suspended. I am experiencing *being with* my client, experiencing how they impact on me, how I impact on them, and how this might change with each new awareness. My explanation of what happens in ego state terms can come later if the client makes this request, or in supervision or my own analysis of the work.

Working in this way can feel very demanding; at uncomfortable moments, I can find myself wanting to talk theory just to fill silences and yet I know that this often disrupts the essence of the work. However, the joy of working in this way is that I feel more freedom to bring the whole of myself to the session, and to work in different ways from some of the people who have influenced me and continue to do so. I do not need to be the perfectly attuned therapist, or the perfectly informed therapist. I am willing to take responsibility for ruptures in the relationship, and to work with the client towards a more healing outcome.

I do this by noticing what goes on for me and by enquiring as to what is happening for them. I encourage my clients to share their ongoing experience of being with me in each session, subtle ego state shifts, and moments of contaminated thinking or clarity that comes from each new awareness. Whilst being aware of my own responses, moment by moment I also make a judgement of what of my own experience I want to share and when it will be therapeutic to do so. I consider that healing comes about through our curiosity and initial acceptance of whatever is there. For me, change is celebrated when it emerges from within the client. Ego state integration, I believe, comes about through these shared experiences and the possibility of new ways of relating, rather than direct confrontation of contaminated thinking. It seems to me that these changes then arise naturally from the process; they are more implicit than the explicit ego state shifts described in some of Berne's earlier writings.

I reflect with pride on some risks I took recently with a client whom I will call Jack. I felt that information that I needed to give him about my own experience would feel very hurtful to him. His presentation was as a man who objectified women; he would often use obscene language to describe the women in his life, being apparently unaware of his impact on them or on me. I knew that this behaviour had to be challenged, yet I knew that to do so early on in the sessions would have resulted in a re-enactment of his other relationships with women. In these, he would have usually stormed off feeling misunderstood and acting abusively towards them. I could also see the possibility of co-transferential relating, where within my own counter-transference, my own Child ego state scare, I would never have the courage to confront this behaviour.

Beneath his bullish exterior, however, I also had a sense of a passionate yet very vulnerable young boy. The healing came about, I believe, because I had enough support through supervision and my own therapy to operate at two levels. At one level, I experienced my side of the co-transferential relationship (Summers & Tudor 2000), and at the other, a confidence to choose the best time for the confrontation. My goal in so doing was to enhance present-centered relating

I knew that I had reached the stage of deciding to act when I was no longer comfortable with consciously withholding my feeling responses to Jack. I explained to him that I was starting to feel offended by the way he was talking. In the event, he did feel hurt, even furious. He was on the edge of writing me off and our relationship. As he left, still furious, I acknowledged his hurt and emphasised that I believed our relationship could withstand this intensity. When he did return for the next session, the quality of our work was transformed. It was only after he returned that I realised that we were both prepared to create new futures that were different from the echoes of our pasts. What is even more satisfying is that he is now established in a loving, intimate relationship with a partner, something that he wanted for a long time. His last 'confrontation' of me was when I remarked that there now appeared to be more Adult in his intimate relationships. He said, "Oh no Steff, there is a rainbow streaming through all three types of ego state". I was very moved.

Mutual transformation

If we are to work in the way I have described, strong commitment from the therapist is called for; a commitment that is well rewarded in the mutual transformations that occur. At the same time, I am absolutely *not* suggesting that we use time with our clients as a substitute for our own therapy. Rather I am suggesting that we consider the significance of the contributions our clients make. This is because I believe that it is the pro-activity of both client and therapist that produces the therapy. Any ego state shifts will be, in part, what we have created together, and in my experience either client or therapist can initiate the shift.

David Mann (1997, p. 180) also suggested that 'Psychotherapy should be considered a mutually transforming process'. This approach helps to redress an in-balance that I think is present in TA literature, in which clients are not portrayed as pro-active, but are often presented as passive recipients of the process. I agree with Allen & Allen (1995), that each person is entitled to more than one story, and that our job as psychotherapists is to enable the client to make/find meaning. Allen and Allen argue that there are numerous possibilities from which we might choose when we construct meaning. Like them, I want to suggest that while we may help clients by 'bringing up interpretations and possibilities, missed or forgotten', it is the client that 'chooses the one with which he or she prefers to identify'.

I recently saw some videos recognising the neural developments of young infants. In one of them, I marvelled at the pro-activity and powerful deter-mination of the newborn baby who was enjoying her father's attuned responses. Although two months premature, she noticed immediately and protested when he was distracted. She was only willing to be soothed when his attention returned and they were re-united in their natural resonance.

I consider this has implications for us to pay attention to the pro-activity of our clients. I also think that we need to act more tentatively when making assumptions or when forming fixed interpretations based on our theories. I regard it to be part of my fundamental respect for my clients that I make my interpretations with consideration. This honours their integrity and makes clear my willingness to remain open to their experience of what is important to them. I recall a session with a client whose mother was dying, to illustrate this.

My client presented with the issue of choosing whether her decision to tell the doctors not to feed her mother through a tube in her stomach was the right one. Her mother, who was suffering from dementia, was vigorously fighting anyone who tried to feed her. My theoretical hunches centred on current and anticipatory grief, but my client's energy was focussed much more on the viciousness of her mother's protest.

As the client's style was to avoid expression of emotion, I could have made an interpretation of this as her defence or her resistance to feeling, and to expressing her grief. I could have directed the session towards resolution of an impasse between P_1 and C_1 and I sensed her resistance to this work.

Instead, I paid more careful attention to her desire to remain strong. As we proceeded with gentle curiosity we found great value in her honouring her mother's spirit at the end of her life. A powerful moment occurred when the client saw her mother as validly protesting and setting boundaries. This was something my client had also struggled with in her own life. The meaning for her was as if, on her deathbed, the mother was communicating strong new permissions and helping her daughter vividly recognise ways she was limiting herself. With her realisation came a quiet grief, in her own time, at her own pace, and a peace with what she knew was to come. She left the session feeling both open to her grief, and that she had brought more dignity to this very challenging time for her and her mother.

In *A General Theory of Love*, Lewis et al (2000) capture the value of the openness required in this way of working.

> The Therapist who cannot engage in this open adventure of exploration will fail to grasp the other's essence. His every precon-ception about how a person should feel risks misleading him as to how that person does feel. When he stops sensing with his limbic brain a therapist is fatally apt to substitute inference for resonance.
>
> (Lewis, Amini & Lannon 2000, p. 183)

Mann (1997) also emphasises the proactivity of the client. He believes that it is often the client who takes the first step and the therapist who then helps him to capitalise on it. As with Jack, the young man I wrote about earlier, his pro-activity was his persistence in presenting me with the very style that could invite a replay of his other relationships. With my willingness to be, as Mann puts it, the new transformational object, we were able to avoid the repetition of our combined histories and take the relationship to a more creative place.

It is in this process that I see our roles as therapists as more about who we are than what we know. In my experience, it is here that we are invited to attend to the unreconciled parts of ourselves, to ego state lesions that remain. In our willingness to honour the wisdom of the unconscious and to attend to these areas, while remaining open to our clients, we can enter into a mutual process in which our clients, ourselves, and our relationships can be trans-formed.

I think it is clear, therefore, that if we are to work in a way that is mutually transformational I do believe we have responsibility to keep our own houses in order. Again I return to an extract from the interview with Ken Mellor (1998):

> From the responsibility point of view, if we're putting out a sign that says 'psychotherapist', then we're inviting people to come with all of their stuff. It's our job to make sure that we're in good con-dition to do the work. The being of the therapist is the primary tool in psychotherapy. Who I am as a person is my major instru-ment in working with people. I need to keep that instrument in pristine condition. If it's not capable of doing the job, I need to modify it, or send my clients to another therapist. We are just like carpenters who routinely have to look after our tools, like

sharpening chisels or saws, to ensure we do the job well. We, as psychotherapists, need to keep clear, physically and emotionally at whatever level the work we do requires.

(Mellor in Oates 1998, p. 29)

In conclusion, I have outlined three areas about which I feel passionately: acknowledging the integrity of our individual experiences and the meaning that each of us attaches to these, recognising the value of theory and using it wisely, and appreciating the importance of our own and our clients' contribution to the process of psychotherapy.

I have deliberately used my own journey and case examples to emphasise the importance of honouring humanity and dignity in our work. I hope it is clear that I enjoy vigorous theoretical debate, which serves to enhance, not limit, the power of the therapeutic relationship.

References

Allen, J.R., & Allen, B.A (1995) Narrative theory, redecision therapy and postmodernism. *Transactional Analysis Journal*, 25, 327-334

Berne, E. (1961) *Transactional Analysis in Psychotherapy*, New York: Grove Press

Berne, E. (1969) *A Layman's Guide to Psychiatry and Psychoanalysis*, UK: Andre Deutsch

Berne, E. (1975) *What Do You Say After You Say Hello: The Psychology of Human Destiny*, London: Corgi. (Original work published in 1973)

Clarkson, P. (1992) *Transactional Analysis Psychotherapy - An Integrated Approach*, London: Routledge

Cowper, W. (c.1800) in *Oxford Dictionary of Quotations* (1985) Oxford, University Press

Erskine, R. (1988) Ego structure, intrapsychic function and defense mechanisms. A commentary. *Transactional Analysis Journal*, 18, 15-19

Gobes, N. (1993) Ego state development in the 'integrated adult' model, in Novey, T.B., Porter-Steele, N. Gobes, N. & Massey, R.F. (1993) Ego states and the self-concept: A panel Presentation and discussion. *Transactional Analysis Journal*, 23(3)123-38

Harris, T. A. (1995) *I'm OK, You're OK*, London: Arrow

Jacobs, M. (1995) *D W Winnicott*, London: Sage

Lewis, T., Amini, F. Lannon, R. (2000) *A General Theory of Love*, New York: Vintage

Mann, D. (1997) *Psychotherapy: An Erotic Relationship*, London: Routledge

Mellor, K (1980a) Reframing and the Integrated Use of Redeciding and Reparenting *Transactional Analysis Journal*, 10(3) 204-212

Mellor, K (1980c) Impasses, A Developmental and Structural Understanding *Transactional Analysis Journal*, 10(3) 213-220

Oates, S. (1998) An interview with Ken Mellor, *ITA News* 50

Staemmler, F. (1997) Understanding regressive processes in Gestalt Therapy. *Gestalt Critique - The Gestalt Therapy Newsletter*. Issue 1

Stern, D. N. (1985) *The Interpersonal World of the Infant*. New York: Basic Books.

Stewart, I. (2001) Ego states and the theory of theory: the strange case of the Little Professor *Transactional Analysis Journal*, 31, 133-146

Summers, G. & Tudor, K. (2000) Cocreative Transactional Analysis, *Transactional Analysis Journal*, 30, 23-40

Wagner, J. (2001) Searching for the soul in psychotherapy *Conference papers from ITA conference, Keele, UK, 2001.*

Winnicott, D.W. (1980) *The Piggle: An Account of the Psychoanalytic Treatment of a Little Girl*, London: Penguin Books

AUTHOR INDEX

SUBJECT INDEX